On Christopher Street

On Christopher Street

LIFE, SEX, AND DEATH AFTER STONEWALL

Michael Denneny

THE UNIVERSITY OF CHICAGO PRESS   Chicago and London

The University of Chicago Press, Chicago 60637
The University of Chicago Press, Ltd., London
© 2023 by Michael Denneny
Published 2023
Printed in the United States of America

32 31 30 29 28 27 26 25 24 23   1 2 3 4 5

ISBN-13: 978-0-226-82461-1 (cloth)
ISBN-13: 978-0-226-82463-5 (paper)
ISBN-13: 978-0-226-82462-8 (e-book)
DOI: https://doi.org/10.7208/chicago/9780226824628.001.0001

Library of Congress Cataloging-in-Publication Data

Names: Denneny, Michael, author.
Title: On Christopher Street : life, sex, and death after Stonewall /
    Michael Denneny.
Other titles: Life, sex, and death after Stonewall
Description: Chicago ; London : The University of Chicago Press,
    2023. | Includes bibliographical references.
Identifiers: LCCN 2022036148 | ISBN 9780226824611 (cloth) |
    ISBN 9780226824635 (paperback) | ISBN 9780226824628 (ebook)
Subjects: LCSH: Male homosexuality—United States—History. |
    Gay liberation movement—United States—History. | Gay men—
    United States. | Gay men's writings, American—History and
    criticism. | AIDS (Disease)—Social aspects—United States.
Classification: LCC HQ76.2.U5 D46 2023 | DDC 306.76/620973—
    dc23/eng/20220728
LC record available at https://lccn.loc.gov/2022036148

♾ This paper meets the requirements of ANSI/NISO Z39.48-1992
(Permanence of Paper).

To Ronald and Johnnie and Tommie too,
and Warren and Bruce and Randy,
and John Purcell and John Preston,
Paul Monette and Paul Baron and Joshua,
Robin Hardy and Franco Zavani,
Richard Rouillard and Allen Barnett
And to my beloved Zaki
—my own greatest generation.

Contents

Becoming Real

Only in the freedom of our speaking with one another does the world, as that about which we speak, emerge in its objectivity and visibility from all sides. Living in a real world and speaking with one another about it are basically one and the same.

HANNAH ARENDT

I am an editor by profession and as an editor I believe that any collection of disparate texts into a single book needs a justification. Sixteen years ago when I first started free-lance editing and had more time on my hands than I'd ever had in the three decades I'd worked for publishing companies, I started looking through these writings, thinking perhaps I could fashion a small book out of the longer essays. But as I started reading, I realized that each piece was utterly grounded in its particular historical moment, often a response to a specific book or article and directed to a specific audience, sometimes even seeking to have an immediate effect on that audience. But the public discussion had since moved on, the particular issues I had addressed were no longer on the cutting edge and I lost interest in the project.

Then, two years ago, at the repeated urging of one particular friend and after I'd done a couple of long interviews that had made me think seriously about the time I'd spent in publishing, I took another look at these pieces. This time, more than a decade later, I saw them as documents of a past era—that is, after getting over the shock of having to consider my own life a "past era." How did that happen, I wondered. "My generation is 20th century. Our time is gone," said the Dalai Lama, expressing a finality I found hard to accept. But after several interviews by younger gay men it was abundantly clear to me that the reality of this period was fast sinking into the mists of history and was in danger of being forgotten. And it seemed to me that a book could be assembled out of these pieces that reflected the great public discussion that had burst out after Stonewall and that had absorbed so much of my adult life.

The history then sweeping us forward lifted a whole generation as if by a great wave and left new ideas agitating the air as they flew from mouth to mouth. And these circulating ideas created a social milieu, a cultural atmosphere I wanted to participate in, as I tried to think my way through the conundrums of an unprecedented historical development—the gay explosion into visibility. I wanted to trace the tremors of that social eruption as it reverberated and was felt and responded to in the part of the world I found myself in—New York book and magazine publishing.

I am, as I said, an editor by profession, and not a writer. My original aim was to publish gay books, not to write about them. But I wanted to be able to think about what I was doing, about what was happening in the world around me. And thinking led to conversations with other gay people interested in these matters; writing was simply one way to continue these conversations. And all the speaking and listening, reading and writing documented here was embedded in an active life that sought to engage in the cultural politics of the moment and to actually change the world in some way, no matter how small.

When I first mentioned the idea of this book to my old friend Chuck Ortleb, he cracked: "Great! I can see it now: longtime student of Hannah Arendt runs smack into gay liberation—results splatter all over the pages of *Christopher Street*!" A bit sardonic maybe, but he hit the nail on the head. I had spent nearly a decade studying with Hannah Arendt at the University of Chicago before moving to New York, partially to be able to keep attending her seminars (I had her permission, as long as I sat in the back and kept my mouth shut). When I left the university I wanted to work in the world, to lock gears with the society I was part of in order to initiate and force change. For me, the events at Stonewall had been a wake-up call, and I saw a political dimension open up, one that I wanted to participate in and to understand. So I left academics and plunged into what Arendt would call the "vita activa."

"But," Chuck continued, "while gay liberation was the main existential event in your life, it also seems to me that in many ways your life always had to answer to the intellectual love of your life, Professor

Arendt." Reviewing these pieces now, I see Arendt's presence everywhere, but especially in the repeated attempt to think through what was happening. "What I propose, therefore, is very simple; it is nothing more than to think what we are doing," Arendt says at the end of her prologue to *The Human Condition*. This is thinking not to achieve knowledge or to generate "theory," but to illuminate where we are in the world at the moment, thinking that could help us learn how to move in the utterly novel situation we find ourselves in.

Thinking what we are doing means paying attention to what we *are* actually doing. This, of course, leads to writing occasional pieces—utterances concretely rooted in specific historical moments, although they are all aligned—as iron filings are aligned by a magnet—to the overriding political objective of gay liberation, whatever it would turn out we meant by that. Each effort is a working out in the actual world of what Hegel called "der Ernst des Begriffs," the serious work of the Concept unfolding into the world and history in concrete and specific detail—i.e., the Idea becoming real, in this case, the unfolding of the idea of gay liberation in the actual world we live in.

But writing occasional pieces also leads to repetition; the same issues, the same touchstones, come up again and again. I find myself circling back, thinking about the same things. And, in a way, repetition is the point of it all—I was trying to come to an ever clearer understanding of what was happening around me. Something was definitely happening and I was watching and trying to think about it.

*   *   *

When I recently went back to read these pieces, I initially tried to organize them in various ways—political essays, personal essays, portraits of individuals, etc.—but nothing felt satisfactory, and the pull of chronology was like an irresistible force of gravity. The pieces felt like they had to be read in chronological order, and when I organized them that way I was surprised to see how easily they fell into coherent sections. So I added short introductions to each section, defined by years. The only exception I made to chronology was to place the essay on *Christopher Street* at the beginning of the book, since the magazine not only originally provided the main forum for me to appear in print, it basically called into existence the very audience I wanted to address. And since each piece is anchored to a specific occasion I have added brief introductory material before the texts, giving the date, occasion, and other context as necessary, to make the historical moment as real on the page as I can.

Rereading these pieces in chronological order felt like taking a time machine on a journey through three tumultuous decades, stopping at moments in my life when some occasion, event or provocation had resulted in my taking to speech or writing, thus making this an autobiography of sorts, not a full autobiography, of course, but a record of my participation in the great public discussion that burst out after Stonewall. The introductions I've added to each piece are meant to function as a sort of voice-over, a commentary situating each event.

And as these live moments followed one another chronologically, I hoped the reader could see—out the window of our time machine, as it were—the unfolding landscape and storyline of our lives and get a feeling for what it was like to live through this period. Which is what I find missing in the historical accounts of these years that I've seen so far. Yes, they capture the facts, the events, etc., but they seem to me to miss what it was actually like to be there then: the vitality, the creativity, the excitement as well as the fear, the loss and the grief that was the core of our lives in those years. Rather than write a memoir of that time from today's perspective, I wanted to try to capture the immediacy of experience. So I have not altered any of the original pieces, even though I winced at some unfortunate sentences. And although the resulting collage may at first glance look like an omnium gatherum of everything I ever published in *Christopher Street* magazine, it is actually a particular selection[1] of very diverse documents that try to show what the unfolding of gay liberation was like for one person, in specific situations and over time. And what unifies the wild diversity of literary forms here is the voice, which remains constant. The essential unity

---

1 Of the 102 pieces of writing in this book, only 10 appeared in *Christopher Street* magazine, 22 in other periodicals or books and 70 were never printed or written expressly for this book.

that makes anything a legitimate book, and not just a collection, is to be found here in the voice, the voice of the man then and the voice of the man now.

Of course, all this particularity runs the risk of getting too far into the weeds. "Too much inside baseball," complained an old friend to whom I showed the manuscript. "Too much inside baseball. Like recounting the theoretical quarrels of the American Anthropology Association in the Sixties and Seventies, interesting if you were there maybe, otherwise, not so much. And who cares now? Some nice ideas here and there, but the discussions are altogether too particular, too specific."

To which I have two responses. First: it turns out that *I* care. As the community falls into the danger of forgetting what this time was like, I found I had the same response James Lapine had when asked what inspired his 2016 revival of *Falsettos*. According to the *New York Times*, "he mentioned the experience of taking his bright, well-educated, 23-year-old assistant to see *The Normal Heart*," Larry Kramer's important AIDS play. "At intermission she looked at me and said: 'Is this based on fact? I mean I know about AIDS, but I didn't know it was like this.' That made me think it was important to tell these stories now to the younger generations."[2]

The Seventies and Eighties are two generations ago now and fast fading. I found that I wanted my experience of that time, my vision of this quite extraordinary episode in gay history and gay writing, to find its way into the historical record. I wanted to say, "Listen, it was like this."

And yes, I know this account is from the specific, limited perspective of one individual. But while history may be a general story it can only be experienced by specific individuals. And it seems to me that the particular, the utterly specific, is where we all actually spend our lives, and where each one of us stands when we think about anything. There is, after all, no place else to stand. So this book takes you into and follows one person's encounter with the upheavals that gay liberation brought us in the last three decades of the 20th century with all

---

2 Ginia Bellafante, *New York Times*, December 4, 2016, Metro Section, p. 6.

the narrowness and contingency that implies, but it is the only life I have immediate access to.

*   *   *

Rereading these pieces gave me the chance to review and reconsider passionately held positions, and to come to some new realizations. It was only in assembling this book that I fully realized that I belong to a very specific generation. Like Cleve Jones, "I was born into the last generation of homosexual people who grew up not knowing if there was anyone else on the entire planet who felt the way that we felt."[3] This was the generation that was faced with the great historical cleavage that Stonewall represented, the generation that would have to bridge the gap between homosexual and gay. It was a generation to whom history offered great opportunity and great tragedy. And it was a generation of remarkable individuals who met the drastic challenge of their time and became heroes. Or so it seemed to me. All around me since Stonewall I thought I was seeing something akin to Nietzsche's transvaluation of all values happening, a creative response to the "nihilism" our cultural commentators had been bemoaning for so long. And when the great disaster of AIDS overwhelmed us, I thought I saw a heroic era in gay and lesbian history and an absolutely shining moment in gay writing, something truly worth remembering. And if the memory of those events is today fading from view, I take solace in Walter Benjamin's comment that "one might speak of an unforgettable moment even if all men had forgotten it."[4] This, I thought, was an unforgettable moment.

Was it a mirage? It seems like a necessary question now, at a time when the surprisingly rapid successes of gay liberation have perversely made its future relevance so uncertain. According to Andrew Sullivan, "the more victories that accumulate for gay rights, the faster some gay institutions, rituals and markers are fading out. And so, just as the

---

3 Cleve Jones, *When We Rise: My Life in the Movement* (New York: Hachette Books, 2016), p. 1.
4 Walter Benjamin, "The Task of the Translator," in *Illuminations*, ed. Hannah Arendt (New York: Harcourt, Brace & World, 1968), p. 70.

gay marriage movement peaks, so does a debate about whether gay identity is dimming, overtaken by its own success,"[5] and this, he thinks, may be "the end of gay culture, which erodes a little more each year." Gay neighborhoods seem to be evaporating like the morning dew as "we observe the disappearance of gay and lesbian ghettos, bookstores, watering holes, and, yes, publications," reports Richard Schneider, editor of *The Gay and Lesbian Review*.[6] Christopher Street itself, writes Andrew Holleran, "is like any other street in Greenwich Village now; in fact, it feels rather sedate. Walking west from Sheridan Square, for people who knew it in the seventies, is a bit like entering a theatre that's gone dark."[7]

Perhaps gay liberation has gone dark, perhaps our "gay ghettos" were only temporary, defensive communities thrown up in haste and now rendered unnecessary because of our "assimilation" as gay life dilutes itself in America. Perhaps. But I miss—*miss* doesn't begin to capture the feeling—that community. That's what hit me hardest in rereading these pieces and revisiting my earlier life. I miss that strong, vibrant feeling of a community (foolishly known as gay ghettos), the presence of so many others, a whole generation more or less spontaneously committed to the common cause. As an old friend said, "There was a moment when we thought we could make the world the way we wanted it to be." And for a while we did, we created a gay world, and a gay culture became a reality, if only a transitory reality, a bubble of shared consciousness that floated on the riptides of history, a bubble that may now be only a memory. But then all life is transitory. That world may now be fading into history but it's worth remembering.

The fact is that the gay community was no *fata morgana*, it became a tangible and concrete reality in response to the AIDS crisis. The community manifested itself daily in countless concrete ways, from groups of AIDS buddies to organizations to take care of the pets of those af-

---

5 *New York Times*, June 25, 2015, pp. 1 and 12.

6 Schneider even wondered whether "gay" is "a 20th-century subculture that appears to be in decline." *Gay & Lesbian Review/Worldwide*, vol. 23, no. 1 (January–February 2016).

7 Andrew Holleran, "Street of Dreams," *Gay & Lesbian Review/Worldwide*, vol. 19 (November–December 2012): p. 49.

flicted, from Housing Works and Project Inform to ACT UP—the list could go on and on and on. This astonishing creation of organizations to meet the crisis and care for the afflicted is a story that has yet to be appreciated, it seems to me. Yes, that generation has just about left the scene. Yes, that feeling seems to have faded, but I think it's worth remembering. We seem to be at the end of an era, the era of gay liberation that stretched from Stonewall to the achievement of gay marriage and gay marines. And yes, we've made remarkable progress, and as we turn the page and enter a new chapter of gay history all this talk about gay identity and gay culture may seem to some anachronistic. All I can say is that this is how it seemed to me at the time, this is what I saw and this is how I reacted to it.

I also realized that the sort of literary collage I am trying to construct with these pieces is, above all, a documentary of the unexpected and startling journey the gay community has been on since Stonewall. The book that resulted stands for me as a tribute to a remarkable generation that I got to participate in, riding the great wave of cultural energy that swept us up and rushed us forward into a new life.

PART 1

Morning in Gay America

1970–1980

The Stonewall Riots, which took place in Greenwich Village in June of 1969, were a thunderclap resounding through the underground gay world of America. That's what it felt like in my life—a loud, startling noise that woke you up. "It was the riot that eventually 'broke the spell,'" Lillian Faderman wrote, the spell of fear, a fear gay and lesbian people had been living with since World War II when the persecution of homosexuals became the de facto policy of the U.S. government. "For Village gays, the riot had been the equivalent of Rosa Parks taking a forbidden seat in the bus to Montgomery, Alabama. The rest of the world might not know it yet, but they knew that there was no going back to the way things had been."[1]

Stonewall's impact reverberated far and wide, ever deeper and ever broader, like the ripple a stone makes thrown in a pond, only enlarging rather than diminishing with time, eventually leading to the largest citizen movement for equal rights in America since the civil rights movement.[2] Frédéric Martel reports in his recent eye-opening book on the global gay movement, "Around the world, in Shanghai and Johannesburg, in Havana and even in Tehran, gays would tell me about the Stonewall Inn. Even if they had never come to the United States

1 Lillian Faderman, *The Gay Revolution: The Story of the Struggle* (New York: Simon & Schuster, 2015), pp. 183 and 184.
2 Lillian Faderman does an excellent job of describing the depth, breadth, and diversity of this struggle in *The Gay Revolution*.

and couldn't place Greenwich Village on the map of New York City, they knew the myth and the place."[3] At the time, it immediately drew contemporaries like myself and many, many others to New York City, anxious to join the "revolution" we thought that event heralded, while initiating the enormously creative gay cultural ferment of the Seventies.

But it's often forgotten that the first impact of Stonewall was one of liberation, *sexual* liberation. The gay movement had its roots in the sexual liberation and feminist movements of the Sixties, and its first result was an absolute explosion of gay sexual *activity*. Our historians will probably concentrate on the history of organizations and political heroes—how the Gay Liberation Front led to the Gay Activists Alliance led to the National Gay Task Force, how Frank Kameny challenged the state, a story of laws passed, elections contested, court battles won and lost—and, of course, this is history. But in the actual fabric of our daily life what was more important and what really *changed* was sex, more sex, *much* more sex. After decades of repression a whole generation suddenly felt free to explore what had been forbidden. Unleashed, gay men (at least, we should let the lesbians speak for themselves) urgently sought experiences they had only dreamed of. A whole generation of young gay men plunged into "the gorgeous confusion and frequent disillusionment of being sexual" (Hilton Als). And not surprisingly, an obsession with sex led to an obsession with romance. The exhilaration and entanglements of sex and romance were what preoccupied and bedeviled me and most of my gay friends in the early Seventies. It took the whole decade for this surge of sexual liberation to condense into a demand for gay civil rights.

But given what followed in the Eighties, an epidemic of death transmitted mainly by sexual activity, I think those of us who experienced the Seventies have tended not to speak about it much, confused and embarrassed perhaps by our part in creating the conditions that made the epidemic possible. And it can be painful to recall lost

3 Frédéric Martel, *Global Gay: How Gay Culture Is Changing the World* (Cambridge, MA: MIT Press, 2018), pp. 5 and 7.

youth.[4] But the Seventies were a truly remarkable decade. "The 1970s were a pretty crazy time in New York," said Calvin Klein recently.[5] "There was Berlin in the 1920s, and Paris in the 1930s, and New York in the 1970s." It was startling to see a whole generation—and not just a small, privileged elite—attempting to unleash and explore the erotic in their own lives. And then go on and redefine what gay male sexuality could be and create new forms of male bonding and new definitions of masculinity. And it was this explosion of sex, promiscuous sex, that made us a community.

And as we went about rehabilitating lust and celebrating romance, the world opened up and seemed new again, as on the first day.

It was morning in gay America, and

> Bliss was it in that dawn to be alive,
> But to be young was very heaven![6]

---

4 A remarkable exception is Cleve Jones' recent memoir: "I had originally thought of this book as having two equal parts: the time before AIDS, and the time that followed. But I soon realized that the stories I wanted most to tell were of the years before the plague, when we were still young and unaware of the horror—and the triumphs—yet to come." *When We Rise*, p. 29.

5 *New York Times*, October 26, 2017, p. D5.

6 As Wordsworth said of the early years of the French Revolution.

Christopher Street Magazine

IF STONEWALL REPRESENTED the great "No!" the refusal to accept society's definition of homosexuality—as a sin, a crime, a sickness, an arrested stage of development, or some distorted and privative form of heterosexuality—then the question naturally arose: exactly how were we to understand it? What did it mean to be homosexual, if we did not accept what society said it meant? What we obviously needed was a forum for homosexuals to speak for themselves, to define and describe the validity of their own lives rather than accepting the view of various experts and authorities whose pronouncements had been so destructive to us. This need became urgent as we tried to understand the implications of the Stonewall revolt.

The first gay book I ever signed up, sometime in the mid-Seventies, was Alan Ebert's *The Homosexuals: Who and What We Are*, a book that let seventeen homosexual men speak for themselves freely and without fear of judgment. By the time the book was published we had dropped the subtitle and replaced it with the sell line: The First Book in Which Homosexuals Speak for and about Themselves. (The book only concerned gay men, since it seemed obvious to all of us at the time that the lesbian and gay male worlds were wildly different.)

This same need for a public forum of our own led to the establishment of *Christopher Street* magazine in 1976, but the magazine had had a brief forerunner in *Out* magazine, which had published only two issues in 1973 before going out of existence.[1] *Out* in turn had been established by four guys who had previously been responsible for publishing *The Gay Activist*, the monthly publication of the Gay Activists Alliance (GAA) in 1971–72. All three publications were direct responses to Stonewall, attempts to establish a public forum for the gay community, a place to discuss and evaluate what was happening to us and around us.

1 See appendix A.

In retrospect, it still astonishes me that we were able to launch *Christopher Street*, given our relative ignorance of everything involved in the magazine business. Sure, there was a felt need for it and growing enthusiasm, but precious little practical knowledge or experience. I was going to describe it with one of the oldest gay clichés—Judy and Mickey saying, "Hey, guys, let's put on a show!"—until I realized that today I'd probably have to add an explanatory footnote. Suffice it to say that it would never have happened except for the extraordinary convergence of a large and open-ended group of gay and lesbian activists, writers, artists and intellectuals who were congregating in New York City after Stonewall and who supported, contributed to, volunteered for and generally made the magazine possible. It was a group enterprise from the beginning.

Christopher Street was always on the verge of bankruptcy during the first five years of its existence.[2] We had started with a woefully inadequate capitalization of $10,400 and did not realize: 1, subscription revenue alone could never support the magazine financially, and 2, there was almost no advertising available to a national gay literary magazine. Consequently, we were constantly scurrying to find any source of revenue we could to keep the magazine afloat. At one point we discovered that we could publish books of the cartoons created by the publisher, Charles Ortleb, and its art director, Rick Fiala,[3] which ultimately led Tom Miller, a young editor at G. P. Putnam's Sons, to suggest a collection of fiction from the magazine, which he then brought out at Perigee.[4] And when a follow-up volume of nonfiction[5] was suggested, we felt we had to take full responsibility for the book's contents, so that book was edited by Charles Ortleb, Tom Steele, the mag-

---

2 See appendix B.

3 Starting with *And God Bless Uncle Harry and His Roommate Jack, Who We're Not Supposed to Talk About: Cartoons from Christopher Street* (Avon, 1978), followed by *Relax! This Book Is Only a Phase You're Going Through* (St. Martin's, 1978) and *Le Gay Ghetto* (St. Martin's, 1980), with the entire advance and any royalties going directly into the magazine.

4 *Aphrodisiac: Fiction from Christopher Street* (Perigee, 1980).

5 *The Christopher Street Reader*, ed. Michael Denneny, Charles Ortleb, and Thomas Steele (Coward-McCann, Inc., 1983).

azine's editor, and myself,[6] although the main burden of rereading five years' worth of issues fell to me.

It seemed a good occasion to try to articulate what the magazine was all about, so in 1982 I wrote the following essay as an introduction to that book. I've put it here, out of the chronological order of the rest of these pieces, because it really frames the whole rest of the book. And because *Christopher Street* (along with its sister publications[7]) was not only the main arena in which I published but was really the basis for my participating in the intense ongoing conversation about gay issues animating and perplexing the newly emerging gay community. *Christopher Street* in fact helped bring into existence the community I was addressing in these writings. These were the people I wanted to talk with and to listen to. *Christopher Street* became a mental space for me, a concrete, if temporary, actualization of the gay community that was emerging. As Arendt said, "Living in a real world and speaking to one another about it are basically one and the same."

Since the 17th century, magazines have been a peculiarly modern device for bringing a public space into existence. Like a town meeting, a magazine enables people to be in each other's company by sharing talk about matters that concern them. And it is through talking with others that most of us start to make some sense out of the world and begin to discover who we are and what we think. Such talk usually does not lead toward general agreement but, paradoxically, to even greater diversity of opinion. Only people who don't talk to each other—or don't do it well—think they agree. In my experience, the better and longer the talk, the more you find yourself in disagreement with others, and if the discussion has genuine quality, eventually in disagreement with yourself—at which point it gets interesting, for this is when change becomes possible and things begin to happen.

6 As was a second volume of fiction, *First Love, Last Love: New Fiction from Christopher Street*, ed. Michael Denneny, Charles Ortleb, and Thomas Steele (G. P. Putnam's Sons, 1985).
7 Which grew to include the *New York Native*, *Theater Week*, *Opera Monthly*, and *Night and Day*. Though I never wrote for *Opera Monthly*.

Publishing a magazine, writing for a magazine, subscribing to and supporting a magazine are all aspects of an activity whose final purpose is not general agreement, a party line, but rather a greater ease and sureness in moving in the world, a firmer grasp of who we are and what we think. *Christopher Street* has never tried to develop a party line; we always thought our task was to open a space, a forum, where the developing gay culture could manifest and experience itself. For people who have been excluded from the social world—gays, blacks, women, any minority group that has been colonized by a dominating culture—this access to public space is basic and urgent. Gays know, or should know, as well as blacks and colonized people, the cost of being "invisible men." We're intimately aware of "the havoc wrought in the souls of people who aren't supposed to exist" (Ntozake Shange). This is no benign neglect, it is an active assault against our persons, a total public denial of the validity of our lives as we experience them. The gap between our inner lives and the socially acceptable version of reality is so wide it makes existence into a charade. It makes you dizzy. It makes you wonder if you're really there.

This experience of displacement and insubstantiality is common to all people society forces to be invisible. The dizziness of the dizzy queen not only expressed the inner confusion of finding oneself constantly forced to play in a charade—"Am I real, honey? Is this world for real?"—it is also a stubborn, insidious, perhaps unconscious but quite effective, political assertion—"Don't you dare think I'm really here, that this is really real, that this is who I am." The celebrated ambiguity of camp is a psychological zap, guerilla tactics for people who can't afford open warfare—not unlike the legendary laziness of blacks or the stupidity of colonized people. Straights are irritated or uncomfortable with it because it's meant to make them irritated or uncomfortable—if you're going to press us down with those values, we're going to camp it up and undermine those values, ridicule them and expose them for the pretentions they are. Those reactionaries who in their heart of hearts *know* we're making a mockery of them are right on this point. You bet. When you can't afford to fight back openly, you ridicule, you undermine, you resist the only way you can.

But the cost is too high. Living in the closet and putting on a mask when you go into the world does not leave your soul intact. Social invisibility reaches inward and causes a confusion of spirit. Our imaginations become closeted *internally*—a phenomenon feminists are pointing to when they discuss "male-identified women." We are no longer able to imagine our own lives. It's well known that we come out sexually before we come out socially, that most of us have been screwing for years before we're willing to say to ourselves, never mind publicly, "I'm gay." After all, homosexuals were undoubtedly sexually active before Stonewall as well as after. But the assertion of gay liberation that started with the Stonewall Riots is not enough. Pecs, track lighting, and brunch do not a soul make. We all know people who dress like clones—and whether they know it or not, this is a militant act, broadcasting the statement "I am gay" not only to gays (we could always recognize each other) but primarily to the straight world—but these same clones wouldn't be caught dead reading a gay book or subscribing to a gay magazine.

This seems to me an enormous strategic mistake. (Of course, being deeply involved in the business of gay books and magazines, I'm not exactly an impartial commentator—on the other hand, who is?) Put simply, I don't think it's possible to have a liberated gay world socially or a satisfying and fulfilling gay life individually without developing a gay culture. Over a decade ago, we found that a private gay life was not enough, that we required some kind of public and visible assertion of our gayness, that "coming out" was the path to liberation and the "closet" a repressive trap, not only politically but in terms of our immediate day-to-day lives. While we may be obscure about the precise nature of this connection, unable even to our own satisfaction to articulate why we feel the necessity of this public assertion—which, quite honestly, most straights and not a few gays still view as a perverse *flaunting* of our lifestyle—still in our gut we knew it was necessary, and this obscure but quite powerful conviction is what has fueled the gay movement for the last ten years.

It is as if liberation proceeds in three stages. The first is the sheer exhilarating discovery of gay sex and same-sex emotional bonding, which becomes the true center of our lives and the ultimate excitement of our souls even if we remain socially in the closet. The second stage is the public and social assertion of our gayness: our demand for the rights and dignity that a decent respect for humanity in all its diversity would grant to everyone. To these, I suggest, should be added a third stage, the liberation of our imaginations from the closet of straight culture. We need to be able to imagine our own lives *as we live them* if we are to have any chance of living them well.

To use a concrete example: for many years I used the term "ex-lover" to name relationships I thought had ended, had failed. It took forever before I woke up to the patent fact that I spent a substantial part of my social time with these "ex" lovers; that these were among the deepest, closest, most stable and rewarding relationships I had. When I looked around and saw that this was increasingly the case with many of my friends, it began to dawn on me that we were in the process of redefining the family, or better still, that we were creating new structures—little tribes—that functioned in our lives in much the same way as, and perhaps in place of, the traditional family. For me this incident encapsulates a general phenomenon: we are in the odd position of having trouble seeing the very lives we lead because we still look at them through the lenses of straight culture, the same straight culture that has gone to such bizarre efforts to deny that we even exist.

Anyone today who thinks he can lead a free gay life without participating in the creation of gay culture is in the same position as those homosexuals of the Fifties and Sixties who thought they could have meaningful and significant intimate relationships while staying in the closet. It won't work. It didn't work then. Untold numbers of homosexuals were severely damaged or driven to distraction by this contradiction between their intimate and their public lives—a situation brilliantly captured by *The Boys in the Band*, an analysis of an emotional pre-revolutionary situation if I've ever seen one. The only way to consolidate the gains of the past decade of gay liberation is to forge a new imagination of our lives and the world, and this can only be done by a serious interaction with our writers and artists, for these, after all, are the people who have elected the task of reporting and imagining and celebrating and criticizing how we live now.

I suppose it's necessary to add that a commitment to a separate gay culture and identity in no way requires the rejection of straight culture. Does anybody think that a Jew who gains sustenance and identity from his people's heritage cannot also be an American? That someone deeply involved in the forging of an American Black culture cannot love Shakespeare and Cezanne? The idea is absurd and is never raised with other groups; when it comes up in discussions of gay culture, in attacks on what's called gay separatism, it's a red herring.

The writings included in this book are among the most interesting and valuable attempts I know at imagining our lives anew. These writers do not agree with one another. They are pushing and probing, thinking and criticizing, celebrating and berating the new lives we find ourselves leading and the new people we have become. To the reader who takes them seriously, they offer invaluable and concrete assistance in the daily struggle we all face to invent ourselves anew, and to recognize ourselves when we've done it.

*   *   *

Any collection of articles from a magazine presents the opportunity for, in fact requires, a reflective interpretation of what exactly that magazine is all about. In re-reading five years of published material one inevitably begins to see the collective endeavor in the clearer light of hindsight. In the case of *Christopher Street*, my own experience of this massive re-reading left me—a bit to my surprise—with a new sense of a roughly coherent public discussion with its own logic and progression. It is this rough sense of the unfolding of an ongoing discussion that informs the present collection, its content and arrangement.

This coherence should not be overemphasized. A magazine publishes articles—glimpses of how we are, brief and tentative surveys of the geography of our lives, sudden clearings of self-awareness, reports from different corners of our world—and a collection of such articles could never offer a systematic and balanced overview. The vagaries of interest, accidents of timing and pressures of circumstance, financial and otherwise, see to that. Yet it did seem to us that an unusual number of articles retained their interest and vitality, that even this scattered record of the attempts of a large and open-ended group of people to make sense of their lives and confront the problems and paradoxes of establishing a gay culture was coherent enough to warrant the permanence of a book.

The final decisions on the contents and arrangement of this collection reflect our sense of the cultural evolution this magazine has recorded and reflected back to the public.

The most striking aspect of this book for regular readers of *Christopher Street* will undoubtedly be the absence of women. From the first issue until today, *Christopher Street* has not only published but gone out of its way to publish articles, fiction, art, cartoons and poetry by and interviews with women writers, both lesbian and non-lesbian, including Bertha Harris, Kate Millett, Rita Mae Brown, Ntozake Shange, Audre Lorde, Blanche Boyd, Mary Daly, Joan Baez, Sheila Ortiz Taylor, Noretta Koertge, Jane Rule, Olga Broumas, and Nicole Hollander, among many others. Yet in reading it all over, it became apparent that this was a secondary aspect of the magazine. The initial selection of material for this book included articles by some nine women and about sixty men, which, sensibly enough, made us all nervous, especially since a third of those women were not gay. It would be easy to charge the magazine with tokenism and this collection with chauvinism—and we shall no doubt hear such charges—but I think the truth of the matter is more complex, less hostile, and ultimately promising.

Christopher Street started with a determined effort at gender parity that lasted about a year and a half. It would be superfluous to recount the demise of this effort—virtually everyone who has been active in any gay endeavor will be familiar with the scenario. What I personally remember with striking clarity was the time one of the women editors, a close friend, told me she actually didn't read any of the pieces by men. She preferred to concentrate her work, energy, and enthusiasm on developing women writers; she simply wasn't particularly interested in what men had to say, unless it touched on a feminist concern. I was startled because I generally found the writing of the women interesting myself. And in fact, we found it to be more or less the case that male readers were interested, even enthusiastic about women writers, but that women had little interest in the work of the men.

Their concern was so intensely engaged in the situation of women that reading the articles by men seemed irrelevant to them. So the magazine was, by and large, never able to win the loyalty of women readers, and the women on the staff slowly drifted away.

At the time all this led to some muttered sound and muted fury and hurt feelings on both sides, but it makes more sense to me now. The connection between gay men and gay women was only ideological; we did not really share a world in common. Women needed their own space, as the lesbian feminists correctly argued, and gay men were trying to create a cultural space to begin with (without the great initial advantage gay women had in the very fact of the feminist movement). The attempt at integration may or may not have been misguided, but it certainly came too soon. Both gay men and lesbians were still struggling to gain some sense of their own identity and apparently neither could afford the effort to try to make themselves acceptable to or even understood by the other.

Where it will all end up is another matter. The relation between lesbians and straight feminists may be changing, the relation between gay men and the feminist movement is certainly changing, and the relation between gay women and gay men seems to be in flux. We can be good allies with anyone who is on our side, but we cannot be good allies, or even good friends, if we confuse ourselves with each other. We need our separate identities and we need to respect the differences between us.

Personally, I think gay men can greatly benefit from reading the several excellent collections like this one, consisting entirely of the work of gay women, which are now available. But to have a few women represented in a dominantly male collection does seem objectionable to me. *Christopher Street* simply has to accept the fact that at the moment it is a gay male magazine; as such, it will continue to publish the best women writers we can find who will interest our readers. And before I'm attacked in print for all this, I would urge people to consider whether any feminist or lesbian magazine has ever opened its pages to as many gay men as *Christopher Street* has consistently to gay and non-gay women—much to its benefit.

Lesbians and gay men have a lot in common, but we're not the same folk. This would seem to be a very simple fact, one that has been abundantly clear for years. Yet confusion over this issue and the attempt to wring from the word "gay" a uniformity that would cover both men and women has led to unbelievable wrangling. It's time to accept our differences with good humor and a genuine interest in each other's lives and work. Lesbians and gay men are natural allies, if only because a generally hostile society sees us as the same—homosexuals. But only if we recognize our differences and can live with the same tolerance of diversity we're demanding from straight society will we be able to work together and enjoy each other's company.

Dead Souls at *The New Yorker*

A PUZZLING CASE

IN 1977 *The New Yorker* published George Steiner's long review of a new study of Nikolai Gogol by Simon Karlinsky, who had become a valued contributor to and friend of *Christopher Street*. Having been a fan of Mr. Steiner for many years I was at first immensely puzzled by his review, until a very careful reading revealed a comedy of errors and good intentions.

In the Seventies a tone of arrogant condescension if not outright hostility coursed through almost all mainstream media discussion of books about or by gay authors. Nowadays I suppose this would be called a battery of micro-aggressions. To someone gay in the publishing industry they were vastly irritating and utterly pervasive. It seemed to me that it was time to start calling out this type of talk in our literary journals. If talking about homosexuality in literature was important, then it was important to consider the quality of such talk—which was generally abysmal in the wider public world, and it was time for us to actively confront and contest that.

So I thought Mr. Steiner's essay ought to be responded to, and was thus tempted into my first contribution to the magazine.[1]

Nowadays (1977) it is always interesting to observe how homosexuality is treated in the media. Previously our response to media tended to be one of unrelieved, and thus dreary, anger; today, however, when the shifting sands of social mores offer such treacherous footing, the spectacle various social and literary commentators make of themselves is often intricately puzzling and sometimes downright hilarious.

We were, for instance, enormously puzzled when we first read George Steiner's review of Simon Karlinsky's study, *The Sexual Labyrinth of Nikolai Gogol*, in the February 28th issue of *The New Yorker*.

---

1 Published in *Christopher Street*, vol. 1, no. 10 (April 1977).

Having read Mr. Steiner for many years with some respect, the tortuous argument of his essay seemed at first blankly incomprehensible.

The first third of Mr. Steiner's essay seemed an inexplicable burst of anger caused by a rather innocuous, if homiletic, paragraph in Karlinsky's book, warning us against the temptation to explain away the prima facie evidence of Gogol's homoeroticism, as has sometimes been done with Shakespeare, Michelangelo, Verlaine and Whitman. Mr. Steiner is severely shaken by the use, in this context, of *these* names (his italics). He goes on to say, "It is just possible—we do not really know—that certain absolutely preeminent achievements in Western culture, perhaps in humanity as a whole, entail some measure of bisexuality or nonsexuality." Considering the book under review, the absence of *homosexuality* in this rather grudging acknowledgment is quite striking—an example of a negative implication making a strongly assertive statement. Professor Steiner then goes on to cite Plato, Leonardo, and Goethe as men of great cultural achievement who in their lives evinced "a dual eroticism," an ability to "experience erotic involvement with both sexes." At this point a sensible reader might conclude that Professor Steiner is willing to accept bisexuality—the old masculine-and-feminine-elements-of-the-soul argument—but is about to resolutely exclude homosexuality.

Mr. Steiner turns immediately to cleaning up the names (or *these* names) so besmirched. As for Shakespeare, in his sonnets there are undoubtedly professions of love to a male reader, but they are (thank God!) "infinitely self-questioning and ironically modulated"—as if those sonnets directed to "the dark lady" were not self-questioning and ironic. In Michelangelo there is "a felt mystery of the flesh, of its enthralling loveliness," which appears "to be concentrated in a masculine rather than a feminine incarnation, or at moments, in a vision of the androgynous." Luckily *his* most impassioned sonnets were to Vittoria Colonna, a bona fide female, and to God, so Steiner can conclude that if there are homosexual sentiments they are registered in a Platonic idiom (somewhat of a dodge, since Plato is the one figure mentioned who's skipped over altogether—I wonder why) and "again we stand partly uncomprehending near a human summit." And without any wild surmises, if you please. With Whitman, "homoeroticism is a triumphant pan-sexuality" while Verlaine's homosexuality "was at most intermittent" (just what did that make his heterosexuality?). In short, homosexuality is for Whitman "self-love" and for Verlaine "self-hatred"—apparently anything is more acceptable than the love of another male.

Having finished with this bit of specious apologetics, Steiner attacks (apparently all) modern literary scholarship for failing to "exhibit an imperative of delicacy." "It ranks and anatomizes," he objects, "it shreds privacy to the winds and speaks loud" (echoes of the love that dare not speak its name). It reeks of "a vulgarity of heart." Although he has not really discussed Professor Karlinsky's book, at this point we are prepared for a real hatchet job; so it is with some surprise that we read that he is "not seeking a quarrel with Professor Karlinsky," whom he considers "an admirably erudite Slavist" with a "thorough and passionate knowledge" of Russian literature who writes with "an unmistakable toughness of mind" and is "an ornament to the teaching profession." In short, Professor Karlinsky is "in the best sense, representative of what should be the most valuable disciplines and aims in the humanities."

If the reader is not thoroughly confused by this point, he soon will be by Mr. Steiner's detailed discussion of Karlinsky's study, with which he apparently agrees on all major points and evidently finds an admirable, even "masterly" work—although he is careful to mention that "there is no firm evidence that Gogol ever consummated his homoeroticism." He asserts that "the case for the prosecution (Karlinsky's) rests and, within its limits, rests solidly." And here is the nub of the whole matter and here our confusion began to subside, for we doubt that Professor Karlinsky ever considered his discussion of Gogol's homosexuality a matter of "prosecution." It is Mr. Steiner who sees it as a "prosecution" and seeing it so, in his own muddled, tolerantly liberal and totally wrong-headed way, he leaps to Gogol's defense. The ensuing argument is hopelessly tangled. So, it goes, Gogol's a homosexual; in the manifestations of his homosexuality (his attitudes toward women, for instance), he's not so different from Macaulay, Byron, Wagner, Hegel, Kierkegaard, or Nietzsche (all straight as nails, if a bit peculiar). Since Mr. Steiner himself has here suggested a reckless number of

"links," of "bonds of style which constitute a psychological and linguistic cluster," with a wildly diverse group of nineteenth-century
figures, it is dismaying to find him complaining that "like buckshot,
the rubric of 'psychological pathology' is indiscriminate (and) makes
it harder for us to read Gogol justly, to make our response a patient,
self-withdrawing attendance to the marvelous singularity of the case."
Of course, implicit in this objection is the unspoken acceptance of the
prejudice that once you know a fag's a fag, you know all you need to
know about him ("no wonder he hated women!"). Since we do not believe for a moment that Professor Karlinsky makes this assumption to
begin with, the whole essay begins to look like a tempest in the wrong
teapot.

Mr. Steiner is quarreling with Professor Karlinsky because the professor has blown Gogol's cover, and his well-intended defense of the
artist forces an unusually sensible man into absurd positions. "Above
all, has (Karlinsky) ever stopped to ask himself whether the vision of the
role and significance of sex in human lives which is now canonic is not,
will not seem one day ludicrously overblown?" *Now* canonic? Shades
of Helen of Troy, of Virgil's Dido, of Dante's Beatrice, of Wagner's
Isolde! If the last 2,500 years of Western culture are anything to go by,
then the answer to Mr. Steiner's rhetorical question is clearly no. "Is
sex that interesting or that important?" demands Mr. Steiner. Well,
to a tortured, suppressed homosexual smothered by the homophobia
of nineteenth-century Russia it is, it may even be decisive—though,
and here we agree with Mr. Steiner, not as decisive as the incredible
spiritual strength and creative ability that allowed Gogol to transmute
his suffering into supreme works of art and, at least for a time, to sur-
mount his anguish before it destroyed him.

But in truth we have no real quarrel with Mr. Steiner. He respects
Professor Karlinsky's work and is reverent before Gogol's achievement. He is simply defending Gogol from being labeled a fag. Unfortunately for Mr. Steiner, in political matters, including cultural politics, it
is always important to know what time it is. In a time when novels written by women were dismissed as ladies' fiction, it was "progressive"
to show that they had a significance independent of the sex of their
creators; today such a stance would be "reactionary." Mr. Steiner has

landed in the foolish position of defending Gogol from an attack that was never made, on a field of battle that has become irrelevant. The case of the well-meaning Mr. Steiner should instruct us once again in the cautionary lesson of *Don Quixote*: in a time of rapid social change, decency is not enough to protect one from being ridiculous.

Lovers

THE STORY OF TWO MEN

AROUND 1977, AFTER *Christopher Street* was up and running and I had started contributing to it, I ran across a couple who had recently broken up, Philip Gefter and Neil Alan Marks, and who had a remarkable photo documentation of their relationship (because Philip was a photographer). Since romance and relationships—particularly surviving their demise—had become a paramount concern to me and to most of the gay men I knew, I decided that interviewing lovers could be an interesting article for the magazine and set out on the project, which soon grew beyond my initial notion.

As I got deeper into it, I thought there was a way I could make something like a literary or intellectual version of a Joseph Cornell box, using Philip and Neil's photographs, the live interviews, and the written self-portraits to capture something—love, passion, and its loss—that I was obsessed with at the time.

Chuck Ortleb had the nerve to devote nearly the entire magazine to the piece in the February 1978 issue ("Anatomy of a Love Affair"), and the next year Susan Moldow at Avon published a longer version as a trade paperback,[1] letting the material take the final shape it wanted.

I'm reprinting here the preface and the afterword.

Preface

The original impulse behind this dual interview stemmed from the state I found myself in after three affairs ended "disastrously" within the same number of years. In this situation the mind has a tendency to play the game of "what if," to repeat the same themes endlessly, like a record caught in a groove, idiotically replaying one line—a psy-

---

1 Michael Denneny, *Lovers: The Story of Two Men* (Avon, 1979).

chological state caught with numbing precision by Kate Millett in *Sita*. I had become a burden to my friends and tedious to myself when I met Philip and Neil, whose own love affair had "ended" some six months earlier. I grew intrigued by the fact that they had an unusual photo-documentation of the two and a half years of their relationship and even more intrigued to find out whether the themes of discord which had plagued me were totally idiosyncratic or whether they were the particularized expression of difficulties inherent in gay love, or perhaps in loving any other person.

Using a selection of the photographs as a focus, I proceeded to interview each, separately, over a series of occasions; the hundreds of pages of transcript that resulted were then edited down to the present piece. These interviews were conducted under the pressure of strong and unresolved emotions, of late night hours slowly turning to dawn, of the urgent need to understand what had happened and why. In the printed interviews I have tried to maintain the surface texture and rhythm of those intimate talks—the confusion and circling around a topic, the pauses and sentence fragments, the contradictions and sudden flashes of insight—for it seemed to me that the living texture of speech was as significant as what was said. This meant running the risk that Philip and Neil would sound less literate and more confused than is usually the case with interviews that are cleaned up editorially, where people speak in whole sentences and even paragraphs. But this risk seemed insignificant compared to the larger question of whether it was appropriate to make such utterly private matters public.

"All happy families resemble one another," said Tolstoy, "but each unhappy family is unhappy in its own way." And in this age of pop psychology and instant sociology, it is relevant to remember that we read novels—stories of very particular individuals, not of the average person—and they are of some use to us. These are not interviews with a "representative gay couple," if such should exist; they concern two very definite individuals. Like most individuals they are quite unlike the rest of us. Whether their story can be of use to the rest of us is for the reader to decide.

For my own part, I feel gratitude and honest admiration for their willingness to share this picture of themselves—for it is not *their* picture; inevitably it is *my* vision of them and there is no way I can maintain that I was merely a disinterested observer. Since they entrusted their self-presentation to me, I want to caution the reader to avoid hasty judgments. Neil says somewhere that he believes we are all made up of very profound and very superficial motivations and hate to admit the superficial ones—a notion I agree with. These two have been willing to expose both their profound emotions and their superficial feelings; their honesty should give us pause.

It is trite to remark that gay relations are uncharted territory, that none of us knows what we are doing. The following interviews are an attempt by two men to understand what happened to them.

Afterword: Interviewing Lovers

> *It is difficult to speak the truth, for although there is only one truth, it is alive and therefore has a live and changing face.*
>
> KAFKA

> *Generally speaking, it is inhumane to detain a fleeting insight.*
>
> FRAN LEBOWITZ

Interviewing

An interview floats in clouds of ambiguity. Neither a portrait of someone by someone else nor a deliberate self-presentation, the interview arises out of the interaction between the interviewer and the interviewee. Thus the question of authorship is perplexing. In plain fact, no one *wrote* these interviews; three people *did* them. If several different people interviewed Philip and Neil, the result would be different interviews. Even if the same person interviewed Philip and Neil at different times, the result would be different interviews. So what makes any one interview better than another? Put it another way. What claim to serious consideration does an interview make?

"Words are formed by the tongue in the mouth," as Sartre once said, and an interview consists of spoken words. Are the words true?

Who knows? Certainly the interviewer can't tell, unless he uses polygraph equipment. And the reader finds himself in an even worse position to judge their truth. The most you could say is that the story hangs together, doesn't contradict itself. But then neither does a good lie. In fact, probability is the hallmark of fiction, more characteristic of it than of reality.

We do know that these words were spoken. By this person. At this time. Or on this occasion—the occasion being the question. ("Ask me a question. I don't know what to say when you don't ask me questions.") So an interview is a selection of moments when a voice spoke out. A selection because the moments were created by the questions. An interview is an attempt to make a particular moment of a particular person *there*, on the page, through the voice. But the "voice" you "hear" on the page isn't the same as the voice electronically trapped on magnetic tape by my Sony. The printed words are a mere shadow of the original, full-bodied, living words "formed by the tongue in the mouth." The pitch, timbre, rhythm, loudness, texture, and silence have been lost— after all, how much can you do with italics, parentheses, dashes, and dots? Furthermore, I've *edited* the transcripts. Diminished things that they were to begin with, I've cut them down to a small fraction of their original length. This selection, the editing, implicitly makes a claim— the claim that these words are worth listening to.

As far as I can see, that's the only claim an interview makes: that this is worth listening to. The interviews in this book certainly don't claim to be a definitive portrait of this concrete individual, Philip, or this concrete individual, Neil. Much less do they claim to be a portrait of that very elusive item, their love affair. Least of all do they pretend to be that most gossamer of all creatures, a portrait of a love affair (elusive) between two representative gay men (abstract)—we should leave such airy items to the social scientists in the wan hope that it keeps them off the streets.

These interviews do not present a love affair. They present two men talking about their love affair. That love was present to them while they were talking. But it wasn't there anymore. It was an absence they felt, like the ache you have when a tooth is gone. These interviews try to make present to the reader what was present to Philip and Neil by making Philip and Neil present to the reader. The claim that this talk is worth listening to can only be tested by the reader. For my part, I feel quite comfortable in making it. I go around all the time telling people they should read this book or meet this person or see something or other. So it is fortunate that I am by profession an editor. Of course, editors publish bombs, too. That's where the readers come in. To publish a book is to ask the public to make a judgment.

Lovers

If the interview is a dubious form, the nature of love affairs is at least as problematic. There are two separate interviews in this book because there are two separate interpretations of the love affair, Philip's and Neil's. This is always the case with love affairs. But any interpretation is an interpretation of a "text." An interpretation is a perspective, and you can't have a perspective without having an object ("text") to perceive. It is precisely that "object" which is missing in love affairs, which is why lovers' quarrels are so maddening and murderous. There is no objective, common ground for mediation.

Love—romantic love or passion—seems to consist of nothing *but* perspective (the two-interpretations-and-no-text phenomenon). Love equals recognition. The lover is the only one who recognizes his beloved—which is why friends can never see what he sees in him. Someday Prince Charming will come along and recognize Cinderella for who she really is—his Princess.

Some evening another Princess will kiss the toad, because she sees beneath his surface ugliness, and—poof!—he regains his real nature. The kiss that woke Sleeping Beauty was the kiss of recognition. Recognition and awakening, the lover and the beloved. For those passed over, Bette Midler wails, "You don't know me, you just don't know me." Love as passion, the mutual awakening and recognition of two lovers, is perhaps the greatest confirmation of our being we can experience. *I want you to be here. I want you to be you. You belong here, with me.* In our increasingly anonymous mass society it's no wonder that love overshadows all other themes of popular culture.

But love is a matter of feelings and a feeling is not a fact. A fact sits there, it stays the same. Two and two will always be four. It's a fact that the Germans invaded Belgium in August, 1914. Facts have a stubborn irreducibility about them, which is both irritating and immensely reassuring. You can count on facts. But you can't count on feelings. Feelings not only change, they seem to *exist* in a state of flow. A feeling is more like a stream than like a pebble. It doesn't stay there, it goes on and in going on, it changes. This sounds pretty theoretical, but it has consequences.

Gays, because of their peculiar social situation, tend to try to build interpersonal relationships—love affairs—on their feelings alone. Without the subtle, numerous sanctions that usually support straight relationships (culminating, of course, in marriage), gay relationships tend to be grounded only on affectional preference, which is no ground at all but a vasty deep whose tides and currents are way beyond our ken, much less our control. Who understands why they love anyone? I can count the ways but not the reasons; you always end up with a *je ne sais quoi* or the banal idea that love is blind. It's because we don't love for any good reason that love can never be deserved. I can owe respect, but not love. All of which does not bode well for lasting relationships. If love is beyond comprehension, it is even more beyond our control. I can promise to do something, but not to feel something. I can control, and thus predict, my behavior but not my feelings.

Which is not necessarily to be deplored. Among other things, it probably makes for our strongest connection with the wild, unpredictable, turbulent life of Nature. Now that the face of the earth has been overrun by man and Nature is on its way to being thoroughly domesticated, the passion of love may be our one remaining experience of the treacherous joy of Nature. It exacts a price, of course. But there's another side. Isak Dinesen found in Africa that she divided all creatures into the good (domestic) and the noble (wild); and while the good are useful, the noble, she felt, upheld the fierce dignity of creation.

And, of course, it would make gays the great romantics of our time.

In any event, these interviews suggested to me such thoughts about the problematic phenomenon of love—two sides but no coin. This elusive quality seemed to demand separate and independent interviews, a bifocal approach that might glimpse the three-dimensional but oddly insubstantial reality. The same desire for "bifocality" led to the use of photographs as well as words generated in response to them. And again, it led to asking Philip and Neil to compose a written self-portrait in response to the verbal picture of them generated in the act of interviewing. If we have to have two sides but no coin, at least we could have two sides three times. So here you have it: the two sides of the story, the pictures and the words, the spoken and the written. In the space between these dualities, slipping through the interstices, something we call passion or love makes its presence felt. Like life, love remains an essential mystery. Talking about it is not an attempt to explain the mystery, but to call attention to it.

"Everything Is Only Ten Years Old"

A CONVERSATION WITH FELICE PICANO

IN THE SUMMER of 1979 Felice Picano and I were both renting in the Pines, a small beach community on Fire Island, really a sandbar off the southern side of Long Island. Starting in the Fifties and intensifying in the Sixties, Fire Island Pines had become what appeared to be (but was not quite) a totally gay community with its own newly emerging culture, separated from the rest of America by the Great South Bay. That ferry ride which began each weekend felt like a magic journey to a liberated area, an oasis in the desert of homophobia that was America in the Seventies.

But this oasis was not a place of relaxation, like the Hamptons for our straight colleagues; rather it was a discipline, as one of my roommates there used to say, "boot camp for gay men." Though another roommate chortled and said, "More like gay high school, if you ask me. We're just learning all the stuff about romance and sexual entanglement that straights learned in high school and college." In any event, it was a gay affirming experience that helped us to live in a homophobic world without becoming reconciled to it. The Pines often reminded me of why those Indians in the Southwest retreated back to their home mesa once a year, there to reenact the rituals that let the spirits of the tribe reappear to them and thus confirm their identity as a community and as this individual Zuni Indian, for instance, before going back out and living as gardeners and house cleaners in a hostile Anglo culture.

That summer there was a lot of buzz in the publishing world about Felice, a popular and successful novelist who was actually able to live on his earnings as a writer, a feat no other gay writer I knew had so far managed. By dealing with intensely gay subject matter in his fourth novel was this man risking his highly successful career? After all, following Ed White's critically acclaimed first novel, *Forgetting Elena*, he had been frozen out with his second, *Nocturnes for the King of Naples*, because of its explicit gay subject matter and the book found no takers.[1]

I took the opportunity one afternoon to interview Felice about the situation.[2]

At 35, Felice Picano is a successful writer, with three best-sellers to his name (*Smart as the Devil*, Arbor House, 1975; *Eyes*, Arbor House, 1976; and *The Mesmerist*, Delacorte, 1977). He has also managed to publish a volume of gay poems, *The Deformity Lover*, and to establish a small gay publishing house, The Seahorse Press.

The following conversation took place in Fire Island Pines and was occasioned by the publication of his new novel, *The Lure* (Delacorte).

MD: The world portrayed in your new novel *The Lure* is the same scene that's covered in "Cruising," the movie that's causing so much agitation right now (1979), and also, for that matter, the world of *Faggots* and *Dancer from the Dance*. But it seems to me there's a real difference in the way you see it and the way it's been depicted in those novels, and probably in the movie, from what I've heard. Yours seems both a more sympathetic and a much more accurate version of this . . . seamier side of the gay world.

FP: Well, I don't know if it's seamy. But I tried to make it as authentic as possible. A lot depends on how I narrate my point of view, how my *character* sees it. For example, I see Fire Island in various ways, having spent a lot of time here. When *he* sees it, he sees it from one particular point of view . . . that is, as somebody who's frustrated, confused and unsure. To him it appears very different than it appears to me. And I specifically chose a different type of character to go into this world, in order to bring out some objective points about it—because he's a so-

---

1 Until I published it at St. Martin's in 1978.
2 Published in the November 1979 issue of *Christopher Street*.

ciologist, essentially. And, of course, he's straight at the beginning of the novel and completely ignorant of the gay world.

MD: Why choose to set it in the sexual demimonde, as it were?

FP: You want to hear what this book grew out of? Because there really was one factual occurrence which set me going. In the early Seventies there were a series of murders of gays in the West Village, murders that were connected with bars and bar owners and clubs. Arthur Bell did some articles on them and then he stopped and nothing more was heard about it. At that time, I was living on Jane Street. A good friend and neighbor of mine was working for the Jane Street Block Association which was very aggressive in neighborhood relations and they met with police liaison units, etc., etc. At that time, he told me that the police had set up a very hush-hush organization in the Village that was going around trying to find out what these murders were all about, what the links were to the Mob and whatever else. This went on for about two years. Later, from friends of mine who were connected with bars or tricks who knew bartenders or other people—it's a floating type of world—from them I heard that this special police unit was disbanded, and I wasn't able to find out why. I began speculating, trying to find out what had happened. It was something that interested me, it was right there in my neighborhood and I wanted to know what was going on.

About the same time that I was putting together the proposal for this book there was an article in the *New York Times* which talked about how the police unit which had been set up to investigate these murders was now being revealed for the first time, and only then because it was being disbanded, and there was an investigation into corruption within the unit . . . none of which was terribly clear. When I called up the reporter who had done the story, he said all the information he had was in his article, and that was all I could find out. At that point I decided a little bit more was going on than what we had been told. And so that was the basis of my novel. I said, let's speculate on what the police did, on what this unit was and why it was disbanded, and why there was an investigation into it. That was how my idea developed.

What I liked about the idea was that it struck a really fascinating metaphor for what being homosexual in our time and place means. Because instead of a gay man pretending to be straight in every aspect of his life, having to build up a second life, what I was interested in was a straight man who had to build up a gay life. The idea of reversing the metaphor for the way gay men live in this country is what actually appealed to me. And the story that worked was all predicated on the fact that this man had to develop . . . something would have to happen to him *internally* as a result of what happened in his dealings with the world.

MD: Do you think you're taking a big risk, as a successful mainline novelist, to turn to this subject matter in your fourth novel?

FP: Yes. (Laughter.)

MD: And especially to try to portray in a popular novel a straight man who essentially is converted to being gay by the end of the novel?

FP: Well, if I hadn't had the support of my agent and editor I don't know whether I would have done it. I felt I had to address the issue at some point. I had done a book of gay poems and I've been doing some gay short stories, but I had to address the issue of homosexuality in a novel. To my mind, there are a lot of really fine writers in their fifties, sixties and seventies who are homosexual, and who could have really taken off if they had addressed the issue. The only one who seems to have done that is Christopher Isherwood, and I think, more and more, that he's going to be the one who stands out. I felt that as a novelist who claimed to be a reporter—which is one of the duties of the novelist, to report on certain aspects of life around us—I had to deal with the subject, which is really close to me. So even at this point of risk, I decided to do it.

MD: But it seems to me you also directed it towards the straight audience without compromising yourself in any way, which is really quite an accomplishment.

FP: Well, there are a certain number of people who have bought books by Felice Picano who expect a kind of book, a book that is going to take them into an area they have not necessarily gone into before. So in that sense I felt that I was being true to the readership I already had. They were going to get another Picano mind-trip into some new area of life today.

MD: Have you had any response? Any idea of knowing how the straight audience will respond to it so far?

FP: Well, I thought straight women would like it because women tend to like the books I write. But straight men also seem to like it a lot! And I think one reason is that it's like escapist literature for straight men, it provides them with what is, after all, a masculine, rather bold and courageous, if sometimes impulsive and sometimes stupid, hero. Someone they can identify with, who goes through an adventurous period of time. He gets to try out all sorts of things they are forbidden to do by their position in society, by their position as family men and by their self-image.

MD: And your publishing house has been totally supportive?

FP: Dell/Delacorte?

MD: Yes, I hear a lot about the difficulty gay writers have because a lot of publishing houses are homophobic, and I'm not sure if that's true or not. I have to say I haven't run into that.

FP: Well, here's the situation. Believe it or not, I originally intended this as a film. I had been talking to a film producer who'd read some of my work and wanted to do a film set in the gay area. When I was out in Los Angeles we discussed it, but this was in 1976 and I really felt that they were not interested in going as far or as deeply as I wanted to go with the material. So we agreed to disagree at that point and I came back to New York. I was handing a completely different proposal to my publisher, and my editor said, "I understand you were out in Hollywood doing something with a scenario." And I said, "Yes, they didn't accept it," and she said, "Well, I'd really like to take a look at it." As soon as I showed it to her, she said, "I really think this is your next book." So the support came real fast. When I did hand in the final draft, I think they were a little surprised by the authenticity and the eroticism and the violence that I portrayed, and I think they were un-sure about who would read the book. But everyone at Dell/Delacorte liked the story, so any hesitation seemed to change real fast.

MD: Well, they seem to be building up the book in a very big way. They seem very much behind it from everything I've seen. Are they going to run this also as a gay book, advertise in the gay press and all that?

FP: Absolutely. We discussed that. Since I had experience with adver-tising as a gay publisher, we got together and discussed what propor-tion of the advertising budget would go to the gay media. And it's a good portion. So it's being run simultaneously as a mainline book and as a gay book.

MD: I think you have this interesting position, because you're working both in mainline publishing through your novels and simultaneously in the gay subculture through your volume of poetry, and now as pub-lisher of Seahorse Press, which does only gay books.

FP: Yes, only gay stuff. And to my knowledge, it's the only gay book publisher in New York. Ashley is out of town.

MD: What else has Seahorse published?

FP: Doric Wilson's book, the two plays that are running at The Spike, *The West Street Gang* and *A Perfect Relationship*, and we're publishing a book of poetry by Dennis Cooper called *Idols*, a wonderful book.

MD: What's interesting is that you can work simultaneously and ev-idently extremely well in both the mainstream and in the gay sub-culture.

FP: I'm hoping that this book is the one that pulls it together. (Laughs.) Because I'm going to continue splitting it apart from here on. I've just started another novel, which is not in any way gay, because that's . . . one of my concerns, but not my *only* concern as a writer. And I'm probably going to be publishing a book of my short stories in a year or two, which are all gay. It's nice to be able to do both. I don't know who else is doing it. I'd like to try to get more people interested.

MD: Ed White, in a way.

FP: Ed White, definitely.

MD: Not as commercially successful yet as you, but he seems to be able to do both of those things. It's interesting: I'm always trying to figure out whether there is in fact a gay literature, a separate and distinct cultural identity . . .

FP: Well, would you consider *Myra Breckinridge* part of gay literature?

MD: I don't know.

FP: Because I think I would. And if that's so, then Gore Vidal is an example of somebody who's done it before, but has done it rather coyly and very carefully because of what happened to him. But he's hiding a great deal, and I don't really see that as necessary from where I am.

MD: That's the feeling I have. But it's odd in terms of other cultural movements. If there is a separate gay cultural identity that would justify these institutions, like magazines, newspapers, small presses, and a separate literature, you'd expect people to get exclusively into that. Look at the Black Movement today. But it does seem possible that gays can work in both simultaneously, which I think is a peculiarity. Like there are all these discussions about ghettoization. And I must admit a few years ago I was totally against it, and now . . . I mean, here we are in the Pines . . .

FP: What a ghetto! (Laughs.)

MD: . . . and I like it. And it's real odd, but it doesn't seem to me in any way to contradict the fact that I work in the mainline world. It seems that "straight" publishing houses, for instance, can serve the gay community perfectly well. Provided the books have sufficient commercial potential, of course.

FP: But I think the real problem is what's happening with gay books that *are* being published: they're coming under an incredible amount of attack, for any and all reasons. Especially from political radicals.

MD: More from the gay press than the straight press . . .

FP: Much more, much more!

MD: That's what's so disturbing. For all the gay books I've published, we get much better reviews in the straight press than in the gay press. I really don't understand it. I realize there are issues . . . I don't think we should only puff stuff that's gay . . .

FP: Right.

MD: . . . but somehow I feel that's not the question. The books really are attacked in the gay press . . .

FP: For not presenting what some people feel is a true picture. If I were to present a true picture of gay life around me it would be Marvin and his lover of ten years finding a new recipe for tuna noodle casserole and inviting their friends over for an evening, and perhaps there's a genius somewhere who can pull that off in a novel, but to me that's not what novels are all about . . . novel means new, and it's supposed to bring something that's new to you, a new viewpoint, a new look at the world, or just new places, new people, new characters. So to a large extent I feel this criticism of gay literature is misplaced. The gay critics are claiming everything that's being done by gay writers now is, in one way or another, sensational. *Lovers* is sensational because it's a failed love affair. And *Dancer from the Dance* is sensational because it over-romanticizes everything. And *Faggots* because it over-criticizes everything. But art is not reality, it's a distortion. And I think you have to choose whether you're going to read something as a document and accept it only as a document, or whether you're going to read it as a work of art. One of the problems may be that the gay audience is, in a real deep sense, illiterate. By that I mean that ever since they have come to gay consciousness they have been fed on pornography on the one hand and gay political rhetoric on the other. And between the two of them there's no space for anything that's judgment or value or setting up standards or criteria. To my mind, that's a really disturbing type of illiteracy. I'm hoping it changes.

MD: It's also happening at a very dangerous time, because this attitude is the opposite of nurturing at a time when we're just starting to get a certain number of gay writers. But the audience is so acerbic and so critical. You know, we'll go back to the Gore Vidal and Truman Capote model.

FP: I don't think that's going to happen though. I'll tell you why. My feeling is that the whole "coming out" idea as a metaphor is so strong and so variable—it's like Sophocles' "Know Yourself"—it can support a huge amount of fictional and non-fictional work and that is going to continue to interest people. It's too good an idea to die. And I think as long as it exists, there are going to be writers who say, "Hey, I can really take this idea and do something fabulous with it."

MD: But there seems to be such a lag. What I seem to see, increasingly, is a greater self-awareness of gay personal identity, which has to do with how people clothe themselves, how they look, what they . . . I mean, all of gay New York has reshaped its body in the last four years. People are not at all closeted, or much less so. There's a very assertive experiment to establish a new type of masculinity as an alternative to the old straight version. But there's such a lag in the literary response to that. If you see how people deal with clothing and lifestyle and everything else, how come their taste in fiction doesn't keep pace? I don't quite understand that. Most of these people do read. And, of course, they'd want to read about their own life, so why don't they?

FP: Right. But look who's doing the criticism. One of the problems that gay writers have at this stage—and I think Andrew Holleran said this first—is that we have to *describe* gay life because it's never been described before. And it's crystallizing around us, it's happening around us, so we have to describe—almost minute-by-minute—what the changes are, what the various points of concentration are. We have to describe what people dress like, what they do, where they go out, how they use their drugs or their alcohol, or what they do for entertainment. A lot of what we're doing is taken up with the description of what gay life looks like and feels like and what it's like to live it. We can only deal with particular areas in one book, you know, between two covers. A lot of people are complaining and saying, "You're not describing *my* life, you're describing some New York queen's life." And I do think that's a problem, I really do.

MD: Except that in literature, nobody sets out simply to describe somebody's life. I mean, that's sociology. Artists, writers use certain material . . . the point you or Andrew or anybody else is finally making is not just to describe a certain segment of life, but to use it as a concrete metaphor, like you would any other material. Well, I suppose not knowing that is the illiteracy you were talking about.

FP: Yes, exactly.

MD: It really is true. Illiteracy is not knowing what the function of literature is in relation to your life; in the most basic way, it's not knowing how to read. And it does seem that we don't. At least the gay critics don't. It's just astonishing.

FP: Well, Pablo Neruda once said that a book is a letter that's written to the world. Some people receive it, some people answer it. And to my mind a lot of the gay critics are like people who've lost their mailbox keys. I don't think they *want* to receive these letters, these books. I don't think they're really that interested.

One of the problems is that a writer, no matter what he's doing, is going to be a rebel. You can't trust a writer, basically. The writer is the gadfly, the outsider, the observer. I think that's the writer's strength, especially in gay society, which is forming itself right before our eyes. I mean, the movement is only ten years old. Everything is only ten years old. If the gay writer comes under attack, as he does so much these days, it's sort of self-criticism. People are seeing what they don't want to see about themselves. And he's pointing it out rather fearlessly and saying, "Hey, look at what you're doing, jerks." I think that's a lot of what's being responded to. Then again, there are some real puritans in the movement. I sort of distrust politics the way I distrust religion. And a lot of the gay criticism that's coming to books is coming from a political point of view, I don't see how the two mix at all. It's a sort of shame.

MD: It's like the literary Stalinism of the late Thirties. On such an appallingly low level.

FP: That's right. Also there is a big question of our enormous heterogeneity. What do I have in common with a gay steelworker in Flint, for example? Very little. And because of that, there are people who are bound to have completely different ideas of how to lead what they consider a gay life. I know people whose only way of looking at gay life is to have a single partner for the rest of their lives. Complete romantics. Something like that is naturally going to color the way they see almost everything that's important in gay life. And they're going to criticize the way we live our lives, the way we party, the way we dress, the way we spend our money, the way we have sex, from that viewpoint. Whereas someone who is promiscuous or someone who decides to have a life that is a series of short and perhaps not terribly meaningful relationships, but which are very pleasant—because people have reached decisions like that, too—he's going to lead as free and independent a life as possible, and he's going to look down on that other person and say, "Hey, I think you're just stuck in straight-world conventionality." And so we're going at it from all sorts of different angles. There's a great variety of lifestyles within this lifestyle . . . and a critic should be able to say where he comes from. He should provide his credentials before he reviews and criticizes a book. (Laughs.) . . . It's a terrible thing to have to say.

MD: It's funny. We could make a checklist: all critics would have to reveal their position on certain questions.

FP: Right! Because I think that's where their criticisms are coming from a lot, they're coming from really root questions of how you define yourself as gay.

MD: Precisely. But this is extremely interesting and, as far as I know, there's no parallel. Take the difference between you and the gay steelworker. What do you have in common? You're both gay. You could try to make analogies, like between an intellectual Jew on the Upper West Side of Manhattan and a Jewish steelworker in Flint. They'll have something in common eventually, because they've inherited this Jewishness, which may . . . I mean there are questions about it, but there is some kind of cultural identity there. And Blacks will fight over the portrayal of "the Black Experience." But again, they have an identity that can't be walked away from. Now, our identity is very odd, because in a way, it's freely accepted. I mean, you could go out and fuck men without making a culture out of it. Obviously. That's what most people have done for . . .

FP: Hundreds of years!

MD: Right. But I can't think of any parallel for that. Andrew Kopkind pointed out recently in his *Village Voice* article that what we're seeing is the creation of an artificial culture, in the sense that it's not necessary. We're not stuck with the Old Testament and 3,000 years of persecution like the Jews. We don't have Black skin. You know, we wouldn't have to be gay. We might have to be homosexual, or not; that's psychological and/or biological question. But being a homosexual—having sex with men—does not necessarily lead to being gay, that is, having a gay culture, shopping at Bloomingdale's, reading gay novels, etc. It really is extraordinarily odd. Kopkind was the first person who made that clear to me . . . the enormous peculiarity of the idea of a gay culture or a gay identity. And it still seems to me very problematic, but I feel it very strongly.

FP: Right. Another problem I think we're dealing with is that there really is a difference between the political critics and what people refer to as style queens, who have in fact shaped all the visible aspects of gay culture, and have done it almost intuitively. They've done it because it looks good, it feels good. The people who are doing the thinking around it, who are trying to formulate an ideology that will work, not only politically but sociologically and psychologically, are quite different. That's where the real split is. The culture's being formed by people who are not necessarily thinking about it, but who *are* doing it because it feels good or looks good, or will make a nice effect. And, in fact, if you take a New York or San Francisco or Houston man who looks gay and lives a gay life, and you strip away the accoutrements, you have just an ordinary man. It's all been put in, it's all styled on top, all surface—the man's haircut, clothing, where he goes dancing, the choice of drugs he takes, and what he will try out in bed.

MD: But what else should there be to an identity, to a cultural identity, but those things—how one looks, how one chooses to move in the world?

FP: The difficulty with people who are trying to build up an *ideological* framework is that there *isn't* any ideological framework. It really *is* surface, it really is a series of attributes, and it seems to work. As you said, we're not stuck with a skin color or a genetic difference, or a religious difference that sets us apart. So gay culture is a distinctive setting apart of ourselves by a whole stylistic framework. And political people criticize that stylistic framework. Part of that is just the distrust of artists, whether they're hairdressers or interior decorators or writers or painters or whatever.

MD: You're saying that the basic division is between what you call style queens and the intellectuals and writers?

FP: Well, my point is that the intellectuals are not necessarily the writers. I think that's where the problem is. The so-called gay intellectuals that I know of are involved in formulating an ideology they hope everyone lives up to. Most gay writers haven't fallen into that camp. They're on their own. They're somewhere between the two, and if they seem closer to the intuitive style gay people, it's because there's more to be seen, more to be commented on—the way people behave, manners, social customs. That's where a writer's real material is . . . it's not in the idea. Writers hope to sometimes expose the ideology. But they're not sitting in the intellectuals' camp, and I think that's a problem.

MD: Well, it gets us very far afield, but it's interesting. If there is an ideology for being gay, more to it than an aesthetic way of being in the world . . . and I think you could dredge one up, I think you could even make a fairly highfalutin' argument where metaphysically the gay condition seems to me—unless I just have blinders on—to coincide with the essential position of "modern man." In a very odd way, in the sense of making it anew, in the sense of not having traditions that are in any sense binding, in the sense of dealing with a great deal of self-consciousness. Other people are encumbered by cultures that seem to be a weight from the past. But it certainly means nothing to me that I'm Irish. You know. Any of that tradition is absolutely . . .

FP: Gone, yeah.

MD: . . . gone, it has no impact on me whatsoever. I don't know what it means to someone else if they're Polish, or if they're German or Italian or something like that.

FP: I was approached by an Italian-American magazine to do something for them and I told them I didn't know what I could do for them. That's not an identity I feel in any way connected with. I didn't grow up in an Italian neighborhood, I learned my Italian when I went to Florence. That isn't one of the ways I identify myself. Whereas as soon as I got in contact with gay magazines, I said, "Yes, I can do it. This is realistic." So okay, I'll grant you that: being gay is one of the most basic ways of defining ourselves.

MD: Okay, then that would mean there's a great deal of cultural content in being gay, that it is not simply a parochial identity crisis or whatever, the formation of a small group.

FP: That's right . . .

MD: A gay culture would have a great deal of relevant significance to the community at large, because the gay situation does seem to coincide with where, on the whole, we are as . . . whatever you want to call us . . . post-modern people.

FP: Well, as soon as we can get mainstream readers for our books, then we'll see whether straight people feel that something is being illumined for them in a gay writer's works. I think that would make the difference. But, you know, this line of thought makes me a bit nervous, just as it makes me nervous when people claim that literature has a function. I don't know if literature does have a function, except to continue. For me, that seems to be a large thing for literature to do in the face of all the demands on people's attention today. I don't know. There are people who really claim that literature, and especially gay literature, should have a meaning beyond its own existence. I don't know if that's true. Someone complained, after seeing one of Doric Wilson's plays that I published, and said, "Well, it does nothing more than mirror our lives." I said, "As far as I'm concerned, that's enough." It would be fabulous if you could see that his play did something more, but the fact that it *does* mirror our lives is important to me, because it hasn't been done before.

MD: Yeah, it's also a question of how far beyond that you could go. I mean, poets are not supposed to be legislators, despite the famous quote. We don't want them to tell us how we're supposed to live. Ideological novels, like socialist realism, are horribly dull as a rule.

FP: Exactly. But that seems to be what most gay critics are demanding. And you'd better agree with them, too!

MD: I've only read one good ideological book, which was *Coming Out* by Wallace Hamilton. I think it was badly misjudged, because nobody considered it as a political book, which it basically was. I mean, it's a very systematic pro-gay novel. You have to go back to Jack London, or some of the Red Chinese writers of the thirties, to really compare it within the framework of literature as a political tract. And I think it compares quite favorably. But I do think you can only go so far with that. And I think probably in the long term seriously literary fiction about the gay world will attract general readers who aren't gay. I'm sure general readers are going to respond to your book. I hope so. I wish they were making the movie from your book rather than *Cruising*.

FP: Yeah, although I really didn't mind that we got no film interest at the time, I'm sort of annoyed now that the producers that I'd originally talked to about it didn't take it on. Just because *Cruising is* being made now, and *The Lure* would have presented what I think is a more accurate version of the same material. So it's sort of a shame.

MD: Because politically it would have been much more—how do we say?—progressive.

FP: Yes, but also because my book asks more questions. Because it goes beyond politics or sexuality, and asks people . . . my character asks himself, "What am I doing? Who and what am I living for?" I think that's something a lot of gay people have to ask . . . and a lot of straight people, too. And we can't help them out too much more than that. But I think people go to a film with a different attitude than they go to a book. I know I do. I don't think people expect to see reality on the silver screen after all this time. I think they expect to see a distortion. Whereas when they go to a book, they seem to want to know more of what is actually going on, and will accept more reality in that form, because it's a private and not a communal experience.

MD: But I do think films have traditionally functioned to show people how to be American. Wave after wave of immigrants have learned what it means to be American, even learned the language, from Hollywood. That's why I think . . . I guess I do think it's legit to use muscle to try to get our own point of view there. Because movies do somehow still reflect and help create the popular consciousness of the whole nation.

FP: Absolutely. But it's a *public* consciousness. I'm not sure whether private attitudes are as affected by films.

MD: Okay, but Hollywood's public attitude is incredibly homophobic. And a gayer industry you can't imagine. But everyone's really closeted.

FP: Yeah, I know from experience.

MD: Well, I suppose we have no more bitch than Black people do in this country. . . .

FP: Whose culture has been misused for years.

MD: And probably never filmed decently except for *Stormy Weather*, the only film I know which was totally Black. I don't know if it was Black-directed.

FP: *Lady Sings the Blues* was to my mind a Black film, inside and out.

MD: Well, if it's taken Blacks so long, and they've gotten so little, I guess we shouldn't despair.

FP: On the other hand, we should be angry because unlike Blacks and women there are gays who are wealthy and powerful and in important positions in this country, including—even especially—in the film industry. And it sort of behooves them, since they're in these extra-responsible positions with all this extra clout that other minorities don't have, to do something a little extra. And I say it's a great shame if people in those positions aren't doing anything. You know, it's really irresponsible. That irresponsibility is really more deplorable than the irresponsibility of a Billy Friedkin (the director of *Cruising*), who seems to be simply after commercial success.

MD: I agree. Do you have something else you want to talk about? Or do you want to go back to the pool . . . an appropriate way to end a conversation in the Pines. (Laughs)

FP: The pool is heaven. It really is.

Decent Passions

REAL STORIES ABOUT LOVE

IN 1978 I was still utterly confused about sex, love, and passion, but now I was struggling to make one particular relationship work. With no (acceptable) traditional patterns to follow, gay men had to invent new rules and consider new possibilities, to reinvent for themselves one of the most basic relationships in life, the human couple. The theme of how to integrate passion, especially sexual passion, into our lives, and how to make relationships work, occupied a whole generation of newly liberated gay men and women. Before Stonewall sex had been hidden and kept so separate from our social lives that such questions never came up; now they arose with a vengeance.

It seemed to me that people all over—not only gays and lesbians but even straights—were dealing with the same issues, as if all of us were trying to reinvent anew the stable structures of intimacy that we traditionally referred to as family. As usual I found it illuminating to discuss these matters. Actually, I became a bit obsessive about it, and over the next two or three years, whenever I could snatch time from my job, I spoke at length with dozens of couples in various cities and locals across the country, and eventually ended up with a book that focused on three couples.[1]

I had a contract with Delacorte/Dial for a cloth and trade paperback edition, with the possibility of a mass market edition with Dell if the sales should justify it. The book was accepted, copyedited and presented to the sales force, who rebelled, saying they couldn't sell such a book to the general (i.e., straight) market since it also dealt with gay and lesbian couples, that the gay male market wouldn't accept it since it dealt with straight and lesbian relationships, and that the lesbian/feminist market certainly wouldn't buy it since half the book was about men. I totally disagreed (then and now), but when I brought it

---

1 *Decent Passions* (Alyson Publications, 1984).

to several other New York publishers, I got the same response. Finally, Sasha Alyson, who had started a small gay press in Boston, came to my rescue and published the book.

I include here the book's introduction and the afterword.

But such reaching out in passion does not simply lift us up and away beyond ourselves. It gathers our essential being to its proper ground, it exposes our ground for the first time in so gathering, so that the passion is that through which and in which we take hold of ourselves and achieve lucid mastery over the beings around us and within us.

MARTIN HEIDEGGER

Introduction: Real Stories

When I embarked on this project, I had reached what seemed like a state of terminal confusion. For some years I had felt most truly alive when I was in love. Although I was intensely involved in my work, enjoyed a group of wonderful friends, and took advantage of the excitement a big city can offer, none of these things by themselves—or even together—seemed to constitute a happy life. If my love life was desolate, everything seemed out of whack. Romance and passion supplied a vitality and happiness nothing else quite matched; without love, life seemed not only barren but pointless. I think I assumed that love *was* the point of life. This can get you in trouble. I not only piled up the usual quota of hard knocks and halcyon days, blissful nights and bitter mornings, I gradually became more and more confused about what I was doing. It was clear I wasn't getting what I wanted; but then again, what precisely did I want? And was it even possible? Or was I only suffering the after-effects of a fading adolescent fantasy?

Thinking about the situation didn't help much. Introspection only muddled me more and talking about it exhaustively to my friends only exhausted them and me. Love seemed to me so confusing, difficult, and ultimately demoralizing that I wasn't sure I wanted it—but without it my life felt somehow empty. For a while I considered the possibility that I was a bit demented about the whole subject, had become a monomaniac or fallen victim to the romantic hype of the media, with its endless stories and songs about love and passion. But as I looked around me it seemed clear enough that love *was* the most important thing in life for most people. It seemed to offer a dramatic intensity and a happiness—from exuberance to ecstasy to deep satisfaction—that most of us can't find anywhere else. Who hasn't felt the astonishment that comes with the first touch of love when everything seems possible again? When the world opens and you feel like you've woken up? The kiss that released Sleeping Beauty, the recognition that allowed the toad to become the prince he truly is—that incredible feeling of passion, which sometimes survives but more often doesn't, is an experience felt by virtually everyone at some moment in their lives.

But who hasn't become entangled in the misery it can cause? The snares of jealousy and the fear of not being loved as much as one loves. The pain of not being wanted sexually when one wants to be wanted sexually. The grating discrepancies in daily habits and outlook that seem so trivial at first but can build up until they affect you like chalk screeching on a blackboard. The furious frustration of not being understood. The dilemmas of personal freedom versus commitment and responsibility. For me, the utter demoralization of losing a lover undercut my sense of self so much I began to wonder if the risk and the grief were worth it, and whether it was ever possible to make things work.

In this state of confusion, I decided I wanted to hear how other people handled these matters, to see if their stories could shed any light on my own dilemmas. It seemed there were endless experts telling me how to do everything, from making love and having sex to building a relationship or at least learning how to make friends with myself. But while these books often have a lot of simple common sense mixed in with the oversimplified nonsense and hype necessary to attract attention, they only work as temporary morale boosters, Sunday sermons that uplift us for an hour and have no impact on how we actually live our lives—or at least how I actually live my life. I wanted to talk to real people who had experienced passion and thought about it, the way we all think about things that matter to us, people who could communicate their experience in its actual weight and density. There are no experts in love as there are no experts in life. We're all in the same boat, and sharing our experience—hard won as all lived experience is—seemed a sensible idea.

So I went out and talked to many couples, some at great length. These people were remarkably open and generous in sharing their lives, as anxious as I to understand what had happened to them, while clarifying for themselves what they had and what they wanted. I made no effort to interpret or analyze what I heard, which may irritate adherents of various schools of psychology or sociology. Frankly, I am dubious about any attempt to penetrate and explain the recesses of the human heart. Anyway, it would have been beside the point. These were stories and I was a listener. I tried not to bring prefabricated *explanations* to what I heard, but to follow the speaker and let the story emerge as it wanted. This led to some surprises: matters I would have thought significant did not emerge on their own, and other themes that I had not considered emerged strongly. The point was not to interpret but *to listen*. You do not necessarily understand a good story the first time you hear it, and your understanding of it may change over time.

It is important that these are real stories; they happened to particular people. There is no attempt here to commit a social science. The six individuals in this book are *not* a representative sample, or a composite portrait, or anything else. They are real people and like all real people they are unique. Their stories are completely individual and particular—which seems fitting. Whether or not there is such a thing as a representative portrait—the average, the norm, the general—you certainly don't find it in love affairs. Love seems to be precisely about the discovery and celebration of the particular person, "who" we are, as opposed to "what" we might be in the world.

Real stories are always unlikely. And love, as common as it is, is the unlikeliest thing of all. By some odd psychological trick—or perhaps it's just mental laziness, a numbness induced by the watered-down social science vision of life the media saturates our world with—we increasingly tend to see ourselves as exemplifying various generalities. We nod our heads as we are told in countless books, magazines, and talk shows that we are alienated from a dehumanized social system, suffering from the frantic narcissism of the "Me generation," fleeing intimacy and fighting responsibility, or suffering the shock of a break-down of values.

But even if true, what in the world do you *do* with this knowledge? This type of thinking leads us to being spectators at our own lives—and inattentive spectators at that. Made drowsy by a surfeit of artificial images of what life is like, we fail to see the reckless improbability of the real thing. Strangeness—peculiarity, singularity—is the hallmark of reality. All we have to do is reflect for a moment on the story of our own concrete lives to realize how odd it is. Everybody has a story and everybody's story is passingly strange. I have found that *whenever* I set out to interview anyone and really concentrated my attention on them, they would be transformed into something "rich and strange" before my eyes. To trade the strangeness of reality—the magic of life—for a likely story that has been processed through the strainer of some grid of interpretation seems to me a poor bargain. I tend to believe that it is the virtue of stories that in them the particular in its very particular-ity can reveal some truths that otherwise could not be grasped. In any event, I have found that some stories have a clarity that is illuminat-ing. This illumination works in obscure ways that I certainly haven't figured out, but I suspect it is the secret of the value fiction has for us.

But these stories are real, not fiction. The following interviews re-veal one moment in the lives of the people interviewed. All these love affairs were ongoing; what happened the next day, the next week, the next year, would, of course, change the story and how the teller told it. That would always be the case, at any point in time. To supply an ending—how did it turn out, did they live happily ever after?—would be precisely to turn these real stories into fiction. Fiction is finished, life isn't. And life doesn't finally make sense the way fiction does, be-cause fiction is one way we make sense of life.

I did not want to force my way of making sense onto these people. My aim is to make sense of my own life; listening to how other people make sense of theirs seems useful. The book that has resulted consists of six interviews that tell the story of three love affairs. Little of signif-icance has been altered and only incidental matters have been omit-ted. I have, of course, edited them; what you will read is only a fraction of the transcripts of the interviews. I have tried to retain the surface texture of spoken speech and follow the rhythm of the stories as they unfolded, with the hesitations and reflective pauses and the sudden onrush of certainty. I sought diversity in age, station in life, geography, sexual orientation, etc., not to construct a representative portrait of love and passion today, but simply to get three *different* stories.

An interview, unlike a fictional story, captures one moment in an ongoing life; thus what comes into focus is what people are striving for, what they affirm in their lives and what they want. The essential question is one of values—what do I want? what can I hope for? what should I accept? I have found these conversations to be of value for myself, especially in clarifying the importance of common decency and the startling idea that it can and ought to be combined with our most intense passion. To talk to people about the ultimate and concrete values in their life always seems to me useful. I hope it proves useful—illuminating, provocative, confirming—to the reader and can serve as a stimulus to the efforts of each of us to make sense of our own lives.

Afterword: Passion and Decency

The six people in this book are all engaged in a fairly astonishing attempt to reinvent love outside the traditional categories, and to reinvent it in ways that actually work in their day-to-day lives. Like most of us today they experience love as a problem, something that generates perplexities and difficulties.

This is a startling state of affairs. The traditional social conventions of love, passion, and commitment don't seem "natural" anymore, they don't just carry us along automatically. It's not that they don't attract us; they just don't seem all that workable in our immediate lives. Many signs—the rise in the divorce rate, the fact that less than a quarter of all American families fit the traditional image (working father, mother in the home, and their two children), the emergence of the women's and gay movements—point to an enormous shift in our lives that increasingly renders our inherited cultural models less relevant. We are confronted willy-nilly with the formidable task of reinventing our lives, searching out and declaring our own standards, starting from scratch. Even those who uphold the validity of the most traditional forms of love and family are engaged in this process of self-creation—after all, in a totally traditional society one didn't have to assert and defend these values, they seemed self-evident, nothing else occurred to people. Today a conventional marriage is as wildly experimental as anything you can think of.

Before I started this project I was particularly interested in the questions of love and passion in the newly emerging gay male culture, not only because it was most immediately relevant to my own life, but because in that context these matters seemed raised with a decided freshness due to the absence of pre-existing social conventions. However, the more I talked with people, the more it seemed to me that we were all in the same boat. Like the pilgrims who set sail for a new world and landed on the shores of an unstoried wilderness, we also must clear a space and build a life relying only on our wits and whatever spiritual resources have survived the journey.

It seems to me worth noting that of all the values our culture has cherished and relied upon to dignify, make sense of, and regulate our lives, the only one that retains broad and concrete vitality today is romantic love. The dignity of work, the satisfactions of the family, the nobility of the professions, the public-spiritedness of patriotism and sense of community—no doubt these values are still alive and effective to some degree in our society, but within the perspective of our immediate and particular lives, they do not seem to inspire us and provide the meaning they formerly promised. Few people today find that their work makes them content with their lives; and while we don't understand what has gone so drastically wrong with the family, most people agree that the contemporary reality falls far short of the Currier and Ives images we still cherish but do not experience anymore. But romantic love or passion offers all of us one of the few opportunities—outside of war—to experience an intensified feeling of reality, "just like the movies," where life makes sense and is beautiful. And everybody, from Mildred Pierce to Marcel Proust, wants their life to make sense and be beautiful.

Passionate love gives us the chance to experience the dramatic in our own lives; as the story unfolds we feel that something is at stake, something matters. In passion *who we are* matters; we matter precisely as this particular individual we are, not as worker, mother, consumer, or any other *role* we might play. All the great folktales and parables about love are about discovery and awakening—Cinderella, Sleeping Beauty, the Enchanted Prince. I think every businessman and housewife, every secretary, engineer, and student goes around most days feeling in disguise—enchanted by daily routines that make us all toads—waiting for the lover who will truly recognize who we are and thereby release us to ourselves (as Heidegger predicted). That particular individuality our society values so highly but doesn't seem to know what to do with finds its place in passionate love; there it flourishes, an oasis in the desert of the modern world. Popular culture is suffused with this theme precisely because it is one of the great possibilities of contemporary life.

All the people in this book experienced the intense value of passion, the inexplicable way it strikes and its nearly overwhelming power, which leaves one grasping for inadequate explanations like "chemistry." We may not understand passion but it hits with such an immediacy and certainty that while it's happening we have no doubt that it's the most important thing in our lives. As something that overcomes us, that we suffer (from *pathein*, to suffer), it is not something we choose. Passion is something that *happens* to us. It is flush with sexuality, that part of us still in the realm of nature with all its arbitrary, inexplicable, exuberant energy.

Instead of condemning the increased importance we've been assigning to sexuality, our cultural commentators might consider that in a time when humanity is overrunning and domesticating the entire earth, sexual passion may be the last wild place available to us. But this final touch of nature still packs a wallop that can knock you on your ear. It's the overwhelming power of the experience that intensifies our sense of reality and generates an exuberant thrill—all radiating from and focused on the beloved. For it is always the particular individual who startles us and awakens the lover, the person "obsessed by a unique image which becomes the absolute sign, equivalent, and definition of his deepest self" (Harold Rosenberg). It is the power of desire to transform the concrete into an ideal that makes passion so important. To condemn sexual desire and passion is to try to block one of the main avenues to human fulfillment and happiness. Passion releases the magic of the concrete, it allows the earth to sing again, magnificently, as on the first day.

None of this is new, of course, but at a time when the so-called helping professions are all bent on making us "healthy"—they would have our souls walk in sensible shoes—it's worth repeating. People have always realized the value of passion, which is why it's a universal theme of the human imagination. But whereas the traditional celebrations tend to be lyrical tragedies, stories of doomed lovers whose experience was transcendent but destructive to the individual, what seems to me new and noteworthy today is the insistence that passion fuse with a decency that respects the person.

Since I had not anticipated this theme, it took me some time to realize I was being repeatedly knocked over the head with it, in interview after interview, and not just the couples here. "Common human decency" was something all of these people demanded and expected to find in their most passionate loves. As I reflected on what I heard, it seemed to me that decency has two components—taking responsibility for one's self and letting the other person be different from you. Taking responsibility for oneself means not acting like a child—not, for instance, demanding the other person read your mind: "I'm unhappy but I'm not going to tell you, if you loved me, you'd know." The common mistake of trying to give yourself away totally to the other person is a falling back to the child within each of us; it doesn't work because the lover is not mother.

Straight men seem particularly apt to make this mistake when they enter a joint living situation and suddenly expect to be picked up after and served—probably because life with mother is their dominant experience of living with a woman—but anyone can make the same emotional mistake. Some part of each of us wants to give ourselves away and return to the emotional security of the child, who knows that he can ultimately leave responsibility for everything to his parents.

It's easy to make this mistake because passionate love does seem to be a total acceptance and affirmation of one's being, which is the great and necessary emotional experience of childhood. But in an adult, trying to give oneself away is a mistake. It is a misuse of the opportunity that love—that spectacular confirmation of our existence—offers us, which is precisely to release us to be ourselves, "in a world which is doing its best, night and day, to make you everybody else" (e. e. cummings). Besides, it doesn't work.

The other side of taking responsibility for yourself is not assuming you have to take responsibility for the other, letting the other person be who he or she is, a person quite distinct from oneself. This fact sooner or later emerges when the early haze of passionate bewitchment begins to burn off. It seems to me this reality leads to disillusion only for those who make their experience of love so self-centered that it leads to a structural paranoia.

The fact that you are hurt does not necessarily mean someone set out to hurt you; not every action of the lover is taken in immediate reference to the beloved—a fact that is oddly clear to us about our own actions, but not about those of our lover. I know that a passing disinclination to sex or a preoccupation or need to be alone does not necessarily mean I am no longer in love; why is it so hard to see that the same is true about my lover? If decency in general means learning to let other people be themselves, it is even more called for in love which is the unmitigated delight that this particular person exists.

It is hard to take responsibility for oneself and it is hard to allow other people to be different, perhaps even to rejoice in that difference. But these are the social demands of adulthood, the requirements of being a decent person. To combine this decency with passion results in a love that is very far from an adolescent fantasy, something, in fact, that adolescents are ill equipped for. Decent passion would require that one be an adult. Love is a matter for grown-ups; for many of us, perhaps, our failed attempts at it are precisely the arena in which we do grow up.

The fusion of passion and decency is what all the people in this book are striving for. It is an extraordinary demand. But it seems clear to me now that it is what I am demanding of my own life and what everyone I know is looking for. On reflection, it seems a worthwhile goal.

Blue Moves

CONVERSATION WITH A MALE PORN DANCER

AS THE SEVENTIES came to a close—I almost wrote climax—commercial as well as non-commercial venues for gay sex mushroomed in various neighborhoods of Manhattan. What emerged was a sexual wonderland that was curiously not visible to straight people, like a secret dimension we could slip into, with portals everywhere. The odd fact that this erotic reality seemed invisible to straight people gave our social lives a weird moiré quality, two social realities superimposed on each other, at a cocktail party or book reading for instance, where the erotic plots unfolding during the evening were simply not apparent to most in the room. In the next decade this apparent invisibility of gay life would return with a vengeance during the AIDS epidemic, much to our detriment. But in the Seventies, it offered a marvelous sort of freedom, and wandering the gay byways of the city one often met interesting people like Robert, whose experience of his gay sexuality I found intriguing. So, one afternoon I asked if I could interview him and he agreed.[1]

I was surprised and embarrassed when I reread the printed version of this interview to see that I had deleted Robert's brief remarks (now reinstated) about how we got to know each other. That strange fit of prudishness strikes me today as totally wrong-headed (especially considering the substance of the interview) and should have then. We're all works in progress, I guess.

In dancing one keeps taking a step and recovering one's balance.

EDWIN DENBY

Robert, how did it come about that you were dancing in a male porn theater?

1 Published in *Christopher Street*, vol. 4, no. 6 (February 1980).

Well . . .

You're a professional dancer?

Yes, I make my living as a dancer. I was very hard pressed for money and this seemed to be an easy way of making money fast, you know, and . . . staying in New York.

What type of dancing had you done before?

Just about everything, classical ballet and contemporary and musical comedy—mainly, though, ballet.

What was the audition like?

Well, what they do is, in the course of the day, if anyone wants to audition, they just put them into one of the shows as if you were part of the show, so the regular audience is there. They just add you on. The manager watches and if he likes what he sees, you're hired.

Were you nervous?

Yeah. The first time I was very nervous. And it was strange because I didn't think I would be. You know, having been on the stage before, and being a professional dancer, I didn't expect at all that I would be nervous. But having to strip—it was hard at the audition, it was hard to separate myself from the audience.

Had you been to a porno theater before?

No, I hadn't, so it was a totally different experience for me.

What was the management like?

Very nice. In fact, I probably wouldn't have stayed there as long as I did, or wouldn't have even taken the job, if the management wasn't as nice as they were. The manager was very up-front and seemed very honest to me. After my audition, I said, "Did you watch the whole thing?" And he said, "Yes," and I said, "I didn't think that I was going to be as nervous as I was." And he said, "Well, you know, it's different taking your clothes off at home and dancing around nude and doing it in front of a roomful of people."

Was this guy straight, gay, young, old?

Young. Young and gay. I'd say he was in his early thirties. Everyone who worked there, with the exception of maybe one or two people, everyone was gay.

Was it owned by gay people?

No, the theater was owned by straight people. I never met the man who owned it, but he was an older man. He wasn't around very much.

How many hours did you work and what did you get paid?

I worked from about two in the afternoon till one in the morning. The thing is that I was at the theater during that time, but I wasn't always working. We did seven shows, and each show lasted forty-five minutes. My individual number was anywhere from eight to ten minutes. So the actual time I was working wasn't much, but you had to stay around the theater and be there for each show. There really wasn't enough time to go out and do anything. And I got $35 a night.

What did you do between sets?

Well, sometimes I would go out and go shopping, just window shopping, or . . . go out and eat . . . sometimes just hang out in the lobby and talk with customers. The customers were always—with me, it was a little different because I tried to really dance, so there were people who would talk to me and compliment me, they obviously saw that I had training, so they were surprised to see someone, you know, present themselves in a theater of that nature. I don't know why, because if more theaters—male theaters—had really good performers, it would add a different dimension. Erotic theater is really what it is, you know.

Like a male burlesque?

Right. So I would have conversations with people. And it was interesting: some of them were really turned on to the fact that I did a good act. And others sort of used that to try and proposition me. But I found that . . . that end hard to get into.

There were people who would just assume that the prices they paid to get into the theater gave them the right to proposition dancers or to have sex with them, or anything. And I found it insulting, in a way, that they assumed that all of the dancers would hustle.

Did many of the other dancers hustle?

A number of them did, yeah, but not *all* of them.

What were the other guys like?

All different backgrounds. I think two others had had dance training and had worked as dancers legitimately. There was one that was a male model.

Legit male model or porn male model?

Legitimate. And they're from all different backgrounds, and they were all really nice, and it was interesting because they were all at different stages in their lives.

What age range, mostly young?

Not necessarily. I would say the youngest was about nineteen, the oldest, forty. A wide range.

Could they dance? Did they take it seriously?

Oh, yeah. Most of them worked hard at trying to come up with something. They worked on what they should wear, the music they should use—everything down to at what point they should take off what individual piece of clothing. It definitely was a form of expression for most of them—the way they choose their music and how they moved to it.

When you started, what was your attitude toward the dancing?

Well, like I said, I was really nervous at the audition, but once I started working there it totally reversed. I really enjoyed it . . . for the most part. It was hard, because being in that atmosphere for that many hours can be very difficult, but I found that if I really worked at what I was doing, like anything else, the audience would appreciate it.

Didn't you feel you'd come down in the world? I mean, you'd done classical ballet, you'd done Broadway shows, and then you worked for the porn theater. Did that bother you?

Not really, because my preconceived thought of it was all wrong. It bothered me before I even worked there, the thought of it. But then, as I said, the management was so up-front and so nice to me, plus everyone seemed to acknowledge me, all the other dancers. They realized that, wow, here was someone who was really a dancer; they were very complimentary and very supportive of what I was doing. So in that respect it made me feel good, because it wasn't like—sometimes in the theater there's less of that, it's a little more cutthroat, and they weren't cutthroat at all, at this particular theater. I found that I could work on things, I could do, almost, what I've always done, and do it for myself and get enjoyment out of that. Sometimes I would do something, and it just didn't work, or it didn't work out the way I wanted it to, but when it did, it was a good feeling. When you're a performer—any kind of a performer—you want to please the audience, otherwise you probably wouldn't be in front of an audience. But when you don't feel that you've pleased them or it hasn't worked out the way you wanted it to, it can be a little frustrating.

So for you it was a legitimate mode of expression?

Yeah, yeah, very much so. At times it seemed almost more honest—you know? Because I was expressing my sexuality and expressing myself emotionally at the same time, but it wasn't like the legitimate theater where sometimes something sexual is sort of glossed over and presented in such a way that it's almost dishonest . . . not as real.

Did that feel hard at first, to present your sexuality so directly on stage, and to an audience of men?

Ummmm . . . it felt a little . . . ah . . . yeah, strange at first. But once I got over the initial shock of having to, of being in front of so many people and being so, I mean, totally naked . . .

And sexual, not just naked but also sexual.

Well, yeah, but aren't we all? I mean, we're all sexual beings, so it wasn't . . .

But we don't get a chance to express it that much, especially if you're gay.

Oh, to express it publicly, you mean? In front of an audience? Ah . . . but see, I always approached it like more of an affirmation of my sexuality, you know? It was a fine line . . . I didn't want to exploit the audience. There's a certain amount of tease that you put in, but I didn't want to . . . ah . . . sort of shove my sexuality in their face, so to speak. I always tried to enjoy what I was doing, to at least *look* like I was enjoying what I was doing, so that, hopefully, people in the audience would connect with that feeling of enjoying their own sexuality, their own bodies, their own homosexuality. And that's what I tried to do. It didn't always work.

Can you describe your act for me, or—maybe that's not the right word—your pieces, or whatever you called them?

Well, when I first started working, my costumes were very sort of everyday clothes. See, I always tried to get two different feelings in a number. I would go from soft to hard: I would come out with a white Yves St. Laurent shirt and black pants—right?—and then I would take the shirt off and eventually strip off the pants, but underneath I would have, maybe, these black stretch bikini briefs and a stretch take top that was cut, so it just went over my chest . . . ummm . . . just over the nipple, and a collar—a dog collar—and then eventually I would take off the top and underneath the briefs I would have either a jock strap—I had this really neat green jock strap—or a black see-through G-string. And musically also, most of the time I would try to start with something slow and my movements would be slow and erotic, and direct it very much toward the audience. More of a soft kind of love thing. But then I would like go into a harder type—either a rock type music or into faster, harder movement music.

Did you take the G-string off?

Yeah. That was one of the requirements, actually, of the management.

Was that hard to do at first?

Yeah, it was. And also I noticed that nine times out of ten even the kids that worked there—I mean, that's what they do for a living, they strip at other places, too—when it came to the point of taking the G-string off, they would be with their backs to the audience. Which I thought was sort of interesting. Lots of times I would do the same thing too, except after a while I got so comfortable that it didn't bother me. But the first few weeks, it was very hard for me to work off the stage. I wouldn't get off the stage; I would work on the stage.

You mean go into the audience?

Yeah, it was hard for me to go into the audience. But then, after a while I even worked that into a number where I did my final strip. I took the G-string off . . . it was to Donna Summer and it was from her *Alive and More* album, and it was a fabulous number because it just worked out perfectly. I had one of those, like a jock strap but without the two back straps? And a G-string underneath that, and I would go from the stage onto the seats and do a strip on the seats. Standing on the armrests. Because then it went from a fast part to a very slow part . . . sometimes that was a little touchy, though.

I was going to ask if people ever tried touching you and . . .

Yeah—well, the reactions were interesting because there were people who had fear written across their faces—just really afraid to touch you. I mean, I don't know what they thought was going to happen if they touched you, but it's like they just did *not* want to have any contact. And there were other people who were grabbing, I mean, they couldn't keep their hands off of you. And there were some people you'd go to and they could enjoy the fun of it, they could just take it for what it was, you know, smile at you and be having a good time. Like you.

What did you do about the people who were grabbing?

At first that bothered me a lot, because I just felt that wasn't supposed to be part of the number, and also like I was up for grabs. You know, for me the whole thing is you wanted to feel some kind of warmth and sometimes that grabbing was . . . there's nothing, no emotion involved with it, they just think you're a body and it's like going to the grocery and feeling the fruit or something. Suddenly you become a commodity.

How did you handle it when it happened?

I learned to play to it, more or less. Because I didn't want to become antagonistic toward the audience, but usually if that happened, if someone was that aggressive, I would just move to another part of the audience. I learned to take it to a point where it looked like I might reciprocate, because that also was a big turn-on. It's like anything else: it's not what actually happens but what people think might happen. That's what excites them, you know. So you can use that, if somebody was in the audience and they were touching you, you could use that to get across that feeling that something might happen. But just as it looks like it might, then you move on. And I found that was the best turn-on for the entire audience. That feeling. Because there were times when things actually did happen. Not so much with me, but with other people. And I think that sort of alienated the audience because it isolated them more.

You told me once about an incident when someone was actually rimming you while you were dancing on the seats?

Oh, yeah, that happened toward the end . . .

How did that feel? I mean . . .

Felt good! No . . . it's very strange. . . . You know what it was, it was—on that particular day, I was very depressed for some reason. After a while, working there, I didn't find it terribly erotic. I mean, it's different for the customer who comes in for a couple of hours, sees a show, watches some of the movie, and maybe connects with a trick or whatever. But the dancer, who has to be there for so many hours and who has to get up and turn on, it's like a sex machine or something and suddenly you have to come out with all this . . . sexuality, sexual feelings. You have to come across with this total erotic feeling and, you know, you don't always feel that way. You *don't* always feel, at every moment of the day, you don't always feel sexual.

So this day you were depressed . . .

This particular day—I don't know why—I felt depressed or something. And, of course, the theater's dark, and that doesn't particularly help to lift your spirits. So I was doing the shows—it was about the second or third show—and there weren't that many people in the audience, and there was this man sitting in the very first row. From the very beginning it didn't matter what I did, or what anybody did, really— maybe he was stoned—he just wanted a good time and he was out to get whatever he could. So I got up to do that number and there was no one really, except sitting way back in the theater, except for this one man, and it was very hard . . .

How many people in the audience, five, ten, twenty?

Like maybe five or ten total. There was no one really to play to, except this one man who was close enough. And I think it was more out of anger, on my part, than anything. I was dancing on the seats and he was just sitting there grabbing and making obscene gestures with his mouth and it was one of those things where I mentally said, "All right, if that's what you want, that's what you're going to get." So I did everything to him, I directed everything to him, and I did the strip. He kept motioning to me to come closer, to stand over him, so I did and I did the whole strip over him, and he started to go down on me and everything. But I did it. . . .

What's everything?

Well, rim me and, you know . . . but I did it more out of anger because I wasn't really attracted to him, and it wasn't a sexual feeling at all for me. I don't know what it was for him. But it was more out of anger, because I wasn't getting anything from the audience, you know, emotionally. I was trying to put out something and nothing was coming back to me except this man. But it was not a good feeling at all. Having him that close. . . .

It didn't feel good, you were saying, having him that close?

No, it didn't, and I think it broke an illusion. I don't think it helped create any kind of feeling with the people who were watching, the people in the back of the theater. And I realized later that the whole thing took place really out of my anger of trying to get through to them. But it didn't help matters at all.

Was that the only time? Or did that happen occasionally?

Ah . . . yeah, that's the only time it happened while I was there, that it was that graphic. Other times—there were times when people would grab your cock or they would feel your ass, but, you know, sometimes that felt fine because it was a different kind of touch. I mean, they really want you, and that, I suppose, is what it's all about. That feeling of being wanted and you're up there and you're creating that feeling of having every man in the audience want you.

That must be a terrific rush.

Yeah, when it happens it is. It is—it's beautiful. But it's a fantasy. It's a beautiful fantasy, you know, because realistically there's a lot more involved with it.

Did you ever meet anyone in the audience or see anyone in the audience that you were attracted to?

You mean besides you? (laughing) . . . Yeah. Yeah, there were a number of times I did.

Did that ever lead to anything?

Ah . . . a couple of times it did, yes. I tried to—which was difficult—but I tried to, as a rule, not do that much in the theater. But I would meet people that I was turned on to and who were turned on to me and . . .

Go home with them?

Yeah. Or we would exchange numbers and eventually get together. It only happened a couple of times, though. The thing is that I found when you meet someone under those circumstances, it's very difficult because you don't know whether what they're attracted to really is the illusion or you. I found it's true in the legitimate theater, too. I mean

I've done things. . . . I've gotten letters, you know. Once I answered a letter, this was when I was doing something legitimate, dancing—and I answered. But it was a mistake, and I find that this can so easily happen, because I was creating an illusion on the stage, and the audience or that person might confuse that with the real me. It's one of the reasons I didn't get together with people. But the people that I did get together with were people that I was very attracted to.

And you did it just for the sex, not for money?

Oh, yeah, yeah.

How come you never hustled?

I couldn't get into it. I think because—I don't know. Really, I don't know. Except I think I figured out that my emotional needs are just too great. I can't separate my feelings from the sexual activity or the sexual being—I can't. I couldn't pretend. Like one of the kids who did hustle said he just put himself in another place or would think of someone else, and that was very hard for me to do. I couldn't—which, when I think of it, might be strange because it's just the reverse when I'm on stage. But then, that's maybe why I'm a performer. You know, when I'm on stage, I feel I can do almost anything. But it was too real for me—hustling—being that intimate, being with one other person, and having sex with them, for money. I guess the money just wasn't that important to me. I don't know. I did question myself because—I mean, I had never thought of hustling before, and in some sense people in the theater hustle all the time. You know, it's not a sexual thing, but in the same sense they're hustling. They're selling themselves all the time—they'll do almost anything to get a part—it's the same thing, in a sense. But I just could not get myself to do it. It's funny because after a while I suppose I felt guilty about it.

About not *hustling?*

Yeah. But . . . I mean, it wasn't—I didn't think anything was wrong with hustling. I don't think I'm someone to judge those things. But I guess I feel that you have to have a certain mentality or whatever, in order to allow yourself to do it. I mean, I tried a couple of times.

You tried?

Sure.

What does that mean?

Well, people offered me money a couple of times, and . . . I went with them . . . but in fact, in one case, I even gave the guy back his money—but he demanded it back—he was very demanding. Because I just couldn't . . .

It didn't work out physically; you couldn't get into it.

No, I couldn't get into it. But I found out later on that there's a whole number that you do in hustling. First of all, people who are going to pay for it, I suppose either feel they have to for some reason, or they do have to for some reason, or they just get off on it—it's part of the fantasy, you know. I found out from someone who did hustle that there are all sorts of tricks you can do, like being aggressive and if someone wants something that you don't particularly do or don't like to do, you just tell them, and nine times out of ten they're still going to pay you. They're really—this is my head, again, but I guess I would like to think this—but I think in the end what they're paying for has nothing to do with, ah . . . the superficiality of it, the body. It has more to do with feelings. They just want something to touch and someone to feel a certain kind of love for. Even if it is for ten minutes or whatever.

When you were on the stage performing, did you fantasize? I'm curious about what it would feel like to feel that erotic publicly.

I . . . there were only a couple of times I fantasized, but when I did fantasize, it had nothing to do with the audience.

What did it have to do with?

It had to do with someone that I knew who was in my own head. I mean thoughts that I had—in fact, there probably were only two occasions that I can remember that I really fantasized to the extent of, you know, practically getting a hard-on. But in both cases it was about someone that I was seeing, and I think both times I had just come from being with him. So I was turned on, mentally, and therefore the audience was tuned into that, and turned on. Now, other times—obviously there were people in the audience who were really turning on to me, to my number, and sometimes, you know, I would go into the audience and I would see a fairly good-looking person, who was turning on to me. And I would play to that, I would play up to that.

Did you get turned on by turning him on?

Ah . . . yes and no, because it was more of a mental turn-on. I mean,

I didn't get a hard-on, necessarily, most of the time. I don't think I ever did, really, when I went into the audience. But the thought that I was turning them on that much and that they were attracted to me . . . ah . . . made me turn on mentally. I think when I was performing—especially in the audience—it was very hard to forget that there were people watching you, you know. In that sense, legitimate theater can be very different, because there's always the wall there, you know, the stage. But working at this theater—or and maybe it's just an aspect of myself that came up—but it was very hard for me to forget the audience was there.

Did you know that you could turn men on sexually, easily, before this?
Yeah.

So it didn't change your feeling about your own sexuality?
Well, it did in a sense, because I don't think I was as open or as ready to admit it before. And I don't know why, except maybe I just thought that that would make me sound terribly vain, or something. Since I was . . . since my teens, at least, I've always known that I was attracted to men and that I was attractive to men, that men turned on to me sexually. But I wasn't as ready to admit it, as much as now. I know, psychologically, doing this work has really helped me tremendously. It's opened me up a lot to my own sexuality.

Did you ever go onto the stage feeling totally non-erotic, like used dishwater, not able to get turned on in the slightest, and what did you do about it? Could you fake it?
Fake what?

Sexiness, being turned on.
Yeah, because, as I said, it was like an act with me. Like some of the kids, I have to say, they didn't all approach it the same way I did. There were a couple who went on stage, like they could have felt like dishwater—I don't know what they felt like, but they looked like they might have felt like that—I mean, they didn't express themselves, either because they were too young, I don't know. I'm thinking of individual people, but they would get up on stage and they would just flaunt themselves. And I found that in most cases it was perhaps the ones with the big cocks, or the better-endowed ones who really weren't

expressing anything sexual up on stage. Now, whether it was because they felt that they really didn't have to, because all the men were there only to see a big cock, or whether they really didn't know how to express themselves, who knows? But I know personally, watching them did not particularly turn me on.

You said you tried not to be a cock-tease to the audience, not to exploit them. What did you try to do with the audience?

Well . . . there's a difference between assaulting someone and making love to someone. I tried to make love to the audience. I wanted them to feel that they were being loved. And not to feel that someone was forcing themselves upon them, sexually or any other way.

Who was the audience? What type of people go there?

All different types. There's no way you could stereotype the people who went there, because they were all different types. Straight-looking men, aggressive-looking men, effeminate-looking, total macho, old men, young men.

There was no particular age; it wasn't older?

A lot . . . well . . . I would say not most of the customers, but the most consistent customers were the older men. But there were all types and ages.

Why do you think they went to the theater?

Well, there were all different reasons. There was a man I had a long conversation with who was married; he was an older man, middle-class —you know, lives in a house with his wife, had a male lover . . .

Had a male lover?

Uh-huh . . .

But still came to the theater?

But still came to the theater. He was totally—and he admitted he was—totally sexual. He had to have sex constantly. Just really hot, I guess. I don't know. Yeah, so he would come to the theater and try to pick up a trick or whatever, but a really nice man. We had a long talk, you know, he propositioned me . . . and there was a young boy, one day who came in.

What do you mean, young?

High school age . . . happened to be off on vacation and . . . really a nice kid, and shy. He lived in the suburbs, was obviously isolated . . . probably it wasn't easy for him to meet gay people, and so this was the answer, for now, anyway.

Did he proposition you?

No, but he was . . . he obviously wanted to get together with me, but I just . . . I don't know, you have to feel something—I do, anyway. And I didn't feel it for him. But I thought he was sweet and I like to get to know people, too. Then there was a man that same day who was dying to have this boy, and he was totally opposite from this young boy. From the minute he came into the theater until he left, it was like he expected to come into the theater and to find someone, connect with someone, and have sex. I mean, from the minute he walked in the door. And he couldn't understand why he wasn't getting any feedback from anybody. But it obviously was the vibes that he was putting out himself, you know. He was just so uptight about it. It's like for him this theater, because they showed pornographic movies and because they had a live show, was synonymous with sex. But this particular man, he didn't have a realistic view of himself.

What were some of the other people like?

There were some—well, I think I told you about him. There was an old man, one day, in the front row. I mean, he was *old*; he was like in his eighties at least, and he was just moving to the music and making all these obscene gestures to different dancers, and he took his cock out and had a hard-on and was just jerking off and everything. It was incredible. This old man.

What was your reaction to that?

Well, it was funny, I laughed. But also, there was something about it that was almost an inspiration, to think that someone—this man, who was really up in his years—was still so full of energy, but even more, his sexual being was still so alive. It's incredible.

What was your general feeling about the audience? I mean, did you like them, did you pity them?

Ah . . . well . . . that's a hard question to answer. I think I had a lot of different feelings. I don't think I pitied them. I think my main feeling was I wanted them to want me, or to acknowledge me, you know, that's my own personal hang-up—where my head is at, I guess. I don't know what some of them might have seen in the show, what it gave them. . . . That's why my act—I tried to do an act and a couple of other kids did an act, which was at least entertaining. But there were other people who were not. The younger guys saw that, and they would either walk out or they just turned off. But the older guys, I think, were more apt to accept just the nudity and the chance to see the male body. You know, it's a hard audience—a body of people—each one there for a different reason; each one has different psychological hang-ups or needs. So it really was hard to feel something for the audience as a whole. I suppose it's why, lots of times, I tried to connect with one individual or a couple of individuals within the audience, playing off of them.

You said when you were doing this you were seeing someone?

I was seeing a couple of people.

Did any of the people you were seeing ever come to watch you at the theater?

One—yes, one did. One I met at the theater, actually. The other one I was seeing had been to the theater but hadn't seen me. We met somewhere else. And he couldn't come to terms with what I was doing *at all*.

I wondered about that—whether they were jealous or sort of freaked by it?

Well, the one guy who I still see at times, since I met him there, it didn't bother him. I think he's into me as a person, so I think nothing would bother him, but the other guy didn't. I don't think he thought less of me, though I have to admit that the fact that he didn't understand what I was doing or really approve of it, bothered me because I was afraid that he was turned on to me only sexually and that he didn't really feel something for me as a person. But, I'm not sure—I mean, that's just a feeling that I had, because it was hard for him to come to terms with the fact that I was working in a porno movie house. But he was honest enough to admit that his whole upbringing and way of thinking had a lot to do with it. He . . . he was totally different from me anyway. He is very into material things, and he was doing a job that he didn't particularly enjoy, but he was doing it because it brought him enough money to live the way he wanted to live. Whereas I'm totally the opposite. I'm not into material things, I'm more into doing what I want to do and trying to be happy doing it.

How about you? Your upbringing was fairly conservative, right? How were you brought up?

Yeah, middle-class, lower-middle-class.

What did your father do?

My father's dead. But both of them worked. My father was an accountant, and my mother still works. She's a combination housekeeper and nanny.

And you were brought up Catholic?

Uh-huh.

Was it a large family?

Five kids.

In Jersey?

Yeah.

So it was pretty conservative?

Yeah.

Italian Catholic?

Italian and Irish.

So you're an Irish Catholic. If this guy had trouble dealing with it because of his background, whatever it was, you must have had some trouble dealing with it, because of your background.

Yeah....

You said that working in the porn theater, dancing, had helped you a lot, had given you a lot of insights. In what way?

Well . . . it made me feel . . . like I had never been able to admit that I might be attractive to men or turn men on a lot, because somehow I always felt that—I don't know—that was being like a real egotist or being terribly vain. But being able to openly express my sexuality, which for a long part of my life I couldn't, I guess this gave me an opportunity to just bare all, so to speak. And also I think it was not only the feeling of identifying the audience as my family and saying, "Here I am; this is me," but seeing it myself. Being able to get up there and just be a sexual male, to enjoy my own sexuality. Which I think a lot of straight men miss out on. It's changing a lot, but—I can't picture my brothers really being aware of their bodies—really being into their bodies, really into looking good. I just can't picture them. In fact, a lot of straight men just totally let themselves go physically, I think more so than gay men. I think it's because they're not into acknowledgment of the male body—to them, it's admitting feelings that they're not allowed to be in touch with.

Do you ever imagine what your mother would think if she walked into the theater? I mean, forgetting why your mother would ever walk into such a theater. Did you ever think of that, or your brothers?

Yeah.

How did you deal with it?

Well, I'm not really that close to my family. My mother, perhaps, but my brothers, no. I've always done what I wanted to do, and I've always felt separate from them, so . . . you know, the thought did come into my mind, what if they found out, but . . . I have to live my own life.

Do they know you're gay, your family?

Not officially. I'm sure they're a . . . aware . . . but they wouldn't admit it, I don't think.

Does that bother you?

Yeah, 'cause I'm . . . I'm trying to be honest with myself, so . . . but, at the same time, it's very difficult. . . . I can't play with other people's emotions.

Is it a number they're pulling, their not knowing? Do you think a number's been done on you?

Oh, yeah, definitely. Quite a bit of a number's been done on me. But . . . but see, I'm dealing with that. I mean, I . . . I've been dealing with that all my life, I guess.

When did you come out as gay?

Uh . . . I guess my early twenties . . . but . . . I knew before then, all through my teens, and I had had experiences, but I don't think I admitted it until my twenties.

Was it hard?

It was hard . . . coming from the family that I did . . . where sex was something that really wasn't openly discussed . . . being in a household full of men.

All five of you were boys?

I have a sister, but she was out of the house when I was a baby. So here are all these straight, conservative, macho types, and me . . . with my feelings, but not really knowing how to express them. Feeling different, you know, and not knowing what exactly that difference was. So that . . . having this . . . having a feeling that there was something wrong with me or wrong with being gay, but yet knowing that those feelings existed, so that it was terribly difficult for me to admit it. I finally did. Of course, it opened a lot of doors. But that's why it was so hard to admit, because of my environment.

Were you going to a shrink during this time?

Uh-huh.

Did you discuss this with him or her?

Uh-huh, yes I did.

What was their reaction? A him or her?

Her.

Her—what was her reaction?

Actually, one of the conclusions she came to was that it probably was good for me because I was getting something there I needed, which I wasn't getting anywhere else. The feeling that I was being acknowledged and accepted.

As a kid did you feel non-acknowledged or just non-acknowledged as gay?

As a kid, I did feel unacknowledged in my family. And this theater was an all-male audience and I come from a household of all males, with the exception of my mother. So I guess I always was looking for that acceptance from my family. And I was getting it at this theater.

Do you think it had any direct impact on your sex life?

Yes, I do.

In what way? Let's be specific.

Well . . . I don't know. It's made my sexual life better . . . it's made me appreciate, I think, someone who is turned on to me. It's made me turn on to them more. It's somehow made me more flexible, more open to a sex partner.

So, are you glad you did it?

Yes, work at the theater, you mean? Of course. Yeah, definitely. I don't know how much longer I would have been able to do it, but I am glad I did it.

Just for the tape, tell us what you're doing now.

Just for the tape?

I mean with the Yiddish theater. I think that's so funny.
What? That I'm dancing with the Yiddish theater in Brooklyn?
Yeah, to go from one to the other.
Well . . .
That's showbiz, right?
It is. You never know where you'll be next . . . so . . . can we play now?
Sure.

PART 2

Beginning to Count Ourselves

1980–1983

Precisely one hundred years before Stonewall, in June of 1869, Friedrich Engels wrote to Karl Marx, "The paederasts [*sic*] are beginning to count themselves and find that they make up a power in the state. Only the organization is lacking, but according to this it already exists in secret," wrote Engels, responding to a booklet by Karl Heinrich Ulrichs, the first modern writer to publicly defend homosexuality. "Thus," Gregory Woods asserts in his book *Homintern*, "at the very time that homosexuality was beginning to be examined and theorized as an individual state of being, verging on an aspect of identity, those who might be called homosexual were also beginning to be seen as a potential group with common interests; if overt, even a political movement capable of collective action or, if covert, a subversive conspiracy."[1] Woods goes on to demonstrate in detail in his remarkable book how during the next hundred years gay social networks spread extensively throughout Europe and America while remaining for the most part covert, leading indeed to persistent rumors of an international gay conspiracy, especially in the arts.

One hundred years to the month after Engels wrote that letter,

1 Gregory Woods, *Homintern: How Gay Culture Liberated the Modern World* (New Haven, CT: Yale University Press, 2016), p. 2.

Carl Wittman in California was writing his *Gay Manifesto*, inspired by Marx's own *Communist Manifesto*,[2] which became a book often called the bible of Gay Liberation.[3] What was significant, said his boyfriend of the time in a recent memoir, was that "it was a call to action directed not at those in power or at society at large *but at gay people themselves* [my italics], urging them to cast off their chains of mental enslavement, their shame for being queer. Everyone knows about the Stonewall Riots of June 28, 1969, but few people know that Wittman's 'Gay Manifesto' was written before the riots (though it wasn't widely published until 1970)."[4]

Evidently the time was ripe. Whatever individual and social changes had been going on covertly for at least the last hundred years would now burst into public view with the gay explosion into visibility.

Stonewall led immediately to what Andrew Holleran has called "The Age of the Clones, 1971 to 1979 A.D."[5] The Clone look—501 jeans, flannel shirts, leather or bomber jacket, boots, short hair—blossomed first in the West Village in New York and in San Francisco's Castro, then, like wildflowers in a mountain meadow, spread to every gay enclave in America. It became a virtual uniform, provoking many jokes, but suddenly we were visible, we could see our numbers and we started to count.

"So how many of us do you think there are, anyway?" Cleve Jones remembers asking a friend.[6] "We were sitting in the bay window of Doug Norde's apartment on California Street between Larkin and Hyde and I was asking a question many gay people were asking in the early months of 1976."

Gay politics became inevitable and we needed to think about it.

---

2 As well as the Students for a Democratic Society's Port Huron Statement.

3 The entire text can be found in the indispensable historical sourcebook of gay and lesbian politics *We Are Everywhere*, ed. Mark Blasius and Shane Phelan (New York: Routledge, 1997), pp. 380–88.

4 See D. E. Mungello's article "Carl Wittman's Place in Liberation History" in the *Gay & Lesbian Review/Worldwide* (November–December 2016): p. 20.

5 Andrew Holleran, "My Harvard, Part 2: New York," *Gay & Lesbian Review/Worldwide* (November–December 2012).

6 In his memoir, *When We Rise*, p. 97.

Archeologist of the Present

MICHEL FOUCAULT IN NEW YORK CITY

OF COURSE, BECOMING visible to the straight society meant we had now become much better targets for the hostile homophobes this society produces in such abundance. We had already seen an organized backlash in the Anita Bryant campaign to "save our children" in Florida in 1977, which led the next year to voters in St. Paul, Minnesota, Wichita, Kansas, and Eugene, Oregon, overturning recently passed ordinances protecting gay rights, as well as the Briggs Initiative in California in 1978 which would have prohibited gay and lesbian teachers. Uneasily aware that Magnus Hirschfeld's homosexual rights movement in Germany had been utterly wiped out in 1933, we were nervous and never sure of the future. But nothing could have prepared us for what became known as the West Street Massacre.

On the night of November 19, 1980, "Ronald K. Crumpley, a homophobic former transit police officer and minister's son, went on a murderous rampage through the neighborhood [of the West Village], shooting a sub-machine gun indiscriminately into a crowd of men standing in front of the Ramrod and Sneakers, another gay bar on West Street,"[1] reported the *New York Times*. Two men were killed and six others seriously wounded. About to launch the first issue of our newspaper, the *New York Native*, we scrambled to cover the story, to memorialize the dead and to interview the wounded. John Preston, who reported for us (since the Ramrod was a leather bar and those were John's people), noted that the overwhelming response of the gay nurses and doctors caring for the wounded at St. Vincent's was "It could have been me!" And Chuck Ortleb in his first editorial for the *Native* wrote, "If people weren't numb, they were thinking, deep and long. They were thinking about the other bars. They were trying to in-

---

1 *New York Times*, July 2, 2016, p. A18.

corporate the image of a man with a machine gun into their notions of gay life in New York City."

The shock that went through New York's gay community in 1980 was similar to the shock and grief experienced after the mass killings at the Pulse nightclub in Orlando, Florida, in June 2016, but at that earlier time it was confined to our own community. The major media paid little attention, and political figures none—"How many times do we have a massacre in this city and your mayor doesn't show up?" asked one gay man.[2] We were left on our own to face the situation.

During this period, the autumn/winter of 1980–81, Michel Foucault had come to New York City, to be in temporary residence at New York University's Institute of the Humanities. Acknowledging the excitement this caused, Doug Ireland, an old friend, invited me to review Foucault's latest book, *Power/Knowledge*, edited by Colin Gordon, for the *Soho Weekly News*.[3]

The day after Ronald Crumpley's Uzi machine gun shattered the windows of the Ramrod bar in the West Village killing two gay men and sending six others to the hospital—Crumpley later explained he "hated homosexuals—I want to kill them all—they ruin everything"—there was a public lecture in Vanderbilt Auditorium, sponsored by N.Y.U.'s Institute for the Humanities, entitled "Sexuality and Solitude" given jointly by Richard Sennett and Michel Foucault. Twenty minutes before the hour the auditorium was already packed, as were, shortly, two additional rooms opened to handle the overflow, and people squeezed into every available inch of floor space. Even for New York City the audience was remarkable—in addition to the expected academics and students, there were poets and playwrights, bohemians, film makers,

---

2 Thirty-six years later, in the wake of the Orlando killings the *New York Times* devoted a long article, "Proper Farewell, Finally, for a Victim of an Anti-Gay Rampage in 1980," to a biography of one of the men killed and invited readers with information on the other to contact the paper—an extraordinary act of apology for our newspaper of record and an implicit acknowledgment of their previous homophobic bias. *New York Times*, July 2, 2016, p. A18.

3 *Soho Weekly News*, February 11, 1981.

architects, ancient emigre ladies, urban planners, editors from a dozen publishing houses and as many magazines, and an enormous number of writers of the most diverse sort—and they kept crowding in. A worried fire marshal tried to clear the aisles but when it became obvious that no one was going to give up their place, Richard Sennett waved away his objections and opened the proceedings. For the next hour and forty-five minutes the audience ignored its discomfort and listened intently as Sennett and Foucault discussed solitude and the erotic imagination, ranging from the Roman Stoics to the 18th-century medicalization of sexuality, from fourth-century Christian monasticism to the bizarre war waged against masturbation by the 19th-century medical establishment. Dazzlingly brilliant, dense, and startlingly original, their talk sketched a novel interpretation of the genesis of society's current sexual ideology, whose immediate impact we all, in one way or another, feel in our daily lives. At the end of the lecture, Foucault, who had only learned of the gay murders when entering the hall, asked an American friend, Mark Blasius, to announce the details of the demonstration to be held that evening, and later both Foucault and Sennett joined some of their auditors in a candlelight march from Sheridan Square to the Ramrod in the West Village.

The surprising diversity and remarkable quality of that audience—the likes of which I hadn't seen since the late Hannah Arendt delivered some of her memorable public addresses—said as much about the peculiar significance of this intellectual event as its striking relevance to the latest action in the street. People had heard of Michel Foucault, even those only vaguely aware of the precise nature of his intellectual endeavors had heard; almost like a rumor, word had spread about this man whose intellectual brilliance and vast erudition were devoted to excavations of the present so startling in their implications they illuminated the entire landscape of western society. The cultural elite of the city had gathered to hear a man whose fusion of scholarship and truly serious thought had already produced a number of works that have had extraordinary impact in Europe both inside and outside the academic world.

The publication of his latest book, *Power/Knowledge*, edited by Colin Gordon, offers a welcome overview of his concerns during the last decade and constitutes the best available introduction to the man and his thought. These nine interviews and three lecture/essays from the years 1972 to 1977 not only acquaint the reader with his major intellectual endeavors—the history of madness and psychiatry, the development of modern medical perception, the evolution and significance of the penal system, the history of sexuality—in a clear and lively form more immediately accessible than his major books, they also situate both the man and his work in its living context, the immensely vigorous and critical intellectual life that has emerged in France largely since, and in some ways in direct response to, the "events" of '68. Whatever else that oddly unreal "revolution" of the imagination did or didn't do, it certainly seems to have shaken the French out of their intellectual slumbers.

These conversations also presented Foucault with the opportunity to slightly refocus his earlier work in the light of his current thinking, for he now sees all his historical investigations of cultural institutions revolving around two terms: knowledge and power. The interaction of power and knowledge becomes the central issue, the way power in the modern world incessantly produces new knowledge which not only reinforces and augments that power but constitutes its actual mode of existence: "When I think back now, I ask myself what else was it that I was talking about, in *Madness and Civilization* or *The Birth of the Clinic*, but power?"

Since "the mechanics of power in themselves were never analyzed," much less the relation of power to knowledge, the concrete way power actually works to produce its effects has never been clear. Foucault focuses on the action of power "in its capillary form" to clarify how power courses through the social body which it animates and organizes. "The eighteenth century invented, so to speak, a synaptic regime of power, a regime of its exercise within the social body, rather than from above it." In his particular investigations into the histories of psychiatry, the penal system, medical organization and sexuality, Foucault sets out to show that power in the modern world works its effects not only through repression (social prohibition, legal sanction, the control, via the army and police, of the means of violence), that in fact our concern with the negative aspects of power has prevented us from seeing the immensely more significant ways power works positively.

He suggests that the emergence of modern society required not only, or even primarily, "the form of control by repression but that of control by stimulation." "Get undressed—but be slim, good-looking, tanned." Power produces its effects "at the level of desire and also at the level of knowledge. Far from preventing knowledge, power produces it." The operations of power have increasingly created new bodies of information (statistical, demographic, psychiatric, medical, penal, etc.) and established new objects of knowledge (the criminal, the homosexual, the deviant, etc.) which in themselves constitute modes of social regulation. Or, as one shrewd anthropological subject put it dryly, "I think this anthropology is just another way to call me a nigger" (in John Gwaltney's excellent book *Drylongso*). "Knowledge" generated by the social sciences becomes the great "disciplinary grid of society" installed by the prodigious 19th-century effort at discipline and normalization.

Foucault's investigations suggest that we should abandon all varieties of the Wicked Witch of the West explanation of history, the attempt to find the bad guys (capitalists, bureaucratic elites, elders of Zion—the form of explanation is identical and equally unlikely). They all boil down to conspiracy theories of history, the absurdity of which was perfectly clear when the government used it to understand political and cultural dissent in the Sixties. The real situation is closer to the story of the Sorcerer's Apprentice: forces and processes have been unleashed which no longer obey a master but activate and reproduce themselves in each one of us. Modern man has become not the agent of history but the site on which social processes take place, often with minimal subjective participation of the persons present. Thus we can have a racist country in which the majority of people may not actually hate or despise Black people, a psychotically homophobic society in which most people probably are not immensely concerned with the way folks unknown to them conduct their sex lives. This form of modern social power has created a world we're forced to live in without subjectively participating in, the origin of that experience of alienation and anomie so many observers have thought characteristic of the last century and a half.

It is as if modern society generates for each person a demographic double, a socialized entity that clings like an aggressive shadow, bent on replacing the concrete and particular person with a bundle of socialized mechanisms. That a world of such abstract golems, soulless bundles of behavior on the march, is more than an intellectual's nightmare was established once and for all by the Nazis' surrealistic Final Solution.

It is against the nightmares of 20th-century history that Foucault works with his historical excavations, his "genealogical" efforts to trace the origins of modern social institutions, for "what is at stake in all these genealogies is the nature of this power which has surged into view in all its violence, aggression, and absurdity in the course of the last forty years." By throwing into relief the historical processes by which power has shaped us, he attempts to demystify the present, to dissolve its opacity, and liberate the future from the curse of a demented past.

It is hard to convey the richly provocative nature of Foucault's thinking, the extraordinary exhilaration his analyses ignite. One reaches back to Marx or Nietzsche to find apt comparisons for the scale and potential impact of this intellectual endeavor. The news is that there is a major philosopher and social thinker at work today, a man who can command the serious intellectual interest of anyone concerned with the fate of the modern world.

Gay Politics and Its Premises

SIXTEEN PROPOSITIONS

FOR SOME TIME I had been hearing from a number of sources about a book John Boswell was writing and I finally called him and arranged to spend a weekend at Yale to discuss it with him. I was bowled over by the book (which was not yet finished, if my memory is correct) and utterly charmed by the author, but after even a brief examination I thought the book was going to require a university press. "Jeb, you have footnotes in more than a dozen languages. I mean you have footnotes in Akkadian, for God's sake! Where are you going to find typefaces in Akkadian? You'll need the resources of a major university, and a press with an extraordinary copyediting and production department to bring this book to the light of day." And I lobbied heavily for the University of Chicago Press, where I had worked for two years in grad school and which had a superb staff, going so far as to write a letter to my old boss, Allen Fitchen, the humanities editor there, and sending a copy to Morris Philipson, the director of the press.

When I received a copy of Boswell's *Christianity, Social Tolerance, and Homosexuality*,[1] and had the chance to carefully read it, it had an enormous impact on me (as it did on many of my gay friends, as I kept finding out in the following years). The book roused in me a deep and clarifying anger and precipitated out these ideas that had been rattling around in my head for a couple of years.

This essay was my attempt to survey the gay political situation at the beginning of the Eighties, a decade after Stonewall and just before the AIDS

---

1 I thought the U. of C. Press had done a remarkably good job of producing the book, but was astonished that there was no author's photo on the back flap (and this was one of the cutest guys I'd ever seen), so I wrote Allen again, saying, "How come there's no author's photo?!! This book is going to sell heavily to gay men, among others, and, believe me, this author's photo will really help those sales." And on the trade paperback, the whole back panel of the book sported a fetching picture of the author.

epidemic was about to break over us.[2] Published in *Christopher Street*,[3] it was meant to provoke discussion, which it did, as can be seen in the next three articles.

---

crackers are born with the right to be alive
i'm making ours up right here in yr face.

NTOZAKE SHANGE

Political reflection must begin with and remain loyal to our primary experience of ourselves and the world or it degenerates into nonsense, the making of idle theory of which there is no end and consequently no seriousness. These thoughts begin with the fact—somewhat startling when I think about it—that I find my identity as a gay man as basic as any other identity I can lay claim to. Being gay is a more elemental aspect of who I am than my profession, my class, or my race. This is new but not unheard of. It corresponds to what Christopher Isherwood was getting at in *Christopher and His Kind* when he frankly confesses his loyalty to his "tribe" in contrast to his desertion of his class and his troubling realization that he had more in common with his German lover who had been drafted to fight in the Second World War than with his countrymen. Obviously being gay was not Isherwood's sole claim to identity. Nor is it mine, but it *is* of enormous significance to how I find and feel myself in the world. Those who do not find this to be the case with themselves will probably find these reflections pointless. And since they are based on the experiences of a gay man, it is unclear how much of this discussion would be relevant to lesbians, if indeed any.

Proposition 1

Homosexuality and gay are not the same thing;
gay is when you decide to make an issue of it.

Homosexual is properly an adjective; it describes something you do. *Gay* is a noun; it names something you are. Gore Vidal, who prefers the

2 And which would, of course, require rethinking the entire situation, especially Proposition 9 and, perhaps, Proposition 10. And, of course, today Proposition 7 couldn't possibly be relevant in a culture suffused with images of gay life.
3 Vol. 5, no. 3 (January 1981).

adjectivally intensified word *homosexualist*, insists on this distinction tirelessly; one assumes he is right in his own case. For him being homosexual is not a central part of his identity, it merely describes some of his behavior, in which case the adjective homosexualist is probably more precise, if inelegant.

Whether or not being gay is a central part of one's identity—one's felt sense of self in everyday life, who I am—*is not a theoretical question.* It is a fact and can be ascertained by fairly elementary self-reflection. There are Jews for whom that fact is an accident of birth and nothing more; Blacks for whom the most monstrous aspect of racism is its bewildering irrelevance to who they are. But there are also gays, Jews, and Blacks who know themselves as this particular gay man, this particular Jew, this particular Black. Such people experience their humanness *through* being gay, Jewish or Black; they do not experience their humanity independent of its concrete manifestation in the world. The following analogy can illustrate, not prove, this position: a person can be an athlete through being a runner, football player, or swimmer; you cannot be simply an athlete, without taking part in some sport.

One can argue about whether one *should* gain a significant part of one's identity in this way; whether one actually *does*, however, is a fact. Facts, of course, can change. Fifteen years ago I did not experience myself primarily as a gay man; today, if I spend more than four days in a totally straight environment, I feel like climbing the walls. I experience myself as a fish out of water, as a "homosexual alien" in the words of the Immigration Service.

Proposition 2

Gays insofar as they are gay are ipso facto different from straights.

Merle Miller entitled his courageous pamphlet *On Being Different*, which was both accurate and apt. The liberal line that gays are no different from anyone else is less to the point than Richard Goldstein's observation that gays are different from other people in every way *except* in bed. Liberals assert that we are essentially the same as them and therefore our oppression is unjust. This passes for tolerance. However, tolerance can only be tolerance of real diversity and difference. The liberal position is not really tolerant—although it is subtle—because it denies we're different, which at bottom is another way of denying that we exist *as gays*. This position is absurd—if we're not different, why all this fuss in the first place?

By relegating homosexuality to the realm of privacy—that which is not spoken about or seen and is therefore unimportant politically (consequently "no difference")—liberal tolerance becomes a perfect example of what Herbert Marcuse called "repressive tolerance" (a concept that seemed to me idiotic as applied in the Sixties). The way liberals have of not noticing one is gay, or if forced to notice, of not wanting to hear about it, or if forced to hear about it, of asserting "that's your private life and no concern of mine or of anyone else," is an extremely insidious tactic that in practice boils down to "Let's all act straight and what you do in the bedroom is your own business."

This is the source of the liberals' famous lament: why *must* you flaunt your homosexuality? (Flaunt is the anti-gay buzzword, as *shrill* and *strident* were the anti-feminist buzzwords.) This position is identical to that of Anita Bryant, who repeatedly made it clear that she was no dummy, she knew that many of those "bachelors" and "spinsters" in the school system were gay, and she wasn't advocating a McCarthy-like witch hunt to have them rooted out and fired; all she wanted was that gay teachers not hold hands and kiss in public, that gay adults not "recruit" impressionable youngsters for the "gay life-style." In other words, get back in the closet and we won't bother you. Anita Bryant was not your traditional bigot; she was something new, a direct response to the emergence of gay liberation. As such, we can expect more of her ilk.

When you point out that this is also the essence of the liberals' position for all its tolerance, they sometimes get infuriated. They have an odd animus against the very idea of gay oppression. People who are otherwise perfectly sensible get uncomfortable and sometimes hostile when you suggest that even *they* might have internalized some of the pervasive anti-gay hostility and prejudice of the larger society. It is hard to know how to respond when they act like you have insulted their honor, but I suspect the best answer is Curtis Thornton's simple observation about white people: "I understand why they don't want us to think they are prejudiced. But if most of them were not prejudiced, it wouldn't be a prejudiced country" (in John Gwaltney's marvelous book *Drylongso*). Liberals in general tend to get upset if one tries to make an issue of being gay or if one says that being gay is an important and central part of one's life and identity. One feels like asking whether their own heterosexuality isn't an important part of *their* lives. Of course, they don't talk about heterosexuality, they talk about sexuality. Which is the whole point.

Proposition 3

The central issue of gay politics is sexuality.

It is sexuality that makes us homosexuals; it is the affirmation of ourselves as homosexuals that makes us gay. Sexuality is not the same as love. Homosexuality is not the same as "men loving men," though it sounds good as a slogan to make us respectable in the eyes of the straight world. Even at our most chauvinistic it's absurd to imply that the straight world is unfamiliar with or unfriendly to the concept of men loving men. They have developed a multiplicity of forms for male bonding, some of which they even regard as noble, some of which even we can regard as noble. What drives them nuts is not love between men but *sex* between men. It is one of the many virtues of Martin Sherman's play *Bent* that he keeps this steadily in mind. Even most gay authors falter in the face of the implacable hostility of society and the deeply insidious homophobia we have internalized and sublimate homosexuality into homosentimentality. Sherman is unusual in being aware of the quite obvious fact that the Nazis did not throw men into concentration camps for *loving* other men but for *fucking* with other men. The theatrically and theoretically brilliant climax of the play is not another noble expression of doomed love but the simultaneous orgasm of the two lovers as they face the audience—a moment that truly shocks the public, including gays.

If the central issue of homosexuality is sexuality, by definition—theirs *and* ours—it should come as no surprise that we are obsessed with sex. Indeed we are, and rightly so. What else would we be obsessed by? Straights throw this at us as an accusation. What they would like—at least the liberals among them—are homosexuals not "obsessed" with sex, i.e., self-denying, repressed, closeted homosexuals, which they've always been willing to put up with (except for a few real nut cases like Irving Bieber, a rabid psychoanalyst intent on converting us all). The only thing wrong with being obsessed with sex is that this obsession sometimes leads to the paltry results we see in too many gay bars. There is nothing wrong with gay bars, but there is a lot wrong with bad gay bars.

Proposition 4

Society does not hate us because we hate ourselves;
we hate ourselves because we grew up and live in a society that hates us.

"The problem is not so much homosexual desire as the fear of homosexuality," as Guy Hocquenghem states in the first sentence of his book *Homosexual Desire*. Many straights—and unfortunately even some gays—have the irritating habit of pointing to one of the more bizarre, extreme, confused or self-lacerating (but rarely self-destructive) manifestations of homosexuality as the reason for their general repugnance and intolerance. But they have it ass-backwards. These evasions of self, confusions of sex and manifestations of despair are the *result* of the implacable hostility of society—"the havoc wrought in the souls of people who aren't supposed to exist" (Ntozake Shange). There is a savage hypocrisy here that reminds one of Bieber's assertion that homosexuals were neurotic because they were, among other things, "injustice collectors."

Internalized self-hatred is deep and pervasive in the gay world and the havoc it can work should not be underestimated, but to compound it by assuming guilt for the sometimes deplorable effects of society's hostility toward us is foolish and self-defeating. It leads to a miasma of depression when what is called for is anger.

The relative absence of clear and cleansing anger in the gay world is surprising and worthy of note; it is probably a bad sign.

Proposition 5

The appalling violence—physical, psychological, social, and intellectual—unleashed against gays by western society in modern times is a clear attempt at cultural genocide.

Most gay men I know will feel uncomfortable with this assertion, which is nevertheless an unavoidable conclusion. The implied parallel with the suffering of American Blacks, the Jews, the Vietnamese and other colonized or persecuted peoples makes us sharply aware of the peculiarities of our own situation, the unusual opportunities for wealth, influence, and a tenuous security that have historically been our options. But the point is not to claim an equality of suffering—pain, physical or psychological, is almost impossible to measure in any case, and the attempt to compute or compare it reeks of vulgarity—still less to assume that a preoccupation with one's own hurt somehow slights or diminishes someone else's. The point is to establish precisely what has been done and to delineate the peculiarities of our own oppression, which are grounded in the peculiarities of our situation.

American racists have inflicted extraordinary suffering on American Blacks but they have not tried to pretend that the Black hero, Crispus Attucks, the first casualty of the American Revolutionary War, was white. The Nazi lunatics systematically sought to exterminate Jews, yet opened perverse "museums" of "decadent" Jewish art (which ironically were very popular). The astonishingly systematic yet spontaneous attempt to *expunge* our very existence from the historical record—through silence, deliberate distortion, and mendacious interpretation—has very few precise parallels; one thinks of some of Stalin's more bizarre insanities or the vicious extermination of the Albigensians, even in memory. Even the cynical will be startled by the catalogue of lies briefly reviewed by John Boswell in his brilliant and seminal work, *Christianity, Social Tolerance, and Homosexuality*. To quote one of the more amusing instances: "Sometimes their anxiety to reinterpret or disguise accounts of homosexuality has induced translators to inject wholly new concepts into texts, as when the translators of a Hittite law apparently regulating homosexual marriage insert words which completely alter its meaning or when Graves 'translates' a nonexistent clause in Suetonius to suggest that a law prohibits homosexual acts."

When one reflects that the Stalinist scholars worked under the threat of totalitarian terror, that the Albigensian Crusades were fueled by a wave of popular hysteria that was transitory, if devastating, and contrasts this to calm, systematic, uncoerced, uncoordinated, utterly pervasive, enduring, and relentless effort to destroy, falsify, and denigrate gay history, paranoia seems a sane response. What are we to do with people who will go to such lengths as to doctor the records of a Hittite civilization which flourished three-and-a-half-thousand years ago?

The attempt to reclaim gay history, so ably argued and exemplified by Robert Martin (on Hart Crane) and Simon Karlinsky (on Diaghilev) this year in the pages of *Christopher Street*, will be accomplished only in the teeth of intense resistance by the straight scholarly establishment. Any ground won will be bitterly contested and we can expect them to get truly vicious as inroads are made. But only the past brings us possibility (for instance, of gay marriage, apparently known in many cultures), and possibility is the air that will save us from suffocating in the present oppression.

In this regard it is important to note that violence *can* destroy things of the spirit. Force *can* destroy culture, as Simone Weil has sharply reminded us. The past can be distorted, even obliterated, it has no force of its own to preserve itself. It is foolish in the extreme to believe gay liberation will *inevitably* triumph.

Proposition 6

All gays are born into a straight world and socialized to be straight; consequently, we have internalized the enemy, and all political struggle must be simultaneously a self-criticism and self-renewal.

COROLLARY: Self-criticism does not mean criticism by gays of other gays who are perceived to be different, as Steve Wolf seemed to assume in a recent Christopher Street Guest Word called "The New Gay Party Line."

The controversy kicked up by *Bent* over whether in fact the Nazis assigned the Jews or the gays to a lower circle of hell was mostly beside the point.

It would be important to know exactly how the Nazis treated gays and how this compared and contrasted to the treatment of other groups—although it is morally tacky for any group to try to lay claims to pre-eminence in suffering in the face of the Holocaust. Sherman's dramatic point was quite different: all gays had been raised as straights, in terms of the play, every queer had internalized a Nazi within and therefore had a spiritual fifth column which could become a collaborator. When Max denies his gay self—denies his "friend" Rudy, fucks the dead twelve-year-old girl to prove he's straight—he has collaborated with the Nazis in his own spiritual extermination, the point Horst eventually teaches him. For Horst, spiritual extermination is worse than physical extermination.

To the Jew, the Nazi is other—an external, if insanely malevolent, agent of destruction. To the "bent," the straight can never be so totally external.

Proposition 7

The elemental gay emotional experience is the question: "Am I the only one?"
The feeling of being "different," and our response to it, dominates our inner lives.

Gays emerge *as gay* in this trauma. One suspects that it haunts gay life in countless subtle ways that we haven't begun to trace. The gradual or sudden but always unnerving awareness that one is "different" leads to the fear of being the only one. One wonders if the extraordinary fear of rejection which dominates the social interactions in gay bars—and which appears so senseless, since we've all been rejected many times and know from experience that it is certainly not devastating—is nothing more than a replay of adolescent psychological scenarios, when natural sexual desire threatened to expose one as "different" and invited the devastating possibility of total rejection, even *and especially* by those "best friends" one was most attracted to. This undermining of sexual and affectional preference, putting into question what one *knows* with immediacy and certainty, traumatizes a person's integrity to the point of making one feel that his very being is somehow "wrong."

This assault on the integrity of the self, which every gay experiences, should never be underestimated. It is the basic tactic our weirdly homophobic culture uses to destroy us—first isolate, then terrorize, then make disappear by *self*-denial. As our archetypal emotional donnybrook, it also helps to explain many things in the gay world—gay pornography, for instance, is by and large a positive fantasy fulfillment that counteracts the nightmarish fears of our adolescent years and, as such, is politically progressive.

Proposition 8

> *"Only within the framework of a people can a*
> *man live as a man without exhausting himself."*
>
> HANNAH ARENDT

If society tries to destroy us by first isolating us, it follows that what is necessary to fight back is not only defiance but the acknowledgment of a community and the construction of a world. Individual defiance may lead to heroism—as we can see in the cases of Quentin Crisp and Jean Genet—but, while we should honor our heroes, the cost is too high. Few individuals have the integrity or the energy to sustain the violence to the soul and the consequent psychological deformations which heroism entails.

The further construction and consolidation of the gay ghetto is an immediate and necessary political objective. The singularity of the gay situation makes this "ghetto" unique, generating perplexities we have barely begun to address and rendering all parallels to the experience of other groups dubious at best. But this should not obscure the fact that "ghetto" is another word for "world" and that "coming out" means asserting our right to appear in the world as who we are. From the Blacks and the colonized we can learn much about the pain of being "invisible men," but we should also learn that if we want to live in the world and not in the closet, we must create that world on every level. It will not be handed to us on a silver platter. We need to create networks of friendship, love relationships, public places and institutions, neighborhoods, art and literature. A gay culture is a political necessity for our survival.

Proposition 9

Gay politics (using politics in its narrow meaning) is a politics of pure principle.

For us there is no "social question." We are not asking for a bigger slice of the pie but for justice. We do not require social programs, jobs, day care centers, educational and professional quotas, or any of the other legitimate demands of previously exploited minority groups. Our demands will not cost the body politic one cent. We demand only the freedom to be who we are. The fact that this demand, which takes away nothing from anyone else, is met with such obstinate resistance is a noteworthy indication of how deep-seated the hostility against us is.

On the other hand, we could expect that gay politics has its best chance in countries which are constitutional republics, where the belief that justice is the ultimate source of authority and legitimacy for the government gives us a powerful lever. It seems to me no accident that gay politics and gay culture have arisen first and most strongly in the United States. This is the only state I know of brought into being by political dissidents. Whatever revisionist history may teach us are the facts of the case, the enormous authority the image of the Pilgrims and the Founding Fathers has for this country should not be underestimated. It often seems that non-American observers simply cannot understand our feeling that *as Americans* it is our right to be faggots if we choose—or as the lesbian novelist Noretta Koertge puts it, "being American means to me being able to paint my mailbox purple if I want." Invoking the ultimate principles—if not realities—of this country is one of our most promising tactics and should be explored and emphasized.

Proposition 10

We have no natural allies and therefore we cannot rely on the assistance of any group.

We have only tactical allies—people who don't want barbarous things done to us because they fear the same things may someday be done to them. Tactical allies come into being when there is a perceived convergence of self-interest between two groups. One can accomplish much in politics with tactical allies, as witness the long alliance between Blacks and Jews—but there are limits that emerge when the group-interests diverge, as witness the split between Blacks and Jews over school decentralization in New York City.

A natural ally would be someone who is happy we are here, rather than someone who is unhappy at the way we are being treated. It would seem that the most we can expect, at least in the immediate future, is a tolerance based on decency. No one, no matter how decent, seems glad that gays exist, even when they may be enjoying works inspired by our sensibility. As far as I can see, even our best straight friends will never be thankful that we are gay the way we ourselves (in our better moments) are thankful we are gay. This is nothing to get maudlin over. It does, however, sometimes seem to limit communication—the sharing which is the essence of friendship—with straights. It is a rare straight friend to whom one can say, "I'm so glad I'm gay because otherwise I never would have gotten the chance to love Ernie," and not draw a blank, if not bewildered and uncomfortable, reaction. It is understandable that they do not see it as something to celebrate, but we should. On the personal level, it is generally unlikely that one's straight family or friends will easily learn genuine acceptance; luckily it would appear that they can, notwithstanding, often learn love. For our part, the paranoia that this situation tends naturally to generate should be rigorously controlled.

Proposition 11

Our political enemies are of two kinds: those who want us not to exist and those who want us not to appear.

Those who want us not to exist are the well-known, old-fashioned bigots, who would stamp us out, apply shock therapy or terroristic behavior modification, cordon us off and separate us from society, and ultimately try to kill us as the Nazis did. Fortunately, these bigots are also a threat to many other segments of society and a number of tactical allies can be mobilized in the fight against them. Bigots are essentially bullies and this bullying impulse seems to be exasperated to the point of massacre by the lack of resistance. This suggests that the best response to them is probably a violent one; unchecked aggression seems to feed on itself and simply pick up velocity, like one of Lear's rages. I suspect that when epithets are hurled at one in the street, it's best to shout epithets back; trying to ignore them with dignity or responding with overt fear seems only to intensify the hostility. Although I am open to correction on this, I have the feeling that the *safest* response to physical assault is fighting back; the bruises one may incur seem to me preferable to the corrosive rage that follows from helplessness, and I suspect they might avoid a truly dangerous stomping. In short, bullies become worse bullies when they are unchecked, and the cost of resistance is probably well worth it in the long run.

Those who want us not to appear are more subtle and probably more dangerous since it is harder to mobilize tactical allies against them. This seemed to me the most significant aspect of the Anita Bryant phenomenon. By carefully explaining that she was only against overt gay behavior—the "flaunting" of our life-style and the consequent "recruitment"—she managed to seem reasonable to a large segment of the public; by disavowing any McCarthy-type witch hunt, she managed to avoid tripping the wire that would have sent large parts of the Jewish community of Miami onto red alert. The difficulty of countering these people successfully is rooted in the fact that we *can* pass, a characteristic that distinguishes us from other minority groups, and is further compounded by the fact that, when you come right down to it, *everyone* would be more comfortable if we remained in the closet, except ourselves.

These matters require much more consideration than we have yet given them. We cannot rely forever on the stupidity of our opponents—for instance, in the over-reaching involved in the wording of Briggs' Initiative in California which led to its rejection for First Amendment reasons that were so obvious they even penetrated the mind of the public. It's urgent to give tactical and strategic thought to these matters—always keeping in mind the fact that in their heart of hearts the overwhelming majority of the American people would prefer us back in the closet. Our only hope is to make it clear that that would be so costly that they will not be willing to pay the price.

Proposition 12

"The only remedy for powerlessness is power."

CHARLES ORTLEB

Economic exploitation, one of the great 19th-century themes of political discourse, has largely been replaced in our own day by the discussion of oppression. Exploitation means basically that someone is stealing from you; oppression is essentially a matter of invisibility, of feeling weightless and insubstantial, without voice or impact in the world. Blacks, the colonized, women, and gays all share this experience of being a ghost in their own country, the disorienting alienation of feeling they are not actually there. This psychological experience is the subjective correlate to the objective fact of powerlessness.

It is odd that the desire for power has for many an unpleasant aura about it, for powerlessness is a true crime against the human spirit and undercuts the possibility of justice among people. In his *Inquiry Concerning the Principles of Morals* (1752), David Hume lays this out quite clearly, albeit without being aware of it, when he speculates that "were there a species intermingled with men which, though rational, were possessed of such inferior strength, both of body and mind, that they were incapable of all resistance and could never, upon the highest provocation, make us feel the effects of their resentment, the necessary consequence, I think, is that we ... should not, properly speaking, lie under any restraint of justice with regard to them. .... Our intercourse with them could not be called society, which supposes a degree of equality, but absolute command on the one side and servile obedience on the other. .... Our permission is the only tenure by which they hold their possessions, our compassion and kindness the only check by which they [*sic*] curb our lawless will ... the restraints of justice ... would never have place in so unequal a confederacy."

Well, we know there are such "creatures intermingled with men"— women first of all, and the colonized races, as well as homosexuals, Jews, and mental patients. It is truly strange that this philosopher, who seems to think he is idly speculating, was quite clearly laying out the premise of the power structure that at that very moment was subjugating so many groups of people. And with two centuries of hindsight, it should be clear to all of us just how effective their "compassion and kindness" is as a check against their "lawless will." If we have to rely on "the laws of humanity" to convince them "to give gentle usage to these creatures," we will stay precisely where we have been, under their heel being stomped on.

I do not pretend to understand the origin and mechanics of this strange social system in which we live. But it seems to me it should be abundantly clear to even the dimmest wit that without power you will not get justice. How anybody could rely on "compassion and kindness" after looking around at the world we live in is beyond me. "Moderate" gays who think we can achieve tolerance by respectability seem to me willfully ignorant of our own history, as well as the history of other oppressed groups. They are the Court Jews of our time, however good their subjective intentions.

Straights who object to our daily increasing visibility are basically objecting to the assertion of power implicit in that phenomenon. They would prefer that we continue to rely on their "compassion and kindness" and correctly sense that our refusal to do so directly insults them. With their record on the matter it is hard to imagine why they are surprised. In fact, our extraordinary explosion into visibility, the spontaneous and visible assertion of our sexual identity that constitutes the clone look, is politically valuable. Not only are we more visible to each other, we are more visible to them. Of course, one would naturally expect a backlash at this point; it is virtually unknown in history for any group to give up power over any other without a struggle.

Proposition 13

Gay life is an issue only for gays, whenever straights address the question, they are attacking us.

The quality of gay life is obviously an issue for us. There are many aspects of the gay world, many peculiarities of gay life that are disturbing; we should face them and, keeping an open mind, try to understand and evaluate them as possibilities for ourselves. (This does not mean attacking gays who choose to live differently than we do; it means deciding how *we* want to live, not how other people should.) But this discussion is totally off limits to straights.

Whenever straights, usually posing as friendly but concerned liberals, address the "issue" of gay life, they are actually raising the question of whether we should exist. Curiously enough, the answer is *inevitably* no. This question is not raised about Blacks and Jews, at least not in polite company, because its murderous implications are at once evident. For instance, in Midge Decter's recent hysterical and hilarious attack on us in *Commentary* ("The Boys on the Beach," September 1980) one finds the following: "*Know them as a group* [her italics]. No doubt this will in itself seem to many of the uninitiated a bigoted formulation. Yet one cannot even begin to get at *the truth about homosexuals* [my italics] without this kind of generalization." To see what is being said here, simply substitute "the truth about Jews" or "the truth about Blacks" and reread. Straights who raise homosexuality *as an issue* are attacking us—about this we should not be confused. From Joseph Epstein's infamous article in *Harper's*—in which this man, a father himself, decides that he would rather see his son *dead* than homosexual—to Paul Cowan's shamefully bigoted review of *States of Desire* in the *New York Times Sunday Book Review*, the position is always the same. Straights who earn their living as cultural commentators, who try to set out the terms for public discussion, display an unholy fear of being peripheralized by us. Perhaps more clearly (not more basically) than any other minority group or culture, gays threaten their cultural power, which is based on preserving and policing a cultural uniformity. To acknowledge diversity or plurality seems to threaten the very existence of their own values. This is sick. We may be bent, but these people are truly twisted. Nevertheless, they are dangerous; they control the organs of cultural definition in this country and they have the power to confuse us with their disguised fanaticism.

Proposition 14

It is absurd to believe that after coming out we are no longer conditioned
by the virulent hatred of gays apparently endemic to this culture.
Homophobia is an ever-present threat and pressure, both externally and internally.

I suspect that by now I will have lost many readers who will feel that these comments are too militant, overblown or emotional. One of the problems peculiar to this subject matter is that it is often hard actually to believe in the reality of gay oppression. The hatred of gays makes so little sense to us, seems so uncalled for and pointless, so extremely neurotic and so easily avoided (by "passing") that we tend to dismiss it from our perception of reality. How very dangerous this can be is apparent to any student of Nazism. In the Thirties most Germans *and* Jews refused to take seriously Hitler's quite explicit and well-known intentions toward the Jews because it was too much of an outrage to common sense. "It's only rhetoric, no one could be that mad." Even during the war, Bruno Bettelheim and other survivors have reported people refusing to believe their first-hand accounts of the concentration camps, to the point where they themselves doubted the reality of the experiences they had so harrowingly survived.

Something similar happens when one steps back to reflect on the clearly documented evidence of homophobia—let us not take the melodramatic examples of shock treatment and forcible sexual reprogramming but the purely prosaic refusal of the City Council of New York, one of the country's liberal strongholds, repeatedly, year after year, to vote civil rights for gays. I suggest that not to give this simple fact its due weight is willfully to blind ourselves to the reality of the situation in which we live.

It is even more painful when this happens in our immediate private life. Often a chance remark or a passingly uncomfortable comment by a good friend turns out to have such devastating implications that we prefer not to think about it. And if we do think it through, the results are so harsh we do not know what to do with them. To dwell on it seems willfully fanatic, slightly hysterical, or "oversensitive," as straight friends are fond of saying. It is less painful to let go, to go along, to accommodate ourselves to these people in spite of their quirks because we value their company and friendship.

The willing suspension of belief in the reality of gay oppression, however, has serious and destructive consequences. Chief among them is the widespread predisposition to believe that once we have accomplished the psychological ordeal known as coming out, we are suddenly and magically free of the negative conditioning of our homophobic society. This is obviously absurd. Nevertheless, we tend to consider our problems—alcoholism, unfulfilling sexual obsession, workaholism, inability to handle emotional intimacy, cynicism, the self-destructive negativism of attitude, and on and on—as simply our own fault. At most, we will trace them to our inability "to accept ourselves." The point of the matter is *no one starts off with an inability to accept himself*; this emerges only after we find other people unable or unwilling to accept us. The conditioning of our homophobic society runs deep and is not easily eradicated; unless explicitly acknowledged and dealt with, it will continue to distort our psyches and our lives. We urgently need to understand the ways these destructive influences continue to pervade our immediate existence, to trace their impact on our behavior in bars and in the baths, in the office and in bed, carefully and without preconception distinguishing what is useful for survival, if not admirable in an ideal society, from what can only demoralize us further. In this connection, I suspect we have, by and large, seriously underestimated the help gay novelists have offered us in books like *Dancer from the Dance*, *Faggots*, and *Rushes*.

Proposition 15

> *The cultural, legal, and psychological assault on gays so weirdly characteristic of our society has not ceased, and there is no reason to believe it will cease in the immediate future.*

Theoretical analyses have absolutely no impact on any social reality. Even the understanding of our concrete situation in the world that they hopefully engender will not, of itself, change the situation.

A Black friend of mine said recently, "If writing a book exposing racism would end it, we would have ended it ourselves a long time ago." All the understanding of homophobia in the world will not make it disappear. We are not omnipotent; neither as individuals nor as a group do we control reality, which is something we share with all those with whom we share the earth. No psychological, interpersonal, intellectual, or spiritual achievements on our part alone will eradicate homophobia, for the problem does not rest only with us—"the problem is not so much homosexual desire as the fear of homosexuality" (Guy Hocquenghem).

What we *can* do is face up to the reality of the situation and begin to change it in our own case. In the Sixties there was much talk of "making the Revolution"; many people seemed to think that somehow this one apocalyptic event would result in the transfiguration of human society. But the Revolution never came. The gay "revolution"—if that term should even be used—can only be made in the daily lives of each one of us. What could gay liberation possibly be but a change in the quality of our actual lives? For better or worse, we create the face of gay liberation in every sexual encounter and love affair we have. With every circle of loyal gay friends established we are manifesting the gay world (the achievements we have been making in this area are well documented in Ed White's *States of Desire: Travels in Gay America*). As we individually come to terms with our straight friends and help them to come to terms with us, we help to dissolve homophobia. While this prospect is not as dramatic or as emotionally satisfying as a "revolution," it does have the enormous advantage of being realistic. We are *already* in the midst of changing our lives and our world, but it will not happen automatically or without our individual participation.

Proposition 16

"We gay people are the alchemists, the magicians, of our time. We take the toxins of a poisonous age, the nihilism that is given us, and turn it into a balm that heals. We heal ourselves, and in that we are an object-lesson for the others."

Declared by a lesbian divinity student at a meeting
at St. John the Divine Cathedral, New York City

In the modern tradition, radical political theory has always assumed that society would be transformed by some group within that society which "carried" the revolutionary impulse. When Archimedes discovered the mathematical laws of leverage, he boasted that given a place to stand he could move the entire earth. When modern political theorists thought they had discovered the laws of society, they assumed that with the proper lever the world could be transformed. The most persuasive scenario asserted that the proletariat, a class totally alienated—that is, outside the society, with "nothing to lose but its chains"—would be the lever that would move the earth. But this theory forgot what Archimedes knew, that there was no such "Archimedean point" on which to stand; the voting of war credits by the German Social Democratic Party in 1914 proved once and for all that the proletariat did not stand outside society; they were as jingoistic as any other group. The truly great vision of political transformation that had animated the West since the French Revolution died with that act.

But as always the debris of broken dreams lived on to confuse the minds of men. There is a constant tendency on the part of people involved in the struggle of their own group for liberation—Blacks, feminists, the colonized, gays—to assume that their group is marked by history to be the liberators of all humanity, the class that carries the revolutionary impulse. It is an understandable error; since no group can be liberated unless the entire society is liberated (because of the simple fact that it is always the *others* who oppress the oppressed, therefore oppression will not cease until the oppressors cease being oppressive), it is easy enough to reverse the argument and say that the liberation of the oppressed group will liberate society. Unfortunately reality does not make such logical errors. Bertrand Russell's witty explanation of Bolshevism—since the proletariat has throughout history always been oppressed by other classes, it is only fair that they now have the chance to oppress everyone else—seems more to the point, as we can see in the unpleasant instance of Vietnamese actions in Cambodia.

At this point in time, it would be silly and tedious for gays to make the same erroneous assertion. Gay liberation has no chance in hell of liberating society sexually. (The reverse argument is, of course, valid, if tautological, the sexual liberation of society would indeed entail the liberation of gays. The problem is only: what will cause the sexual liberation of society, who will bring this about? You can see how one could fall into thinking about the agent or carrier of historical change.) Gay liberation will not be the carrier of the revolutionary idea if for no other reason than the fact that by "revolutionary idea" is meant the revaluation of all values, and values are not "things" that can be "carried" like shoulder bags or diseases. A discussion of the nature of value, however, would take us too far afield.

If gay liberation is not going to liberate society, has it any meaning beyond that of promoting the self-interests of the individuals who make up this particular group? (I hasten to add that defending and promoting the self-interest of any oppressed group is in itself totally justifiable.) I think the answer is affirmative, if somewhat speculative at this point.

It has been known for well over a century now that something is drastically wrong with our culture; our values seem to be working in reverse. Western civilization looks more and more like the sorcerer's apprentice: it has unleashed powers that threaten to overwhelm it. Nihilism is the name usually applied to this phenomenon. Our values have turned against us and threaten devastation, if not extinction. This sounds rhetorical. It is not. It is a simple description of the current state of affairs, as a moment's uncomfortable reflection on the Holocaust, the threat of nuclear annihilation, the consequences of pollution and irreversible ecological intervention, genetic engineering, or a dozen other phenomena reported daily in the papers, makes quite clear. We need a revaluation of all our values, but how can this be accomplished if there is no Archimedean point on which to stand? If the salt has lost its savor, wherewith shall it be salted?

I suggest that the complex, subtle, everyday transformation of values that we gays have been engaged in for the last ten years, the self-renewal that constitutes gay liberation, is a creative response to the viciously negative values of our culture. As such, it would be *a part* of that urgently necessary revaluation of all values and could serve not as a historical catalyst that will save anybody else, but as an example of what is necessary and as a welcome ally to those already engaged by this challenge. In the struggle for gay liberation we come home to ourselves and our world and take our place among the ranks of decent and responsible people everywhere who stand together at this decisive moment in humanity's career on the planet.

*   *   *

No doubt other propositions regarding the contemporary gay situation might be added to the sixteen I have sketched. My purpose, however, is not to be exhaustive but to give examples of the type of matters we must think about if we are to grasp the dynamics of our own lives.

These are things which directly affect all gay men; what may seem at times overly theoretical or abstract is nonetheless an attempt to come to grips with the dilemmas that structure our sexual experience, shape our patterns of socializing, and all too often distort our psyches and blight our loves while simultaneously bringing us a reckless joy at being alive. These are matters that our writers and artists think about, as well as philosophers and gays on the street—whether they know it or not. They are important. For if we do not measure up to the unprecedented novelty of our current situation, we will piss away a golden opportunity to improve the fate of gay people in our culture, for both our own and future generations.

Sixteen Propositions

AN EXCHANGE

CHRISTOPHER STREET RECEIVED a number of letters about the *Sixteen Propositions*, most lengthy and some quite heated. Given my day job, it was impossible to answer all of them, nor could the magazine devote the space to it that would be required, but it seemed to me important to acknowledge disagreement and respond to it. I choose to answer Barry Bergen's letter, which I thought the most trenchant and intelligent. And which raised the most interesting issues.[1]

Michael Denneny's "Gay Politics: Sixteen Propositions" (January 1981), while thoughtful throughout and often perceptive, establishes priorities which, if followed, would ultimately take us no further than we have already come. His "propositions," taken as a whole, while providing an interesting series of reflections on the nature of being gay, do not present a coherent political program for gays. Denneny offers us no solutions to the problems he himself raises, only contradictory means and ends.

The fundamental problem with Denneny's position derives from his attempt to abstract gays from the society in which they live. Thus the problems of gays, for Denneny, stem from the fact that "insofar as we are gay we are ipso facto different from straights," that we have no "natural allies" in politics, that we are different, that the knowledge of this difference "dominates our inner lives," and he makes the source of that difference, our sexuality, the central issue of gay politics. It is for this difference that we are subject to physical and psychological violence, and "cultural genocide."

Denneny's analysis ignores the place of gays in society as a whole.

---

1 *Christopher Street*, vol. 5, no. 7 (July 1981); reprinted here with Barry Bergen's permission.

Denneny may feel that being gay is his most significant identity (his "imperative status," as anthropologists would put it), but this does not justify the formulation of a politics which ignores both the other components of his social status, and social categories which are significant to other people. He sidesteps our samenesses, and the potential strengths of our differences.

This criticism is based on two related ideas. First, being gay does not negate one's other social identities, and there is no good reason for giving it priority in one's politics. Doing so both neglects the problems of gays who are oppressed in other ways—Lesbians, Black, Asian and Latino gays, to name only a few—and denies the relationship between the oppression of gays and the oppression of non-gays. A gay politics which does not address the problems of Blacks, of the poor, which cannot (in Denneny's own words) even claim to be relevant to *lesbians*, cannot serve as a gay politics for the 1980s.

Second, as Mary McIntosh first demonstrated in her pioneering 1968 article, "The Homosexual Role," homosexuality as a category of social existence—as something that someone *is*—is a recent historical development. Until relatively recently, in historical terms, people in the West did not inhabit a world of heterosexuals and homosexuals. Rather the world was populated by people, undifferentiated in this sense, who could commit a variety of sexual acts which did not define their place in society (except perhaps temporarily as sinners). Indeed, the word "homosexual," as Jeffrey Weeks has pointed out, was not invented until 1869, and did not enter into English usage until the 1880s and 1890s. In fact, the emergence of the homosexual role seems to coincide with the growing categorization and classification of people within the developing bourgeois ideology: race, gender, childhood/adulthood, sane/insane, criminal/law-abiding. These differentiations were then institutionalized in various forms: asylums, prisons, schools, the bourgeois family, etc. Many of these distinctions were, however, mere abstractions, not physical facts. Homosexuality, like race, is not at root an objective condition. Many may balk at this. But, as Lorraine Hansberry wrote nearly twenty years ago, race is a device. Or, as Barbara J. Fields has brilliantly explained more recently, race is a purely ideological notion, not a physical fact. And as an ideological notion it is a historical product. (My apologies to Ms. Fields for this simplification of a complex argument, to which mine owes a great deal.)

Homosexuality as a category of social existence is, too, an ideological construction. As Hocquenghem and Mieli have each shown, following Freud, erotic desire is universal, and the libido does not differentiate the gender of its object choice. We are all people capable of engaging in a multiplicity of sexual acts which do not define us. The homosexual role, and the heterosexual one, are products of the historical development of a particular ideology. This does not mean that gays have not been persecuted and oppressed through the operations of this ideology. But it suggests to me important directions for gay politics and gay history. For the latter, it suggests the need to study the historical development of the homosexual role, and its link to other such differentiations. As a historian, I am sensitive to Denneny's desire to reclaim our past. But I do not believe that this consists in the glorification of particular historical figures as "gay." Rather, we must discover the historical roots of our oppression. This means the search for the development of homosexuality as a category of social identity, and for the emergence of exclusive heterosexuality as the norm in Western civilization, which, though difficult to locate precisely, is nevertheless a historical development. As for gay politics, the production of such an historical knowledge of the roots of our own oppression will provide us with a basis for a political theory that will attack our oppression at a more fundamental level. This must, I believe, link the oppression of gays with that of non-gays. And I strongly believe that this will occur when we come to understand the complex relationship between ideological constructs such as race and sexual orientation and objectively identifiable bases of oppression like class and gender.

These beliefs, then, lead me to an understanding of the nature of our oppression and how to combat it that is far different from Denneny's. Denneny feels that we are not exploited, but oppressed, that we are the objects of attempts at "cultural genocide," and subject to the double-edged sword of internal and external hatred. His remedy is a "politics of pure principle." We, as different, must band together into gay ghettos, create and protect a gay culture, fight for our right to be who we are, a fight we must fight alone.

I take issue with most of this. We are both oppressed and exploited. This is precisely the implication of Herbert Marcuse's concept of "repressive toleration," which Denneny seems to misunderstand. The tolerance which we receive in Western society is repressive insofar as the illusion of freedom which it produces circumvents the problems and tensions which might otherwise erupt into revolt or revolution. But it is also exploitative, because what most of us do with this freedom is adopt the values of consumer capitalist society. Not shackled with the reproduction of the species, which society no longer requires of us, most of us become consumers *par excellence*, archetypal representatives of consumer culture. Therein lies the root of our freedom: it is only the freedom of the ghetto. And that "freedom to be who we are," which amounts to sexual freedom for Denneny, is only another example of the same, or more precisely, what Marcuse called "repressive desublimation": sexual freedom can be repressive too. Should we band together in the ghetto and expend all our energies in wanton sprees of consumption and sex without emotional attachment? This is not the aim of my gay politics. Moreover, I'm not sure what Denneny means by "cultural genocide," but we are not a culture. And genocide means the extermination of a people. We are not a people. True, some of us function within a kind of gay subculture in major urban centers. But many, perhaps most of us, do not. People with some homosexual desires are born and raised in straight families all over the country, the world, regardless of the attempts to suppress (or promote) it. We cannot be exterminated, for we do not constitute a people; we do not reproduce ourselves. Gay people, in the popular conception (and Denneny's), are only a handful of those with homosexual desires who choose to make that desire the centerpiece of their existence. Mr. Denneny's politics may do something for that small group, but it does little for the majority, or for the new generations of "gays" being born into society every year.

A gay politics centered on the ghetto thus can never solve the problems of gays in the society as a whole. It can never fight the double-edged sword of internal and external oppression because it does not attack its roots in the values of the larger society. And it ignores the problems of other groups in society and the relationship between our oppression and theirs. And finally, it does not liberate the gays of the ghetto, because even for them it merely replicates the values and structures of the larger society. Liberating ourselves first, cutting ourselves off from society (even from our lesbian sisters), seeking for the few the hedonistic illusion of freedom of the ghetto—these were the hallmarks of gay politics for most of the 1970s. They produced no real liberation, no real freedom, no real power, and thus (as we now see), no real security. A gay politics for the 1980s must seek to discover the real roots of gay oppression, to reintegrate our understanding of gays into understanding of the whole society in which we live, and thus it must seek to link the struggle of gays with other struggles against oppression. We do have natural allies. For a gay politics which does not seek to radically alter the structure and content of our society will never achieve true liberation of gays, or anyone else.

BARRY H. BERGEN
University of Pennsylvania Department of History
Philadelphia, Pennsylvania

Michael Denneny responds:

I think Barry Bergen's letter is interesting because it epitomizes for me the cast of mind of many of our gay intellectuals and illustrates—at least to my mind—why our intellectuals are so out of touch with the rank and file of gay men. (I know it's repetitive, but I have to say it again: I'm only speaking to the situation of gay men. The situation with lesbians seems to me different—the work of their theorists seems much more immediately relevant to their sisters—and in any event, I'm in no position to comment on their scene; we can perfectly well listen to their analyses of their situation.)

Mr. Bergen asserts that "being gay does not negate our other social identities and there is no good reason for giving it priority in one's politics." I don't think Mr. Bergen has been noticing how our society actually treats us. To take two examples (everyone can add their own): There are many gay teenagers for whose parents that one fact of being gay does indeed negate their children's other social identity—of *being their own children.* Or, to take a personal example, I have published a gay book that was reviewed in *The Village Voice* by a writer using a pseudonym. When I actually met the author of the review, I asked why he had not written under his own name; because, he told me, he feared he would lose his job, or at least any chance of advancement, if the Catholic university at which he worked suspected he was gay.

I don't see how Mr. Bergen can maintain his position when the majority of gays continue to live—more or less—in the closet because of their fear that they will lose their jobs, the affection of their family, the respect of their co-workers, or their relationship to their children. Does he think these fears are ungrounded? Are we all a bunch of foolish paranoids? As long as such enormous social sanctions are directed against open homosexuality, I think it's quite sensible for a gay person to think being gay is a significant identity, an "imperative status." Hannah Arendt once said, "When you are attacked for being a Jew, you cannot say, 'Please excuse me, I am not a Jew, I am a human being.' This is silly."

Of course I realize how irritating it is that others can and do define us, can by their attitude and actions decide what is our "imperative status," as the Nazis decided the question for the Jews in the Thirties. But any Jew who didn't realize that being Jewish was his paramount identity in Nazi Germany, the one social fact that outweighed all others, was refusing to face the facts of the situation, and to refuse to face the facts—especially when those facts are stupid—is politically foolish in the extreme.

Mr. Bergen seems to think that because homosexuality is a social construct that emerged historically—he cites McIntosh and Weeks, and could have added Plummer, Altman, and Foucault—it is somehow less real, less "objectively identifiable (than) class or gender." Now this makes no sense to me. Clearly class is a social construct; classes come into existence historically at certain times, as he well knows. And unless we accept the argument that anatomy is destiny, gender (in the relevant sense of social-constructed roles) is also a product of history. He himself cites the fact that race is a historical and cultural construct, an ideological notion, a political device to oppress people, which it clearly is. However, try telling a Black man in Mississippi that because of that being Black is not his "imperative status."

Now I find all these historical and theoretical studies Mr. Bergen cites to be enormously interesting, but there is a side effect to them that I find extremely unfortunate. Mr. Bergen, for instance, finds that they "suggest the need to study the historical development of the homosexual role . . . (to) discover the historical roots of our oppression. . . . As for gay politics, the production of such an historical knowledge of the roots of our oppression will provide us with the basis of a political theory which will attack our oppression at a more fundamental level." And, meanwhile, while we're waiting for this historical knowledge that our scholars and intellectuals will presumably provide, what are the rest of us supposed to do, sit on our hands? Should the Jews in the Thirties have waited for historical research on the origin of anti-Semitism? Did Blacks need to wait for an analysis of the roots of their oppression before they acted to gain their rights? This is simply old-fashioned intellectual elitism, the belief that you have to have a theory before you can act. But oddly enough, these theorists always call for more *theoretical research*, not political action. I'm sorry, but no "political theory (will) attack our oppression"; it will be attacked only by politicized gay people.

Mr. Bergen shares a quite general prejudice of many professional intellectuals—that we have to understand our oppression and its roots before we can fight it. Luckily, this is not true. If we had to understand evil before we resisted it, we'd all be dead.

This is not to argue for a mindless politics; it is to argue for a politics based on a common-sense appreciation of our social situation, an understanding open to all gay people whether they've had the chance to read these theoretical and historical researchers or not. Such scholarship is useful; it is not, in my opinion, a prerequisite for gay political action. It would be good if we could all remember that scholarship, and even thinking, is not the same as, or even a good substitute for, real political activity.

Mr. Bergen says I did not offer "a coherent political program for gays" and he's right. He himself offers a program of historical research and theoretical synthesis in which ninety-five percent of the gay population cannot be actively engaged. I offered a series of propositions that I thought we should all consider and argue about if we hope to achieve some clarity about and control over our lives.

If I were to suggest a political program, I think I would advocate the creation of political action committees everywhere possible with the function of channeling money and energy into electoral races, the running of gay candidates for any and all offices whenever this possibility might arise, and (failing to have our own candidates) the active participation of gays in any relevant electoral race. Most elections in this country are decided by a few percentage points; the ability to swing even five percent of the electorate can give a well-organized minority group real power, as the far right has recently so clearly demonstrated. These actions—and others like them—have the great advantage that, whether they achieve their immediate aims or not, they achieve as a by-product the further consolidation of a real community among gay people, which increasingly seems to me the real end of all gay politics.

To put our differences in a nutshell: Mr. Bergen believes that when we understand things—how society works, how the homosexual role came into being—we will be in a position to change them (and, presumably, automatically will—and for the better). I find this wildly optimistic. I'm much more modest in my hopes for how much we will be able to understand—or, at least, how much I will be able to understand. But I don't believe that prevents us—or excuses us—from trying to change things that we know ought to be changed. Politics is not based on knowledge—scholarly or theoretical—but on principles. The clarification of our principles and our values is our most urgent task.

Personally, I have the impression that a number of brilliant intellectuals working on these matters—in a book like *The Making of the Modern Homosexual*,[2] for instance—have concentrated their energies on an analysis of "the homosexual role" as a category of repression, a social identity that maims and limits the individual, without noticing that what has in fact happened in the last ten years is that gay people have transformed that category into an existential possibility of great

2 By Kenneth Plummer (Hutchinson, 1981).

richness and potential fulfillment, a human possibility, so not without its dangers, drawbacks, and pitfalls, but, for all that, one of great joy and beauty. In an earlier, simpler time, we used to say gay is good, gay is proud, gay is beautiful. It's taken ten years for that to begin to sink in, but for those willing to meet its challenges, live it, and create it, gay life is simply the guise in which life itself confronts us today.

Scaring the Horses; or the Question of Gay Identity

AS THAT ISSUE of *Christopher Street* sold out, discussions seemed to spring up across the country and I heard back a few scattered reports that people were Xeroxing and stapling the article and handing it out free on a corner in the Castro, as well as in a bar in Houston and at a gay community center in Chicago. Later in the Spring I was invited to give a talk at the Southeastern Conference of Lesbians and Gay Men, at the Louisiana State University campus in Baton Rouge (April 10-12, 1981), organized by the Louisiana Gay Political Action Caucus. That weekend was an exhilarating experience. Hundreds of gay men and lesbians from the South had gathered to talk about our current situation; l was speaking to a live and concrete community of activists and intellectuals and I had never felt so grounded and so engaged. I remember those three days as a highpoint of energy, enthusiasm and community, the culmination of a decade of gay progress since Stonewall, with a bright future not yet darkened by the looming threat of AIDS.

Although never published—*Christopher Street* had already devoted enough pages to my framing of the issues—this talk was my most personal take on the whole matter.

I should like to talk about gay identity and gay culture, two issues that come up a lot in my life and that have caused me some perplexity. Straight friends and co-workers often seem uncomfortable at what they consider my *over-emphasis* on being gay. Although they're genuinely sympathetic, they simply don't understand why I have to drag my sexuality into everything; after all, they're heterosexual, but they don't constantly emphasize it—or so they think. The idea of a "gay identity"—something that would say as much about you as your ethnic or professional identity—strikes them as unfortunately narrow and parochial; it overlooks too many aspects of one's personality which they find much more significant than sexual orientation. While some gays share this attitude, most of my gay friends and colleagues do understand the pervasiveness of homosexuality in our day-to-day lives. It doesn't seem odd to them that on meeting a new person I immediately want to know if he's gay or straight; they understand that this is a much more relevant fact than his ethnic or class origin. It is self-evident to them, and to me, that homosexuality pervades a person's life and character and is a central aspect of one's identity.

But many of these same men are often dubious, if not exasperated, by all this talk about gay culture. Often talented and successful people, they appreciate Balanchine and Beverly Sills, read the *New Yorker*, *Architectural Digest* and John Irving, and don't see why they should be interested in gay novelists or support gay magazines. Many doubt that there could even be such a thing as gay culture, though I suspect they all think that, if it existed, it would be a parochial and peripheral affair. It often seems to me that these people want to act gay but have a straight sensibility (a very *refined* straight sensibility, to be sure), while paradoxically, the larger society wants you to act straight, but can appreciate a gay sensibility (provided they don't have to deal with it in an immediate day-to-day fashion).

There seems to be an evasiveness here I find hard to support. When a gay writer urges us to "transcend our merely homosexual identity" and reach "to the general experience of mankind," I am perplexed. Our homosexual identity is not something that can be put aside in the interest of general solidarity, like being a Republican. Gay life is not a small part of our lives, like bowling, something we do in our spare time. Gay life is simply life as experienced by gay people. Nor does mankind have "general experience" (except in the debased forms studied by mass psychology); all experience is particular or it is not real; what mankind has in common are universal *situations* which are experienced in particular ways. Certainly the death of a parent or the fact of ageing are universal situations we all face; but gays will experience these situations quite differently; our experience of these events is enormously colored by the fact that we are homosexuals.

Identity and culture are two sides of the same coin, or to use a more precise metaphor, they are the same thing viewed from opposite ends of the looking glass. Looked at from inside, on an individual level, it's called an identity; looked at from outside, on a social level, it's a culture. A culture is simply a group's identity; an identity is an individual's culture. Either way, an identity is a set of characteristics by which a person recognizes himself and by which others recognize him.

It seems to me beyond question that ever since Stonewall, and beginning perhaps before, a large-scale social movement has been going on in this country for the last decade in which gay people have been creating both an individual and a cultural identity; that is, we are becoming recognizable as never before. From Greenwich Village to the Castro to Baton Rouge to Portland, Maine, we have been building a gay "lifestyle" and sometimes gay "ghettos" at breakneck speed and with unsure consequences. Whatever else it may be, this is something entirely new, with no historical precedents to serve as guideposts to us. As Charles Silverstein and Ed White noted in *The Joy of Gay Sex*, "Whereas many scholars have looked for historical continuity . . . the startling truth only now is becoming apparent: modern gay life has no antecedents."

Like anything utterly new, this has led to many confusions and some misgivings. It is not only social reactionaries like Anita Bryant who object to this development and, in the words of Jerry Falwell, "do not want people to promote homosexuality as an alternative or acceptable lifestyle." Many liberals—and I suspect we will see an increasing number of them—are put off, if not actually repelled, by this developing gay "lifestyle" *and* by its new visibility. Liberals are in an increasingly uncomfortable position—on the one hand, often willing to support civil rights for gays (much as they might support civil rights for mental patients) but still as unwilling as Anita Bryant or Jerry Falwell to consider homosexuality an "acceptable life style."[1]

On a cultural level, virtually the entire straight press in America—with a few, notable exceptions—refuses to review gay novels as a legit-

---

1 Reading this today, I think I was wrong here; it turned out to be just a wobbly moment (or year or two) for the liberals before they increasingly began to rally to our cause.

imate expression of a minority culture. Behind almost any discussion of a gay book in the straight press one can find a hidden evaluation of gay life—and it is *invariably* negative. This would never be allowed in reviewing Black novels or Jewish novels for the obvious reason that it would be transparently racist, though something similar does happen in reviewing women's, and especially feminists', novels.

Although I suspect the liberals' position will be a key factor for our political fate in the next few years, it is still not as significant as the confusions and profound ambivalence that gay people themselves feel about this new phenomenon—gay culture, lifestyle, ghetto, identity or whatever you want to call it. More than a few men I know wonder whether working out at a Nautilus health center, discoing away their weekends and redoing their apartments with track lighting actually reflects who they are on any serious level. Going to the barricades to defend the right to be promiscuous gives many people pause, especially when it's so easy to "pass" and still enjoy a comfortable life.

What is really at question here is whether being gay—whatever we may mean by that—is a sound basis to gain a significant sense of one's identity in the world, or whether sexual orientation is really a detail of one's private life, like being a heterosexual foot fetishist, of no great concern to anyone but oneself. It seems to me obvious that the gay movement in the last ten years has developed *as if* the former were the case, *as if* homosexuality was indeed a basic element of individual and social identity, *as if* gays constitute a hitherto disenfranchised minority group, with a right to its own culture and lifestyle. But the lack of explicit discussion of this proposition leaves us totally unprepared either for the subtle and overt resistance of the dominant straight society or for the demoralizing misgivings that arise among ourselves.

The *question* of gay identity has arisen precisely because we have rejected the answers offered on our behalf by any number of self-appointed experts. What does it mean to be gay? Within our own lifetime, homosexuality has been seen as a sin, a crime, an impairment, a sickness and a perversion. Having rejected those answers, both politically and personally, and often at no small cost, we found ourselves smack up against the question: What does it mean to be gay if it doesn't mean what we've been taught it meant?

In the early Seventies, right after Stonewall, there was an energetic attempt to answer this question on a theoretical level, generating much discussion of neo-Freudian ideas of polymorphous perversity, inherent human bisexuality, and universal sexual liberation, as well as neo-Marxist ideas of the social arbitrariness of gender roles and the coercive function of sexual repression in a capitalistic system. But as time wore on, the question "What does it mean to be gay?" tended to be displaced by the more immediate and practical questions of our day-to-day lives. Having asserted ourselves as militant homosexuals and denounced the oppression of straight society, we had to face the question "What do we want, anyhow?"

Well, sensibly enough, we wanted to be let alone, we wanted society to stop hitting on us, we wanted to lead our own lives the way we saw fit, discovering ourselves as we went along, making mistakes and messing up like anybody else, and learning from our experience. Politically in America, this naturally led to converting an enthusiasm for sexual liberation into a demand for gay civil rights. It was concrete politics rather than theory that led to our current assertion that gay is a minority life-style, the natural conclusion of our political demands for the same civil rights and cultural acceptance that other minority groups (supposedly) enjoy.

However, from the pre-Stonewall era of the closet to today's assertion of minority group status represents such an enormous shift in self-definition that the continuities between these two stages are often obscured. For instance, it seems to be widely thought that gay people are asserting a novel proposition when they insist that sexual orientation is central to one's identity. Most straights I know, and some gays, react as if this assertion were a new *theory* that some—the more radical among us, perhaps—are proposing. This strikes me as absurd. The decisive significance of homosexuality is a *fact* not a theory, and it was first insisted on by straight society, not by militant gays.

I can clearly remember being a teen-ager in the mid-Fifties when a dawning sexual awakening drew me to those little, pseudo-gay physique magazines that had started appearing and realizing the enormous social consequences that loomed ahead if I were to be a homosexual. At the time all men had to register for the military draft at age eighteen and if you were discovered or thought to be gay, you got a 4-F draft status, with a big "H" stamped on your draft card. And in those days to get any job one had to show one's draft card; and with a 4-F one could not work for the government in any capacity, no large company would hire you, no union would allow you to become a member, your chances for any kind of decent career would be blocked and you would be branded for life. At the time I decided to enjoy the pornography and assume this was just a stage I was going through—as was the phrase of the day—and blithely thought that if I was still homosexual by the time I graduated college, I would commit suicide.

Far from saying anything new when we insist on our gay identity, we are simply acknowledging the facts of the matter. *In this society*, sexual orientation *does* overshadow any other aspect of a person. To insist on this point is not to deny that other aspects of a person exist and are important, it is not even to agree that in truth sexual orientation *should* be considered more important than these other aspects. It is simply to say that our society generally acts as if this fact were decisive. And if society thinks being homosexual is decisive, then for all practical purposes it *is* decisive.

It is important to be clear about this: the overwhelming significance of homosexuality is a social fact, not a theory. You can be put in jail, denied an apartment, or fired from your job because you are a homosexual. Today. You can lose your standing in the community, be denied public office, be thrown out of the military, and lose your children because you are homosexual. Today. In an astonishing number of cases, you can be disowned by your parents and lose the love and support of your family because you are homosexual. And according to the Congressional Research Service, a government agency that reviews the impact of proposed legislation, in their analysis of The Family Protection Act, which Paul Laxalt will shortly introduce before the United States Senate: "No person who was a homosexual or who even intimated that homosexuality might be an 'acceptable' lifestyle could receive any federal funds under such programs as Social Security, welfare, veterans programs, or student assistance." It seems clear enough from how straights treat us or allow us to be treated that *they* think homosexuality is decisive. Nobody is proposing denying Social Security or veterans benefits to heterosexual foot fetishists.

Of course, most of us have known the socially decisive significance of homosexuality since our adolescence. We knew it when we hid our sexuality from our best friends, afraid that they would desert us. We knew it when we were clever enough to hide our sexuality in order to get into the schools, jobs, or professions we chose. Many of us know it today in our continued reluctance to acknowledge the fact to our parents. We do not have to wonder whether homosexuality is central to our social identity in this society; we know it is from our concrete experience.

Straight friends who doubt the fact and complain that we overemphasize our homosexuality and dubious gays who manage to confuse themselves about the issue are invited to wear a large button saying "I am a lesbian" or "I am gay" to work or school and to all social occasions for one month. The facts of the matter will emerge clearly enough and we will save a lot of time spent in tedious argument.

Long before there was any gay liberation, society insisted on the decisive significance of homosexuality and used that insistence as a weapon against us. It is perversely ironic that now, when we have faced this fact squarely and are bent on transforming the values imputed to homosexuality, the straight world hastens to argue with us that no, after all, homosexuality is not that important. "You are making too big an issue of it," they say; "You are so much more as persons than just your sexual orientation." Well, we're not being attacked because we're persons, but because of our sexual orientation, because we're homosexuals, and we can reply to this line or argument with a comment of the late Hannah Arendt: "If you are attacked as a Jew, you have got to fight back as a Jew, you cannot say, 'Excuse me, I am not a Jew, I am a human being.' This is silly."

Of course, no one is only a Jew; and "the Jew" in capital letters is a social construct that never actually existed. This truth, however, was irrelevant to Jews in Germany in the thirties, and anyone who insisted upon it at the time was simply refusing to face reality. Not to face reality—especially when that reality is debased, false, and stupid—can be a very costly political mistake.

Like "the Jew," homosexuality is a social construct. Social constructs are very palpable things. They've been using this one to hit us over the head with for quite a few years now. And whatever the reasons, and whether or not it's a good idea on some theoretical level, sexual identity happens to be as fundamental and central as you get in this society. "Is it a boy or a girl?" they ask and you're well on your way to having an identity.

To put it in a nutshell, we have no choice; as homosexuals we are involved in a struggle over self-definition. They have *already* defined us. Only a counter-definition can work. Attacked for being homosexual, we can only defend ourselves by being gay, that is by making a public avowal of our homosexuality. And it is *precisely* this public quality that so upsets society.

That we are being attacked seems obvious, but it is peculiar to the nature of gay oppression that most straights don't really believe such a thing is going on; even many gays are oddly uncertain about the existence and intensity of gay oppression. It seems peculiarly hard to grasp the concrete nature of this oppression. We can, after all, slip fairly easily through society; our social domination is not expressed as starkly or as concretely as that of Blacks, for instance. The oppression of Blacks is systematically actualized in economic hardship and social limitation—realities so palpable you can feel them. But the domination of homosexuals has been accomplished mainly through *threats*—by holding out the dire possibilities of what will happen if we are, or acknowledge that we are, homosexuals. Threats are, in essence, a subclass of possibilities; they are negative possibilities. Possibilities are peculiar. There can be possibilities that are never actualized, which remain nevertheless real, real as possibilities. The threat or possibility that a rich father may disinherit his son may never be actualized and yet be real enough to control the son's actions for years. I think it is because gay oppression is for the most part expressed through threatening possibilities that makes it seem so elusive and renders the whole issue so weirdly psychological.

One of the strange consequences of this is that a person can have a fairly decent life objectively speaking—with the average portion of happiness and misery, striving, failure and success—and still consider himself a miserable fag—a state, peculiar to closeted gays, which has been captured with numbing precision by Merle Miller in his novel *What Happened*. Politically speaking, the peculiar nature of this form of cultural oppression is that it obscures the line between the miseries caused by oppression and the unhappiness which is an expression of the inherent limitations of the human condition, the common fate of all mortals. The transient nature of physical passion, for instance, is generally acknowledged to be virtually universal. Yet when we gay men experience it, there is an overwhelming inclination for us to see it as somehow our fault, a sign of the shallow nature of homosexual attraction. Militant Blacks and women often have the same difficulty distinguishing between the negative consequences of perverse social arrangements and the inherent limitations of life.

For the most part, it is through threats rather than hard social realities that straight society tries to keep us in line, and for them that means to keep us pretending to be straight. As long as public appearances are maintained society seems willing to tolerate an enormous amount of illicit activity. The attitude might be summed up by Pat Campbell's remark at Oscar Wilde's trial: "I have no objection to anyone's sex life as long as they don't practice it in the street and frighten the horses." In this light, gay oppression might seem negligible. At first glance. But what appears to be a reasonable demand for decorum boils down to a formula for the closet. And we all know that the closeted existence has a schizophrenic effect, which denies us our reality. At the culmination of Martin Sherman's play *Bent*, Horst shouts, "We made love. We were real. We were human." It is our human reality that the closet robs us of, leaving us "invisible men," interlopers in someone else's world.

I don't think it's necessary here to discuss the evils of the closet, the psychological damage and spiritual havoc "wrought in the souls of people who aren't supposed to exist" (Ntozake Shange). It is because we are so vividly aware of these miseries that we are here—scaring the horses. As we should be. For in an existing homophobic society the only possible liberation from the oppression of the closet is the public assertion of a gay identity and culture.

In the early Seventies, many of us thought that the way to gay liberation was through the sexual liberation of the whole society. For a while, we could even imagine that history was on our side. Today, however, I think we are all much more dubious about the possibility of an immediate social transformation—at least, for the better. The liberated society may remain the ultimate goal, if anybody can figure out a way to get there. Meanwhile we have to deal with the fact that we live in this existing society and we must cope with our immediate day-to-day lives. This has not only led to our current demands for civil rights and minority group status, but to the spontaneous generation of a multiplicity of new ways to be gay. Claiming the rights of a minority group has paralleled the development of a minority culture—from the clone look, disco sensuality, and what can only be described as new forms of homomasculinity to lesbian publishing companies and farm collectives, the emergence of totally gay neighborhoods in several cities, and the establishment of gay choruses, gay marching bands, and gay literature. All of these—and others—are creative and concrete attempts to manifest new ways of being gay in the world.

As an identity, being gay is today a cultural *opportunity*. Finding ourselves already labeled, we have been engaged in a modern alchemy, transmuting a perversion into an existential theme. As Ed White noted in *States of Desire*, "gay life . . . is obligatory existentialism forced on people who must invent themselves." Being gay is a way to be in the world—like being a Jew or being a man or being a woman. What we make of this fact is what counts, but the question, "What does it mean to be gay?" cannot be answered with any definitive content, just as the question, "What does it mean to be a woman?" cannot be answered. Whenever an answer *is* given, a little poking around will always reveal an underlying attempt at the social control and domination of women. To answer the question, "What is a real man?" is to attempt to organize and dominate all men for some ulterior purpose. There is no room for this sort of thing in any gay culture worthy of our respect. The task and the opportunity before us is not to establish what is *really* gay, not to set up a new social orthodoxy which would inevitably classify all divergence as perversion. It would be disastrous if the gay culture that is emerging took on the same moralistic, unitary shape and dominating function as the straight culture we are fighting against.

It seems to me that the one thing you *can* say about gay culture is that it has to be pluralistic and cosmopolitan. It should not only tolerate diversity but welcome it. For not only are we everywhere, as the slogan goes, but we are *everybody*—all races, all genders, all ages, all classes, all religions. The root principle of any gay culture and community must of necessity be cosmopolitanism, a respect for and a joy in human diversity. And this is the core of the matter and the nexus of our struggle with straight society.

Finding ourselves homosexual in a straight world endows us with a fundamental insight into the nature of our society—its driving insistence on uniformity and its obsessive fear of difference. The different as such is so threatening to this society that for centuries it has attempted to deny that we even exist. Surely the most bizarre and remarkable aspect of homophobia is the near pathological reluctance of straights to even *name* this behavior they detest so much. In the first recorded incidence of homosexuality in New England in 1629, we read about a "wickedness not to be named." In 1631 in England, the Earl of Castlehaven was executed for crimes "so heinous and so horrible that a Christian man ought scarcely to name them." This latter phrase in Latin—*peccatum illud horribile, inter Christianos non nominandum*—was in fact the standard formula for referring to homosexuality in the law, which after all had to talk about it in order to make it a crime. The rest of society simply passed it over in silence.

Now this is remarkable. There are other heinous acts that society has abhorred—from patricide and cannibalism to mass murder and treason. What is peculiar here is the reluctance to even give a word to the activity—as if denying it a name would deny it reality. John Boswell in *Christianity, Social Tolerance, and Homosexuality* has briefly inventoried the ways our culture has attempted to *expunge* the fact of our existence from the historical record, to deny that we have ever been here. While I do not fully understand this peculiar impulse, I am convinced it is somehow at the heart of the matter. Even the more recent attempts to categorize us as deviant, or cases of arrested development, or in some sense sick—all share the underlying impulse to deny that homosexuality is really real in itself and attempt to see it as an immature, deformed or twisted mode of heterosexuality. Over and over again straight society has exhibited this distinctive impulse to refuse to acknowledge the reality of what it perceives as fundamentally different.

We, on the other hand, are in the reverse position; we homosexuals absolutely know that there is such a thing as heterosexuality. Sometimes I think we're much surer of this fact than the heterosexuals themselves. They often talk as if, once you let down all the social barriers to homosexuality, no one would remain heterosexual. This, for instance, is the only conclusion one can come to after reading Midge Decter's hysterical, and hilarious, attack on us in a recent issue of *Commentary* magazine (Sept., '80), where she defines homosexuals as "males undomesticated by women" and clearly implies that without the discipline of straight women, all men would go gay. How one can explain this utter nonsense is beyond me.

But the essence of the matter is that from the moment we awaken to the fact that we are homosexual—often first experienced as a vague sense of being "different"—we must learn to live with the fact of difference. Since we cannot deny that heterosexuality exists, any gay culture will have to make room for difference, will have to accommodate diversity and be built on plurality, unless we want our lives and culture to be no more than a travesty of the straight society that has caused us so much grief.

This does not mean that, faced with a truly startling diversity of values, from fairie circles to the S&M leather scene and far beyond, we cannot criticize one another, that we cannot argue together over questions that are vital to our lives. It does mean that there are some guidelines for this type of discussion. It is inappropriate, for instance, simply to try to impose our tastes and sensibilities on other gays, as Sally Gerhardt did in an essay in *The Advocate* last year that essentially declared most forms of male gay sexuality "invalid" and "wrong." Or again, it is vacuous and invidious to declare a lifestyle different from one's own to be "sick." Illness is a medical concept; it signifies a temporary inter-ruption of natural processes. Anything that could be a permanent con-dition cannot, by definition, be an illness. Being blind is not an illness, nor is being a lesbian sadist.

There is always room for discussion among peers about our val-ues and about the wisdom of leading our lives in this or that manner. I believe more such discussion is urgently needed, for I believe the ho-mophobia we grew up with and continue to live with today has infected our lives in subtle ways that we often don't recognize or understand. However, when some form of gay behavior appears to us to be the in-ternalized and disguised form of social oppression, we must remem-ber that only the oppressed person himself can be the judge. To insist on seeing manifestations of oppression when the alleged "victim" sees none is simply another form of oppression. To insist that gay promis-cuity is a manifestation of internalized self-hatred or that a monog-amous domestic relationship is a crippling imitation of heterosexual norms is to arrogate to ourselves the responsibility for someone else's life. If you don't want to be promiscuous, don't be. If you don't want to live in a stable marriage situation, don't. But why in the world attack other people who do? That is to be infected by the malady we are try-ing to recover from. This imperialistic drive in our society to legislate for others, this moral busybodyness which has recently expressed it-self in the disciplinary grids of the normative social sciences, which Michel Foucault has so clearly revealed for us, is somewhere near the heart of the spiritual canker which afflicts our civilization. It is not only the specific content of certain social valuations such as "queer"[2] that we must fight, but the form in which these values are cast.

If heterosexuality—presently constituted by this society as a sexual/social identity—is somehow actually threatened by the existence of a gay lifestyle, there is something wrong with the values of heterosex-uality. If the family is threatened by the existence of homosexuals, there is something very wrong with the family. If the domestic com-fort of permanent coupling is threatened by the existence of a lifestyle of elected promiscuity, there is something wrong with the structure of

---

2 How times do change, and language with it.

the couple situation. If our values are threatened in their essence by the existence of different values, then our values are poor ones indeed. Not attacking others but only criticism of our own values will ever be productive of any wisdom or insight, any help in the endless task of living a decent life which is our common concern.

Who Are We? What Do We Want?
How Best Might We Get It?

THE NEXT YEAR, on May 17, 1982, Larry Gross and Scott Tucker organized a panel discussion on gay politics in Philadelphia, sponsored by Giovanni's Room Bookstore. The panelists included Felice Picano, Ed White, Dennis Altman and myself. We were given these three questions to address: Who Are We? What Do We Want? How Best Might We Get It?

What I have now is the handwritten notes of my introductory remarks and a few notes jotted down during the very lively discussion that followed (once again, I hadn't talked about lesbians! Why did everybody keep harping on that?). What I notice now is that just as the public discussion of the contemporary gay political situation seemed to be gaining widespread traction across the country, the first note of AIDS sounds distinctly at the end of this talk, the coming catastrophe that was going to increasingly absorb our attention and energy. And the political awakening I thought I was seeing in the early 80s was soon diverted into concern with medical and scientific matters and immediate issues of survival.

The organizers of this event went to some pains to impress upon me their hope that we would address the topic of why theory is important. Behind this seemed to lay an anxiety that this meeting might degenerate into a squabble about the importance to the gay movement of mainline electoral politics, and their apprehension—correct in my opinion—that such an argument would simply not be productive in any real sense. It would seem silly to me if seventeen of us tried to convince the other eighteen of one opinion. First of all, that's very unlikely to happen in this group. Secondly, even if we did, so what? What would be the result of that? Now thirty-five of us would share one opinion. This will have very little impact on the world.

I think the intention behind this meeting was to try to get us to turn our attention to the basic questions and assumptions that lie at the heart of the actual situation of gay people in America today. This, I think, could be useful. It's always useful to try to articulate the situation we find ourselves in and the various options for responding to it that suggest themselves. The decisions among these options, of course, will be made by every individual—consciously or by default—and politically and historically they will be made by the entire body of gay people, not by any small group such as is assembled in this room. But this group—whatever you want to call us: activists, intellectuals, writers—could serve a useful function if we could help focus the situation intellectually and help articulate various concepts, principles, and strategies that could be useful to gay people confronting the concrete and problematic reality of their own lives. In other words, we can either act elitist and squabble in a vacuum, or we can try to provide conceptual tools and to articulate options—a modest but useful contribution to the on-going gay movement. This approach also has the advantage that we only have to improve our own thinking through open-minded discussion, we don't have to convince others of our opinions—a disagreeable and questionable task in any event.

In this spirit, I would like to consider some of our basic assumptions about your three questions: who are we, what do we want, and how best might we get it. But before we approach these matters, it is necessary to give some analysis to what it is that oppresses us. I doubt very much whether homophobia created homosexuals—there's a mad, *Alice in Wonderland* quality to the otherwise quite brilliant work of some scholars, mainly English, who seem to maintain this position—but homophobia *is*, without a doubt, the basic condition under which the modern homosexual emerged, and as such, homophobia conditions (even if it does not create) every aspect of homosexuality. And it continues to do so to this day.

Recently my boyfriend returned to his hometown of Bismarck, North Dakota, for three weeks. Bismarck has a population of about 38,000 and is a society totally organized by family. You are real—i.e., invited to dinner, introduced, known—as a member of a family. A single woman in her mid-twenties, like my boyfriend's sister, feels totally out of place, peripheral in this social world. Her social reality is still being a daughter of the family and will be until she starts her own family. The situation with the several hundred gays in Bismarck is much more desperate. Although they share the reality of straight society—after all, they too are sons and brothers, employees and partners, and, quite often, husbands—they can scarcely share the reality of being homosexual. Currently, there are no gay bars in Bismarck (or, for that matter, in the entire state of North Dakota), no public meeting places, no publications, not even a dirty bookstore or a cruise strip. Their social reality becomes problematic—these homosexuals live in a place where homosexuals don't exist. They cannot even share the reality of their homosexuality with each other, for there is no community.

It is the absolute peculiarity of homophobia, what seems to distinguish it from other forms of social domination, that it denies the existence of the object of its oppression. The Nazis did not deny that Jews existed—quite the reverse, they tried to kill them, which at least implies that they were there. American racists didn't deny the existence of Blacks, rather they wanted to exploit them and keep them in their place. But homophobia, in all its forms, whether it sees us as an aberration, a passing stage, or an illness, is always somehow denying that we really exist, always seeing us as a temporary, stunted or twisted form of heterosexuality.

This is why I agree with Arnie Kantrowitz' assessment of the last ten years in his essay, "The Day Gay Lib Died":

> Even if "gay liberation" is no longer in style, its dream of gay community has just begun. For all our theoretical differences, for all the disparate worlds we inhabit, there is one link between us. We have made ourselves real. Even if we have to live through target practice and scapegoating, we are still tangibly here.

And this, I agree, is the great accomplishment of the last decade.

There may, however, be a deeper connection than Arnie indicates between our being tangibly here and the scapegoating and target practice we're subjected to. I think the reason it has been the right tactic to turn the struggle for gay sexual liberation into the struggle for gay civil rights is its impact on the nature of our oppression. This tactic reduces a pervasive cultural attitude—homophobia—into concrete people— homophobes, fag haters—and specific actions—anti-gay legislation or ordinances, physical attacks on persons or legal attacks on organizations. What happens is that an element of culture, which is by nature amorphous and about which you can do nothing, gets crystallized into concrete actions that specific people do. You then pin the responsibility for those actions squarely on those people and you're in a position where you can begin to fight back. This, it seems to me, has been the tactic of the gay movement in the last ten years and there's no question that it's been overwhelmingly successful.

Now, after that digression, let's turn to our original three questions. To the question "Who are we?" I would like to append a motto from Hillel: "If I am not for myself, who is for me? If I am for myself alone, who am I?" Nobody can be gay without the presence of other gay people. Unlike being a homosexual (or bent or queer), which only requires the presence of straight people, being gay implies a community of other gay people with whom we share our reality, who confirm us in the reality of our existence. The task of gay liberation cannot be accomplished within the horizon of the individual; we can only be delivered of our oppression if we emerge into a community of other gay people. Theoretically there might be such a thing as a single homosexual, but it's impossible there could be a single gay person, just one. Gay implies a community, a public space that arises between people and in which we can appear to others as who we are. Reality is a function of social existence and the validity of our reality is what, on its most basic level, has been denied us. We can only become real insofar as we are members of the gay community. As gay people we are a community or we are nothing.

Now, question 2: "What do we want?" As gay people I think our aim has always got to be the strengthening and deepening of the gay community. The establishing of a gay culture and the forging of a gay personal identity are two sides of the same coin, and they are simply the articulations of gay community. What we need is the social reality and consequent self-respect that only a community makes possible.

In this task of strengthening the community and consequently our personal identity and reality, the use of influence and power (and these are two different things) has an important but not exclusive function. The use of influence (economic, political, literary, or educational) on the dominant society to protect the community is obviously important, but it has its pitfalls. The history of the European Jews in the last two centuries should teach us some of the limitations of this tactic. Influence, personified in the figure of the Court Jew, no doubt helped and protected the community at times, but at the *decisive* time, this tactic was disastrously inadequate. I suspect that influencing straight politicians or the straight media will be, in terms of real change, as severely limited for us as it was for the European Jews.

In response to your third question, how best might we get it? I'd say the use of power, which is exclusively political, is more promising. In our terms, power means the election of gay people to public office. This has two distinct results. First, it has the type of impact on the straight world that no exercise of influence and no educational campaign could ever achieve. When the first elected Black representative sat down in the Mississippi State Legislature, the social force of racism in that state was dealt a severe blow—the situation, though not resolved by any means, would never be the same again. It seems to me obvious that Harvey Milk was essentially right—imagine the impact if one openly gay person was elected to the United States Senate.

And the impact of such victories on the straight world pales in comparison to its impact on the gay community itself. Power arises when people come together in voluntary association to achieve common ends—power empowers the people who generate it. The exercise of power would strengthen the gay community as perhaps no other single tactic could.

But it should be noted that it is the politicization of large numbers of people and their experience in having some impact on the issues that affect their own lives that is decisive—not whether or not one gay rights bill is passed or whether we win or lose on any particular issue. These discrete and particular ends are ultimately only a means for the further empowering of the gay community.

Win or lose, it's the fight that counts, that strengthens us, which means we win every time. I would go so far as to suggest that this ought to be the standard against which we can measure the worthwhileness of any gay praxis: to what extent will this action contribute to the consolidation of the gay community and the further development of individual gay identity? Of course, if we adopt this as our yardstick of judgment, it becomes clear that politics can not and should not be the only avenue of activity. Action or praxis must always be judged in terms of the specifics of time and place. In America today it seems to me, a concern with the medical situation of gay people should rank at least as high on our priorities as political action, for the medical situation now poses a threat of internal demoralization which is probably more pressing right now than any threat from the straight world.

One closing comment: In a recent article in the *New York Native*, with which I found myself in almost total agreement—much to my surprise—Dennis Altman stated that:

> These (electoral victories) are at best steps in a much larger process, namely the creation of genuine acceptance of homosexuality both among lesbians and gays themselves and in society at large.

In an effort to find at least *some* area of disagreement between us, let me suggest that this is putting the cart before the horse. Not the creation of a genuine *acceptance* of homosexuality but the creation of a genuine *homosexuality* is the task that faces us immediately. Each and every one of us has to construct our own life and identity, as a group we have to construct our own community, before we worry about whether or not they accept it. In a deep sense I believe that the straight world surrounding us is largely irrelevant, an irritating distraction at most.

A little further in his essay Dennis says we have to change the values of the straight world. Now the nature of values, what they are and how they exist, is too complex a matter to go into here. But I think that the only values you can change are your own (that is, without the use of force and violence, which can destroy but not create values). We can only change the values of the straight world by changing our own values—which is only another way of saying that the creation of a gay community—a gay culture and gay identity—is the immediate task on our agenda and the essence of a gay praxis.

PART 3
The State of the Tribe
1983–1987

The first report of what would turn out to be AIDS was published in the *New York Native* in the Spring of 1981, but even before this report appeared people in our community were getting sick with strange new diseases (which is why it got our attention and we started to cover it), and by the time the news made it to the paper people were starting to die. There was virtually no discussion of these matters in the mainstream public media or medical press—for months, then years!—but in the private world of friends and gossip, rumors started to spread like wildfire. The illnesses seemed to have epicenters—Fire Island Pines, where a number of houses were particularly hard hit, or the members of the private dance club, The Saint (an overlapping group), or, some said, guys into S&M or guys into heavy drugs, or one particular drug—the rumors were endless and incessant, but no one knew anything for sure and the result was a period of confusion, panic, denial, anxiety and fear. And increasing dread, as people all around us fell ill with a bewildering variety of strange new diseases and died, while our doctors seemed helpless. Something was happening, but what?

For me, and I think for many of my peers, this period of confusion was swept away by the publication of Larry Kramer's famous essay, "1,112 and Counting," also published in the *Native*.[1] Two years of an-

1 *New York Native*, issue 59, March 14, 1983.

guish, uncertainty and dread coalesced into a hard determination to respond to this new and mortal danger. It was now clear we faced an existential threat to our new way of life and our newly emerging community, a threat that required the total mobilization of the gay community to confront it. And since it was unclear what one could do about the external threat, indeed it was unclear precisely what the external threat was, I was most concerned about the internal morale of the community. I feared that the internalized homophobia we had absorbed from society could weaken our response at a time when we needed to fight for our survival.

Gay Pride and Survival in the Eighties

THIS PIECE WAS written three months after Larry Kramer's essay had sent shock waves through the national gay community—that essay was reprinted in virtually every gay newspaper and magazine across the country. Kramer's impassioned alarm rang loud and urgently and made it clear to the gay community that a new and dangerous era was upon us, one that could mean the end of any sort of gay liberation.

At a time when the idea of gay pride seemed more than questionable, Tom Steele asked me to write a piece for the 1983 Gay Pride issue of the *Native* and I did.[1]

Today the gay world is facing an outbreak of history, one of those rare moments in time when things can actually change in a fundamental way. Perhaps the first such "moment" in our history was the Second World War, when the gay community was precipitated out of the vast social turmoil caused by a national mobilization. The second was surely Stonewall, both the actual event and the impact it had on our collective imagination as we woke up and became conscious of ourselves as a community. Now, after more than a decade of relative stability, we can feel the ground moving under our feet, always a sign that history has started up again.

The AIDS epidemic may threaten the very existence of the gay community. With the grand perversity of true history, AIDS has made our sexuality a threat to our lives and has brought us back under the medical model we spent three decades escaping. AIDS could destroy the gay community, not through killing each and every one of us, but by attacking our deepest values, which concern sex, and by isolating us into

1 *New York Native*, June 25, 1983.

homosexual monogamy. Of course, homosexuals would still exist—isolated and dispersed among the straight population, leading private monogamous lives—but the gay *community* could disappear.

Gay pride calls for our courage in responding to this crisis. We must remain loyal to our community; we must protect and cherish those of us stricken with this disease; we must fight for the medical treatment, the research programs, and the government assistance that are our right as citizens and taxpayers of this country. Individually, we must realize that we are in the midst of a great emergency and we must respond appropriately. The gay community is under siege today as the city of London was under siege during the Blitz. Emergency measures are called for. If promiscuous sexuality is now threatening our lives and the lives of our friends and lovers, monogamy (serial or not) and even celibacy are reasonable precautions to take during this attack. Who is dumb enough to keep cruising Regent's Park while bombs are falling in London?

But it is important to understand that this is an *emergency* measure. I do not believe we will, or should, give up our sexual freedom. For all the confusion and dead ends that sexual freedom has led to, I still believe it is somehow our main achievement and at the heart of who we are as gay men. But AIDS, and the epidemic of amoebiasis (amoebic dysentery) that preceded it, has made clear that our urgent task is to make our world safe for sexuality. Since these are sexually transmitted diseases, social diseases, it does little good for the individual to get himself cured; we need to cure the whole community. Health must become as prominent a value in our culture as physical beauty. We may have to invent new institutions to monitor and insure our sexual health—gay health clinics that would have the same place in our lives that gyms do now. We may even have to mobilize massive funds for scientific research, an effort on the scale of the Jewish community's support of the state of Israel.

At first thought, these proposals may seem unlikely, even utopian. But the astonishing response of the gay community to the AIDS crisis—a response on the part of a medically threatened population unparalleled, to my knowledge, in the history of medicine—should teach us better. We are a remarkable community, quite capable of doing what has never been done before. AIDS is a lethal threat to our way of life and our community. But if we measure up to the challenge history is presenting us with, then our response will mark the coming of age of the gay community.

The State of Gay Criticism

AS THE NEW gay fiction started to appear it was still met with condescension in the mainstream press, which was to be expected. What
was not expected, by me at least, was the response of gay reviewers
and critics, who unfortunately too often echoed the hidden prejudices
of the larger society. Reading an extended essay in *Bay Windows*[1] on
"The State of Gay Male Fiction" by Robert K. Martin, a distinguished
gay academic and literary critic, triggered this somewhat exasperated
response.[2] I thought Martin's essay offered a good occasion to consider how the pervasive homophobia of the larger society still worked
havoc in our minds, obscuring the novelty of our lives and preventing
a clear-eyed view of the remarkable writing being produced by gay authors.

In a recent essay in *Bay Windows* on "The State of Gay Male Fiction,"
Robert K. Martin writes: "Holleran's work is entertaining and moving,
gracefully written, occasionally suggestive about the meaning of contemporary urban gay life, but finally lacking transcendence. These are
novels that seem likely to die with the times they depict."

In spite of my increasing irritation at the wrong-headedness of this
essay, I was still astonished when I came to this sentence. The unbelievable arrogance and condescension that shine through these words
so clearly made me wonder exactly what type of critical discourse Mr.
Martin thought he was writing. What sort of writing would this type
of judgment fit into? To Mr. Martin, it seems, the critic resembles no
one as much as Pirate Jenny in *The Threepenny Opera*, before whom
are brought the citizens of the town so she may decide who shall live

1 Vol. 4, no. 27 (1986).
2 *Christopher Street*, no. 104 (September 1986).

and who shall die—"Hoop-la!" she cries happily, off with their heads! But Jenny is a nihilist who wants to destroy the old order and execute them all. Mr. Martin is something different. Mr. Martin is interested in creating a new order, in defining what shall be the future face of gay literature. And it seems so clear and self-evident to him that this task belongs by right to the academic critic—and not to the writers themselves, not to the people who have worked to establish gay magazines, newspapers, and publishing houses, and not to the gay reading public—that it doesn't occur to him to argue the point. The academic critic is here not to argue with us, not to join the public discourse on gay writing, but to *tell* us what is worthy and what is not—what possesses or lacks "transcendence" and therefore what is of real worth and will survive.

Gay writing has survived years of malign neglect, tendentious interpretation, and barely veiled scorn and hostility at the hands of straight reviewers and critics who have done their damnedest to convince themselves *and us* that these books are marginal, of only parochial interest, and not worthy of being included in the great and noble mainstream of our literary culture. More surprisingly, gay writing has survived almost fifteen years of reviewing and criticism in the gay press that has been shamefully marked by sour grapes, sheer incompetence, and the most petty sorts of factionalism, all decried with great accuracy in Ethan Mordden's recent sharp-tongued and brave essay "Gay Writers and Their Critics."[3]

As if that were not enough, it would now seem that gay writing must survive yet a third assault, the attempt by our newly minted gay literary academics to take over the field of gay writing and make it serve their own parochial self-interest—which, of course, has to do with building new curriculums, new courses in gay literature they can present to their deans as justifications for their inclusion on the faculty and on the payroll. And in fact Mr. Martin begins his essay with a strange lament: twenty-five years ago, in 1961, when he was an undergraduate, he read works by Truman Capote, Gore Vidal, James Purdy, and Tennessee Williams in his college English course; today, he asserts, "a glance at

3 *The Advocate*, issue 447 (May 27, 1986).

most undergraduate reading lists will show them they (the successors to this impressive list of gay talent) are not there." One can understand why this—if true; myself, I have not glanced over most undergraduate reading lists lately—would be distressing to a gay academic. Everyone, after all, has to make a living. Furthermore, this disappearance of contemporary gay writers from the academic curriculum is, according to Mr. Martin, the fault of the gay writers themselves. Now, since I am convinced that gay literature is here to stay (and to prosper), and that, unfortunately but inevitably, this means that gay studies and gay academics are probably here to stay, this argument is worth looking into. In the good old days of 1961, according to Mr. Martin, when college students were forced to read Capote, Vidal, Purdy, and Williams (but not Isherwood or Genet or Ginsburg), these guys were "not only gay writers, but artists whose work was taken seriously by a larger intellectual community." Gay Writers, you muse. Well, not actually "gay and proud." Mr. Martin concedes that "the price of that acceptance was a reluctance to talk too frankly (*too* frankly? They were frank, right? Just not *too* frank) about these men in sexual terms." Odd that Mr. Martin doesn't mention Vidal's second novel, *The City and the Pillar*, which almost torpedoed his career. But still things seemed better then to Mr. Martin, for these writers were *taken seriously* by "the larger intellectual community."

It never seems to occur to Mr. Martin that the "larger intellectual community," which can only be taken to mean the dominant powers in the culture at the time, were the same people responsible for reinforcing, reproducing, and handing down homophobia through their control of the organs of cultural definition. The "larger intellectual community" created and perpetuated a power situation in which writers who were gay had to resort to subterfuge and innuendo to disguise their concerns, and in which only extraordinary talent could gain them a provisional place in the literary pantheon—provided they were not *too* frank.

Unfortunately, our gay writers today seem to be driven by a compulsion to be *too* frank: "Gay fiction these days seems too aggressively (the word 'too' gets a lot of use in Mr. Martin's essay) concerned with a very narrowly defined vision of gay life." Seems *to whom?* you might ask. Why to "the larger intellectual community," of course, the dominant and dominating culture to whom Mr. Martin would willingly give the last word in these matters. To these people, our gay writers seem to be *flaunting* their concerns with life as they find it as gay men. They are no longer willing to resort to that "irony and wit that once allowed gay writers to deal with their own situation and at the same time rise above it." It seems terribly important to Mr. Martin, and "the larger intellectual community" to which he aspires, that gay people rise above their situation. Through the use of irony and wit. Or find their work lacking Mr. Martin's cherished "transcendence." And here he seems simply to have missed the point altogether: what the movement for gay liberation and the consequent flourishing of gay literature intend to do is not transcend but *change* that situation, once and for all.

Given this agenda, it is self-evident why gay books have, temporarily I suspect, disappeared from the curriculum. The only mystery is why it is a mystery to Mr. Martin. "Have gay writers simply become too blatant (another buzz word, like flaunting) for inclusion in college courses?" he asks, without for a moment considering the cases of Norman Mailer or *Portnoy's Complaint*—two perfectly fine examples of "blatant," if you ask me. "Have we come out of the curriculum as we have come out of the closet?" he wonders. *Of course* we have. What did the man expect? In the Fifties American culture, including literary culture, was systematically, pervasively, and actively homophobic on just about every level you can imagine, which even the briefest acquaintance with the cultural history of the period makes perfectly clear. Mr. Martin might refresh his memory by taking a look at John D'Emilio's *Sexual Politics, Sexual Communities*.

Oddly enough, Mr. Martin simply drops this line of inquiry. It must seem perfectly self-evident to him that the answer to these two rhetorical questions is no. The real reason for our absence from the curriculum, according to Mr. Martin, is that this new openness about gay life has led to an "increased parochialism." "Writers are apparently now writing for their gay friends, rather than for some larger, more general readership." (Throughout this essay, Mr. Martin exhibits a remarkable tendency to scamper after the majority opinion.) "Introspective, self-indulgent, closeted in a surprising new way, these works fail to reach the reader of fiction, as they address themselves more and more to *gays who read*." Since Mr. Martin himself italicized those last three words, one gets the impression that this is truly a dastardly thing for gay writers to do. What precisely, do you think, is the difference between "the readers of fiction" and "gays who read"? Evidently, gays who read do not constitute any part of that abstract phenomenon, the readers of fiction. Perhaps, since Mr. Martin is always so concerned with the majority, he means the majority of the readers of fiction. In which case, I have some very sad news for him: the majority of readers of fiction in this country today vastly prefer schlock romance or suspense novels that Mr. Martin wouldn't be caught dead reading. No, he can't mean that. I suspect that Mr. Martin used this empty abstraction, "the reader of fiction," to refer to and at the same time disguise a small class of people who read fiction professionally, who make their living from it, either reviewing it in newspapers and magazines (excluding gay ones, of course) or teaching it in universities. Since Mr. Martin himself belongs to this class of professional readers, who, like all professionals, wants to achieve a monopolistic control over their field and exclude all non-professionals, it is not surprising that he is aghast at the thought that gay writers might now be writing their books for *gays who read*. Presumably, writers should know by now that they are writing for professors of contemporary literature.

I am reminded of the infamous review of Toni Morrison's *Song of Solomon*, on the front page of the *New York Times Book Review*, in which the reviewer, a man, asserted that Toni Morrison had now, after *The Bluest Eye* and *Sula*, written a major work of general interest to "the reader of fiction" because, for the first time, her central character was a man. It seemed self-evident to this benighted soul that novels which concern themselves exclusively with the lives of women or of little girls could not possibly be of more than marginal interest to the "larger intellectual community"—i.e., the middle-aged, white, heterosexual men who currently control the organs of literary discourse in this country.

So too with Mr. Martin: "the failure of most contemporary gay writers to see beyond the narrow confines of their own ghettoized world means that *they* have failed to reach a larger readership" (my italics). This is the type of hogwash we have come to recognize under the rubric of "blaming the victim." The fact that the dominant literary power structure in American culture today *still* has not awakened to the extraordinary renaissance of truly first-rate writing by something like a dozen Black women, the fact that they do not recognize that this is the major event going on in contemporary American writing, similar to the explosion of male, urban, Jewish writing that occurred in this country after World War II, is not the fault of the writers. These Black women authors have not *failed* to reach a larger readership. (This repeated emphasis on the importance of reaching a larger readership, which seems to be the touchstone of literary worth for Mr. Martin, is truly strange coming from a man who has just written a book on Herman Melville, a writer whose "failure" in that sense can only be bested by the "failure" of Emily Dickinson.) The *readership* had failed, as it has time and time again in the literary history of the past century, to recognize the most significant writing of its time. And it could be said that they failed because *their professional readers failed them.* One can become truly irritated with Mr. Martin as one reads, again and again, statements like "gay writers no longer seem to want to speak to the general reader, even as more and more gay lives are lived exclusively in the gay world." Would he say the same about Black writers who write about exclusively Black societies, do you think? How do you suppose he would handle the case of Isaac Bashevis Singer? "The result is a loss for the larger world of contemporary fiction, where the gay voice is heard less and less often." If this man does not know that straight readers do not particularly want to read about faggots, as to a lesser degree white people don't want to read books about Blacks, and if he doesn't know that this can be changed and must be changed and is being changed, then he simply doesn't know the first thing about the real situation of gay literature today. And if he thinks that the gay voice is heard less often today than it was in 1961, Mr. Martin is simply not living in the same world that I am. If he wants to settle this disagreement objectively, I would suggest that he go through all the reviews in *Publishers Weekly* for the year 1961 and then do the same for the year

1986. I think it would be clear enough that the gay voice is heard more often nowadays—by those who want to hear it, of course—than it was in 1961.

For God's sake, many of us *remember* 1961!

What could account for the perverse wrong-headedness of this discussion coming from a man whose academic concerns have been staunchly gay? Robert Martin is the author of *The Homosexual Tradition in American Poetry* and *Hero, Captain, and Stranger*, a study of Melville in which he explicitly argues that American culture is founded on the "subordination of women by men, colored nations by white, and of nature by law." Surely Mr. Martin would add to that list "the subordination of gays by straights." Why, then, would he write an essay the burden of which—I swear!—is to recommend to gay writers a renewed subordination to the dominant straight culture, to the "larger intellectual community"?

I think the heart of the problem lies in Mr. Martin's idea of fiction. "One task of fiction with any claim to permanent importance is the ability to see through the particular to the general." Here Mr. Martin is working with the classic academic model of art. The academy has constructed in its collective imagination a transcendent realm in which reside immortal works of art, torn from their distressing, almost sinful, roots in particularity and redeemed by universal applause. Thus Mr. Martin thinks Proust transcends the world he writes about and thereby "makes his work one that is of large appeal," while Andrew Holleran does not. Of course, there is no way to prove this transcendence except its consequent "wide appeal" and this sort of argument always runs the risk of being nothing but a fig leaf for the majority opinion of the moment. Just how wide an appeal does Mr. Martin think Proust had when he was first published? For that matter, how wide an appeal did Melville's *Moby-Dick* have? (In the U.S. *Moby-Dick* sold fewer copies during Melville's lifetime than any of his previous five books: 3,215 copies in its first 34 years; and in the U.K. it sold only 500 copies.) Of course, Mr. Martin could throw in the time variable and say that *in time* the whole culture came to see the value of these writers. But this is precisely what he doesn't seem willing to grant to Andrew Holleran and other gay writers whose works he complacently consigns to oblivion almost immediately upon publication.

It is *never* the task of fiction "to see through the particular to the general"—except perhaps for a few misguided attempts such as Socialist Realism. The "general" is the object of the social sciences. But it could be said that fiction's task is to see through the particular to *the universal*. This error in terminology is significant. You only write novels about highly particular, never "general," people. Nothing could be more radically particularized than the characters of Dostoevsky, or Henry James, or Mark Twain. And for a very good reason that has to do with the nature of human life—human beings exist only in the mode of radical particularity. It is not possible to be a person in general, just as it is not possible to be an athlete in general. To be an athlete, you must participate in some particular sport; you must be a swimmer or a basketball player or something. To be a person, you must, in America today, be Black or white or Asian or Native American or something. You cannot just be "a person in general" in this society without belonging to a particular race. True, this thought does not usually occur to the editors of the *New York Times*. When they think of people in general, they think of white people (and usually of white, middle-class, middle-aged, male people); seldom would they think of eight-year-old Black girls.

If the history of literary culture teaches us anything, it is that only the most intensely particularized works of art ever achieve universal stature. Dostoevsky is as intensely Russian as Sophocles is intensely Greek or Synge intensely Irish. And if people who are not Russians or ancient Greeks or Irish can enjoy and benefit immensely from reading these works, I'm suspicious of any "larger intellectual community" which turns away from gay novels in despair at their "increased parochialism." I have a lot more in common with a straight man in this society than either of us has with Sophocles. And as far as I know, no one is complaining about parochialism in John Updike's novels about middle-class Connecticut white people.

The real problem with the academic model of art and its "transcendence" to an imaginary timeless realm of immortal works is that the make-up of this pantheon is always and only a reflection of the minds who dominate the organs which articulate that culture at the moment. And since literary creation is at most times in history inextricably involved with efforts by groups of individuals to seize control of those organ of culture from their predecessors, this model almost always lands one in a reactionary position, i.e., supporting the cultural status quo and giving preference to those artists and works of art that are most easily assimilated by the dominant culture of the time. The academic model insures that any critic using it—gay or not—will adopt, no matter how subtly, straight interests and evaluation. Thus at this point in his essay, anyone could have predicted how Mr. Martin would rank the writers he discusses—Robert Ferro, Andrew Holleran, David Leavitt, David Plante and Edmund White. And just to prove the point I stopped and wrote out that ranking myself—surprised to find that I couldn't anticipate how he would deal with Ed White. And sure enough, it was exactly the ranking he gives us, the only unexpected turn being his truly strange treatment of White at the end of his essay.

Predictably, Mr. Martin does not like Robert Ferro's *The Family of Max Desir* and takes a few unfair potshots at the style, "but the worst problem is that the novel is finally about so little." And what is this novel about, you ask. "Will Dad accept Max and his lover Nick? Do they have a place on the family tree?" Mr. Martin talks as if it is self-evident that the disruption of a son's relation to his father, the possible reconciliation of a father and son, the question of whether a man still *has* a family once he's come out as gay, is utterly trivial. Why? you might fairly ask. After all, Jane Austen wrote novels on the much more limited theme of courtship in early nineteenth-century rural England, and one somehow feels sure Mr. Martin would award the coveted "transcendence" to those books. As far as fathers and sons are concerned, there's *Oedipus* and *The Brothers Karamazov* and . . . but why go on? The fact that the novel deals with the plight of a *gay* son drives Mr. Martin to scorn: "Meanwhile, Mother is dying and Father is thinking about joining a monastery. . . . Tune in tomorrow." Such sarcasm is evidently provoked by the irritating triviality—to Mr. Martin—of anything having to do with gay issues. Mr. Martin likes Andrew Holleran a bit better because he is "not so superficial as Ferro in thinking of his hero's relationship to the family in terms of 'us' and 'them.'" How this could be said about the author of *Nights in Aruba*, in which the protagonist's whole life is dramatically, even *geographically*, divided between his gay life in New York City and his family life in Florida, is totally beyond me. That division is what the novel is all about! But as we have seen, Holleran's novels are finally dismissed for their lack of "transcendence." David Leavitt is much more to Mr. Martin's taste, which should make David Leavitt nervous. "No one is likely to think of these stories as 'gay fiction' in the same way that one does Holleran's or Ferro's novels. (I wonder what Mr. Martin makes of *The Lost Language of Cranes*?) For they manage to move beyond the *merely* gay by their ability to imagine other lives"—presumably by "other" he means straight lives, which David Leavitt does depict quite well. How do you think Mr. Martin would speak of Toni Morrison's novel *The Bluest Eye*, in which there are no white people? Would he say it was "*merely* Black" (and those were his italics)? Would he say Philip Roth's novels were *merely* Jewish? Isn't it odd that Mr. Martin is so anxious to have our gay writers move so quickly beyond the *merely* gay? What's the rush? Gay writers have barely *begun* to describe gay life. It's like that ploy straight reviewers have been using for the last couple of years: "Oh no, not *another* book on the trauma of being gay!" As if there were hundreds of such novels. As if anyone said, "Oh no, not another book on the traumas of being a middle-class, suburban white person!" Mr. Martin is simply nervous in the presence of anything gay; the less gay a novel is, the better. How else could you describe this, except by saying that it is the attitude of a straight-identified gay?

Thus, according to Mr. Martin, David Plante is by far the best writer he's considered so far. True, he hasn't managed to find that coveted "large readership," but he is "a much more established writer, although one whose reputation has not often gone beyond the literary world." Mr. Martin especially likes *The Francoeur Novels* and their "protagonist, Daniel, who comes of age as an artist and also (although this is more discreetly presented) as a gay man." That "discreetly" is very important to Mr. Martin, just as it is important not being "too frank."

It is odd that Mr. Martin thinks that the "artist" can serve as a useful metaphor for modern man, but that being a gay man cannot (as being an eight-year-old Black girl cannot). After all, one out of every ten (or twenty) American men is gay; artists are *much* rarer than that. It is because "Plante is willing only to suggest his sexuality, and not to see it as an important part of his fictional self" that "Plante's work gives us, more than that of any other contemporary gay writer, the sense of a larger world." One wonders if he would demand that women not see their sexuality as an important part of their fictional self. But then what about Jane Austen, Colette, Virginia Woolf? If Mr. Martin does not want our gay writers to see their sexuality as an important part of their fictional self, then Mr. Martin simply does not want gay fiction. He may want what he read in college in 1961, established fiction by gay men, but he does not want gay fiction. Such are the confusions to which the academic model of art can lead when applied to contemporary, living literature.

It is reassuring, finally, to see in Mr. Martin's strange discussion of Ed White that gay writing itself still has the power to wreak total confusion in the minds of those who follow the academic model, the power to make the discussion twisted to the point of true silliness. It reminded me of Rose Mary Woods' tortured demonstration—one leg flung out, one shoulder nearly dislocated—of how she could possibly have caused the gap in the White House tapes. Mr. Martin declares that White is "the writer who has come closest to achieving that kind of gay fiction" (the kind Mr. Martin likes) and asserts that "*A Boy's Own Story* is the most important American gay novel in a long time, if not ever, and it has quite rightly been almost alone among gay novels in gaining larger readership." Note that "quite rightly" with its unpleasantly smug and Calvinistic tone—it was commercially successful because it *deserved* to be. (Once again, one wonders what this man thinks of the failure of Melville's books in his time—was that deserved too?) Of course, he is simply factually wrong here. Gore Vidal's *Myra Breckenridge* certainly achieved a much wider readership, as has John Rechy's *City of Night*, for that matter. Once again Mr. Martin assumes that the public is right (and that *that* makes Ed White right) and the writers are wrong—which only demonstrates his ignorance of the realities of commercial publishing today.

But what really makes Mr. Martin enthusiastic about *A Boy's Own*

Story is that it "is an important work in the history of the American novel, the conventions of which it adopts and transforms." And here the academic has found his home ground, in the Never-Never Land of the history of forms. For the phrase "the history of the American novel" does not point to any concrete reality—it points to an academic course: "The History of the American Novel, 112." This is a totally mental construction that changes every time the dominant textbooks used in our schools change. The "history of the American novel" is simply the shadow the present casts on the past; a suitable rearrangement of valuations that will always retrospectively confirm the cherished notions of the present. "The history of the American novel"— that's *really* reality to people like Mr. Martin—not the real-life situation of gay and straight people living in today's world.

Oddly enough, his discussion of *A Boy's Own Story* has nothing whatsoever to do with form, and the comments Mr. Martin makes on its content do give one pause, to say the least. How in the world could one describe this book's protagonist as "a lustful Candide in a world of hypocrites"? I mean, Mr. Martin goes on to say this character "learns to control the world by mastering it" (*Candide?*), giving "the lie once and for all to that myth of American boyhood innocence." Has Mr. Martin read *Candide?*

But more puzzling by far is his general treatment of White. To fit Ed White into his overall scheme, Mr. Martin has to dismiss White's previous two books—"two highly mannered novels of lush prose and opaque meaning"—and totally *ignore* White's latest novel, *Caracole*. Now *Caracole* was published in September 1985, Mr. Martin's essay on the state of gay fiction in July of 1986, and we all know that *Bay Windows* does not have *that* long a lead time. Using Ed White, who "has quite rightly been almost alone among gay novel(ists) in gaining (a) larger readership," to illustrate his argument, Mr. Martin has to ignore *three* out of the man's four novels. The argument is tortured beyond belief.

This type of academic discourse when applied to the creation of contemporary works of literature is wrong-headed to the point of silliness. It understands neither the conditions of cultural creation nor the realities—personal, social, political, cultural—which give weight, meaning, and significance to writing. Above all it does not understand the vital symbiosis between the individual act of writing and the public consciousness of the community. And worse than that, it's dangerous. It endeavors to turn the sheer creative act of writing into the production of "literature" precut to fit the mold of the academic mind. Such critics, in the words of Harold Rosenberg, "cause the mirror of modern literature to be turned to the wall, so that events take place blindly, while art becomes a copying of monuments in the oversized scale of the 'humanist perspective.' The net effect is a pervasive Philistinism."

No doubt my response to Mr. Martin's essay is overheated. But I am exasperated beyond endurance by the treatment our gay writers are subjected to at the hands of gay reviewers and critics. It's about time we cleaned up this mess. And I would suggest the best way to start is to consider seriously the nature and function of criticism. There is certainly no place, as Ethan Mordden declared, for the petty snipping of envious egos settling imagined scores. But neither is it the task of the critic to assert personal taste, for which support is sought in pedantic references to "the history of the novel." Nor is it the task of the critic to pass out grades like a school marm—you get a B+, you flunk—or act as a policeman endeavoring to keep gay writing in line by reporting misdemeanors and holding up the virtues he does discover as examples to the wicked. And above all, it is not the task of the critic to tell writers what to write about or whether their sexuality should be an important part of their fictional self.

The task of the critic is to write about writing he responds to—and to shut up about writing he doesn't respond to. The task of the critic is to contribute to and improve the quality of public talk that goes on about books. The task of the critic is to improve the cultural ambiance that forms the matrix in which new works of literature emerge and are received and read.

And it's about time—it's past time—we got on with it.

Oedipus Revised

DAVID LEAVITT'S *THE LOST LANGUAGE OF CRANES*

IRRITATION, IT TURNS out, is a great spur to writing, and the critical reception of David Leavitt's first novel, *The Lost Language of Cranes*, provided plenty of irritation. Sarcasm can be fun! The enormously positive literary reception to Leavitt's first book of short stories had built great anticipation for this novel, especially among gay readers, but the wacky response of national reviewers in the mainstream media to Leavitt's attempt to address the gay situation head-on was all over the place and bewildering in its confusion. Surveying the whole spectacle, one sees how homophobia works its insidious way into the minds of men.[1]

Not the least interesting thing about David Leavitt's first novel, *The Lost Language of Cranes*, is the way it's being handled by reviewers in the mainstream press. Given the critical and commercial success of *Family Dancing*, Leavitt's first book of short stories, and the media exposure lavished on its author, this was one gay novel that could not be ignored, or dismissed in a brief review—two favored methods of dealing with the emergence of our contemporary gay literature. At least this book would have to be dismissed at length, which gives one a nice opportunity to observe homophobia in action, to watch the feints and ploys by which the dominant culture in this society tries to maintain its power position and monopolize the right to define reality. It is an irritating—if informative—intellectual spectacle.

The mugging started with *Publishers Weekly* deploring "a dragged out plot and characters whose sexual orientation seems more important than their humanity." The separation of "humanity" from "sexual orientation" is not something that *Publishers Weekly* normally de-

---

1 *Christopher Street*, no. 105 (October 1986).

mands of, say, women's novels, but it's virtually a leitmotif in the public discussion of this novel. *PW* signs off on a note of sobering absurdity, regretting that "the narrative displays little of the maturity or subtle touch" of Leavitt's previous collection of stories, which this 25-year-old author wrote four years ago when he was in college. Evidently Leavitt has regressed, and above all, he has ceased being "subtle."

Christopher Lehmann-Haupt, writing in the daily *New York Times*, takes issue. With a pervasive condescension that seems utterly unconscious, he says, "What a miracle it is, then" (considering "that both father and son are homosexual"), "that *The Lost Language of Cranes* is neither comic nor bizarre." One imagines ruefully that liberals of another age had the same reaction to the early work of Black writers like Zora Neale Hurston or Langston Hughes. Mr. Lehmann-Haupt asserts happily "that a reader nearly forgets the issue of sexual identity and identifies with what is universal among any set of lovers." "We have come a long way," says he, parodying a certain cigarette commercial, "from the work of, say, Tennessee Williams or Edward Albee . . . writers . . . forced by convention"—not prejudice, of course, or homophobia—"to disguise homosexuals as heterosexuals." It's hard to believe that a *New York Times* reviewer would actually use this old canard. Only a straight man would think that *Streetcar*'s Blanche DuBois or *Virginia Woolf*'s Martha was a faggot in disguise.

Lehmann-Haupt's enthusiasm for Leavitt's novel is limited, however: "It pretends to show everybody's point of view, but it is subtly biased in favor of Philip's outlook"—a fatal flaw in a novel, as we all know. "Thus Owen, Philip's father, comes out as a mere accessory to his son. In the novel's final scenes, their roles are reversed and the son ministers to the father, while Rose, the mother, is dismissed from the scene along with the rest of the straight world, which in any case is under-represented—another shortcoming." Bet you didn't know we now have a quota system for straights in gay novels, did you? I'm waiting for Lehmann-Haupt to extend his principle and demand a quota for whites in Black novels, for Jews in Catholic novels, for Catholics in Jewish novels, for middle-aged men in the works of Bret Easton Ellis!

But Phillip Lopate, writing in the Sunday *New York Times Book Review*, couldn't agree less about Rose, Philip's mother, being dismissed from the novel. "A strange Oedipal tale, in any case," he admits, "with Oedipus and Laius going off to do their male bonding while Jocasta is left in the cold." More strange than the *original* Oedipus tale, one wonders? Perhaps straight men really don't think it strange to murder their father and have sex and children with their mother. "Yet if Mr. Leavitt seems to opt for that fashionable plot solution"—now quick, name three fashionable novels in which father and son ride into the sunset, deserting the mother—"the subtext is quite different," Lopate continues, "for the real electricity, the edgy mutual respect, occurs in the mother-son encounters. In a curious sense, theirs are the only true love scenes in the book." In a very curious sense, indeed. "So the novel's underlying dynamic may be classically Freudian after all; the father is killed (that is, made weak as a character) to order that mother and son may celebrate their passionate dialogue in an ongoing agony." Well, that's certainly one way to read the novel. Since a distinct note of relief can be detected in this last sentence, maybe straight men really are that strange. One always knew they were peculiar.

In spite of Lopate's enthusiasm for the classically Freudian Oedipus legend, he thinks "it is debatable whether the question of sexual orientation alone can sustain the whole novel." I guess he means that although Oedipus has always seemed to work as a play, the story wouldn't sustain a novel; for unless I'm wrong *Oedipus is* a tale of sexual orientation, one might even say a classically Freudian tale of sexual orientation. Lopate goes on to say: "When Philip tells his parents, 'My sexuality, my attraction to men, is the most crucial, most elemental force in my life,' I found myself impatiently thinking: surely there are other tasks for the self to address." It's too bad Mr. Lopate wasn't around to set Madame Bovary straight, or Anna Karenina. One would like to hear him lecture the French Lieutenant's woman (and her author) the way he lectures Leavitt; "For the most part there is no work," and we know how that ruined Jane Austen's novels—"there is no world, there is no intellectual or spiritual striving, no interest in art, no engagement in politics—except sexual politics." Take that, Nabokov!

Given Lopate's avowed belief that the passions and conundrums of the erotic life are simply not interesting enough to sustain whole novels, it is not surprising that he feels that "the coming out to one's parents scene is becoming an overworked convention in contemporary fiction." We all know how many novels have appeared in the last year that contain major coming out scenes to one's parents. I'm sure Lopate could instantly name five, if we asked him. Why, it's becoming more common and overworked a convention than falling in love and getting married was once, or getting separated and divorced is today. Why don't those gays follow the lead of straight writers and work on some original conventions, I wonder.

Of course, Matthew Gilbert, managing editor of the *Boston Review*, writing in the Boston *Sunday Herald*, totally disagrees: "*The Lost Language of Cranes* is not simply a gay coming out story, nor is it written for a gay audience." And that takes care of us. "As in Leavitt's popular short stories, homosexuality appears but doesn't overwhelm. His characters are human beings first." And gay second, just as so many of Norman Mailer's characters are human beings first and heterosexual men second. You see how important it is to them to separate humanity from sexuality. Of course, some people might say that's like saying Dwight Gooden is an athlete first and a baseball player second. Some people might say that's like saying Portnoy is a human being first and a Jew second, or that Alice Walker's characters are human beings first and Blacks second. Some people might say that's a distinction without a difference. Some people might say that the people who make that distinction don't like Jews or don't like Blacks.

Raymond Sokolov, writing in *The Wall Street Journal*, doesn't seem to like gays and particularly David Leavitt, "someone *The New York Times* and *Esquire* have gone to for the latest word on letters," who "rides a crest of publicity and approbation" "thanks to the rapturous response to Mr. Leavitt's first book . . . that last year turned him into a spokesman for homosexuals and for his generation at the age of 23." One smells sour grapes here, but it would probably be bitchy to wonder if Sokolov's own age and degree of media success have anything to do with his opinion of this "unremarkable story about love in Manhattan." Sokolov disagrees with just about everybody: "*Cranes* is a gay manifesto for gays of the '80s," says he, "a sentimental fable whose central issue is sexual inversion," "at best skillful melodrama." Mr. Sokolov, whose review is titled *The Love That Can't Shut Up*, is quite tired of all these gay novels he evidently has to read. The one good thing he finds to say about Leavitt's book is that "it makes the case, once and, one hopes, for all, that gays can be as banal as everyone else—given half a chance." So it's a gay manifesto for the '80s, but Sokolov doesn't think being gay is all that big a deal. He goes on to invite the reader to try to imagine earlier gay writers' reactions to the Philip-Eliot love scene. "What would Oscar Wilde, Marcel Proust, or W.H. Auden have made of it? Fun, I think. They would have mocked it." Which is evidently the only respectable and literary way to treat a gay love scene—mock it. Do you suppose Sokolov ever wondered why gay writers developed such skill at mockery and irony? Do you think he ever wondered who the classic queen is mocking, and why? Probably not.

To someone who works in the publishing world, it's depressing to say that the only review I came across that was not riddled with these inane prejudices was Dorothy Allison's long and perceptive essay in *The Village Voice*. Leave it to a lesbian to make the simple but central point that "the coming-out story is the essential homosexual theme, as persistent as the romantic love story and the coming-of-age novel, containing as it does elements of both." I don't like the feeling—and I'm sure David Leavitt doesn't either—that only another gay person will give a gay novel a fair and decent reading, but it sure is the impression you get. Which is not to say that there are not a number of sharp and insightful comments made in most of these reviews; unfortunately they're embedded in a cultural attitude of arrogant condescension, prejudice, and homophobia that twists their perspective and severely distorts their literary judgment.

It's worth watching precisely how this happens, how homophobia manifests itself, makes its impact and thereby reinforces itself "on the capillary level," as Michel Foucault would say. To assert that homophobia is at work in these reviews is not to say that the authors necessarily hate gays personally and on a subjective level. Homophobia is a cultural reality, a fixed pattern of social power relations. These specific individuals, these writers talking about this gay novel, are merely the sites on which the homophobia of our culture manifests and realizes itself, reasserting and reinforcing the dominant power relations of the society (i.e., the supremacy of the white male heterosexual). Cultural realities by their nature exist across a spectrum of individuals. The individual participates in the culture. The culture speaks through the individuals, often making the person say something more than and different from what he intends to say. And this is still a homophobic culture, if one in process of change.

Oddly enough, individual people change before their imagination, their culture, does. (Otherwise cultural change would be impossible.) These individual reviewers are probably much more likable than their imaginations would lead you to believe. Probably a gay person could get along with them fine in a concrete situation. Nevertheless, their imagination—riddled with the homophobia of the culture—is a danger to us because their imagination affects *our* imagination. We too participate in the social reality of the culture. And we know the results of internalizing in our imagination the homophobia of the dominant culture: it leads to self-hating gays, to the phenomenon of internalized homophobia which is the precise mechanism by which the society has been able to suppress homosexuality by getting homosexuals to suppress and deny it themselves. The war to rid our imaginations of this alien attack has to be carried into the public culture, for imagination is inherently a social and cultural construction as much as a subjective faculty. Our imaginations have been colonized by a homophobic culture; we have been invaded by an alien spirit which we must eradicate. We must do this because our imagination is the faculty by which we recognize the reality of our lives.

Oddly enough, this is just what I would say *The Lost Language of Cranes* is all about—though I suspect I'm being seduced by the sheer perversity of finding myself more in agreement with Sokolov than any of these other reviewers. He's right, it *is* "a gay manifesto for gays of the '80s, gays who can come out without waving feather boas or chains to prove their liberation, because the generation before them made it possible to drop a lot of the fear and defensive 'lifestyle' so often enveloping gay life." Any reviewer reflects the bias of his own perspective, and to this reviewer *The Lost Language of Cranes* is about gay culture, why it's necessary, and the disasters that occur in its absence.

The most persistent image of the book is the fate of foundlings, children taken from their natural home and raised in an alien social setting, and Leavitt's overriding concern is the cost to the child, the loss of its natural language (language, of course, being the primary as well as the ultimate expression of culture). The Black lesbian Jerene, apparently so loosely connected to the novel, marks the center and core of the novelist's concern. When we first see her, "she stood up, unbending from her sitting position like a crane stretching itself to demolish a building." She has been working on a doctoral dissertation for seven years, at one time focused on the private language invented by a pair of famous twins who were separated by social workers so they could "pick up the new language." Jerene wonders if they remember the private language of their childhood, and concludes, "Probably not. Probably their early childhood is like a dream to them, the way it's supposed to be for children who are kidnapped and raised by different parents." "In a different kind of world," Jerene muses, "the twins' language could have flourished, could have become the language of a culture."

Jerene herself was not kidnapped, but adopted, as was Philip's lover, Eliot. Presumably the child of a poor Black woman, she was raised by a wealthy lawyer and his wife, the only Black couple to own a home in Westport, Connecticut, in 1957. Her parents themselves have migrated from the culture of Black poverty to a white middle-class milieu, and they pay the cost for "passing" in this world: dining in an elegant restaurant, "everyone—the waitresses (elderly Black women in white aprons) as well as the other patrons—gave the family curious, condescending glances, as if to question whether they belonged there. Still, for two hours they stuck it out, sitting stiff-backed in their chairs, smiling, pretending enjoyment as if their lives depended on it, and in certain ways their lives did depend on it." Nor are they more at home in the working class world of her father's parents, "the tiny apartment of his childhood, with its cracked, impossibly narrow halls, and there they sat for an hour on stiff-backed chairs in the little sitting room, eating cookies and drinking lemonade." Without a world of her own, Jerene spends seven years sitting in stiff-backed chairs in the library, fascinated by lost languages, quitting only when she finds a lover, gets a job as a bouncer at a lesbian bar, and starts doing volunteer work for the Gay Hot Line (where one of her distraught callers is Philip's father).

Structurally, Jerene is balanced by Philip's boyfriend, Eliot, who was also adopted, but when this child's parents died in a car crash they had left instructions that he be raised by their best friends, a gay couple. And it's Eliot's seeming naturalness—as if his spirit had not been breached in childhood—that fascinates Philip. "Philip understood that there were people in the world like Eliot for whom love and sex came easy, without active solicitation, like a strong wind to which they had only to turn their faces and it would blow over them." Being gay is natural to Eliot, a natural language, one that he shares with his parents. Gay life, or at least gay sex and love, is something that *happens* to him, like a wind blowing, not something he *does*. But Philip has grown up, like most of us, in a family of straights, consequently his erotic life had to be kept a secret, a secret language he shared with no one. "His sexual life had been bred in secret, he had never spoken of it with anyone, not even himself. Could something so private be real, he wondered?" Consequently, Philip's attempts to be gay have a painful over-eagerness to them, a tense anxiety about whether he's doing it right, and it's not surprising that the most common words out of his mouth are "I'm sorry."

Like virtually all young gay men, Philip is an intense romantic, someone whose deepest longings could exist only in the world of fantasy, for at the very onset of adolescence the realm of desire and the realm of experience had parted company. "Before Eliot, Philip had lived so long without physical love that he believed it to be the only thing in the world he needed." It is natural that when he has the luck to reunite desire with experience in the person of Eliot, he becomes intensely nervous and unsure of himself, for "he was living at that moment the strongest wish-fulfillment fantasy he could muster; his dreams ran parallel to his reality."

Balanced opposite Philip stands his father Owen, who removed his dreams as far from his daily life as possible, containing them within the narrow confines of his furtive Sunday afternoon visits to a gay porn theater. Hoping to stifle his homosexual inclinations, Owen had married Rose and fathered Philip, seeking above all safety: "For years he had felt safe only in his apartment, only with Rose." But the apartment is going co-op and his sexual urges seem to be gaining in strength, so when Philip finally decides to come out to his parents he begins a process that topples their carefully constructed life. And it topples because it is based on a lie: "That he had lied to her—that he had built a marriage with her on the basis of a sexual lie—was a regret of such magnitude that he could not get around it." And so had Rose—though curiously none of the straight reviewers, except Matthew Gilbert, seem to have noticed it. Not only did Rose have an affair with the couple's best friend the year they lived in Italy, she later maintained an office liaison for seven years (broken off not by Rose, but by the man). More significantly "there had been moments when a great desire for change welled up in Rose, moments when as she had long ago read in Proust (and she always, always remembered), the heartstrings yearn to be plucked at any cost, the soul tires of contentment, the body craves any kind of change, even decimation, even death," and "during those rare episodes of wanting, Rose had always looked to someone else, not to Owen."

"With prolonged denial comes passivity, a psychic numbing," observes Matthew Gilbert; "for 26 foggy years, Rose and Owen Benjamin have lived in the dark of the New York City apartment, afraid to look at the furniture of their marriage straight on. They are most comfortable ignoring each other's infidelities." They have built their life on a lie because "the idea of safety," as Lopate points out, "as the primary value in life—rather than, say, independence—is never questioned." So when Philip decides to come out to his parents, his assertion of erotic truth threatens the entire family structure, which is why the coming-out novel invariably becomes a family novel.

"Americans tend to write about families," states Ethan Mordden in his recently published *Buddies*, "gay Americans particularly. The gay writer's unique contribution to literature, the *Bildungsroman* of gathering self-awareness and coming out, is essentially a family novel." In the last analysis, it is probably the family that is the source of homophobia, and thus the family is the area where the gay issue must be fought out and established. Philip is looking not only to realign his position as a gay man within his family, but to find ways to include his gay life within the family, within the settled structure of domestic love that defines the meaning of family. "He fantasizes taking his lover home to his parents the way other people dream of having sex with movie stars," remarks Dorothy Allison, just as the characters in Mordden's *Buddies* are working to establish extended gay networks that function as a familial structure in their lives.

What is remarkably striking about Leavitt's *The Lost Language of Cranes* and Mordden's *Buddies*—for my money the two major events in gay literature this season—is that both books end with the conversion of the father generation. In both it is the sons who have the spiritual courage to try to base their lives on the erotic truth of their being and to stumble ahead trying to create new patterns of love, thus enabling the son to lead the father out of the dark morass of self-denial and self-deception.

It is indeed a new twist on the old Oedipus story of sexual orientation, as, of course, one would expect it would have to be. Considering how the original Oedipus story ends with its implications that male rivalry—to the point of murder and mother-fucking, self-mutilation and blindness—lies at the core of the traditional family—one might think that straight reviewers would pause before rejecting the vision of reconciliation between fathers and sons that is the common note sounded in both these books. In any event, their simultaneous publication marks to my mind a high point in the emergence of our new and remarkable gay literature. I agree with Dorothy Alison that "in *The Lost Language of Cranes* Leavitt has plotted the slow, stumbling passage of coming out with a richness and power that give me new hope" for gay fiction.

Paragraph 175, or How Dark Can It Get?

WITH DARKENING CLOUDS threatening our skies, when an early bound galley of Richard Plant's *The Pink Triangle: The Nazi War against Homosexuals*[1] came into *Christopher Street*'s office for review, I grabbed it. This I wanted to consider. At a time when things looked like they might get bad, it was worth considering just how bad things could get. How bad things actually *did* get. And only forty years ago, in my parents' generation—that was the shocking thing.[2]

Given the potential situation AIDS was creating—in 1985, twenty states debated legislation for quarantining or otherwise controlling people with AIDS[3]—I thought this was a book that all gays should read, but I knew they wouldn't, so I tried to offer a very condensed version of Plant's message.

At a time when the AIDS epidemic has introduced a wild card into the politics of homophobia in this country, it would be wise for all of us to give some serious thought to the passions and prejudices that fuel anti-gay political action. It is one of the great peculiarities—and one of the great dangers—of the social situation of gays that many gay people find it hard to believe in the reality of homophobia. Although paying lip service to the concept of gay oppression, many gay people do not experience it in the day-to-day reality of their lives—unlike, say, the oppression of Blacks, which is systematically actualized in terms of economic hardships and social limitation so concrete that most Black people feel them daily. Gay people can *pass* in this society, that is, act like straights and thereby avoid the more concrete consequences of homophobia,

1 A New Republic Book, Henry Holt and Company, 1986.
2 Published in *Christopher Street* (September 1986).
3 Abigail Trafford and Gordon Witkin, "The Politics of AIDS," *US News & World Report*, November 18, 1985.

and that tends to remove the whole discussion of gay oppression to a weirdly insubstantial and psychological realm, the realm of the merely possible. But, even if they are not actualized, possibilities can be quite real, and they can have far-reaching consequences; threats, after all, are possibilities and, even unfulfilled, they can be very effective indeed in controlling people's actions. In these circumstances it is useful to turn to history, to what *has* happened, for once anything has actually happened, we know it is a real possibility.

Thus, in terms of gay history, one would think that the historical attempt the Nazis made to exterminate German homosexuals would be the single major event preoccupying our historians. After all, what could be more important than the fact that at one time, and fairly recently at that, forty years ago, there was a coordinated and sustained effort by a modern state to wipe homosexuals off the face of the earth? After the Holocaust, Jews realized that this event was at the center of their fate in the modern world, that no Jew in his right mind could avoid considering it. Unfortunately, this has not been true of our gay historians and theoreticians. Considering the possibility that antibody testing could quite conceivably—and soon—make it impossible for the majority of gay men to continue passing, a reconsideration of the Nazis' war against German homosexuals is urgently needed. This is why the gay community should be especially grateful for Richard Plant's new book, *The Pink Triangle*. It deserves a wide audience and thoughtful consideration. At a time when the notions of quarantine and the tattooing of people with AIDS are being thrown about recklessly, it is worth considering how bad things can get. Richard Plant was lucky. His father, a physician, a socialist and a Jew, was arrested almost immediately after Hitler came to power, but released after a few weeks, thanks to the intercession of some of his patients who were nominally Nazis. His father insisted that Plant leave Germany immediately and enroll at the university in Basel, Switzerland, and Plant fled Frankfurt am Main on February 27, 1933, the day the Reichstag went up in flames. "Only years later did I realize how lucky I had been," says Plant in his Prologue. From the vantage point of neutral Switzerland, he watched, horrified, as events unfolded in his homeland. He learned of the Nazi war on homosexuals from his friends, quoting at length one startlingly vivid letter from Eric, his best friend in *gymnasium*:

> Before I come to what has happened to some of our acquaintances, here is some news not published by anybody in Frankfurt (Eric wrote in 1935). Have you heard about the Roehm murders? With that it started, the rounding up, the closing of the bars, and so on. No place is open here in Frankfurt. In return we are blessed with new sex laws. Our old buddy Harold said they can get you if you smile at another boy. This he told me before he went underground—I have no idea where he is. If he is alive. Remember the G.G. brothers? Arrested a week ago, put into Preungesheim jail. Remember Max? Supposedly in Dachau, near Munich. What little contact I had with Ferdi is lost but I'm afraid his SA uniform is no protection with Roehm gone. A few he seduced on his endless expeditions would rat on him quickly. Richard, you could never guess how many told on their former friends when they were thrown in jail and "reeducated" by the bullies. Kurt, the pharmacist near your house, was dragged out of bed at 5:00 A.M.
>
> They found his address book—the fool didn't burn it or throw it in the river. What happened at headquarters I can only guess—I haven't seen him and I don't have the nerve to ask his mother. . . . Now don't worry about me. I'm going to enlist in the navy. Yes, I know, I should stay with you in Basel and perhaps later we could get away from all this, far away, to Australia, Canada, or California. Mother wants me to, but how can I leave her?

Soon the two friends lost touch but "in an important way," Plant declares, "It was the memory of Eric that kept urging me on, decades later, to search out that rather little known area of the swastika tyranny, the hounding and slaughter of homosexuals under the Third Reich." The book that resulted does honor to that friendship, even if Plant insists on the preliminary nature of his study. "Although it was painful, I had accepted the fact that someone like me, working alone, with limited time and no assistance, could never dream of doing justice to the wealth of evidence on the fate of the gays under Hitler." The reader may agree with Plant that "what follows is only a beginning and cannot be considered the definitive chronicle of homosexuals kept behind the barbed-wire fences of the Third Reich," but all the more reason to honor those who make the beginning and point the way.

The disquieting fact is that during the first third of the twentieth century Germany had the most advanced homosexual rights movement in the world. In 1897, the year Magnus Hirschfeld founded the Scientific-Humanitarian Committee, the central Berlin police compiled a list of between 20,000 and 30,000 known or suspected homosexuals throughout the country. On the basis of his 1909 survey, Hirschfeld concluded that there were about 1.2 million gays in Germany, or about 2.2 percent of the male population. By 1914 there were some forty gay bars in Berlin, and by 1933 when Hirschfeld's Committee, wisely, destroyed its roster, its larger organization, The Friendship League, had some 28,000 members who paid regular yearly fees. In American *today* The National Gay Task Force has about 8,000 paying members.

Throughout his career Hirschfeld fought tirelessly for the repeal of Germany's anti-homosexual laws, and tried to do so by changing the perception of homosexuality in the public mind. Already in the nineteenth century homosexuality had gone through its first transformation in public perception: from being a vice, that is, a criminal *act*, it became a criminal *class* of people. Krafft-Ebing, the leading psychiatrist of the late nineteenth century, could write: "Such degenerates have no right to existence in a well-regulated bourgeois society, and they have no gift for doing so. They endanger society to a high degree and they do so as long as they live." Sodomy was no longer seen as a criminal act, like the act of theft, but as a criminal state of being: not something you do, but something you are—"as long as they live." Hirschfeld struggled to change this perception of homosexuality from a criminal state to a medical state. "Hirschfeld's tireless efforts, while in many respects enlightened, nevertheless, did much to establish the notion of homosexuals as a medically defined, vulnerable, and official minority." The good doctor believed not in politics but in the education of the straight community: "Hirschfeld's motto was 'Justice Through

Knowledge'" and he "optimistically declared that ninety percent of the German people would vote to repeal the nation's anti-homosexual laws if only they had a chance to learn the truth." Unfortunately, this transformation of the criminal act to criminal class to medical class was disastrous when faced with the Nazis' own pseudo-medical theories of eugenics. With the bitter wisdom of hindsight, the evolution of the public perception of homosexuality, engineered by the newly emerging field of psychiatry along with the burgeoning homophile movement itself, looks like a perfect set-up.

The Nazi Party made their position on homosexuality clear very early. In 1928, when questioned about its stance toward reform of Paragraph 175 (Germany's anti-homosexual law), a reform which, at Hirschfeld's urging, the Social Democratic and Communist parties had gotten through a crucial parliamentary committee so it could be brought before the Reichstag, the party declared:

> It is not necessary that you and I live, but it is necessary that the German people live. And it can only live if it can fight, for life means fighting. And it can only fight if it maintains its masculinity. It can only maintain its masculinity if it exercises discipline, especially in matters of love. Free love and deviance are undisciplined. Therefore, we reject you, as we reject anything that hurts our nation.
>
> Anyone who thinks of homosexual love is our enemy. We reject anything which emasculates our people and makes it a plaything for our enemies, for we know that life is a fight, and it is madness to think that men will ever embrace fraternally.

In 1929, when the Nazis gained 107 seats in the Reichstag, parliamentary reform of Paragraph 175 became impossible.

On January 30, 1933, Hitler was named Chancellor of Germany. Less than four weeks later, on February 23, pornography was banned along with all homosexual rights organizations, and by the summer, Ernst Roehm's SA goons were raiding gay bars throughout Germany. However, the Nazi war against homosexuals did not shift into high gear until 1935, after Roehm himself had been disposed of. Roehm and many of his cronies were homosexual and Roehm had built the SA into a private army that rivaled the Reichswehr. Hitler had used the SA to gain total power within Germany, but if he wanted to conquer Europe he would need the full support of the German army, and thus a bargain was struck: in exchange for the destruction of Roehm and the SA, the army would swear loyalty to Hitler personally. And on June 28th, 1934, "the Night of the Long Knives," Roehm was assassinated and the bloodbath began. Precisely one year later to the day, on June 28th, 1935—that is, *before* the anti-Jewish laws were announced in Nuremberg—stringent new laws concerning homosexual conduct among men were promulgated.

With Roehm dead, Heinrich Himmler and his SS became the main organ for the Nazi war on homosexuals. In 1933 Himmler had established the first concentration camp at Dachau, to which were sent a few criminals, Communists, Catholics, Liberals, Socialists, Jews and homosexuals. Himmler had a special horror of homosexuals and he was determined to exterminate them. On June 17, 1936, Himmler was appointed chief of all SS and police forces and three months later he established the Federal Security Office for Combating Abortion and Homosexuality—a startling juxtaposition that should give pause to readers today. Homosexuality and abortion are constantly linked in Himmler's mind, nowhere more clearly than in a speech he gave to his elite SS training academy on February 18, 1937, declaring Germany's need of a "National Sexual Budget." Having lost more than a million men in World War I, "Germany had suffered the sharpest decline in its birthrate of all European nations, reaching an exceptional low in 1933." Ignoring the battered economy as a possible cause, Himmler concentrated on an estimated two million homosexuals, who in his belief did not reproduce, as well as the half-million babies he estimated to have been lost through abortion. If these twin vices continued, he warned, "it will be the end of Germany." Germany's Teutonic forbears "know what to do with homosexuals: they drowned them in bogs. No, it should not be called punishment. It was 'extermination of abnormal existence.'" "Like stinging nettles," he vowed, "we will rip them out (the homosexuals), throw them on a heap, and burn them." So worried was Himmler about the homosexual threat that this former puritan, who had once advised chastity before marriage, now declared prostitutes to be necessary to prevent young men from having to "turn to homosexuals for gratification."

Animated by their own version of "The Family Protection Act," the Ministry of Justice issued new guidelines in December 1934 stating that homosexual offenses did not have to be actually committed to be punishable; intent was what mattered. And on June 28, 1935, Paragraph 175 was revised to extend the concept of "criminally indecent activities between men." It permitted the authorities to arrest any male for the "offensive touching of another male." Mutual masturbation was declared a felony; a kiss or a touch could be interpreted as criminally indecent. Later, as Eric informed the young Richard Plant, "courts decided that a lewd glance from one man to another was sufficient grounds for prosecution." And "in at least one instance, a man was arrested not because he had been watching a young couple make love in a park, but because he had been seen observing the actions of the man more than those of the woman."

Such are the lengths to which an aggressively heterosexual society can go in its madness.

Nor is this merely a cheap shot. The point is that in this society heterosexuality had become a state concern. The state declared the protection and propagation of the family to be a matter of national security and consequently the regulation of the sexual lives of its citizens a legitimate sphere not of moral suasion but of legal prescription and criminal prosecution. At bottom, there is no difference between the essence of these politics and the slippery slope the Catholic church in America has embarked on today, when, having failed to convince the majority of their *own* believers that abortion is immoral, they would use the power of the state to make it illegal for everyone, Catholic or not. Overall, we may "reasonably estimate the number of males convicted of homosexuality from 1933 to 1944 at between 50,000 and 59,000," says Plant, "of which nearly 4,000 were juveniles. (Also recorded were the arrests of six lesbians—a bewildering statistic, since sex between women was not against the law.)" Altogether, according to Plant, somewhere between 5,000 and 15,000 homosexuals perished behind the barbed-wire fences of the concentration camps.

In absolute numbers, gays constituted a small minority of the concentration camp population but, according to the testimony of survivors, "gays and Jews were considered the lowest, most expendable group," and insofar as statistics can be tabulated, "those we possess show that in 1945 when the camps were liberated, the mortality rate of the homosexuals was higher than that of the other units investigated." This was evidently due to the heterogeneity of the group, who had nothing in common besides their homosexuality, and to the pervasive homophobia not only of the guards but of the other inmates. Plant quotes Eugene Kogon, who survived six years in Buchenwald and wrote the still classic account of the camp experience, *The Theory and Practice of Hell*: "Homosexual practices were actually very widespread in the camps. The prisoners, however, ostracized only those whom the SS marked with the pink triangle. The fate of homosexuals in the concentration camps can only be described as ghastly." Plant comments that "homophobia flourished everywhere, making it nearly impossible for gays to join any effort by prisoners to improve conditions in the barracks. They were suspect as a class. Whatever assistance they might offer was thought to mask a sexual motive."

The testimony of survivors is indeed ghastly, but it is worth reading even if one has to constantly remind oneself that what one is reading is real, that these things did indeed happen. They happened to Jews simply because they were Jews and they happened to homosexuals simply because they were homosexual.

It happened in June 1942. In Camp Sachsenhausen, there started one of those special operations designed to get rid of a few hundred people. This time, they worked out the final solution for the homosexuals; they would be put into a special liquidation command, where forced labor and starvation would bring about a slow, painful end.... After roll call ... our throats dry from fear.... Then the guardhouse door of the command tower opened and an SS officer and some of his lackeys stroke toward us. Our *Kapo* barked: "Three hundred criminal deviants present as ordered." ... We learned that we were to be segregated in a penal command and the next morning would be transferred as a unit to the cement works ... We shuddered because these bone mills were more dreaded than any other work detail . . . "You don't have to look so dumb, you butt fuckers," said the officer. "There you'll learn to do honest work with your hands and afterward you will sleep a healthy sleep. You are a biological mistake of the Creator. That's why you must be bent straight. . . ." Guarded by staff sergeants with machine guns, we had to sprint in lines of five until we arrived . . . They kept beating us with rifle butts and bullwhips. . . . Forced to drag along twenty corpses, the rest of us encrusted with blood, we entered the cement quarry. Then the martyrdom started. . . . Within two months, the special operation had lost two thirds. . . . To shoot someone "trying to escape" was a profitable business for the guards. For everyone killed, they received five marks and three days special furlough. . . . Whips were used more frequently each morning, when we were forced into the pits. . . . "Only fifteen are still alive," whispered the man next to me. . . . When I weighted not more than eighty-five pounds, one of the sergeants told me one morning: "Well, that's it. You want to go to the other side? It won't hurt. I'm a crack shot."

Perhaps, for a gay person, the darkest chapter of this story is the fact that "very few families seem to have been willing to stand by sons, brothers, husbands, or other relatives convicted of crimes against Paragraph 175." Since gay friends would endanger their own precarious existence by any attempt at communication, this meant that homosexuals in the camps were totally cut off from contact with the outside world.

The final bitterness was that once gay prisoners were liberated, they found themselves in a world still officially hostile. Hard as it is to believe, "according to German law, homosexual ex-prisoners were to be treated as criminals," since West Germany did not abolish Paragraph 175 until 1967. And "in at least one instance, a homosexual camp detainee was given a stern lecture by an American colonel, informing him that the United States also considered what he had done criminally offensive."

The Pink Triangle is a hard book to read, but it is a reading experience I would recommend to every gay man. Not so much for the purpose of drawing facile "lessons from history"—though Plant's work utterly confirmed my hunch that the idea of educating the straight majority (Hirschfeld's "Justice Through Knowledge") is a useless tactic, and we ought to concentrate on organizing our own community for political and economic power. Rather, the importance of this book, it seems to me, lies in saying over and over again to yourself as you read, this *really* happened. This actually *really* happened. Such a thing is possible in the world we live in. Which is, after all, the essential lesson of all history. One does not need to draw easy parallels to the political situation in America today, but one does need to know that such things are not only possible, *they have happened.*

This is a chilling thought, but in its power to unsettle it may help clarify our vision as we try to come to a sober and accurate assessment of the situation in which we find ourselves today.

A Culture in a Crucible

MY MEMORY IS hazy about the origin of this piece, but I believe Jim Marks, editor of the *Lambda Rising Book Report*, offered me space in a forthcoming issue[1] to highlight my next publishing list. Instead, or in addition, he got this little diatribe. A bit intense. I was increasingly frustrated that in the face of the crisis AIDS was presenting us with gay men by and large were still ignoring the extraordinary efforts and accomplishments of our writers in facing up and responding to this threat to our very existence.

Such were the times. But I did get to my books in the end, even mentioning a few books brought out by other publishers.

"Oh, I don't read *gay* books," said a roommate of mine on Fire Island a few summers ago. Like most of the men who took shares in the extraordinarily beautiful house in which I was lucky enough to spend seven summers, this man was educated as well as handsome and gorgeously gymned. An upwardly-mobile professional in his late twenties, he was quick to read the latest novel by Gore Vidal, kept up with the theater and ballet, and knew more dish about the opera world than I had ever thought possible. Here was a literate, well-educated guy who managed to keep abreast of the current culture in New York City to a much greater extent than I, and I could never understand why he showed no interest whatsoever in the new gay literature which, it seemed to me, was being born under our very eyes. So I prodded him one August afternoon as we lay by the pool smoking a joint and drinking vodka tonics.

"Oh, I don't read *gay* books," he said.

The scorn and dismissal I heard in his voice—aided perhaps by the

1 *Lambda Book Report*, no. 101 (1987).

well-known associative properties of marijuana—suddenly reminded me of discussions I'd had with gay men in the early Seventies, at 2 a.m. on a Thursday night in The Ninth Circle, for instance: "Rex Harrison, oh, she's a raging queen, darling!" Somehow the fact that this or that actor was gay was enough to diminish him, make him an object of scorn. And this was in 1972, on a night when we had all just come from a GAA (Gay Activists Alliance) meeting at The Fire House, supposedly gay revolutionaries militantly tearing down all the lies society has used to oppress us!

Naturally, we were naïve then. Or more naïve then than we are now. We did not yet realize that society oppressed people by getting them to oppress themselves—it's much easier and cheaper that way. We did not realize that it was not the overt homophobia of society that was our deadliest enemy, but the internalized homophobia that could cripple us. And perhaps we still do not recognize that point sufficiently today.

Recently a friend and I were talking about the gay writing scene and he told me a story that I'd never heard before about a quite successful and well-known gay editor who had turned down a superb gay first novel—and he admitted it was a superb novel—because he was already publishing two gay writers. He didn't want to be known as a "gay editor." I was startled because I had later published this novel—quite successfully for all concerned—and I'd never known the book had been turned down elsewhere. I was also interested because of another story I'd heard about this same author; in conversation with Richard Howard, I'd been told, this man emphatically asserted that he did not want to be known as a "gay writer."

"But you're gay, aren't you?" Richard asked.

What's interesting to me is that none of these people—reader, editor, writer—made any bones about being gay. Each in his own way was "gay and proud"—I mean it, I know these people. Yet each bought into the homophobic propaganda that saw in "gay" a diminished thing, something peripheral, minor, parochial, not worthy of consideration by the mainstream. It's depressing to see our own people co-opted this way, unwitting agents duped into participating in their own oppression, an oppression of the imagination (their *own* imagination!), which is far more serious, far more basic than the stupid laws or the social insults used against us. Depressing because you would think that by now we would have learned about this trick from the experiences of other oppressed groups.

Listen, for instance, to Toni Morrison in a recent article in *The New York Times*: "Ms. Morrison said that unlike some authors, who despise being labeled a Jewish writer, for instance, or a Southern writer—she does not mind being called a Black writer, or a Black woman writer. 'I've decided to define that, rather than having it be defined for me,' she said. 'In the beginning, people would say, "Do you regard yourself as a Black writer, or a Black woman writer?" and they also used the word woman with it—woman writer. So at first I was glib, and said I'm a Black woman writer, because I understood that they were trying to get me to accept their view of bigger and better. I really think the range of emotions and perceptions I have had access to as a Black person and as a female person is greater than those of people who are neither. I really do. So it seems to me that my world did not shrink because I was a Black female writer. It just got bigger.'"

Seems to me a writer who fears being labeled a "gay writer" is letting other people—hostile people—define for him what is "bigger and better." In which case the fight is over before it began. A gay writer or a gay editor or a gay reader who buys into this is in the same miserable condition all gay people were in before Stonewall. They may be liberated socially but their imaginations are still locked in the closet.

And none of us can afford this self-hating stupidity right now.

Our friends and lovers are dying. Many are already dead. We are living with a grief and fear that most people only experience in times of war or prolonged natural disaster. It has become clear by now that the AIDS crisis is an historical event that will have the same impact on the gay community that the Holocaust had on the Jewish community. Our survival is at stake. What it means to be gay is at stake. Our values and the meaning of our lives are at stake.

The gay community has risen to meet this disaster with a heroism and solidarity that amazes me, and our gay writers are responding with works of astonishing courage. I'm thinking of the books coming out in the next nine months, and only the books that I've heard of. By the time this piece is printed Randy Shilts' massive narrative of the AIDS crisis, *And the Band Played On*, will be in every bookstore across the country. Shortly thereafter, *Strategies for Survival* (by Peter Goldblum and Martin Delaney, with Joseph Brewer) will appear, sort of a gay male version of *Our Bodies, Ourselves* written in the context of the AIDS crisis. In the winter comes Paul Monette's extraordinary *Love Alone: Eighteen Elegies for Rog*, a cycle of poems on the death of his lover that is one of the most powerful pieces of writing I have ever read in my life. Adam Mars-Jones and Ed White will present a collection of their stories on AIDS in *The Darker Proof*, and Andrew Holleran will bring out a collection of the extraordinary essays he has been writing for the last few years in *Christopher Street*, entitled *Ground Zero*. Also in winter Lon Nungesser offers a desperately needed self-help book for people facing a terminal diagnosis and their loved ones and friends, *Notes on Living until We Say Goodbye*, as well as a paperback edition of his *Epidemic of Courage*. In the spring I have heard Robert Ferro has a new novel about AIDS coming out and George Whitmore, a book of nonfiction which, word has it, stunned and overwhelmed his editor at New American Library. And Christopher Davis offers a second novel, *Valley of the Shadow*, a story about lovers and AIDS which is both shattering and consoling. And I'm sure there are more books that I haven't heard of yet.

These books are important to all of us.

This is a time of absolute crisis for the gay community. It is a time when we cannot afford to neglect the help our writers are offering us, at God knows what cost to themselves. These are the people who tell the stories, who sing the songs, who remember the battles and who can tell us what is happening to our people and our souls. Not to listen to these voices would be a dreadful mistake and a foolishness beyond comprehension. This is why "culture" was started to begin with and what it has always offered: to recapture through the imagination the reality of our lives. It is the only way we ever know where we are, who we are.

PART 4

Workaday Publishing, or Hegel's Ernst

1985–1988

Way back in the early Seventies, one Sunday morning around dawn, I found myself at the little lunch counter in the St. Mark's Baths on East 8th Street having a hamburger and getting involved in an intense conversation with Vito Russo, who worked there as a towel boy and short-order cook. We'd been discussing the problem of leadership, which had so bedeviled the Gay Liberation Front and then the Gay Activists Alliance (as well as so many activist groups of the Sixties). But rather than relying on leadership and organizations, we concluded that the gay movement would only be successful if there was a spontaneous assumption of responsibility by individual gay people in every walk of life, in every profession, in every state and city and town— spontaneous, freely chosen, decentralized and autonomous.

"Look," said Vito, "it'll only work if we each do our part. I'll research homophobia in films, in Hollywood,[1] Arthur [Bell] does what he can as a columnist at the *Village Voice*, Barbara Gittings takes care of the librarians, Chuck Silverstein is working on the psychiatric profession, Chuck Ortleb is hell-bent on getting a literary magazine going. This is what will make the gay revolution: the spontaneous assumption

---

1 Which ultimately became *The Celluloid Closet: Homosexuality in the Movies* (New York: Harper and Row, 1981), now a revered classic in gay studies.

of responsibility by individual gays and lesbians working in their own backyards. Which takes advantage of the fact that, as the slogan says, we are everywhere and we are everybody."

It was a conversation that I never forgot, and as the Seventies proceeded it seemed to me that was precisely what was happening—individuals in their own corner of society spontaneously taking on the responsibility of asserting gay rights, working in their own sphere but in parallel to so many others. And gradually we would get to know one another and a sort of loose network arose. For me, besides *Christopher Street* magazine, the normalization of gay writing in mainstream publishing seemed like a reasonable task to take on. I remember John Preston interviewing me for *The Advocate*, in 1977 I think, where I laid out my plans and suggested it would take five or six years. Well, it actually took about twenty, but aside from the time factor my analysis was pretty good.

Further Down the Road

THIS WAS THE introduction to the second volume of fiction from *Christopher Street*, *First Love/Last Love*, published in 1985.[1] A full decade had passed since the magazine had been launched and it seemed like a good time to take stock, to consider how far we had come.

The publication of a second volume of fiction from *Christopher Street* magazine seems to me a significant occasion. It marks another point in the development of gay writing, the promotion of which was the main reason *Christopher Street* was established. Back in 1974–1975, when Charles Ortleb began talking with people about founding a magazine, we were all caught up in the excitement and turmoil of transforming our lives, confused yet exhilarated at the astonishing prospect of creating new ways of living as gay people, ways we hadn't even been able to imagine a few years earlier. The great surge of communal energy released by Stonewall was opening all sorts of spaces in the society where we could unbend, stretch out, and breathe. In our social lives we had started to undo the damage caused by years of being forced to live in the closet. Yet our minds and imaginations were still bound by the mental constraints of the larger society, for we naturally still saw the world and ourselves through the spectacles of the dominant—and dominating—straight society.

Many years ago feminists began exploring the concept of the "male-identified" woman. This notion was very useful in pointing out the subtle and insidious ways in which a dominating culture co-opts even the imaginations of those who are dominated. Other groups—women, Blacks, the colonized—had already recognized the danger: if you see

1 *First Love/Last Love: New Fiction from Christopher Street*, ed. Michael Denneny, Charles Ortleb, and Thomas Steele (New York: G. P. Putnam's Sons, 1985).

the world through the eyes of your enemy, the fight is over before it's begun. What is at stake in these struggles is always the right to exist as yourself—the right to declare the reality of your own experience rather than having it defined by others. For some reason still obscure to me, this society has tried desperately to make homosexuals, as well as Blacks, "invisible." The earliest laws against our "offense" refused even to *name* the crime and commonly spoke of a "grave and heinous sin whose name is not spoken among decent people." The peculiar stubbornness of this refusal to accept our homosexuality as real constantly surfaces when we are told it is only a phase, a deviation from the natural and normal scheme of things, an arrested level of personal growth, or a sickness. In other words, homosexuality doesn't really exist in itself, the argument always goes, it is a distorted form of something else, a privative (and deprived) form of heterosexuality. While this may have been true for some sailors now and again, we knew from the reality of our own lives that this talk was baloney, that these "explanations" were really attacks on our right to exist. So while heterosexuals went around busily doing things like changing the pronouns in Michelangelo's love sonnets from "he" to "she," we homosexuals searched furiously through the cultural record for any sign of our existence, even if we could only find it in the back pages of *Esquire* magazine in those tiny but wonderful advertisements for Parr of Arizona and Ah, Men Swimwear. Ah, men, indeed, we would sigh with relief. Somewhere out there were others like us.[2]

I think all the people Charles Ortleb mobilized to establish the magazine agreed on this: We wanted, we *needed*, to see our lives reflected in the books and magazines we read. We wanted to see ourselves and not some caricature in the mirror that culture holds up to life. And this is important. We can recognize reality only in our imagination, for the

---

2 I suspect young gay readers of today who have grown up in an environment suffused with gay images and characters will have no comprehension of how arid the pre-Stonewall culture was in this area. There was almost no indication anywhere you looked in the common (above ground) culture that gay people even existed, which resulted in the emotional experience of wondering whether you were the only one and the enormous thirst to find others like oneself. This has got to be the most radical change in the gay condition.

imagination, as Spinoza once noted, is the mental faculty by which things become real to us. It was the reality of our own lives we were seeking, the reality that had been so long and so perversely denied us. So it seemed like a good idea to start a gay literary magazine, a useful piece of the work to contribute to the ongoing endeavor so many were engaged in to recreate our lives and our world.

We probably all assumed that if we could establish the magazine and clear a public space for serious gay writing, then the material would come flowing in, all those gay stories and poems and essays that writers had left in the bottom of their desk drawers because there was no place to publish them. As it turned out, this was not quite the case.

After having launched the magazine fairly recklessly with an obvious homage to *The New Yorker* in style and format—after all, you might as well make your intentions and ambitions crystal clear—we occasionally found ourselves embarrassed at the paucity of riches we had to lay before the public. As Ethan Mordden indicates in his short story, "Interview with the Drag Queen," the fact that there was no place to publish such a story too often led to its not having been written. It turned out that there wasn't all this unpublished material lying around; there was all this *unwritten* material lying around, which is quite another problem. Our Mr. Steele often found himself echoing the earlier Mr. Steele (of *The Spectator* and *The Tatler*), who, in danger of running out of material at one point, warned his audience that unless they contributed to the journal, it would have to close. And our writers—as well as our art director, copy editors, production people, and just about anybody else connected to the office—rose mightily to the occasion. In one issue Ed White wrote four pieces under as many different names to help us out in a pinch.

Often the magazine went through lean times, barely surviving as a financial entity. Only the iron will and apparently inexhaustible energy of Charles Ortleb and the extraordinary support of a large and open-ended group of writers allowed this magazine to survive. And in turn the magazine began to fulfill its basic function of nurturing and supporting gay writing. A quick glance over the list of books that, in one way or another, originated in *Christopher Street* is instructive. It would include:

Alienated Affections by Seymour Kleinberg
Who Was That Masked Woman? by Noretta Koertge
Lovers: The Story of Two Men by Michael Denneny
Setting the Tone by Ned Rorem
The Movie Lover by Richard Friedel
States of Desire by Edmund White
The Mayor of Castro Street by Randy Shilts
The Confessions of Danny Slocum by George Whitmore
Modern Love by Roz Chast
Jailbait by Brad Gooch
Entre Nous by Tim Dlugos
I've a Feeling We're Not in Kansas Anymore by Ethan Mordden
Male Fantasies/Gay Realities by George Stambolian
The Wit and Wisdom of Quentin Crisp by Quentin Crisp
Cruising the Movies by Boyd McDonald

There are perhaps a half-dozen more currently in the works, and it seems to me that most if not all of these books would never have been written if *Christopher Street* magazine had not existed.

In addition, of course, the magazine has offered a forum for already established writers. It has also excerpted and celebrated the best gay fiction and nonfiction being published by both mainstream and gay publishing houses. I can testify from my own experience in publishing that this has had the subtle but quite beneficial effect of legitimizing the publication of gay books. What once seemed daring has now, on the whole, become almost routine business, which is all to the good.

Christopher Street is now ten years old—a truly startling fact to those of us who have been involved in it since the beginning. Under the leadership of Charles Ortleb and the editorial direction of Tom Steele, it has survived its first decade and I think fulfilled the promise made in its first issue. Of course, we were not immediately the magazine we set out to be, but a look at any current issue should convince the skeptical that *Christopher Street* has indeed become the magazine it originally promised its readers. And gay fiction, the very notion of which seemed dubious to some (who oddly seldom had the same doubts about the validity of Black or Jewish fiction), seems firmly established. This should be a cause for great satisfaction, even celebration, for without our storytellers and poets we would never be able to recognize ourselves and regain through the realm of the imagination the reality of our lives, which is the great gift all culture, including gay culture, offers to those who participate in it.

The Universal Voice of Gay Writers

BY 1987 THE number of gay books appearing had increased mightily. So much so that I was able to launch a trade paperback line at St. Martin's Press devoted entirely to gay fiction and nonfiction. On that occasion Daisy Maryles, an editor at *Publishers Weekly*, the book industry's trade journal, invited me to write a "My Say" column to explain the move.[1] They changed my original title, "Stonewall Inn Editions," perhaps because it sounded like an advertisement and cut it a little (but not badly); here is the original. For the reader of this book it contains a bit of repetition, but I was talking to a different audience here, people professionally involved in the book industry who would mostly be straight and I thought these points needed to be made.

Today an extraordinary ferment among gay writers is bringing forth a body of literature that seeks, in both fiction and non-fiction, to map the new world of gay life. In so doing, gay writers are both articulating and responding to the larger social movement that has brought a new community into existence, for it is the function of writers to be the consciousness of society. Eighteen years after the riot at the Stonewall Inn, anticipated by nobody yet immediately recognized as a decisive act that would change the lives of gay people everywhere, the surge of social energy unleashed by that event continues to gain momentum: gay communities have sprung up in major cities and even in small towns, gay newspapers, magazines, and theaters proliferate, gay business groups, choruses, marching bands, softball leagues, and community centers are emerging across the land. Even the AIDS epidemic, rather than destroying this movement, has been met by a dramatic mobilization of the whole community, which has in the last few

1 *Publishers Weekly*, July 3, 1987, p. 48.

years created almost three hundred organizations dedicated to fighting the epidemic and helping those afflicted. It is clear that since the Stonewall Riot in June 1969 a new gay community has come into existence and continues to grow in spite of all adversity.

From the beginning, gay writers have been in the forefront of this shared effort to forge a new identity for gay people. Our novelists and poets, historians and essayists have sought to reflect the new realities of gay life and explore the conundrums of the emerging gay identity. In the Seventies, self-declared gay writers were a small band of explorers, a loose-knit group, mostly friends, who took the risks of being cultural pioneers. In the Eighties we are seeing a second generation of gay authors—novelists and poets and philosophers, anthropologists and historians and political commentators—who constitute a cultural movement that matches and reflects the emergence of this new community.

Why literary and cultural movements happen at a certain point in history remains a mystery, an enigma based on the deep symbiosis between the individual act of writing and the public consciousness of a community. The emergence of urban male Jewish writers to such prominence in this country after the Second World War, which I think could not have been predicted by anyone, not only enriched the Jewish community but contributed mightily to broadening American literature and reinvigorating the literary world. Similarly, the remarkable renaissance of superb work by Black women writers that began some fifteen years ago—a literary movement which, it seems to me, has still not received the recognition it is due—continues to enrich American culture and nourish the spirit of readers of all races.

It is to be hoped that the dramatic surge in creativity among gay writers will likewise enrich American culture in general, even as it reflects the aspirations of this new community to see its life and innermost soul reflected in works of art. People *need* writers, which is why this whole culture business got started in the first place. Writers offer us the images and stories that reflect our lives; they hold up the mirror which shows us who we are and make us question the lives we are living. And gay people need gay writers, for without our storytellers and poets we would never be able to recognize ourselves and regain through the realm of the imagination the reality of our lives, which is the great gift all culture, including gay culture, offers to those who participate in it.

Unfortunately, there is a tendency today to think that gay writing is only relevant to gay people. And some critics are even dubious about the very concept of gay fiction, though oddly they seldom have the same doubts about the validity of Black or Jewish fiction, which leads me to think that this line of argument is only a fig-leaf for prejudice. If the history of literary culture teaches us anything, it is that only the most intensely particularized works of art ever achieve universal stature. Dostoevsky is as intensely Russian as Sophocles is intensely Greek or Synge intensely Irish. And if people who are not Russians or Ancient Greeks or Irish can enjoy and benefit immensely from reading these works, I'm suspicious of readers, and especially reviewers, who turn away from gay books in despair at their "parochialism." I have a lot more in common with a straight man in this society than either of us has with Sophocles. And as far as I know, no one is complaining about parochialism in John Updike's novels about middle-class Connecticut white people.

I would think that this is a fairly elementary point, but evidently it is not understood by most reviewers in this country. Gay writing has survived years of malign neglect, tendentious interpretation and barely veiled scorn and hostility at the hands of straight reviewers and critics who have done their best to convince themselves *and us* that these books are marginal, of only parochial interest, and not worthy of being included in the great mainstream of our literary culture. At times this reaches the point of silliness, as when the reviewer for the daily *New York Times*, discussing David Leavitt's *The Lost Language of Cranes*, complained that "Rose, the mother, is dismissed from the scene along with the rest of the straight world, which in any case is under-represented— another shortcoming." *Which in any case is under-represented?* Bet you didn't know we now have a quota system for straights in gay novels, did you? How do you think this man would respond to the works of Isaac Bashevis Singer? Would he criticize Toni Morrison's *The Bluest Eye* because the white world is under-represented? But even this absurdity was topped by the *Sunday Times* review of the same book:

"A strange Oedipal tale, in any case," admits this reviewer, "with Oedipus and Laius going off to do their male bonding while Jocasta is left in the cold." More strange than the *original* Oedipus tale, one wonders? Does this man remember what the original Oedipus story is all about, or do straight men really not think it strange to murder their father and have sex and children with their mother?

But there is no end to complaining about reviewers and no doubt I'm overly sensitive, as my colleagues sometimes tell me. "You would be too," I say, "if they made similar cracks about Jewish writers. And everybody would be appalled if reviewers talked that way about Black writers." Fortunately, in my experience the publishing industry is not beset by these inane prejudices. From editors to salespeople to bookstores, our industry has, on the whole, welcomed gay writers and their books, which is a good thing. For if we ever want to build a truly decent and pluralistic culture, it means welcoming people who are different, not only letting them be different but rejoicing in that difference and in the unique visions that difference brings. As a white person, I owe an incalculable debt to Black writers and musicians, who have expanded my world and shared with me the treasures of *their* culture. And if the books of Alice Walker and Ntozake Shange, Philip Roth and Saul Bellow hold riches for all of us, so too do the works of Andrew Holleran and Edmund White and the whole generation of young gay writers who are now appearing.

A Conversation with Allen Barnett

ALLEN BARNETT, A young writer who became a close friend and eventually one of my authors, absolutely loved conversation about publishing and literature, especially gay literature. Since he lived in the neighborhood he often came over for dinner and conversation, or at least gossip. One night in 1989 he wanted to tape a conversation about the new Stonewall Inn line, so he could use parts of it in an article he was doing for *The Advocate*.[1] Later he gave me the original transcript. I've edited it down somewhat and polished our language a bit.

Stonewall Inn Editions, why now?

I got tired of publishing gay books and selling the paperback rights to NAL (New American Library). I had actually tried gay trade paperbacks nine or ten years ago when I first came to St. Martin's. We published three novels—*Special Teachers/Special Boys, A Queer Kind of Death*, and *David at Olivet*—at $4.95 in trade paperback. That experiment was a failure in that they didn't sell enough copies for me to make a reasonable argument for continuing that kind of publishing to the gay audience. So I switched to cloth.

The experiment ten years ago might have been premature.

Yes, for sure. Then trade paperbacks went for $4.95, today they are $7.95 and $8.95. But, more importantly, the mistake was publishing them originally in trade paperback. Now I publish first in cloth and even if I only sell three thousand copies I make a certain amount of income. Three thousand copies is basically the breakeven point at St. Martin's. At that point I've usually amortized all the costs, so I can bring out a paperback without having to typeset it again and there's nowhere near the amount of overhead, so it becomes much more prof-

1 *The Advocate*, September 15, 1987.

itable. By publishing first in cloth and then in trade paperback and putting the figures together on both, it becomes economically a much different picture. It doesn't make vast profits, as some people think, but it *is* viable—it makes a neat little profit (and there's almost no risk of loss—which is important to your bottom line). And basically NAL paved the way by proving it, giving me sales figures for the paperbacks.

Also, there are more gay books available now, for NAL and for you. If you were talking about starting up a gay trade paperback line ten years ago, that was just the beginning, the emergence of the new gay writing.

(Laughing.) You're right, that's the other big difference. At a certain point, the second generation of gay writers started coming along who weren't there in 1976 and 1977. So I guess I jumped the gun.

We didn't have Dancer from the Dance *until 1978, and* Faggots *came out the same year.*

And *Nocturnes for the King of Naples* and *Taking Care of Mrs. Carroll* and *The Lure*—all in the same year. And five or six years later you saw the emergence of more gay writers. There seems to be two generations of gay writers; there is the generation of the Seventies, mostly from the Violet Quill Club—Ed White, Felice Picano, Robert Ferro, Andrew Holleran, Michael Grumley—plus Paul Monette and Larry Kramer, and for almost a decade when you spoke of gay writers that is who you were referring to. That didn't change for quite a few years. We weren't seeing that many new writers coming up. Then, at a certain point, there was a second generation—John Fox, Ethan Mordden, David Leavitt and so on—I'm not going to name all of them, there were just many more gay authors.

Plus, when I had started up the original gay trade paperbacks, there were only eight or nine gay bookstores. There are now nineteen. If that doubles, you could make gay publishing profitable without any other kind of stores—I wouldn't need the straight stores. One could serve that part of the market quite viably as a major house. And the increase in bookstores means there are more people supporting the bookstores by buying the books, people who weren't there ten years ago. I think that in the last ten years we have been engaged in building an audience, and at this time the writers are ahead of the audience, which puts a cramp in the writer's income, which is unfortunate. But I think that the audience is coming into existence—in a way the writers are calling it into existence—and it is expanding and that is the base that makes the whole thing possible.

It seems to me there's a different attitude in buying paperbacks than in the past. They're more beautifully designed today, given prominent space in bookstores and original fiction in paperback is given equal weight by the reviewers.

Not really. There may be a few exceptions like *Bright Lights, Big City*, but I don't think the review media treats original trade paperbacks on a par with cloth books.

What about the Vintage Contemporary Authors series?

We'll see how far that goes. That was the exception. But now that everybody has a trade paperback line, we'll see. This has been the complaint since the early Seventies: that trade paperbacks are not given the review space that cloth books are. I don't think that has really changed. I think that Vintage Contemporaries had an edge when they were the only one, but there are now eight lines like that.

Basically, there are three avenues of publishing today: there's the cloth book which is now $17.95 to $19.95; there's the trade paperback at $6.95 to $9.95; and there's the mass market at $3.95 to $4.95—three tiers of publishing, which makes sense to me. Certain books will do better in one than the other, but I think it will be difficult to publish gay books originally only in trade paperback. If you're getting that much less of a cover price, you have to sell many more copies.

That seems to be the case with the Men on Men *series. George (Stambolian) couldn't do a second volume until he sold 20,000 copies, which really seems high to me.*

It would be highly unlikely that you could put out a first novel and expect to sell twenty thousand copies, be it a straight or a gay novel. It would be phenomenal to sell 20,000 copies of a straight first novel, be it in cloth or trade paper. It may happen, but that will be the rare exception. So, if you want to publish a greater number of authors you're going to have to do it selling smaller quantities of each title. I'm interested in being able to publish more authors and to publish these authors successfully. Which I do if I sell four to five thousand in cloth and 8- to 10,000 in trade paper.

Not only are you going to be able to sell more books, you're also going to be able to sell more authors.

Yes, and that has to do with overhead and other things. At most publishing houses today, if you publish a novel, you have to say that it will sell 7,500 copies. Now for a first novel that is almost never true, so you lie. You know it won't sell 7,500 copies, they know it won't, you know they know it won't, and they know you know they know it won't. The result is self-censorship. You bring out one first novel a year.

At St. Martin's we have—for a number of technical reasons, a different overhead structure, a different way of doing things—for instance if you print four books with a 5,000 copy print run at the same time, you get the unit cost you would printing 20,000 copies, which is very helpful, and they only have to be the same size and ready at the same time. So we can publish books successfully that sell 3,500 to 4,000 copies. That's not a raging success, not a windfall profit, but that's what we do with the mysteries and it turns out to be a profitable little thing, with, as I said, very little downside risk.

And that's one reason I stay at St. Martin's—if I were at another house, I would be publishing gay books on sufferance. Once a year I could publish a gay novel and we would all pretend that it would sell 7,500 copies, when it actually sold 3,500 copies, and that would limit me to one a year, and they would put up with it as long as I was making money on the other books I published. (That's the tactic certain other gay editors have taken at other houses.) I like St. Martin's because we can make things work with smaller unit numbers, and that means more editorial freedom in what you can publish. St. Martin's not only publishes more gay books than anybody else, we publish something like 38% of all the first novels published in America.

Which is why all young writers like St. Martin's so much.

It's because we can do this, and I think the more people you can get published, the better the literary culture will be. That's one reason I like the company.

You've been at St. Martin's fifteen years?

Eleven. I'm a stick in the mud. I've only worked for two companies in New York: Macmillan for five years and St. Martin's for eleven. I don't understand all this moving around because you lose about a year—at least!—when you move to another house. Each house is different. It's like a machine, you have to learn how it works, what it can do well. It's never been quite clear to me why, but different houses can publish different types of books successfully. The things I was doing quite successfully at Macmillan didn't work at St. Martin's, and I had to adjust to St. Martin's and St. Martin's had to adjust to me. I had to find things that I wanted to publish and things that they could publish successfully. Each time you change houses, you have to retread. And you have to nudge and push the social machine to make it do the types of things you want it to do. Right now at St. Martin's I have a sales force that is so gung-ho for gay books that they go out like crusaders. If there was homophobia in the company ten years ago, there isn't now. They are a very well informed company. They know all the gay buyers, all the gay bookstores. If I were to go to another company, I would lose all those years of educating the company and the sales force to the gay market. I have an odd situation where I am at a straight house that knows a great deal about gay literature and gay publishing and gay bookselling because we have done it consistently for a decade now. If I went to another house it would take years to have an impact on the company such that they would do as good a job.

Did you go to them with a proposal for this line? Did you say to them, listen, NAL is publishing all my books, can't we do it ourselves?

Yes, and the figures were very convincing. It was silly to sell *The Boys on the Rock* to NAL and let them make a small fortune on the paperback when we had taken the risk of publishing a first novel—they used our typesetting, they used the reviews we got for the cloth edition. It just seemed foolish to do all the work, take all the risk, and just hand it over to some reprinter who had a much easier job publishing it in trade paper, which is much more profitable than publishing the original in cloth. I argued we should do both together.

You're taking some of Plume's authors away from them.

I hope. But Plume will still be there. They have a different sort of editorial profile than I do. We'll compete for some books and for some we won't. It strengthens me that there is another major publishing house publishing gay books systematically in trade paperback. It's much better for me that I'm not the only person doing it. It's much better for me that Knopf is going to be publishing Ed White. That Morrow publishes Andrew Holleran. If St. Martin's were the only house publishing serious gay books we would not be in such a good situation. I don't want to beat the competition. I want more people to publish more gay books. That can only help me in the long run. Of course, I think that I will publish the best ones, or that's the game we play.

St. Martin's has had a long commitment to gay books and has really put themselves behind you.

Yes, the president, Tom McCormack, is a remarkable man. When I went for my first interview I made it real clear that I had published one gay book in five years at Macmillan and that that was a huge struggle. I wanted to make it clear when I went around for interviews so that everyone would know: I wanted to publish gay books. If it didn't work out, fine, it didn't work, but I wanted a couple of years backing to see if we couldn't publish these authors for these readers, so it was an explicit discussion before I was hired. And Tom has always backed me, for eleven years now, sometimes dubiously, but he's kept to that commitment. We have now published or signed up eleven books on AIDS.

Who wants to read that many books on AIDS?

You will.[2]

We've talked about institutionalizing gay publishing . . .

In terms of that I think it's real important that there be specialized gay presses around. Publishing is like an ecological system, there are lots of different niches. It's helpful to me that Sasha Alyson is there, and hopefully it's helpful to him that I'm in a mainstream house. But I think it would be a mistake if all gay books were published only in gay houses. We wouldn't be using the organs of society to serve our community, and I don't see why we shouldn't. But at the same time, that doesn't mean it isn't important for there to be gay houses around. For one thing, they are able to do even smaller print runs than I can. They are able to do gay poetry much easier than I can—it can be economically viable because their overhead is so small.

You know, in the mid-Seventies I used to go to these panel discus-

---

2 Allen Barnett, of course, became the author of *The Body and Its Dangers* (1990), one of the most powerful works of fiction to address AIDS.

sions on gay publishing and I was the only person from a mainstream house and I would get a lot of political flak about that, but I thought we had the right to be in the mainstream houses as well as having presses of our own.

And the gay presses will always do things you couldn't do yourself.

What I can't publish is the erotica. Boyd's [McDonald] collections have probably kept more gay bookstores afloat than any other author. And I don't think I could have published the genre novels.

Why did you call the new paperback line Stonewall Inn Editions? That means something to me that it's not going to mean to most straight readers. Isn't that pigeon-holing, ghettoizing gay books?

We had the same argument about *Christopher Street* magazine—people thought we would be ghettoizing. As a name, I thought Stonewall Inn would work a lot like Christopher Street—a signal to gay people that straight people would not necessarily pick up on.

Stonewall Inn makes it sound like Random House.

OK with me. On the subject of pigeon-holing, I think it's odd that so many writers are worried about it. There's a parallel to this: in the early nineteenth century in America, there was a big controversy over whether we were going to have an American English literature or an English English literature. It was a division articulated in the 1820s between Washington Irving and John Neal, who was really the first in a line of people like Mark Twain, Herman Melville and Emily Dickinson, these weird, odd American authors. Whereas Washington Irving was another strand of American literature that goes down through Henry James, etc. Anyway, it was the same argument. There were the Americans who felt a cultural inferiority versus these people who had just gotten their independence and wanted to start something new. And the books I most value from the nineteenth century almost all come from the stream that believed in American American literature. And I can't imagine Mark Twain or Walt Whitman saying they did not want to be known as American authors, although clearly there were people at the time who thought it a put-down to be referred to as an American author. That seems to me a literary parallel.

Today I can't imagine any of the Black authors I know—Toni Morrison or Gloria Naylor or Ntozake Shange or Alice Walker—saying they don't want to be known as Black authors. It did come up with some of the Jewish urban male authors after World War II—Saul Bellow, for instance—that they didn't want to be known as Jewish writers, but most of them certainly claimed first and foremost that they were Jewish writers, and then Jewish American writers. This whole idea that you can be sent to the periphery and not be an important part of the mainstream is propaganda from the people who control the organs of culture in this society at the moment and who want to have a culture about white, middle-class, heterosexual men. Isn't that clear by now? I mean, that's who heavily controls the cultural levers in this society. And they want their culture to be the universal culture. I'll say it until I'm blue in the face, but I think the only way that something becomes universal is by being infinitely particular. Sophocles is infinitely Greek, Dostoevsky is infinitely Russian, Synge is infinitely Irish. When our own writers believe that propaganda it is very unfortunate. It means that their minds have been colonized, their imaginations colonized essentially by a dominating culture.

And I should point out that when I publish gay books, they come out in cloth first, where they are in no line whatsoever—so no ghettoizing. It is only in paperback that they come out in a gay library. And I saw this as a paperback library of interest to gay people *and* to straight people. If I have no trouble reading Black novels, I don't see why straight people should have trouble reading gay novels. And any concession to that sort of *New York Times* stance that what is universal happens to be white, middle class, heterosexual and male is, if you are not white, middle class, heterosexual and male, a treason to the self. Women have had to fight this out. Black people are still having to fight this out.

I got into publishing gay books in 1975 because I was publishing women's books, quite successfully and enthusiastically, but I never got to read novels that dealt with my own life and that of my friends. At the time I was going to the Pines every summer, which was an extraordinary experience that I thought and talked about a lot, and that was reflected nowhere in the literature available to me, and I wanted that reflection. Culture is a mirror that you hold up to see yourself. Spinoza said that we can only gain in the imagination the reality of our lives. I think that is the nexus of culture. It is only when you see in a story the reality of your life that you really are given it back, that you have realized what has happened. This has been the engine driving culture all along. People are not marginalizing the work of Black women writers anymore, saying that this is only, or merely, a Black book. They did say that some years ago, but it has been knocked out of them. And we have to knock it out of them in reference to gay books.

Why is it that when we talk about drawing on gay particulars to get to the universal—and all gay writers do it—that this is a problem?

It's a problem because the label gay, meaning "merely gay," is put on it by the dominant culture. And yes, it's an offensive label, as it would be offensive to say merely Jewish, or merely Black, in a diminishing sense, as if the reality of these people's lives is not as interesting as the reality of middle-class white people's lives in Connecticut. This is an insult from the people who are in control of the organs of the culture at a given time. Gay writers have a legitimate fear that they will be marginalized by critics calling it merely gay fiction. But I really think that's changing. A lot of my straight friends are asking for gay fiction; a lot of my straight authors are reading gay fiction.

That did not happen five years ago. I think we are going through the same process that women went through, and Black women certainly went through. And I think that we are going to win. We'd better win if we want a pluralistic culture. We live in a pluralistic society and should have a pluralist culture. The uniform white middle-class culture of the Fifties seemed to me a disaster and gave nourishment to nobody.

But in my experience . . . for instance, a story I am working on now is coming from anger at heterosexuals and I don't want it published in a gay publication but in The Atlantic *or* The New Yorker *because I want them to hear me.*[3]

I can understand that. But when I write I am much more interested in gay people hearing me. I think that gay people need to hear gay writers much more. Of course, I hope that that will be a benefit to straight people, too. I think that Shange or Morrison write primarily for a Black

3 And indeed, they did hear him. St. Martin's got two stories from Alan's *The Body and Its Dangers*, first serialized in *The New Yorker*.

audience, which doesn't mean that the rest of us can't enjoy those books immensely and benefit from them. But those authors are writing for their community. I think that that's the great advantage that gay writers have, and Black writers have, that there is a community and that there is a felt sense of community and that the literature *matters*. Publishing a first novel from one of my straight authors is like dropping a rose petal into the Grand Canyon and waiting to hear an echo. You're publishing one of the 2,000 first novels published in 1987. The chances of being heard and developing a readership I think are much *greater* for a gay person today. And that's a huge advantage. I think culture and writing are stimulated by and inextricably involved in the larger community, and one of the problems in mainstream literature in America today is that there isn't a national community. I have talked to non-gay authors again and again and this is always their problem. They *envy* gay authors for having a community out there, that their books matter to people's lives, that something else is being judged other than aesthetic perfection, which always ends in sterile academicism.

I remember once seeing a young Black girl carrying The Bluest Eye, *a book I liked immensely, although it seemed more important that she read the book than I.*

It would matter to her and her life and her spirit in a way that it would never matter to you. For you, it would be an aesthetic product as opposed to a product of the living culture.

It seems to me right now that gay writers have the chance of making a real cultural movement precisely because the community needs them. You have an opportunity when writing is important to people's lives, their sanity, their values, to what they have to get through daily. And the option of cultural products having meaning rather than being simply commodities in an aesthetic, or an academic, or a commercial system, is a great benefit to any art. It means that an art can be real. Painters don't paint for collectors or academic specialists, although a system has evolved that makes it seem that way, which must be a source of despair for painters.

What I see coming in response to the AIDS epidemic, whether it's Paul Monette's poem cycle or Chris Davis' new novel, I think these will be works of art that will get people through the night. I think these books will be vitally important to get you through the weekend, through the next funeral.

And it's remarkably fast. The last national crisis was the Vietnam War, where an entire generation was affected by it. But you didn't start getting a lot of books for fifteen years. Yet our writers are responding almost immediately. Which means that writers can be important in a way that they seldom can be important, the way that the underground writing since the Russian Revolution will be one of the great literatures of the twentieth century. It's very unusual that writing can be such a vital part of the ongoing life of the community. I think that's why we may see an extraordinary renaissance of gay writing, and if I'm right about that it's because of this odd and terrible situation. It's one of the few times that literature can carry a national soul, or the soul of the community. It's why people started telling stories and having culture to begin with, before it got into such an elaborate system that the point often gets lost.

There's a lot more to say about AIDS. It will have an impact on every aspect of our life—psychological, social, ethical, legal. It offers a fertile and diverse opportunity for writing.

It's going to change everything. It *has* changed everything. And that includes who we think we are as gay people. The future of any such thing as gay identity, and the obverse side of that coin, gay culture, is up for grabs now, and will be determined partly on how our writers respond and partly on how the community responds. I mean, they are sort of separate factors. From what I am seeing, I think that the writers are rising to the occasion. Once again, the writers are rising before the audience, but that's okay as long as the audience gathers around.

I think that there is an incredible task and burden on gay writers today, and an incredible opportunity. There is a great crisis that the gay community is experiencing, there is a crisis in the soul and the spirit today. And how our future history gets shaped is going to be determined by how the community is responding now; and how the community responds will depend heavily on how the writers respond. I think it's an enormous opportunity for producing an astonishing literature.

AIDS is becoming for the gay community, unfortunately—and I possibly could be wrong, and I hope I am wrong—but at the moment

I think that AIDS is an event that is going to have an impact on the gay community and gay culture that the Holocaust had on the Jewish community and Jewish culture. The event and how we respond to the event is going to define who and what we are. Even whether we continue to exist.

Now you're making a distinction between an aesthetic and social revolution?

It's both. The enormous heroism that you are seeing now in everyday life, with people doing things . . . you would have to go back to London during the Blitz, or Walt Whitman in the hospitals during the Civil War, this type of daily heroism, of the whole community, is going to have an enormous impact. If it were just the writers, it would be a different thing. I think that the gay community is responding extraordinarily to the enormous challenge that history is facing us with right now, and what I see is that the writers are responding as well. It is not a happy occasion, but it is not the happy occasions that give birth to the greatest literature or to the noblest moments of human history.

How do you think the AIDS crisis is making it possible for the New York Times *to treat us with more dignity, and publishing houses to do more of our books?*

Paradoxically, I believe that AIDS has established the "ethnicity," as it were, of the gay community more than anything else. I remember in the Seventies when Dennis Altman was arguing that we were not a minority group the way Blacks are a minority group. You could take that argument seriously, for a short time. But it seems to me that argument has now become totally moot, that whatever is going to happen in terms of the spread of AIDS to the heterosexual population, the way it crashed first into the gay community—still only two percent of the people diagnosed today are from the "general population," it is a minority disease, at least the first five years of it—aside from what we know in Africa—it is hitting the gay community. Oddly enough it has legitimized the whole idea that we are a minority group, like Black Americans. The combination of that and the response of the gay community to this crisis is something I don't think that most good-willed Americans can fail to be impressed by. The thing is, this is also happening to the people who are our mothers, our brothers, our co-workers, our nieces and nephews, and they don't want to see their gay relatives and friends and colleagues dying, even if AIDS is going to be contained within the gay community (and a few other subgroups). I don't think I have a single straight sales person who doesn't know someone who has died or is dying of AIDS, and this is amazing because they are scattered all over the country. It has hit everyone.

More gay books are coming out and the books are getting better and better, and yet the state of gay criticism has not kept up with the writing.

Personally, I think the level of gay criticism is appalling. Unbelievably low, and the pettiness! The type of discourse this is bothers me a great deal. It reminds me of the gay talk from the late Sixties in which one might assert that a movie star was gay in such a way that you would be tearing him down. It wasn't that you were proud that he was gay or that you were proud of him, but that you were diminishing him. I find that type of attitude in a whole lot of the gay reviews. I think that Ethan Mordden is right and is one of the few people who has the balls to say it. It is partially because these reviewers are incompetent, and partly because they are young, unpublished and envious. A lot of people don't get paid to write these reviews, so you get smart-alecky 24-year-olds just out to tear down with no sense of what a writer is doing for the community, and often no sense whatsoever of the literary quality of the books.

This recent review by Daniel Harris of Andrew Harvey's *The Web* is an insult. He goes on for three columns trashing the book. "Wiping my butt with (this) book is a fate far more majestic than (it) deserves." This is a string of insults. I'm not making a claim on how good Andrew Harvey's book is, but this review is just an opportunity for this man to vent his spleen and to show off. I am very sorry that *The Native* published it; I think it is exactly the type of critical discourse that we <u>don't</u> need. I think there is a great deal of vicious, petty, backbiting, ill-informed arrogance—the arrogance is really surprising. I mean, this man is *not* a good writer, so from what position does he think he is judging and condemning Andrew Harvey's work? It is not illuminating, it is not useful. I don't know what type of writing he thinks this is. It's nothing but opinion holding.

What's really disturbing is that it's coming to the point that I am getting better reviews in the straight press than in the gay press. Whereas years ago it was an uphill fight, now we are winning some sort of respect. Even the *New York Times* has reviewed every piece of fiction I've published in the last two years. The books may not always get the respect that they deserve, but we're making progress there. It bothers me that we are not seeing this progress in the gay press. I don't know what to do about it. [George] Stambolian has been yelling about it, Ethan [Mordden] has been yelling. But I don't know if it does any good.

I think we have to set standards and that the major writers have got to be doing the reviewing. Of course, that has its own problems too.

I doubt this person knows what writing a review is.

Seems to me that the only reason you could ever give for critical writing—other than daily reviewing, which is just a public notice, really, news—critical writing's only justification is to improve the ambience of talk in which works of art are conceived and in which they are received by the public. Harold Rosenberg articulated that very clearly. Critical writing is not to compete with or replace the work of art, it is to somehow illuminate the space between the viewer or the reader and the work of art. It is to improve the quality of discourse, of the talk that goes on about the art that is being created. One can thereby perhaps improve the quality of the art that is being created, and one can certainly improve the quality of reception and attention that that art is given by its appropriate audience.

For some of these reviewers it's as if the enemy is the gay writer who has had a book published. And this is wrong. The act of writing any book is, in the final analysis, an act of generosity, the impulse is to share, that's what all artists have in common. There is something inherently communal about art—it is private, but the impulse to write is an impulse to share, and never deserves this kind of reception that you see in Harris' review.

How to Review a Gay Novel

THIS PIECE EXISTS as only a few pages from a legal pad, handwritten and undated. Handwritten obviously in a fit of pique, and thankfully never published. Perhaps it was just a private koan to calm my nerves. Such were the irritations.

The following pearls of wisdom are offered in the hope that the burgeoning number of people who now review gay novels will memorize them. It couldn't hurt.

Pearl # 1 Novels do not tell you how to live — Mildred Newman and Bernard Berkowitz do.

Only gay reviewers and bookish adolescents with over-heated imaginations make the mistake of thinking that Dostoevsky or John Rechy or Andrew Holleran are presenting life models for emulation. Gay reviewers looking for spiritual guidance should be directed to the appallingly vast section of psychological, interpersonal, and spiritual self-help books to be found in any large bookstore.

Perhaps gay reviewers would find the following mantra useful: You do not read gay novels to learn how to make quiche.

You do not read gay novels to learn how to acquire, keep, or train a lover.

You do not read gay novels to learn how you ought to be gay.

If gay reviewers do not know precisely *why* they read gay novels, perhaps they should stop reviewing them.

Pearl # 2 New York is a place, not an idea. To which one might add: nor a conspiracy, movement, school, or clique.

It has occasionally been noticed by literary historians that a sense of place will sometimes inform a writer's work. Usually the place where s/he lives. Maybe half the authors in the U.S. live in or around New York City. It follows that maybe half of the gay writers in the U.S. live in or around New York City.

A disproportionate number of novels published in America are set in or around New York; a disproportionate number of gay novels now being published are set in and around New York City. This is undoubtedly unfair in some vague sense. What about Toledo? What about a proportionate number of gay novels set in Toledo? Certainly we can all agree with Richard Hall that California with its vast wealth, power, and population *deserves* more gay novels.

Perhaps President Carter's famous statement should be amended to read: culture is unfair.

Pearl #3 The reason more good gay novels set in Toledo are not being published is because they are not being written.

I can say no more.

Pearl #4 A book is a generous act, however misguided.

Corollary: Book reviews are often not. Unfortunate, but true.

Chasing the Crossover Audience and Other Self-Defeating Strategies

---

AS GAY NOVELS began to have a bit of success, new issues arose to bedevil us all. It turns out that success might create as many problems for gay writers as being ignored or shunted aside. I was attempting to think through one of these problems in this talk, originally delivered at the Second Annual Conference of the Lesbian and Gay Studies Center at Yale, "Pedagogy and Politics/1988," held on October 28–30, and published in the Winter 1989 issue of *Outlook*.

The production of any writing necessarily takes place within a cultural and social context. Language is peculiarly and primarily a social fact, rooted in one of the most elemental aspects of the human condition: plurality. If only one person existed on the face of the earth, language would never have arisen. Linguistic creation, though an individual act, remains forever inextricably related to the social reality of the community in which it takes place. This guarantees that the act of writing, the decision to publish and disseminate writing, and its evaluation by the critics and ultimate reception by the public (often divergent responses, at least initially) will be permeated and shaped, facilitated or distorted, by the specific social situation and the cultural politics of the moment. It is unwise to ignore these issues of cultural politics, for their influence is utterly pervasive. It is the nature of such issues that they cannot be "solved" once and for all; rather they are like fault lines that articulate the underlying stresses of a given situation and so trace the hidden geography of the cultural moment. But if they cannot be solved, they *can* be thought about; one can strive to reach not an answer but perhaps greater clarity about the issue, and in the process better locate oneself in the contemporary world. And it is always useful to know where one is, for knowing where one is standing often leads to knowing what one stands for and even to the emergence of standards, those banners around which we rally that they may prevail even as they give us direction in this confusion we call life.

The issue I want to discuss is that *fata morgana* of gay writers—and, to a lesser extent, gay agents and editors—the fabled crossover book.[1] Having been one of the founding editors of *Christopher Street*, working today as a book editor deeply involved in the publication of gay writing, and as a gay writer myself, I have had the opportunity of watching a virtual parade of gay writers through the last decade and have followed with interest the changing fortunes of gay books in the marketplace, as well as the changing attitudes and intentions of the writers themselves.

With the recent breakthrough to national visibility in the mainstream media—both *Newsweek* and the *New York Times* have within the last year published several articles about gay writing "reaching the mainstream"—and the critical and commercial success of a (small) number of gay books over the last few years, has come a new and startling ambition by many gay writers, to achieve success with a wider audience. No longer are many of these writers content to seek out a gay audience for their books; increasingly I hear about "the crossover audience" and "the crossover book," the book that will appeal to gay *and* straight audiences alike. Indeed, many of the younger writers resist being categorized as "merely" gay writers, that territory being a "literary ghetto" which they feel unfairly limits both their audience and their income. Considering that only a few years ago it was a struggle just to get a gay book published or to sell enough copies to break even in a commercial sense, this is a notable development, undoubtedly a

---

1 For the purpose of this discussion, I am referring only to gay male writers. None of what I have to say is directly applicable to lesbian writers. Because of the historical connection of gay women to the (non-gay) women's movement, the crossover situation for lesbian writers is completely different, and perhaps more promising. My own impression is that gay women writers—like the remarkable surge of Black women writers—can more easily find an audience for their work among non-gay (or non-Black) women influenced by the feminist movement. There is nothing analogous to this in the situation of gay men.

sign of the enormous and underappreciated distance we have come in a very short time. Still, it raises some new and troublesome issues that can be seen more clearly in the context of our recent history.

In the beginning, that is, in the mid-Seventies when gay authors as we know them began to be published, there was not much, if any, talk about crossover books or crossover audiences. When Edmund White and Andrew Holleran, Larry Kramer and Felice Picano and Paul Monette and others decided to write and publish gay fiction they were taking what was at the time a huge risk that their literary careers would be distorted or derailed, marginalized or altogether aborted by that decision. These people were not under the illusion that the straight world was eagerly waiting to read about our lives. At the time it was quite clear that the straight world would rather not know we even existed, and when they were forced into that awareness their general response was hostility. And this was only to be expected. After all, the mechanism by which this society implemented the oppression of gay people was to extend a blanket of invisibility over most gay life, while simultaneously promoting lurid images of marginal figures—the doomed drag queen, the sick child molester, the pathetic sissy. This cultural manifestation of the dominant social and political power was buttressed by laws that made sodomy illegal, as well as by harassment from organs of the government (such as the Post Office and the House Un-American Activities Committee), and the occasional prosecution and jailing of deviants. However, since it is clear that all these police measures and punishments did *not* in fact stop homosexual activity but only inhibited the assertion of a public gay identity, I think it's equally clear that the major and most effective weapon used against us by this society was the cultural war of enforced silence mixed with false images and derogatory definition. Since this war was carried out by the cultural—and especially the literary—organs of society, it was unlikely that those same organs would suddenly welcome a new literature that attempted to free gay people from the false consciousness fostered by the dominant society—a consciousness consisting of society's hatred of homosexuals internalized into self-hatred. Gays were oppressed by society, but more important, society through the use of its cultural power *got gays to oppress themselves*—not only a neat trick but perhaps the most efficient means of oppression.

What motivated White, Holleran, and the others was not a naïve belief that a straight readership was out there waiting for gay writing, nor the hope that the literary establishment, which had promulgated and reinforced the homophobia of the society for years, would, or even could, give a fair hearing to the new gay writing. What impelled them to jump into the arena of gay writing was the enormous energy that had been released by the Stonewall Riots and that, to our amazement, seemed only to gain momentum in the years that followed. Stonewall was the critical point, the unpremeditated and still somewhat inexplicable event that unleashed a vast reconstitution of gay society: gay bars, baths, bookstores, and restaurants opened, gay softball teams, newspapers, political organizations, and choruses proliferated, gay groups of all sorts popped up, while gay neighborhoods emerged in our larger, and many of our smaller, cities. This was and is a vast social revolution that to my mind has received nowhere near the attention it deserves: a new community came into being in an astonishingly short period of time. The excitement of those days captured the imagination of the writers, while the emergence of the gay community provided the beginning of a public as interested in reading about gay life as the writers were in writing about it. I believe that in the mid-Seventies the first generation of gay writers wrote primarily for a gay readership, and I know that the first generation of gay editors published gay books primarily for gay readers and in the teeth of outright hostility on the part of the literary establishment and indifference if not scorn on the part of the general public.

Time passed, struggles were won, and gradually, grudgingly, the literary establishment ceded some marginal room to gay books. More important by far, a new generation of gay writers emerged by the early Eighties whose talent, diversity, and sheer numbers exceeded our wildest hopes—we are now in the midst of a burst of gay writing such as has never been seen before. And, of course, the social and political situation has changed. The mayor of New York now walks in the Gay Pride Parade, The Gay Men's Chorus performs at Carnegie Hall, Harvey Fierstein charms everybody's mother on television talk shows, and AIDS has made us relentlessly visible to mid-America. As the situation of gay people in this country has changed, so the situation of the gay writer has changed, and almost entirely for the better.

The critical respect and, even limited, commercial success of a few gay writers entirely changed the situation within the publishing industry—the net gain being to normalize the publishing of gay books, that is, books consciously intended for a gay readership.

Whether it was the visible success of these first writers, or whether it was another manifestation of the unfolding cultural energy that has powered this movement since Stonewall, we soon saw a "second generation" of younger gay writers appearing as the Eighties got under way. These writers did not share with their predecessors the initial experience of confronting a homophobic literary culture head on, when it was a victory simply to get a gay novel published or reviewed (no matter how condescendingly) in the mainstream national media. This work had been done, the situation was improved, the issue now was the age-old plaint of any writer: how to make a decent living.

And here arose a problem. A gay book is defined in the publishing industry as a book directed toward a gay readership—the gay public. And while this gay public *is* expanding (for instance, when I started publishing gay books a decade or so ago there were some nine gay bookstores in this country; today there are thirty-two), this market is still limited. For the gay writer trying to earn a decent income, there were two possibilities: the continued growth of the gay public, which would provide more readers, or the chance to sell their books to the more numerous straight audience.

So it is not surprising when one increasingly heard about the crossover audience and the crossover book—from agents and publishing people, but mainly, it must be admitted, from gay writers themselves. More and more I meet or hear of gay writers who bridle at being labeled "gay writers," writers who now wish their books to be marketed to the so-called general public, writers whose ambition is to see their books in the chain stores rather than in their local gay bookstore.

What could possibly be wrong with this, you might wonder—every writer, after all, wants to make as much money from his or her book as possible, that is only reasonable. They do not want to be labeled gay writers or have their books categorized as gay fiction because of commercial considerations. Like all writers, they want to reach a larger public and sell more books. Which seems fair enough at first glance, but I think this position has some implications worth noticing. The premise is that a book will be more successful, a writer will make more money, if the work is not identified as gay. Now, why is this? Because, evidently, the so-called general public and the literary establishment prefer not to buy or read books by explicitly gay authors, books "only" about gay life, books, that, in some sense, *are* gay. And, by and large, I think this is probably true. They don't. It has been true for a good long time now, in fact; there is nothing new in this analysis of the situation. What is new—and to me discouraging—is the idea that instead of *changing* the situation, some members of this second generation believe the best strategy is to avoid the outright identification, the specific and glaring label "gay."

Now, I ask you: what is this except a literary version of the old strategy of "passing," or not calling undue attention to the fact that one is gay. Because to call undue attention to the fact that one is gay is to open oneself to homophobic attack, to insist that one's book is a gay novel is to risk . . . having the public label it a gay novel. And gay novels they don't rush to read. It's the old blanket of silence.

The basic flaw with this strategy is that it would leave the homophobic response intact. It would not change the basic situation. But the basic situation is what must be changed if there is to be anything like a gay literature or a gay culture. These writers believe they can sidestep the issue, that they can ask that their books be judged from an exclusively literary point of view, as if the literary establishment were neutral, somehow above the politics of the larger culture, instead of, in fact, a constituent and active part of the homophobic culture of this society.

Even more to the point: the pursuit of the crossover market means that these gay writers worry more about what straight readers think of their work than about its impact on the emerging gay community. Increasingly it seems that a number of our younger writers are willing to gauge their own literary merit by the standards and judgments of the current literary establishment, that they wish at all costs—and the costs may be considerable—to avoid being described as *merely* gay writers who "only" write about gay life.

To me this seems shortsighted and self-destructive, for homophobia still courses through the structures of this cultural establishment. To believe that the homophobia that reached demented proportions in this country in the Fifties and Sixties could be eradicated in the last twenty years is simply silly. Like racism, homophobia has been endemic in the West for many centuries and like Black people we must face the fact that it will not disappear soon—face the fact, live with the fact, and produce our work and structure our ways of life in the teeth of that fact.

Black authors do not get joy from the fact that they have to do their writing in what remains, both subtly and blatantly, a racist society. But they do it, and often with more grace than anybody has the right to expect. A couple of weeks ago, I watched the almost classically "liberal" Bill Moyers on his television show ask August Wilson, "Don't you ever get tired of writing about the Black experience?" A question of such breathtaking stupidity that even Wilson paused. Would he ask John Updike whether he ever gets tired of writing about the White experience? Would he ask Dostoevsky if he ever got tired of writing about the Russian experience? Would he ask Sophocles whether he ever got tired of writing about the Greek experience?

Just think for a moment about what is really being said here. The implication is that "the Black experience" is somehow limited, is something one could get tired of, is not inexhaustible the way life is. After all, one can't quite imagine even Moyers asking, "Don't you ever get tired of writing about the human experience?" I mean, what else is there to write about? And unfortunately the reason one cannot imagine Moyers asking Updike, "Don't you ever get tired of writing about the White experience?" is that he probably equates "the White experience" with life itself. And this is the crux of the matter, in this case the crux of cultural racism. The idea that somebody's life is of less extent, of smaller consequence, carries less weight, is at the heart of racism, or, in our case, of homophobia. Black writers have much practice dealing with this type of idiocy. Listen, for instance, to Toni Morrison in an article last year in the *New York Times*:

> Ms. Morrison said that unlike some authors who despise being labeled, she does not mind being called a Black writer, or a Black woman writer. "I've decided to define that, rather than having it be defined for me," she said. "In the beginning, people would say, 'Do you regard yourself as a Black writer, or a Black woman writer?' So at first I was glib, and said I'm a Black woman writer, because I understood that they were trying to suggest that I was 'bigger' than that, or 'better' than that. I simply refused to accept their view of bigger and better. I really think the range of emotions and perceptions I have had access to as a Black person and as a female person are greater than those of people who are neither. I really do. So it seems to me that my world did not shrink because I was a Black female writer. It just got bigger."

Ethan Mordden makes the same point in regard to gay experience: "Despite straights' lack of comprehension and outright intolerance, gays inevitably comprehend straights, because, whatever our sexuality, we all grow up within the straight culture as participants. . . . Gays understand straights; but straights don't understand gays any more than whites understand Blacks or Christians understand Jews, however good their intentions."

There is much confusion about this topic of minority writers (or regional writers). This confusion stems from the insistence of those straight middle-class white men who control the organs of cultural definition in this society that the only valid, universal image of the contemporary human condition is . . . the straight middle-class white man. Now this is simply what Marx called ideology, in the purest sense of the word: the specific conditions for the liberation of a segment of society are universalized into the conditions of liberation for all, when in fact the interests of all other groups in the society are subordinated to the interests of the one dominant group. Or, in the bald words of its most succinct example: What's good for General Motors is good

for the country. This is pure cultural politics—the use of culture to re-
inforce the politically dominant position of one group within the society.

But as well as being a power struggle, this attitude has a much
deeper, more insidious effect, one that would be especially deplorable if it confused the writers themselves. To demote our literature to
a peripheral status, to try to make our writers "merely" gay writers,
is not only a classic power play, it also entails a basic and total misunderstanding of the nature of literature. As Jean Strouse pointed out
recently in the *New York Times Book Review*: "Louise Erdrich's novels, regional in the best sense, are 'about' the experience of Native
Americans the way Toni Morrison's are about Black people, William
Faulkner's and Eudora Welty's about the South, Philip Roth's and Bernard Malamud's about Jews: *the specificity implies nothing provincial or
small.*" (Italics added.) (One might note parenthetically that we don't
see the words "Edmund White's and Andrew Holleran's are about gay
people" in this otherwise lucid and sane declaration.)

Specific does not mean provincial. A sharply delimited subject matter in no way prevents a work of art from achieving universal statue.
My God, think of what Jane Austen was able to do within the narrow
confines of courtship rituals in early nineteenth-century England. Or,
to take an example from our own day, consider how the most successful musical in all of Broadway history is described by Charlie Willard,
a dance captain for that show: "*A Chorus Line* managed to find an uncanny kind of universality in the specificity of that white line on the
stage. Dealing with the very specific milieus and ambience of chorus
dancers, it somehow spoke to everyone, and from the very beginning,
it cut across the gypsy story. Because of that, it's often forgotten that it
was intended to be a show that celebrated a subculture."

Specific and concrete reality is indeed the origin of all great works
of literature. And if Dostoevsky is not diminished because he wrote
"only" about the Russians, or Synge the Irish, or Sophocles the Greeks,
then gay writers are in no way diminished because they write about
life as it presents itself to and is experienced by gay people. The idea
that this is somehow a failing, a limitation, is simply absurd and would

never have gotten into circulation if it were not a disguise for a political agenda. To allow ourselves to be confused by this nonsense would be sad indeed, because it's quintessentially self-defeating. Those gay authors who are so anxious to cultivate the crossover audience should realize that the task before us is rather to help bring into existence and further develop a new audience, the gay audience. And the reasoning behind this assertion is very simple. Given the fact that at the moment we live in what continues to be a homophobic society, the idea that gay writers could achieve success with the general public implies either that the general public cease being so homophobic or that the gay writer cease being . . . so gay. The first—that the general public become less homophobic—is unlikely unless we *do* something about it, for instance, publish and buy and read gay books, do our bit to strengthen and enrich the gay community, while making our lives and our art a more public and therefore more accepted fact. The second—that gay writers become less gay—unfortunately is always a possibility. When I was in college it was classically known as selling out, a cliché admittedly, but a cliché that might fit the situation of someone who doesn't want to be known as a gay writer because he will sell more books or gain a greater literary reputation that way.

The task before us is to create a gay literature and a gay culture in the midst of a situation that is hostile to that literature and that culture, and to bend every effort to facing up to and eradicating homophobia in this society. The way to do that is to encourage the further emergence of a literate gay public that supports and involves itself with the quite remarkable gay writing that is now being created. That and only that is the way to the crossover audience. Once there is a sizable and substantial gay reading public, the books they buy and read and value will attract the interest and the curiosity of the so-called "general public." The way to the general audience is through the specific audience, the way to the general public is through the gay public.

The present generation of gay writers, both those who emerged in the Seventies and those who appeared in the Eighties, were called into existence, *whether they know it or not*, by a remarkable social revolution, the unexpected and mighty upsurge of collective energy that started with Stonewall. Of course, it's better to know it. Not to know it, to ignore or forget it, means not to know where one is, means to cut yourself off from the historical roots and the cultural energy that sustains the creative act and sets it within a social and political context that gives it not only meaning but value.

Editing Fiction and the Question of "Political Correctness"

IN 1991 JERRY Gross, a veteran book editor and an old friend, invited me to write a chapter on the question of political correctness and the editing of fiction for the third edition of his essential book, *Editors on Editing*.[1] Since I had been battered around by the issue for years, I welcomed the opportunity to have my say.

In rereading this (and other essays) I've become sharply aware of how my close and abiding relationship and editorial work with Ntozake Shange—forty years now, the longest collaboration of my editing career—has permeated and clarified my thinking on these matters.

The recent squalls over politically correct speech that have swept through various college campuses and on into some of our national news magazines give some indication of the turbulence generated when a culture undergoes profound realignment. In the case of the P.C. debate, we see some of the strains attendant on the quite remarkable social changes occurring in American culture in the last few decades. For most of our history, American culture was dominated, defined, and evaluated by a relatively small segment of the population: English-speaking male persons with a deep grounding in and loyalty to the Anglo-Saxon literary and cultural tradition. Although there has always been some tension between the dominance of this so-called genteel tradition and various nativist, regional, or immigrant self-assertions, the main line of American culture has been emphatically Anglo, as has been the case with other countries that began their history as British colonies.

1 Published in 1993 by Grove Press.

However, since World War II this country has witnessed seismic shifts in both the culture—consider the emergence of urban male Jewish writers in the Fifties, African-American women writers in the Seventies, and gay and lesbian writers today—and in the demographic and social substratum upon which that culture rests. For instance, on the Berkeley campus in 1960 only three percent of the students were nonwhite, whereas in the autumn of '91, over fifty percent of the incoming class came from non-Anglo traditions. This opening up of the educational and cultural establishment to hitherto disenfranchised groups, the emergence of what is known as pluralism, appears today to be an irreversible trend. If it is indeed irreversible, this would mark a profound—and, in my opinion, a highly desirable—shift not only in the composition, but perhaps even in the basic nature of that culture.

Times of such basic transitions naturally generate confusion, conflict, and trouble for those of us who work in cultural fields such as publishing. The recent insistence on politically correct speech, or more precisely, the attacks on writers found guilty of being politically incorrect, i.e., offending members of one or another minority group, is a case in point. Its effects are felt on both ends of the publishing process, as a pressure on the individual author and as an influence on the opinion of the reviewer as well as the response of the reader, and they raise nice questions of judgment for the working editor.

*   *   *

When an author from a hitherto marginalized group succeeds in raising her voice in the public space, she feels not only the weight any author feels—the dreadfully public nature of publication—but also the burden of being a spokesperson for her community. While attempting to speak in her own unique and authentic voice, she is constrained by the realization that she will be heard and read as a representative of her group. This is a dilemma that is inherent in the historical situation and cannot be avoided; each author must negotiate her way through these dangerous waters, finding a balance between the claims of her own voice and her responsibility to the community. There are in my opinion no hard and fast rules here, and the responsibility of the editor is to be sensitive to the issue while acting as a sounding board for the writer. The decisions taken are so basic that they must be thrashed out by the author rather than imposed by the editor, who in this instance, as in so many others, plays a part oddly reminiscent of the nonjudgmental but supportive therapist. At times this can be a rather tedious role—editor as echo chamber—but it does have the great advantage of adhering to The Supreme Rule of Editing: Always remember that this is not your book but the author's.

The truth of the matter is that serious works of art can be neither propaganda nor public relations efforts, no matter how urgently needed or how well intentioned. It is curious that this is not abundantly clear to everyone today, given the dismal results of the fifty-year literary experiment with socialist realism in the USSR. I mean, "Man meets tractor, man falls in love with tractor, man marries tractor" just doesn't cut the mustard. If we want art—and whether or not we want art has indeed been a serious question to political thinkers since Plato—we must give up this absurd notion that art can provide role models for anyone. It is beyond me how this idea ever achieved currency, since a moment's reflection blows it away. Homer's Achilles, whatever else he was, was certainly no role model for the ancient Greeks, as he rejected all counsel of moderation and stormed against the limits of mortality, which for the Greeks defined the human condition. Nor was Madame Bovary intended to be a guide for the lives of provincial French women. This role model theory of literature boils down to a simplistic notion of monkey see/monkey do, which reveals a profound misunderstanding of the relation between literature and life.

Nevertheless, there is an understandable tendency on the part of social groups who have not previously achieved visibility in the culture or who have suffered under negative public images generated by others to feel intensely possessive about how they are portrayed, especially by their own. Ever since the furor over Philip Roth's *Portnoy's Complaint*, various communities have shown a tendency to judge works of fiction by the impact they assume such works will have on the community's public reputation. This is both a remarkably short-sighted and a remarkably persistent tendency, as can be seen in the initial reaction to Ntozake Shange's *for colored girls who have consid-*

ered suicide/when the rainbow is enuf or Larry Kramer's *Faggots*, both of which were attacked most bitterly by members of each author's own community. As far as I can see, the author has no choice but to endure such emotional buffeting and critical riptides, while preserving the authentic honesty of her own vision; the editor's job is to support the author against all comers. This can sometimes be a bruising experience for an editor—though nowhere as bruising as it is for the author—but it comes with the territory, as my mother would say. To my mind, the most apt response to such a situation was that of Spike Lee after the storm of advice and criticism unleashed by the announcement that he intended to make a movie about the life of Malcolm X: "If you don't like the movie I make about Malcolm, go make your own."

In such situations both the author and the editor will constantly feel the pressure to conform and be politically correct. But this is merely another expression of the essential dialectic of the creative imagination, the tension between the author and society, between individual talent and the tradition. Society, tradition, and the currently politically correct always have the advantage, both of weight of opinion and of numbers. It seems reasonable to me that the editor do what he or she can to redress the balance by standing behind the author's individual talent and unique vision.

*   *   *

In addition to protecting the author from the demands for political correctness emanating from her own community—"Is it good for the Jews?"—there are other, more subtle issues that arise when publishing writers from a community different from one's own. As Joan Pinkvoss of Aunt Lute Books has pointed out, the great danger when, for instance, a white editor is working with a writer of color is the sometimes almost unconscious temptation to make the writer's voice more intelligible or acceptable (the one sliding into the other) to white readers. This temptation must be resisted absolutely. It is the integrity of the writer's voice and vision *alone* that can provide the editor with a true standard for the editing process. The goal of editing is to make the book better, not different. From the history of Black music in this country, we know fairly well the mechanics of producing a white "cover" for a Black song. This is essentially a commercial and cultural rip-off, which to my mind would be a serious offense if committed by an editor. Even if the writer is willing—or eager—to make such changes in an effort to be more commercially successful (which we used to call selling out), it seems to me that such pandering to the marketplace negates the reason you would sign up such a book in the first place—your delight in the power and freshness of a voice and message that expand your own horizon.

The temptation to make a Black author more acceptable to white readers, far from making the work more "universally" available, is a subtle but serious betrayal of the author, for it masks the attempt, however innocent, to change the audience the writer intended to the readers the editor has in mind. This truly negates the purpose of engaging in pluralistic publishing in the first place and is reminiscent of the early explorers and anthropologists who brought back samples of the "exotic" humanity they encountered around the globe for the amusement or edification of Europeans. This is abhorrent since it would ultimately turn literature into a zoo. The purpose of pluralistic publishing is to open the realm of the written word to hitherto excluded groups, while at the same time letting people from other communities hear these new voices. Of course, the first time you listen to someone who speaks in a dialect or accent new to you, it takes some time to get the hang of it. But the editor's job is never to make everyone speak in the same way, but to rejoice in the richness that a variety of different voices offers us.

*   *   *

Although most of the conflicts over political correctness emerge from differences between the writer's vision and the convictions of the more vocal members of her own community regarding how members of that community should be portrayed publicly, there is also the question of writers characterizing members of "other" groups in what could be considered a negative way—for instance, the presentation of African-American men in the media mainly as criminals or drug addicts, thus slandering a whole group. One gets the impression from public discussions of the topic that this is the major problem. Whether or not this is still true of the media in general is another question; however, in my experience it comes up remarkably rarely in publishing. Negative stereotypes of African-Americans are now unusual and generally arise from clichéd thinking and lack of imagination (the signs of a poor writer of fiction) rather than from racism. And, except for an occasional British book, one simply doesn't come across casual anti-Semitism in novels today.

One does still see unthinking homophobic comments now and then, in which case the editor's job is to point these out to the author. If there is no justification for such comments in either the plot or the portrayal of the character, the author should be made aware of the possible impact on the reader. (Obviously portraying a homophobic character or a homophobic act does not make the author homophobic.) Recently I was working on a mystery in which one character asserted, "I'm not queer," and I flagged it for the author. In context the use of the word "queer" instead of "gay" would to my ear indicate one of the following: (a) this is a bad guy because bad guys use bad language (which he was, but at this point in the plot the reader should not have been tipped off to that), (b) this character is homophobic and that will somehow be relevant to the plot, or (c) this character protests too much, which means he's uncertain or conflicted about his sexuality and this fact will somehow be relevant to the plot. Since the second and third explanations did not seem to me to fit the plot, I thought the author had made the mistake of tipping the reader off to this man's character too early in the mystery. However, after some discussion the author realized that he did mean to indicate some severe sexual repression in this man; it was a theme that he had intended to bring out more but that had gotten lost in the writing and rewriting, and a few further changes in the manuscript made it fit smoothly (without giving the plot away). The fact that such words are today freighted with more significance in fiction than they may carry in real life *is* a fact, and the author has to take this fact into account. A woman executive swearing in the office is common; a woman executive swearing in a novel will probably signal things to the reader that the author might not intend. As always, the editor's primary task is to clarify the author's intention.

It is certainly possible that one would come across an author who was actually homophobic, racist, or anti-Semitic, in which case you have the option of simply not publishing him. But let us be clear: the option of *my* not publishing a given author can *not* be called censorship. Censorship is a general prohibition against publication, usually requiring the power of the state or a similar social institution, such as the church. As specific editors, or even specific publishers, a disinclination to publish a certain book is a matter of taste, of whom we choose to be associated with, not of censorship. As long as the author has the option of taking the book elsewhere, or of publishing it himself if all else fails, there is not a question of censorship, only of commercial or social success, which is a different matter entirely.

There is, of course, also the possibility that one might find a homophobic, racist, or anti-Semitic author who was a truly great writer—consider the cases of T. S. Eliot or Ezra Pound. I have always wondered what I would do if I came across a fiction writer whom I believed to be truly excellent who was also, say, homophobic; but since this has never happened, I honestly don't know how I would react, although I'm very curious. I could certainly imagine publishing a nonfiction book by an author I thought was significant although he was homophobic—the autobiography of Louis Farrakhan, for instance.[2]

*   *   *

As a rule, I firmly believe that an editor's own politics, opinions, and prejudices have no place in the editing process, which can lead to some strange situations. While editing G. Gordon Liddy's autobiography, *Will*, I found myself in the odd situation of helping Gordon rewrite his attack on the student radicals who had converged on the Democratic Convention in Chicago in '68. There we were, sitting at my dining room table as I urged Gordon to cut the rhetoric and hone his comments on

2 But my attempt was ultimately quashed by the upper management at Crown.

the anti-war demonstrators into a substantive attack, an irony not lost on either of us since Gordon knew well I had been there myself, rioting in Grant Park. Luckily, we had become good friends despite wide differences in some of our political opinions, and in return for my editorial help I extracted a promise that he would read Hannah Arendt's *On Revolution*, which salved my non-editorial conscience somewhat.

In some respects it is easier to edit someone whose experience in the world or political convictions are widely different from my own than it is to edit someone who stands closer to me. The very distance creates a discipline and an alertness: you can feel yourself making the effort of imagination and empathy required by the task; the discipline is palpable, indeed sometimes mind-wrenching. When dealing with a closely allied sensibility or political orientation, the temptation to slide oneself into the text is more subtle. Before signing a contract with Dennis Altman for *The Homosexualization of America: The Americanization of the Homosexual*, Dennis and I had to have long and frank discussions, for this was an area I was actively involved in, had in fact written about, and Dennis was understandably nervous that precisely this closeness could represent a danger to the integrity of his views, the individuality of his opinions. Thus prepared, we managed the process quite well and, while I do not agree with everything written in that book either, I was proud of the fact that in the end Dennis assured me that he felt the book had remained totally his.

Perhaps the most tender area of P.C. sensitivity in gay fiction today concerns the portrayal of unsafe sex in gay novels set in the era of AIDS. On the one hand, there is the strong stand taken by Sasha Alyson, who will not allow any descriptions of unsafe sexual practices in any fiction published by Alyson Publications. On the other hand is the position taken by Warren Singer, an old boyfriend of mine who had AIDS and with whom I discussed Sasha's position: "Lord, the only place we ought not to have to practice safe sex is in our imagination!" said he. This quandary could lead to endless philosophic discussion, but the question is best addressed on a concrete basis, case by case. Recently I read a story of gay romance between an HIV-positive and an HIV-negative person—their antibody status clearly established in the text—in which the protagonist who is positive realizes after withdrawal that the condom he was using had broken. Neither the protagonist nor the author made any comment about this and the story simply went on, but I didn't. I had been brought to a full stop because I didn't know how to interpret this incident. It would certainly be a significant event if it happened to you in the course of a romance and it must be significant in the course of this story, but the author had left unclear what that significance was supposed to be. This is a bit like saying offhandedly that there is an elephant in the living room and not mentioning it again. This will not do. As Chekhov informed us: if you introduce a gun in the first act of a play, it had better go off before the end of the last act, otherwise it shouldn't have been there in the first place. If a character practices unsafe sex in a contemporary gay novel, that fact carries an interpretive weight that the author has to take into account, because the reader certainly will. Similarly, if a character casually uses words like "Jew boy" or "nigger" today, the reader will inevitably feel the author is making a rather strong point about that character whereas we would not necessarily assume that if the text were written sixty years ago.

The point, I think, is not to have general rules, which never work very well in editing anyway, but to point out to the author in each case what implications the reader will likely draw from the incident and to make sure that the author does not inadvertently create an effect that was not desired. The author may well intend a character to be obnoxious, but authors seldom intend to present themselves as obnoxious. As always, the editor's role is to help the author achieve her aim, not to insure that the writer is politically correct.

In general, the attempt to make any fiction politically correct is a misguided one; it is an attempt to police the imagination. This inclination has been quite prominent among the politically committed since Plato first banished poets from his ideal republic; its resurgence today is merely an unfortunate but quite predictable by-product of a valuable surge in political activism, the dangers of which have always been self-righteousness and intolerance.

The political activist and the poet have always marched to different drummers. As an editor my loyalties lie with the freedom of the individual imagination, the fruits of which have done very little harm in the real world. Unfortunately, the same cannot be said of political action. Until the politically correct can actually produce a better world in fact rather than in theory, I for one am not willing to grant them control—or even veto power—over the realm of imaginative literature.

PART 5

On the Raft of the Medusa

1988–1990

Sometime in the late Eighties while walking through the Metropolitan Museum with a friend on our way to an exhibit, I was startled by a huge historical canvas called "The Raft of the Medusa," a classical French early nineteenth-century historical painting depicting the starving survivors (barely) of a shipwreck, clinging to a disintegrating raft as they're thrown about in a turbulent storm. Although not the type of art I usually look at, this painting froze me in my tracks and I stared. And said to my friend, "That's the way we live now. That's a perfect depiction of our emotional life. Shipwrecked, starving, dehydrated, dying, being tossed about by this furious storm of history."

It's not a painting I've gone back to see, but it is a painting I've never forgotten. For by the late Eighties our life had become like that: huge waves of hope, despair, anger, loss, betrayal, abandonment, and terror constantly slammed into us among riptides of ignorance, prejudice, fear and panic. "As we realized the magnitude of the epidemic," the writer Robin Hardy recalled, "we were horrified, angry, terrified and pathologically depressed."[1] We could see a wall of death coming.

At the same time, the crisis brought out the best version of our selves. Care groups formed spontaneously around each new ill friend—to cook meals, walk the dog, wash the dishes, arrange visits to the doctor,

---

1 David Groff and Robin Hardy, *The Crisis of Desire: AIDS and the Fate of the Gay Brotherhood* (University of Minnesota Press, 1999), p. 32.

whatever needed to be done to keep a person's independent life going as long as possible. Six, eight, ten people—ex-lovers, ex-boyfriends, gym buddies, work colleagues, perfect strangers (volunteers)—would somehow get in touch with each other, divvy up what needed to be done, and keep everyone up to date with round robin phone calls every night (someone had early introduced phone trees, to divide the task, which made things a lot easier). And by the end, when there was nothing more we could do, we could be there. We could be company, so they wouldn't be alone. The AIDS crisis triggered an outburst of caring and communion, a daily heroism, that demonstrated to me that we had a living gay community taking care of its own in the worst of times. The AIDS epidemic paradoxically made the gay community a living reality and a source of strength.

But the shadows were lengthening and darkness was coming, along with heavy hearts.

The Death of a Generation

THESE ARE ROUGH notes hurriedly jotted down in pencil on a legal pad during the subway ride to an interview with Kathryn Loomis of "Performance Today," a National Public Radio show that in June 1988 she devoted entirely to AIDS, a breakthrough of sorts at the time. I've included them because they struck me as a bulletin from the front, as it were, a scrap ripped from the pages of living history. But sometimes a scrap, like an evanescent bolt of lightning, can reveal a whole landscape.

1) Overview – AIDS might have depressed or inhibited gay writing, but instead it's galvanized it.
   A A remarkable literature is emerging: Randy Shilts: And The Band Played On
      Chris Davis: Valley of the Shadow
      Paul Monette: Love Alone: 18 Elegies for Rog & Borrowed Time
      Robert Ferro: Second Son
      George Whitmore: Someone Was Here
   B What's remarkable is that these voices are being raised in the very midst of the disaster—usually there's a time lag.
      As far as I know books on the Holocaust came after Hitler's defeat & it took a decade before novels about the Vietnam War began appearing.
      But the real parallel is to the poetry written in the trenches during World War I—Siegfried Sassoon, Wilfred Owen—but it's as if this writing was being broadcast *from the trenches*—this is a literature of engagement—"engagé," as the French say—the people who are writing are taking part in the battle, the writing is part of the fight, a political act.

C For an editor, this puts you in an odd position—this AIDS writing
is not just a matter of aesthetics.

- I never thought I'd have regular discussions with authors about
whether they would live long enough to finish their book—it's
a race against time and death—editing in hospital rooms after
visiting hours were over, writing between funerals, etc.

2) You have to understand this disaster is happening to a whole
generation—three out of four gay men in NYC are affected, caught
up in this medical holocaust (73% seropositive). My generation,
the first post-Stonewall generation of gay men, is going to be wiped
out—and we will not go in silence—we owe it to everyone who's
died, everyone who's medically in danger, to make this event public,
to force people to know it's happening.

- ourselves, so we don't go mad.
- others, so that this doesn't happen the way the Nazi Holocaust
happened, in silence, with many people not knowing in the 30s
and 40s that the Jews were being destroyed. It was this not knowing that allowed the world not to come to the aid of the Jews.
  As the motto of Act Up says: Silence=Death Silence today is a
crime

3) And in one of those terrible paradoxes of history, the AIDS holocaust
is going to firmly establish the existence of a gay culture—it will be,
it already is, a central event, a shared memory (which is what all culture is), a shared memory held by all gay men.

- that's why I'm encouraging writers to write—not so much for the
straight, so-called general audience—but for each other, for their
peers, and especially for the gay kids who are coming up—free of
the disease—the gay teenagers, gay kids in college.
- Our first generation of activists, the people who made gay liberation and who started gay literature, this generation is going to be
wiped out, this generation of writers is doomed.
- What we have to pass on to the kids is our response to this
catastrophe—they have to see that we battled it, that we fought
society's neglect—they have to see that our spirit was strong
enough to rise to the occasion, to respond to the disaster with
words and deeds that matched the occasion and give us back our
dignity.

- This is what our writers are doing—at God knows what cost to themselves—this is what we have to leave to the next generation, and every gay writer I know is responding.

4) The AIDS epidemic is over among gays, except for the dying which will be monumental in the next five years. But a new phase of the epidemic is looming—i.v. drug users to Black women and children.
    - Black and women writers have got to carry the ball now, our writers are dying.
    - This disease could be devastating to the Black community.
    - one out of 61 women of child-bearing age in NYC are infected
    - one out of 43 women of child-bearing age in the Bronx are infected
    - These are poor people, people without access to the media, people who are not well organized to fight the society for what they need.
    - Black writers and entertainers and sports figures have got to organize, to speak out on behalf of these people.
    - And I hope the women's movement. Seems to me it's the perfect issue for the women's movement to mobilize itself around. If "sisterhood" means anything. . . . These women need allies, people who can articulate their cause.

An Intellectual Ambush

ON THURSDAY, APRIL 13, 1989, the Center for Lesbian and Gay Studies at CUNY held a public panel on Randy Shilts' *And the Band Played On*, which drew several hundred gay writers and activists, to Hunter College if memory serves. The panel was clearly stacked against Randy: four people who had already publicly taken critical stances against the book and me for the defense. But since I was always arguing we needed more public discussion about serious matters there was really no way I could avoid the challenge.

Larry Gross of the Annenberg School of Communications, University of Pennsylvania, was the moderator; the other panelists were Douglas Crimp, an editor of *October*, Cindy Patton, the author of *Sex and Germs*, and Melinda Cuthbert of Yale University. I was seated at the very end of the table and spoke after the other three panelists had had their say. I have only a handwritten copy of my introductory remarks that night, which I'm reprinting here verbatim. This was followed by a fairly intense discussion that went on for some time. I have no recording of it and only a few jotted notes about comments that really irritated me, but I remember being startled by the intensity of the audience's response to (and, I thought, obsession with) the Patient Zero story.

Patient Zero was one of the earliest known cases of what would later be called AIDS, an extremely attractive Canadian airline steward who was enormously successful sexually in the Seventies. When on the verge of *Band*'s publication, it appeared that this book with its massive attack on the AIDS policy of the Reagan Administration and the CDC was not going to get any attention in the national media—I had been told by the *New York Times*, *Time* and *Newsweek* that they were not going to review the book—I stooped to using yellow journalism to trick the media into covering it. Knowing (too well) the *New York Post*'s homophobic stance, in the publicity materials we sent them I highlighted the story of Patient Zero (mentioned in 12 pages of a 630-page book), a story that had everything they wanted: sensational sex, glamor, death, and, best of all from their point of view, he was a foreigner, someone they could blame, the man who brought AIDS to America! It was a low move, I admit, and it took me a week of arguing with Randy, who hated the idea, to get his grudging consent, but I thought of it as a sort of cultural karate, using their homophobia to get AIDS onto the national agenda. If they were only going to run homophobic stories, so be it!

And it worked! Within two weeks the *Times* had run two reviews and five news stories on the book, which forced the rest of the media, both national and local, to cover it. And thus put AIDS front and center of the national conversation for the first time in five years.

But I continued to be surprised during the next three decades by what seemed to me to be an obsessive, and somewhat inexplicable, focus on what was in my opinion a minor episode of media manipulation (on my part) and yellow journalism on the media's part (sensationalizing and mis-reporting a story). There's no need to rehearse my version here. If one is interested in this topic, there are at least three books which deal with it at length—Priscilla Wald's *Contagious: Cultures, Carriers, and the Outbreak Narrative*, Richard McKay's *Patient Zero and the Making of the AIDS Epidemic*, and Phil Tiemeyer's *Plane Queer: Labor, Sexuality and AIDS in the History of Male Flight Attendants*—the last two of which gave me much space to present my side of the story. There are also an astonishing number of essays, the best of which is Guy Babineau's "The Prettiest One: Remembering Gaetan Dugas," an author who, although Gaetan's best friend who criticized me severely, also gave me full space to tell my version. There's even a film, *Killing Patient Zero*, by Laurie Lynd, who interviewed me. I've had the chance to have my say.

I think it was only when I read the reminiscences of Ray Redford,[1] Dugas' former lover and life-long friend, that Gaetan really came into focus for me and I suddenly could understand this obsession. But that would be another essay.

---

1 Which Richard McKay wisely used to end his book on Patient Zero.

First, let's be honest about this: this panel was stacked against Randy Shilts. When it was first proposed to me, I asked Larry Gross whether he wanted me to get Randy himself to participate, which I could have easily arranged, but he thought that was not appropriate. Then I asked if we could add one more person, someone perhaps a little more neutral than the current panelists, like John Preston, say, or Larry Bush, but he had no enthusiasm for that suggestion either.

So, this is a panel set up to *trash* Randy Shilts and his book. What we have here are four academics taking potshots at a non-academic who has managed to accomplish something.

In fact, the first title of this panel, printed on the original flyer I received, was "*And the Band Played On*; History as Mini Series?" "History as mini series" is a phrase taken from Douglas Crimp's article "How to Have Promiscuity In An Epidemic," which is mainly an attack on Shilts, Kramer and Ortleb—three people who, to my mind, have done more work—and more important work—for the last eight years than any of the members of this panel.

Perhaps that original title was too obvious, because it was soon replaced by "How Will the History of AIDS Be Written? Critical Responses to Randy Shilts' *And the Band Played On*." Which is an interesting title.

The word "history," of course, has two meanings. History can mean

1) the acts and suffering, the *events* that are worth remembering or
2) the study of those acts and events, i.e., the academic discipline, the study of history.

In its first meaning—history as the reality of events—the history of AIDS *is* being written now, and by people like Shilts, Kramer and Ortleb. In fact, with these people the act of writing, the use of language, has become a political act and thus a historical fact.

These political acts of language will be, and already are, constituent parts of the real history of this epidemic (history in the first sense of the word). They are, among other things, what the historians will study and write about when they write *their* histories.

Michel Foucault once said that we are doomed to live in an epoch of secondary discourses, discourses about discourses, and while I think this is an incorrect analysis, the distinction between primary and secondary discourses is useful.

Shilts, as well as Kramer, Ortleb (and, of course, many others) are participating in, are creating, the primary discourse about the AIDS epidemic—that is, they are engaged by their acts in the history of the AIDS epidemic.

The scholars on this panel are engaged in secondary discourse, that is, discourse about discourse. Now, there's nothing wrong with this activity—it is the essence of scholarship and it has been with us for a long time. Already Montaigne complained, "There is more to do to interpret the interpretations than to interpret the things."

Shilts, Kramer and Ortleb are actively engaged in interpreting the things, while the scholars on this panel are engaged in interpreting the interpretations. The inherent danger of secondary discourse, the interpretation of interpretations, is that occasionally, especially in the hands of the ambitious, it falls prey to an inherent tendency to cannibalize its subject, the primary discourse. Art criticism, for example, or literary criticism, shows a deplorable tendency to want to *replace* the art it's about with itself. This might be called "primary discourse envy."

And as Quentin Crisp might say, "This will simply not do."

- *And the Band Played On* is a work of investigative journalism.
- Randy Shilts is a reporter who is also a gay man.
- As a gay man, finding himself in that profession at a time when the gay community came under an extraordinary threat, he used his profession and his career to do what he could to respond to that threat.

This was not an easy task, nor was it one without risk to himself:

- After I could not generate a sufficient advance at St. Martin's to realistically underwrite the project, every other publisher in Manhattan, twelve other publishers, turned this book down flat.
- When Randy came back to St. Martin's he got an extremely modest advance of $16,000 to underwrite what was four years of work.

- He put himself heavily into debt to get the time to write this book.
- And he worked incredibly hard.

In my opinion what he did was an act of professional heroism, an extraordinary job, and deserves respect. And it certainly has had impact. I've already heard from three gay reporters at major American newspapers that they can now cover the AIDS beat because of Randy's example.

I think that if gay people in other professions would dedicate their professional lives in a similar way, the gay community would be in much better shape today.

And that brings me to scholarship. It seems to me that the task of our gay scholars is to do with the fields of scholarship what Shilts has done with his profession of investigative reporting.

I'm not sure what this new gay scholarship would look like—in fact, I thought that's what this series of panel discussions was supposed to be about. But I suspect it would look something like Boswell's *Christianity, Social Tolerance, and Homosexuality*, or Jim Saslow's *Ganymede in the Renaissance*, or Jonathan Katz' *Gay American History*. In other words, I don't think gay scholarship should consist of only "primary discourse envy."

If you don't like Shilts' book on the AIDS epidemic, write your own, as Cindy Patton has done. We need more voices and more perspectives on what has turned out to be the major event for our community in this decade.

And you can rest assured that time will sort out these books[2]—that the best will remain as the others fade.

This seems to me a much better use of your energy than the type of criticism we've heard here tonight.

---

2 In 2012 the Library of Congress published a list of 88 books that had "shaped America." Not necessarily the best books, according to James Billington, Librarian of Congress, but "books that have influenced our lives." Randy would have been very happy to know he appeared on that select list, since investigative journalism's innermost engine and ultimate purpose is to effect change in society.

A Quilt of Many Colors

PRIMARY DISCOURSE AND THE
CREATION OF A GAY CULTURE

MY OLD FRIEND, Dick Howard, who had listened to me ranting on at a dinner about what was happening with gay literature under the onslaught of AIDS, suggested I give a lecture on the subject for The Humanities Institute at Stony Brook where he taught.[1] I jumped at the chance to try to sketch an overview of the remarkable events I thought I was witnessing. All around me I watched writers respond to the threat of the AIDS crisis, a whole generation of writers rising to the community's mortal threat, something I could find no parallel for in literary history. The ferment was intense and utterly serious, the stakes ultimate. Secondary issues that usually obscure the writing life were burned away. I wanted to try to think through the radical situation I thought gay writers were in. Absorbed by this unfolding phenomenon, I failed to watch where my feet were going, and fell into Thales' old well.

Although I usually take care to make my public comments relevant to the specific occasion and audience I'm addressing, I went badly astray in this instance. My attention totally absorbed by the subject, I misjudged both audience and occasion. The audience consisted of one nervous undergraduate and four or five graduate students or young instructors. The minute I pulled out my typescript, I realized the rhetoric was totally wrong for this small audience in an average size lecture room with people who had probably never heard of any of the writers I was going to talk about. I must have been thinking of an audience that hadn't come into existence yet—and wouldn't until the first Outright Conference for gay and lesbian writers was held the next year—or maybe I was just not thinking, a mistake I could have kicked myself for at that moment.

I tried to make adjustments, lower the intensity of the rhetoric and

---

1 I did, on October 23, 1989.

cut many passages, but it was basically a disaster. The sole under-graduate scurried out the second I was finished talking, and, although a couple of guys came up to ask about individual books and authors, it was clear they'd never heard of any of these people. Which served me right for not keeping the audience and the occasion in mind while writing.

But the mangled talk got a second chance as an essay when Chuck Ortleb published it in *Christopher Street*[2] that October (1989). It was later republished in Judith Pastore's *Confronting AIDS through Literature: The Responsibilities of Representation.*[3]

Rereading it today I realize it was my more worked-out response to the previous panel of academics, at attempt at an in-depth defense of primary discourse, against the secondary discourses of the academic world.

I.

In the Preface to *The Birth of the Clinic* Michel Foucault wrote: "It may well be that we belong to an age of criticism whose lack of a primary philosophy reminds us at every moment of its reign and its fatality: an age of intelligence that keeps us irremediably at a distance from an original language. . . . We are doomed historically to history, to the patient construction of discourses about discourses and to the task of hearing what has already been said."[4]

It is perhaps unfair to continue an argument with a man after he is dead but it is increasingly necessary, and I doubt Foucault would have minded, especially considering the gusto he displayed in late night discussions about this issue of primary discourse in our time, specifically the emergence of the possibility of such a thing as gay culture and its corollary, gay literature. I would not presume to try to reproduce Foucault's subtle—and, to my mind, shifting—position on this topic; for

2 Issue 141, vol. 12, no. 9 (October 1989).
3 University of Illinois Press, 1993.
4 Michel Foucault, *The Birth of the Clinic* (New York: Vintage Books, 1975), pp. xv–xvi.

my part, this despair about primary discourse seemed to me a result of the commanding position the academic mind has achieved in our culture, reigning over the recording and evaluation of the activity of intelligence in general. The academic mind, I argued, looks out and sees reflections of itself and its interior processes, not the world as it is happening around us. We are doomed not historically but academically to the patient construction of discourses about discourses, to the task of hearing what has already been said. History dooms us to something else altogether.

Acknowledging the enormous loss to this discussion caused by Foucault's death from AIDS, I would like to try to extend this argument to the extraordinary surge of writing that has been occasioned by the advent of the AIDS epidemic, acts of primary discourse whose nature, depth, and value seem to me in danger of being obscured by the natural bent of the academic mind. It is noticeable that secondary discourses about AIDS—how the media speaks when it speaks about AIDS, studies of the metaphors used in AIDS discussions—naturally float to the surface of academic journals or serve as the occasion for thematic issues, while the primary acts of speech uttered in confrontation with the thing itself are neglected or misunderstood.

What history dooms us to is the shock of events, happenings that break over us and challenge the human spirit to give back an answer— "answering back the hammer blows of Fortune," in the words of the final chorus of *Antigone*. This urge to answer back, to declare one's presence even at the cost of acknowledging the original blow to the spirit, lies at the very heart of what we mean by culture, that shared collection of individual acts of the spirit that articulate who we are and how we find ourselves in this life.

History dooms us to the shock of events, and an epidemic is an historical event, the unleashing of an infectious—in this case, lethal— disease in a population. AIDS is not a condition to be managed, like high blood pressure or poverty. AIDS is not just a disease, like cancer or sickle cell anemia. AIDS is not a chronic medical state, like diabetes— though it may become one. AIDS in our time is an *event*, a calamity, like a forest fire, like the Blitz of London. AIDS is an epidemic and an epidemic is an event.

More precisely, an epidemic is the occurrence of death as a social event. Usually death is one of the most individualizing and private experiences a person can undergo. But death is sometimes a social event, a shared reality; it was so in the trenches of World War I, in the gas chambers of Auschwitz, in the killing fields of Cambodia. When death becomes a social event, the individual death is both robbed of its utter privacy and uniquely individual meaning and simultaneously amplified with the resonance of social significance and historical consequence. When death is a social event, both the individual *and the community* are threatened with irreparable loss.

An epidemic is a shared social disaster played out on the bodies of the afflicted. AIDS, of course, is not a gay disease. But, given the means of transmission, AIDS managed to gain momentum and achieve epidemic force first in the gay community. As John Preston has said, "AIDS is not a gay disease. . . . It is, however, a catastrophe for gay men."[5] Although it has ravaged other individuals (hemophiliacs, transfusion recipients) and diverse social groups (Haitians, Africans, IV drug users and, through them, the mostly Black and Hispanic inner-city underclass), it was the happenstance of history that the disease should first achieve epidemic proportions in the gay community. The world, motivated by a disastrous combination of prejudice, vicious self-righteousness, murderous indifference to the fate of a group mistakenly thought to be "other," and massive, panicked denial, ignored the problem and blindly allowed the epidemic to get out of control, with grim consequences that have not even begun to be perceived, much less tallied. For the gay community, it meant that the AIDS epidemic was to become the central fact of its history at this moment, as elemental an event for this fledgling community as the Holocaust was for Jews all over the world.

It is clear now that the history of the liberated gay community in America is divided into two phases.

First was the original act of constitution as a self-acknowledged

5 John Preston, "An Essay," *Tribe: An American Journal*, vol. 1., no. 2 (Spring 1990): p. 4.

community, initiated by the Stonewall Riots in June 1969 and unfolded in the Seventies when a vast act of social transformation reshaped the lives and attitudes of millions of Americans—a social event of such magnitude that it can only be compared to the half-century-old civil rights movement, but which has characteristically received virtually no attention from our so-called social scientists. The second phase commenced with the advent of the AIDS epidemic at the beginning of the Eighties, an event that threatened to destroy this community both physically and spiritually.

The initial shock at this dawning social disaster was compounded by the peculiar relations of the gay community to the surrounding society, which has always favored resounding silence as the most effective means of gay repression. Thus, when gay men found themselves in the middle of a social catastrophe, found themselves and their friends wasting away from an unknown but clearly rapidly spreading disease, their panic was compounded by the hostility of the Reagan Administration, the indifference of the national medical establishment, and the virtual silence of the media. The shameful silence of the *New York Times*, the nation's self-proclaimed "newspaper of record" as well as the hometown paper for the city that was the epicenter of this catastrophe, left gay New Yorkers in a near schizophrenic situation: on the one hand, friends were falling ill left and right, life became a surrealistic series of medical disasters, hospital vigils, and memorial services; on the other hand, everyday life went on as if nothing were happening, the media were nearly silent, and straight friends and co-workers, going about their normal lives, seemed to be living on some other planet. "It was as if a war was going on in our city," said William M. Hoffman, "and half the city was in rubble, but people weren't mentioning it."[6]

Piling the insult of silence on top of the grotesque injuries wreaked by AIDS left the gay community in a state of political confusion and spiritual despair, for the impact of any social disaster is mute until it is articulated in words, reflected in the imagination. Only then do we

---

6 Quoted in David Kaufman's "AIDS: The Cultural Response," *Horizon Magazine*, vol. 30, no. 9 (November 1987): p. 14.

realize what is happening to us; only when we can relive in the imagination what has happened to us in life does it become real for us. As Hannah Arendt observed, "The impact of factual reality, like all other human experiences, needs speech if it is to survive the moment of experience, needs talk and communication with others to remain sure of itself."[7] It is precisely for this reason that gay writers became pivotal players in the second act of gay history.

During the first decade of gay liberation, the community itself seemed to undergo a process of spontaneous transubstantiation: when the drag queens and the boys in the bars initiated it all by fighting back, it was as if a signal went out, heard by all, calling everyone to the colors. The process of transformation ignited everywhere, and the enormously complex act of redefinition—sexually, politically, morally, psychologically, interpersonally, spiritually—was spontaneous, decentralized, and multiple. Something akin to Nietzsche's "transvaluation of all values" was happening all over the place. This enormous ferment unleashed in 1969 gained velocity during the Seventies, creating new social spaces, new relationships, new institutions, even new sexual acts, and igniting the imaginations of the first generation of gay writers who emerged in the late Seventies avid to reflect in their writing these fundamental changes that were already clearly sweeping through our lives.

With the advent of AIDS in the early Eighties a new and heavier task fell to the writers: the job of sounding the alarm, mobilizing the community both politically and spiritually, delineating the shape of this disaster breaking over us, and initiating the discourse of AIDS in the face of the silence of the national media and institutionalized medicine. It is notable that it was a gay newspaper, *The New York Native*, which first announced the existence of this disease—before the Centers for Disease Control did—by insisting that a handful of cases of a rare cancer in gay men must be connected to the unheard-of pneumonia that was

---

7 Hannah Arendt, "Epilogue: Reflections on the Hungarian Revolution," chapter 14 of *The Origins of Totalitarianism* (New York: Harcourt, Brace, Jovanovich, 1957), p. 495.

striking gay people down.[8] It was Larry Kramer's famous 1983 essay in *The Native*, "1,112 and Counting," which swept away the confusion and mobilized gay people from one end of the American continent to the other.

Taken completely by surprise, enraged and demoralized by what seemed like a malevolent symbolism in a disease that not only appeared to target gay men, but that seemed to zero in on sexual activity, the locus of most of the hard-won liberation of the previous decade, the gay community reeled. One of the first to confront the panic and grief that the sudden appearance of this new and almost unbelievable disease engendered was William Hoffman in his play *As Is*. "Personally, I was trying to cope with the death of friends—four in particular at the time—and the illness around me," he said.[9] At almost the same time, Larry Kramer, furious at the inaction of the gay community, the medical establishment, and political "leaders" from City Hall to the White House, took to the stage with *The Normal Heart*, an intensely political play that rang out with a stinging indictment of official indifference and a near-maddened call to arms.

As the epidemic expanded, as more people fell ill and died, as visits to the hospital and the funeral home became regular, if bizarre, social occasions for gay men, the community moved into life in the war zone. Like other gay men in major urban areas, gay writers spent an increasing amount of time caring for the ill; confronted by the epidemic every which way they turned, it began to seem the only serious thing to write about. Robert Ferro's novel *Second Son* was written while the author, ill himself, was caring for his dying lover, and published only months before his own death from AIDS. Christopher Davis, in his novel *Valley of the Shadow*, sought to present the human reality behind the impersonal—and increasingly frequent—obituaries of young gay

8 Randy Shilts, *And the Band Played On* (New York: St. Martin's Press, 1987), p. 67. The *Native*'s first article ran on May 18, 1981; the CDC's first report ran on June 5, 1981, in "The Morbidity and Mortality Weekly Report," Centers for Disease Control, Atlanta.
9 Quoted in Kaufman, "AIDS: The Cultural Response," *Horizon Magazine*, vol. 30, no. 9 (November 1987): p. 14.

men appearing in the newspapers. This first-person fiction sustained with remarkable beauty a clear-eyed depiction of the grief, loss, and love that would soon become common throughout the gay world.

Randy Shilts, determined to set down the objective record so long ignored by the media, produced *And the Band Played On*, a massive, relentless, hypnotic, and epic narrative of the first five years of the AIDS epidemic that laid bare the unfolding politics and history of this disaster with such persuasive force and detailed accumulation of fact that the book itself became a political event.

Paul Monette, seeking to make personal sense of the holocaust that had swept over his life, wrote *Borrowed Time*, in which he etched with passion and anger the impact of AIDS on two lovers, while his great poem cycle, *Love Alone*, raised a shattering paean to the death of a whole generation of gay men, "the story that endlessly eludes the decorum of the press."[10]

George Whitmore learned of his own illness while writing *Someone Was Here*, a book of personal reportage in which he managed, before his death, to show people with AIDS (PWAs) as the concrete individuals they were, not just statistics and categories, and not just gay men. At the same time, his friend Victor Bumbalo was working on *Adam and the Experts*, a play about their friendship during the crisis. "Writing the play was a painful experience," Bumbalo told an interviewer, "but also very, very cathartic."[11]

"Did you have to wait a long time after your friend died to be able to write it?" he was asked.

"No, he was alive when I finished it. He read the play. This was George Whitmore. We talked about it, and he loved the idea of the play. And then he said an interesting thing to me. He asked me, 'Is Eddie going to die during the play?' And I said, 'No, I don't think so,' because I was nervous and trying to avoid it. He said, 'Then as a PWA, I would be very uncomfortable watching your play, it would be denying what may happen to me.'"

---

10 Paul Monette, *Love Alone* (New York: St. Martin's Press, 1989), p. xii.
11 Victor Bumbalo, interviewed by Michael O'Conner, *Mandate* (January 1990): p. 87.

"And what did he say when he read the play?" asked the interviewer.

"He really liked the play a lot. But then, George is George; he's also a writer. So first, of course, he had his emotional experience with it, and then he looked at it as a writer. I mean, I was writing this play and he was writing *Someone Was Here*. We were two of the most depressed people in New York!"

Around this time, according to Andrew Holleran, "there came a strange point—this was years into the epidemic—when I realized that all the writing that was not about AIDS that I myself was reading seemed so irrelevant and pointless, that it really was like playing bridge while the *Titanic* was sinking. It was just impossible to talk about anything else."[12] Holleran's monthly essays in *Christopher Street* became a lifeline to many readers like myself who felt like they were clinging to the Raft of the Medusa. Collected in *Ground Zero*, these essays charted the wilderness that life with AIDS had become, probing, exploring, grieving and mapping the way we live now.

Robert Patrick's searing one-act comedy *Pouf Positive* (printed in *Untold Decades: Seven Comedies of Gay Romance*) was a final gift to an ex-lover whose last request the author found on his answering machine when he returned to the city shortly after the man's death: "You ask if you can do anything for me, Robert? Yes, write a comedy about this absurd mess." And Harvey Fierstein, in his comic trilogy *Safe Sex*, explored the new social conundrums AIDS has established with a rare blend of wit and anger.

Larry Kramer weighed in once again with his *Reports from the Holocaust*, a collection of passionate essays and thunderous calls to action that proved just how mighty the pen can be. Not since Emile Zola's *J'accuse* has the sheer power inherent in the spoken and written word been used with such polemical skill and political impact.

In *Personal Dispatches* John Preston, who had stopped writing for over a year after he was diagnosed, found a way out of his own panic and despair by collecting essays from some twenty writers who had to put their personal and professional agendas on hold and turned to the

---

12 Andrew Holleran, "Personal Dispatches: Gay Writers and AIDS," *Tribe*, vol. 2, no. 2 (Spring 1990): p. 15.

written word to confront the plague that increasingly threatened their circle of friends, their lovers, their own bodies. "The drive of each author was to bear witness," said Preston in an interview, "and in rereading the book, I was struck by how often that word was used . . . and the word 'witness' is not a passive word, it's a very active verb. To 'witness' is not simply to make note, not simply to record, although there is a power in that. It is to go out and see what is going on."[13]

Two of the contributors to Preston's anthology died before the book could be printed. And well over half of all the writers mentioned here are sero-positive, ill, or already dead.

These writers—and many others I have not mentioned[14]—registered the initial shock of AIDS as an historical event, that moment when a deep shudder seized the soul of the gay community. Because of criminal neglect and indifference, this eminently preventable epidemic, which should have been treated as an emergency but was not, spread throughout the land and became a medical fact and an omnipresent threat. By the late Eighties the emergency had become a condition of life, particularly for gay men. "We seem to have reached a plateau of some sort," commented Holleran in 1988, "in which people have adapted to it in a strange way. . . . It's a way of life now."[15]

A way of life that Paul Monette, who, against all odds, continued to be able to write, explored in two further novels:

"It's never going to be over, is it?" asked Mark, not really expecting an answer.

"Someday. Not for us."

---

13 John Preston in an interview with Sarah Pettit, "Bearing Witness," *Outweek*, no. 25 (December 10, 1990): p. 43.

14 Of course, the people I discuss do not exhaust the list of courageous writers who have responded to the epidemic in their work; there are many more, and with time we will no doubt get more balanced overviews of the subject. I have concentrated on the works and writers I have been most involved with, through the happenstance of friendship, admiration, or professional association.

15 Andrew Holleran, "From the Dance to Ground Zero," an interview with Damien Jack, *New York Native*, December 5, 1988, p. 21.

"Will anyone understand what it was like?" It was curiously easy, perched on the mountain of death, to speak about the future when all of them would be gone.

"Maybe the gay ones will."

"Yeah, but they'll have to see through all the lies. 'Cause history's just white folks covering their ass."[16]

Beyond even anger and grief, gay writers realized they now stood in the full noon of disaster, unrelenting, unending, inevitable; and, like Michael Lassell in his great poem "How to Watch Your Brother Die"[17] they set down a record to stand against the lies.

Peter McGehee in his two extraordinary comic novels, *Boys Like Us* and *Sweetheart*, describes what life is like when you live amidst a circle of friends, an elective family, that you know is soon going to disappear, when imminent absence is a palpable, felt pressure affecting every present moment. It was his great achievement to wrest comedy from material saturated with such intense mortality. Edmund White described the new situation with a precise clarity: "Mark thought this summer everything was just as it had been the twelve preceding summers. The only thing different was that this summer would end the series. He wanted to know how to enjoy these days without clasping them so tightly he'd stifle the pleasure. But he didn't want to drug himself on the moment either and miss out on what was happening to him. He was losing his best friend, the witness to his life. The skill for enjoying a familiar pleasure about to disappear was hard to acquire . . . knowing how to appreciate the rhythms of these last casual moments to cherish them while letting them stay casual—demanded a new way of navigating time."[18]

This growing body of work defining the face of AIDS, limning it in

---

16 Paul Monette, *Afterlife* (New York: Crown, 1990), p. 264. See also his novel *Halfway Home* (New York: Crown, 1991).

17 Michael Lassell, "How to Watch Your Brother Die," *Gay & Lesbian Poetry in Our Time*, ed. Carl Morse and Joan Larkin (New York: St. Martin's Press, 1988), p. 224.

18 Edmund White, "Palace Days," in *The Darker Proof: Stories from a Crisis* (New York: New American Library, 1988), p. 164.

our public and collective imagination, seems to me more than a literary accomplishment. These are individual acts of language performed in the full light of the community's crisis. They are, I would argue, the primary discourse of AIDS, a public dialogue that articulates the experience of the community and constitutes, beyond the shadow of a doubt, the creation of a culture. This new writing is not "discourses about discourses"; indeed, it was impelled into being by the urgent necessity to put speech where there had been cultural silence, for in our present circumstances, as the motto of ACT-UP succinctly puts it, "Silence=Death." The task was not to "hear what has already been said" but to utter the new word, the word that would reveal what was happening to us and, at the same time, would constitute our answer, our response, our resistance.

This writing lays before us an example of a living culture, culture as a spontaneous act, for culture is a complex social event that creates the public space in which a community comes into being through participation. Generally, we tend to think of culture either objectively, from the outside, as an anthropologist might look at Samoa, or passively, as a tradition that's there, that is somehow fundamental and undergirds our intellectual life today. But we are not outside this culture that is ours, we have no disinterested Archimedean point of view from which to study it; we *are* the Samoans. Nor is culture any longer a tradition handed down to us, shoved at us by the previous generation; indeed, a great portion of the cultural activity of the last century has centered on the collapse of this tradition and its consequences. Insofar as it exists today, culture is an event that requires activity at both ends, on the part of the initiator who raises a voice to speak, and on the part of the hearer who actively attends to the word. Culture *is* the relationship between these two, and that relationship is an activity, of speaking and of attending, and that activity creates the bond that is what we mean by the word *community*.

II.

The writing that is emerging from the AIDS crisis is, to my mind, startlingly different from our normal understanding of writing and books in this society—that is, writing as a literary career or profession, on the one hand, and books as a commercial commodity and the object of esthetic appreciation, on the other. Virtually all the writers I know of who have grappled with AIDS in their work have experienced this as an interruption of their career.[19] They speak of putting aside their personal agendas to care for friends, to do political or volunteer work, to manage their own illness, and finally to confront this disaster with the tools of their trade, to use the imagination and the capacities of language and its forms to comprehend what is happening.

"Many of the contributors to (*Personal Dispatches*) are activists," said Preston. "They are doing things that must be done. There's a quote at the beginning of the book, 'For some of us must storm the castles. Some define the happening,' that I hesitated before using because it seemed to imply a separation of roles. Writing on the one hand, action on the other. I kept it in because I came to understand that it was a corporate statement; that both must be done and that much of it is done by the same people."[20]

"Write as if you were dying," admonished Annie Dillard in the 29 May 1989 *New York Times Book Review*, evidently not imagining that a whole generation of gay writers might be. "At the same time," she added, "assume you write for an audience consisting solely of terminal patients."[21] When this is actually the case, profession and career do not begin to define or situate the activity of writing.

"The purpose of AIDS writing," declared Preston, "has to be found outside of any conventions that contemporary criticism and publishing might try to impose on us. The cannons are proven to be ineffective, inappropriate. What is 'literature' becomes a meaningless academic question when what is defined can't accommodate what is happening in our lives. . . . Those of us who are writing about AIDS can't worry about these definitions anymore. We can't be concerned with career-

---

19 See for instance the comments of John Preston, Paul Monette, Edmund White, Andrew Holleran, and Larry Duplechan in *Tribe*, vol. 1, no. 2 (Spring 1990): pp. 3–29.
20 Sarah Pettit, "Bearing Witness," *Outweek*, no. 25 (December 10, 1989): p. 43.
21 Annie Dillard, "Write Till You Drop," *New York Times Book Review*, May 28, 1989, p. 1.

ism, with academic acceptance, or with having the fashions of the day dictate how we write. We can now only deal with being witnesses."[22]

The poems in *Love Alone* that coursed out of Paul Monette in the months immediately following his lover's death were not conceived as a literary strategy: "Writing them quite literally kept me alive," said the author, "for the only time I wasn't wailing and trembling was when I was hammering at these poems."[23] When Randy Shilts took a leave of absence from his job as an investigative reporter to write *And the Band Played On*, he intended to change the world, to shock the country into taking action that would end the epidemic. That all he achieved was another book, albeit a best-seller, does not alter the original intention; indeed, the sardonic, even bitter, tone with which he recounted in *Esquire* magazine the story of the book's success and his own utter failure starkly reveals his original intentions.[24]

If it is an inescapable irony for the artist that acts of the spirit when put into the world, immediately become transformed into exchange commodities—for instance, books to be sold and bought—still, this does not change either the author's original intention or the work's essence. In fact, it only creates more paradoxes. "Who wants to read this fiction?" asked Allen Barnett, whose harrowing stories remind us that reading is sometimes a courageous act. "It hurts me to re-read them."[25] Kenneth Lithgow, who has produced some of the most powerful depictions of AIDS on canvas I know of, says, "My fear is these works are going to die in the studio. People see them and cry. Who would want to live with these paintings?"[26]

And Holleran writes of books about AIDS, "I really don't know who reads them for pleasure."[27]

Aesthetic appreciation is neither the intention nor the relevant response to such works. "I don't consider myself an artist," writes Larry

22 John Preston, "AIDS Writing," comments made at the 1990 Out/Write Conference, San Francisco, unpublished manuscript sent to me by the author.

23 Monette, *Love Alone*, p. xii.

24 Randy Shilts, "Talking AIDS to Death," *Esquire* (March 1989): pp. 123-34.

25 Spoken in a personal conversation with me.

26 Kaufman, "AIDS: The Cultural Response," p. 18.

27 Holleran, *Ground Zero* (New York: William Morrow, 1988), p. 12.

Kramer. "I consider myself a very opinionated man who uses words as fighting tools. I perceive certain wrongs that make me very angry, and somehow I hope that if I string my words together with enough skill, people will hear them and respond. I am under no delusion that this will necessarily be the case, but I seem to have no choice but to try."[28] And Paul Monette says of *Love Alone*, "I would rather have this volume filed under AIDS than under Poetry, because if these words speak to anyone they are for those who are mad with loss, to let them know they are not alone."[29] Whatever it is, this writing is not about the making of well-wrought urns.

What distinguishes this AIDS writing from other literary production in our time is not only the writers' intention but the unique situation in which the act of writing occurs. This is not strong emotion recollected in tranquility; these are reports from the combat zone. AIDS writing is urgent; it is engaged and activist writing; it is writing in response to a present threat; it is in it, of it, and aims to affect it. I can think of no good parallel for this in literary history. As far as I know, most of the writing done about the Holocaust was published after 1945, when the nightmare was over in reality and began to haunt the imagination. And while the closest parallel might be the poetry that came out of the trenches of the First World War, the bulk of that writing was published, reviewed and read after the war; whereas this AIDS writing is not only being produced in the trenches as it were, but is being published, read by its public and evaluated by critics in the midst of the crisis. It is as if Sassoon's poetry were being mimeographed in the trenches and distributed to be read by men under fire—the immediacy of these circumstances precludes the possibility of this being a merely aesthetic enterprise. The aesthetic requires distance and the distance is not available, not to the writer, not to the reader.

Because of this peculiarity, the truth or beauty—that is, the inherent excellence—of this writing will not wait upon posterity for judgment. In this onrush of death, posterity—even posterity as an imagined

---

28 Larry Kramer, *Reports from the Holocaust* (New York: St. Martin's Press, 1989), p. 145.
29 Monette, *Love Alone*, p. xi.

frame for the activity of writing—is a luxury. The time is not available. Writers who are facing death are writing for an audience that is dying. Never could I have imagined ten years ago having *regular* discussions with writers about whether they would live long enough to finish a project. Never could I have imagined feeling, on a daily basis, this terrible urgency to get the book out while the author is still alive. "During the year after Roger died," Monette told an interviewer, "I spent the next eight or nine months writing the book *Borrowed Time*, assuming I would be dead in a year. I felt that I should get up in the morning and write the best I could that day and put it to bed that night, for who knew what would happen the next day. It was a sense of urgency, a calamitous urgency throughout the writing of those two books."[30]

Many artists and art movements in the twentieth century have tried to shake themselves loose from the deadening context of posterity-as-judge, to avoid the specter of the eternal museum outside time to which art is consigned, in order to free the creative act and its inherent energy. It is a terrible irony that for gay writers AIDS has knocked to smithereens all such constraining cultural frameworks.

A comparison may make clear the unparalleled circumstances in which this work is being written. Anne Frank's diary, which might at first be thought a good literary parallel, has its own special beauty; but, on the one hand, it was written without her really knowing what would happen, and, on the other hand, we read it knowing there is nothing we can do about the course of events. But AIDS writing is about something we know *is* happening, *now*, and about which we must in fact *do* something. Of necessity this writing arises from the moment and intends to have its impact in the present. As Sarah Pettit has pointed out, what is "wholly different about the present sort of bearing witness is that it's witnessing *in the midst* of the nightmare. Speaking out *in the midst* of an event has to hold with it the notion that witnessing can effect change."[31] Preston agrees:

---

30 Mark Stomberg, "Deliriously Unique," an interview with Paul Monette, *New York Native*, March 26, 1990, p. 19.
31 Pettit, "Bearing Witness," p. 43.

The purpose of AIDS writing now is *to get it all down.*

The purpose of the writer in the time of AIDS is *to bear witness.* . . . To live in a time of AIDS and to understand what is going on, *writing must be action. Writing must be accompanied by action. Writing is not what our teachers told us, something that stands alone.*

To be a writer in the time of AIDS is to be a truth-teller. The truth is more horrible than anything people want to hear. . . . The truth is devastating. The truth can't be contained in a pleasantly structured short story that will satisfy the readers of a literary magazine.[32]

III.

"This writing about AIDS reports from the thing itself. It unsettles all the assumptions culture codified about how art is supposed to work and how long it is supposed to take for it to work and who decides whether what is working is really art," writes Robert Dawidoff in *Personal Dispatches.* "The reader and writer community of AIDS has rediscovered the roots of any kind of writing, the roots in human survival, expression, ritual and need. We need to have these things written. The information, the truth, the anger, the philosophy, the history, the fiction, the poetry, the spirituality do a job now. Their place in history will be judged by their success in helping to keep the community the writing serves alive, safer, together, comforted in sickness and in loss."[33] Holleran agrees: this writing will be judged "as writing published in wartime is, by its effect on the people fighting."[34]

The idea that the appropriate measure of writing is its impact on the continued existence and well-being of the community is the validating principle of any ethnic or national literature. It is why Isaac Bashevis Singer is important to Yiddish culture, why the slave narratives undergird all African-American writing in this country, why the

32 Preston, "AIDS Writing."
33 Robert Dawidoff, "Memorial Day, 1989," in Preston's *Personal Dispatches: Writers Confront AIDS* (New York: St. Martin's Press, 1989), p. 174.
34 Holleran, *Ground Zero,* p. 17.

underground Russian writers of the last fifty years will be treasured by generations of Russian readers. All such writing has as its innermost principle the act of bearing witness. To bear witness is to declare oneself, to declare oneself present, to declare oneself in the presence of what has come to be. This is the original discourse, the primary word, the logos that opens a space in which we can be present to one another. It is this space that allows a community to come into being, for this is the site of the action of culture and the possibility of memory. Those who bear witness carry the soul of the community, the stories of what it has done and what it has suffered, and open the possibility of its existence in memory through time and beyond death.

This understanding of writing and its inherent nature and excellence stands in opposition to all ideas of universal literary standards, the presence of which is always an outstanding characteristic of the hegemonic urge of any dominant and dominating class, group, or nation. In literary culture the assertion of universal standards of judgment is always the tip-off to the urge to dominate, to subdue the different, to draw all into a uniform order. You reach for the universal when you don't want to tolerate diversity, politically speaking, when you want to abolish the existential fact of human plurality.

This is, of course, an outstanding fact about the literary culture in America today, as anyone who has the misfortune of being in a profession that requires the reading of a large cross-section of book reviews can testify to, or as a brief glance at the furious defenses of the canon coming from our reactionary, but still dominant, cultural commentators attests to. In spite of the fact that this country is composed of a loose assortment of variegated and astonishingly numerous communities all superimposed upon one another, that virtually every individual American participates in a number of overlapping communities, each with its own culture—as a woman, say, who is also Jewish, a lesbian, and an academic—the organs of cultural definition in this country seem hell-bent on asserting a uniform and shared culture, which is in fact a myth, an obfuscation, a curtain drawn over the real mechanics of cultural creation today. The purpose, of course, is to assert control—to absorb those creations which can be assimilated to the cultural amalgam of the dominant class without upsetting the applecart, and, at the same time, to peripheralize the rest into a marginal, regional, special interest, minority reservation—colorful perhaps, worth a visit as a tourist, but in some basic way not the real thing.

This has been the root problem with the reception of works of gay writers by the mainstream press in the last decade. And it is only heightened when the writing concerns AIDS, for as long as the mainstream press does not participate in the community of crisis, which may be defined as those who choose to be affected by AIDS, as long as the mainstream press sees AIDS as something that happens to "other people," it will continue to judge this writing and these writers in terms of conventional aesthetic categories: is this aesthetically pleasing; does it constitute an advance in the career of the writer? In short, the media will continue to miss the point.

A revealing instance can be found in the long, joint review that *Time* magazine printed last year of three books provoked by the AIDS crisis: Paul Monette's *Borrowed Time*, Andrew Holleran's *Ground Zero*, and Alice Hoffman's *At Risk*, a novel by a heterosexual woman about an eleven-year-old white girl, a gymnast no less, who got AIDS from a blood transfusion—what they call "an innocent victim." It was utterly predictable that the book that had the strongest impact on the gay community and on those affected by AIDS, Monette's *Borrowed Time*, was the book *Time* found most disagreeable. "*Borrowed Time* demands a sympathetic response instead of inviting one," complained the magazine, as if this constituted an unwonted imposition on the reader by the author.[35] Would they have made the same complaint about Nadezhda Mandelstam's memoirs or the tale of any Holocaust survivor, one wonders. Oddly enough, the reviewer didn't notice that the reason Holleran neither invites nor demands sympathy from straight readers is that he assumes that all his readers are gay, for this is clearly whom he is speaking to when he sits at his typewriter.

Of course, the best book of the lot, according to *Time*, was Hoffman's account of an "innocent victim." "Hoffman gets the blend of hope and despair just right," approved *Time*, as if the author were whipping up a cake. What can this possibly mean? Is there a mixture of

---

35 R. Z. Sheppard, "Journals of the Plague Years," *Time*, July 18, 1988, pp. 68–69.

hope and despair that is just right? Is it right in all cases, or just in this instance? What precisely constitutes hope when your eleven-year-old daughter is dying of AIDS? What the reviewer really meant is that his sensibilities were not unduly disturbed, that his spirit was agitated but still soothed in a pleasing manner. If you want to see the essential vulgarity of this purely aesthetic response, just imagine someone saying, "Anne Frank got the blend of hope and despair just right."

In the gay literary community there was much heated debate about *At Risk* and a good deal of bitterness about the fact that this work of fiction far outsold any other novel on AIDS. While I believe that no author can be told what he or she can or cannot write about, this anger did not seem a surprising response. One could imagine a novel about an eleven-year-old Christian girl in Berlin who, through some mix-up one day on the street, is caught in one of the round-ups of Jews and "mistakenly" sent to Auschwitz—the "mistake" here is equivalent to "accidentally" getting AIDS. This is a perfectly legitimate subject for a novel, but if the book detailed the suffering of this child and her family while virtually ignoring the fate of the Jews at Auschwitz, one would not be surprised to get a chilly reception in the Jewish press. And if that book far outsold any other novel about the Holocaust, one would not be surprised to find bitterness in the hearts of many Jews. This is a hypothetical example, but there was in reality a quite similar debate over *The Confessions of Nat Turner*. All arguments aside, the point of the matter is that there *was* a heated public debate—as there should have been—but I did not see one reviewer outside the gay press even raise the issue with *At Risk*, and, in fact, few reviewers in the gay press did either. And surely the matter was worth discussing.

In fact, it raises a serious and troubling question about the judgment of contemporary works of fiction. When I read Allen Barnett's extraordinary story "The *Times* as It Knows Us"—the title signals the sheer contempt this gay New Yorker has for our so-called "newspaper of record"—the author's unblinking vision of the harrowing events that take place during one weekend in a not untypical gay summer house in The Pines both exhausted and impressed me. The story's power derives from its understatement, its lack of hysteria, and its unbending courage to imagine things as they are right now for many of us. It is not an unfamiliar story to me or to my friends; it's one I recognize only too well, yet I found it almost unbearable to read. The fact that Barnett's imagination did not buckle under the weight of this horror steadied me and convinced me of the magnitude of his achievement. But what, I wondered, would a straight reader make of it? Would such a reader feel the unstated pressure that made it difficult for me to breathe? And, if not, was I saying that a straight friend of mine would be in no position, would have no right, to judge this story because she did not have first-hand experience of what the story was about, a position that made me very uncomfortable. When I raised the issue with Barnett himself, he thought a moment and said, "You know, I saw a teenager, a Black girl, on the subway today reading Toni Morrison's *The Bluest Eye*, a book that had an incredible impact on me. And I realized that the book could never have the meaning for me that it would have for her. And I was very glad she was reading it, for she is the audience."

For me this little story neatly raises the question of the plurality of cultures in which we live. In one of the last great works of the imperial spirit, T. E. Lawrence wrote in *The Seven Pillars of Wisdom* that to try to view reality simultaneously through the veils of two different cultures would drive a man mad. Though this sounds convincing when you come upon it in that remarkable book, one remembers that Kierkegaard and Nietzsche, the first two thinkers for whom modernity as such was a problematic issue—indeed, a crisis—both characterized modernity, or perhaps the crisis hidden within it, as the ability or the necessity of holding contradictory ideas in the mind simultaneously. "Contradictory" was perhaps inexact, but the collapse of a unifying tradition that could take disparate elements and order them into a more or less uniform, or at least non-contradictory, whole, this collapse of tradition is indisputable and glaringly the fundamental datum of twentieth-century culture, articulated over and over again in the works of our thinkers, poets, and artists. By now it should be quite clear to everyone: the center did not hold. And with the collapse of the authority of tradition, all cultures, not only all present but all past cultures, regained a certain viability as a veil that one might borrow to see certain aspects of reality more clearly, as when Picasso raided African art for forms and principles that could rejuvenate his own.

The resulting situation, it seems to me—with all due respect to Lawrence of Arabia—is that today we see reality precisely through a multitude of veils simultaneously. And while this may require some fancy footwork and a greater mental and spiritual dexterity by no means will it necessarily drive us mad.

All the questions, objections, and arguments about the existence of a separate and distinct gay culture—and the deep-seated hostility with which the spokespeople for the dominant culture in this country react to this possibility—rest on a mistaken notion of the relationship between the two. It is not, as they think, a question of the Greeks versus the barbarians, which in essence boils down to those who have culture versus those who don't, *hoi barbaroi*, the barbarians who babble, who have no language (don't speak Greek) and thus no culture. This paradigm of how a plurality of cultures co-exists always comes down to a power relation, a hostile power relation: us versus them. But we *are* a them, each one of us. I am a white American gay man. I participate in gay culture, but I also participate quite actively in mainstream American culture. And, in fact, through my reading of the remarkable burst of superb writing by African-American women in the last decade and a half, not to speak of Black music in general, I get to participate in Black culture. And when I read Maxine Hong Kingston and Amy Tan, I get to see life in this country through the veil of Chinese-American culture.

These cultures all exist simultaneously, inexactly superimposed upon each other, a great palimpsest, creating a moiré effect in the soul that is the basic texture of cultural life today. And when suddenly groups of us—urban male Jews or African-Americans or Chinese-Americans or gay people—spin our veils, we are creating garments for the spirit that can be shared.

Allen Barnett can share *The Bluest Eye*, though perhaps it will never have the resonance and depth for him that it will for a Black girl. Then again none of us can participate in Greek tragedy with the transparent clarity it must have had for contemporary Athenians. But still we read it. Which is precisely why we have Greek scholars, specialists who not only tend and preserve the work and its meaning but try to clear away the obscurity that an ever-lengthening distance between us and the work creates.

Time, of course, is not the only type of distance; there are psychic distances, between, for instance, the souls of Black folk in America and the dominant American culture, between an emerging gay sensibility and straight America, between those who are living through the maelstrom of AIDS and the rest of the country. But we can bridge these distances by the active power of the imagination, that power, as Hannah Arendt used to say, that makes present that which is absent, that makes near that which is far, that power which is the root and source of all human understanding.

Those who are living through AIDS are spinning an astonishing garment for the spirit, one that offers its gift not only to those stricken but to all who care to reach, to participate in the great life of the imagination and spirit that is human culture. Gay culture is a necessity for us and an offering to the rest. At the moment, the dominant culture mainly rejects the gift and spurns the giver, which is a great foolishness.[36] The gift asks only to be taken, and in that sharing we begin to participate in the communities of all peoples. In that sharing we begin to learn how to live among a plurality of peoples and to move among a multiplicity of cultures with whom we share the Earth even as they share with us the riches of their experiences and the wealth of their spirit.

---

[36] See, for instance, the remarkably shallow essay by Edward Hoagland in *Esquire*, "Shhh! Our Writers Are Sleeping!" (July 1990, p. 57), in which he bemoans the fact that American writers of fiction avoid the major social issues of the day. Although he mentions AIDS in passing, he seems utterly unaware of the extent and depth of the literature responding to this particular issue of the day. It would seem that it is Mr. Hoagland who is asleep, especially since he also seems quite unaware of the central themes of African-American women writers in the last decade. Or perhaps the problem lies in Hoagland's understanding of the phrase "our writers."

Preaching to the Choir

THESE REMARKS WERE delivered at "Outright '90," the first National Lesbian and Gay Writers Conference, held in San Francisco on March 4, 1990. Virtually everyone who was involved in the writing and publishing of gay and lesbian books was there. I was astonished at the size of the audience and the Chautauqua spirit blowing through the assembly. This would have been the perfect audience for "A Quilt of Many Colors," I thought. Instead, I ended up in the role of cheerleader, urging gay and lesbian writers to go out there and build the audience, make the revolution! A necessary task, of course, but nowhere near as interesting intellectually.

I should note here the discrepancies in the number of gay bookstores mentioned in various pieces. At different times there were full-on gay and lesbian bookstores; then there were women's bookstores and feminist bookstores, some of which were glad to stock our gay/lesbian titles; then there were independent bookstores which were neither gay/lesbian nor women's bookstores but which carried all our gay/lesbian titles; then there were chain bookstores, some of which developed separate sections for gay/lesbian books and carried much of our inventory, backlist as well as current titles. If they did enough volume, all of them became gay and lesbian specialty stores from the point of view of the salespeople. The number I used in each place probably depended on the last person I'd talked with about the issue or the last thing I'd read. However, the main point was always the same: the number was constantly increasing.

The remarkable boom in gay and lesbian publishing we are currently witnessing is, in my opinion, neither illusory nor a fad. It is, quite simply, the literary manifestation of a much larger event, a vast transformation in social reality as wide and deep as the civil rights movement that has reshaped the face of American society in the last half century. The emergence of the gay community in America is one of the major domestic events happening in this country in the second half of the twentieth century. That our so-called social scientists and media commentators are oblivious to this fact should not obscure our own vision. When twenty million people go from considering themselves sick, sinful or criminally deviant to self-affirming members of a totally new, historically unprecedented, voluntary community, you have a social transformation of enormous magnitude.

The emergence of gay and lesbian writing is the literary mirror of this social transformation, a transformation that shows no signs of slowing down in any area. The sheer number of younger gay and lesbian writers now appearing on the scene provides further reassurance that this process will continue. The fact that there are 1,300 people registered at this conference—just think of it: 1,300 gay and lesbian writers in one place!—that would have seemed inconceivable fifteen years ago. But if these numbers are reassuring, they also raise some disquieting problems.

If all of you are going to become published gay and lesbian authors, who is going to buy your books? As David Groff of Crown said yesterday, the reason there aren't more gay and lesbian books published is that there aren't more gay and lesbian book buyers. And while I personally rather liked his own solution to this dilemma—that from now on we all agree not to sleep with anybody who owns more record albums than books—I doubt the majority of us would have the self-discipline required. Besides, it would be the end of sex in our time.

The crucial question for the future of gay writing is the development of the gay and lesbian audience. Let's face it: we are not going to convince the people who buy Dick Francis, Rod McKuen or Danielle Steele to suddenly start buying Michael Nava, Judy Grahn and Armistead Maupin. If you all want to be published authors, we are going to have to create a new and larger book-buying public.

If we don't, gay writers may end up in the dismal situation that, by and large, poets find themselves in today—i.e., the only people who buy books of poetry are the people who write books of poetry. And I admit that in my darker moments I have considered the possibility that the only people who buy gay books are the people who write gay books—not necessarily get them published, but write them.

Most of the time I don't think we are headed in this direction. Our book-buying public *is* expanding—ten years ago there were nine gay bookstores in this country, today there are about thirty-seven, and maybe another hundred stores that have gay sections.

Still, I have the impression that at the moment the number of gay and lesbian authors is increasing faster than the number of gay and lesbian book buyers and somehow we have got to address this problem. We have got to find a way to reach the boys in the bars and the lesbians down the street. We have got to expand the literary culture further into the gay and lesbian community. And, although I expect it will be unpopular to say it here, this is something authors have to do themselves, publishers cannot do it for you. If you want to be a successful writer, you are going to have to take the responsibility of fashioning your own careers and developing your public. Judy Grahn and Armistead Maupin, John Preston and Sarah Schulman have developed their own publics, people who have read their last book and want to read their next book, and that is why they get published. A publisher cannot do this. A publisher can exploit an existing market—for women's romances, say, or male adventure novels—but they cannot bring a new market, a new book-buying public, into existence.

Writers do this—by giving readings and workshops, by writing for magazines and newspapers, above all by digging deep enough into their psyches that what they come up with resonates in the minds and souls of their readers, making the writing *matter* to their audience. And no editor and no publisher can do this for you.

Too many writers today seem to think that their audience is the publisher—and I don't mean to limit this to gay and lesbian writers, it is just as true of straight writers. Writers in general seem to think that the crucial nexus is the writer-publisher connection, that their main task is to get the publisher to offer a contract, or a bigger advance, or a larger advertising budget. But the publisher is just the middleman. The decisive connection always has been and still is the connection between the writer and the reading public.

But I don't want to give the impression that the prospect is grim.

Actually, I think the situation for new gay and lesbian authors today is better than the prospects for new straight writers. Really excellent straight first novels can often garner no more than five or six reviews across this *whole* country and sell 1,800 copies. In contrast, a gay book will get many more reviews and will almost certainly sell more copies. In fact, a month ago I did an analysis of the first novels I'd published for the last five years, gay and straight, and the gay books definitely sold better than the straight books. And, even more important, the gay authors got a *much* bigger critical response, often garnering twenty to thirty reviews and giving the writer the sense that there was some response from the world, which is immensely important for a writer's morale. In fact, my straight novelists are downright envious of the situation of the gay writers—and with good cause. The audience is more articulated and coherent, more immediately present at readings and signings, even the controversies are more real and meaningful. When gay writers—and editors—dwell on the problems of being a gay writer in this country today, the framework is often unrealistic expectations. Probably less than five percent of the writers in this country are able to support themselves on their writing—a fact that we often forget when we deplore the fact that so few gay writers can support themselves from their writing.

A further reason for optimism is the first stirrings of gay and lesbian studies in the universities, which is just beginning and which I hope—and pray, actually—is going to explode in the next few years. It is very clear that the economic substructure for feminist publishing in this country is the fact that women's studies courses are taught in virtually every university and community college across the land. There are literally thousands of women who teach women's studies. This creates a solid base for women's books—both among the students and especially among the faculty. More important, it creates a cultural climate—the women who take these courses will tend to continue to buy books in this area. If the gay kids in college now start taking gay studies courses, they will become the audience for your books in the years to come. If developments follow this path, the economic substructure for gay publishing will get put on a firm basis and things could look very bright indeed.

The Present Moment

IN THE SPRING of 1990 Malcolm Boyd, an author of mine as well as an old friend, invited me to participate in a conference at UCLA called "The Claiming of World Citizenship: Gay and Lesbian Literature Explodes Into the Nineties," held on April 21 of that year. This was my contribution.

When discussing this panel, Malcolm Boyd suggested that it would be useful if I could cover the history of gay literature from the past to the present (in approximately ten minutes).

However, this charge presented me with several difficulties, the main one being that the past, *this* past, has not yet fully come into existence. For it is the present that contains not only the seeds of the future, but the seeds of the past. The remarkable emergence of gay and lesbian literature today is even now calling into being its past by reclaiming its predecessors and uncovering its hidden tradition. The buried genealogy of gay literature is rising into view like a submerged continent, as a huge reassembly and reinterpretation of historical fact is underway—from new historical analyses of Pater and Swinburne to new readings of Thornton Wilder's *Our Town* and Emily Dickinson's poetry. This reclaiming of our past, the taking back of gay and lesbian voices that have been appropriated by the dominant society for its own purposes, is a complex and subtle task, but it is far more a consequence than a cause of the flowering of gay writing today. So if the past is a reverberation of the present, I propose we look at that present.

Gay and lesbian literature would not be possible, obviously, without the presence of gays and lesbians. Gay literature presupposes the existence of both a gay identity (or, as some would prefer to say, a gay sensibility) and a gay community. Now these two—gay identity/ sensibility and gay community—are not the same thing but they are inextricably connected and they arise simultaneously. Gay identity, the self-declaration of the individual which we encapsulate in the simple phrase "coming out"—but which is, in fact, as subtle, complex, varied, and rich a theme for our writers as "coming of age" is for non-gay writers—this declaration of personal identity is possible only in the face of the community; gay identity presupposes the gay community. Conversely, the gay community presupposes the existence of gay individuals who make it up. And gay literature presupposes them both. Thus gay literature is inherently political—it rests on the political existence of a self-acknowledged community and the political act of self-declaration that constitutes an individual's gay identity. And this brings us back to the political moment that ushered in our presence—the Stonewall Riots of June 1969.

It used to be that in meetings like this one could say: it is not necessary to recall what life was like for gays and lesbians before Stonewall. However, as many of us get younger and some of us get older, this has changed and it is increasingly necessary to recall the nature and quality of our lives pre-Stonewall. This life seems to me brilliantly captured in Mart Crowley's play, and movie, *The Boys in the Band*, which came out just before Stonewall and which depicts a pre-revolutionary situation if I've ever seen one. Those of you who have not seen it for a while should rent the videotape—it's a startlingly prescient work in which six very angry homosexual men essentially attack one straight man. The play gets its tension and drama for this explosive but submerged anger pervading the psyches of these homosexuals, who are not even aware how angry they are until a trivial incident sets off an explosion. What is so moving—and startling to realize—is how the characters have no horizon of possibility. Their discomfort, anger, rebellion they can feel, but they don't know what to do with it—the idea of gay liberation is as absent from this play as it was from the lives of most of us in 1966 or 1967—although an astute observer, seeing the play in '68, might have been able to anticipate that something like Stonewall was imminent.

Which is not to say that Stonewall was inevitable. There is something ultimately inexplicable about any event, why it happened when it happened, and why it had such consequences. John Preston told me of a very similar event that happened in a bar in, I believe, Chicago a year or two earlier—he describes this incident in *Franny, the Queen of Provincetown*—which seemed to have no historical impact whatsoever. But as Kant told us in his writings about the French Revolution, what is of decisive significance is not so much the event itself as its impact and meaning for the spectators, those who watched and perceived the truth being manifested in the event.

And surely Stonewall was an event that manifested the truth, and the political imperative of the moment, for gay people all over this country. Stonewall was the shot heard 'round the gay world. Michael Scherker, who was working on an oral history of the Stonewall Riots until his recent death, told me one story he had heard of a man who was a communications officer in the army in Danang, Vietnam, in 1969. Sitting by the teletype machine in the middle of the night, this man watched with disbelief as the story came over the wire: "Homosexuals Rioting in Greenwich Village, Police Injured and Retreating from Parts of the Village." This one moment changed the course of his life for the next twenty years, and he knew it would *instantly*, though, of course, it would take decades to work out the implications concretely in his life. Historical events of the first magnitude have this quality of revelation, and, as we are realizing more and more, Stonewall was a historical event of the first magnitude.

As the implications of Stonewall unfolded in the Seventies, we increasingly realized that not only had we been oppressed, but our very imaginations had been hijacked. We saw life through the lens of the dominant, heterosexual imagination—the very people who, for some odd, berserk, unfathomable reason desperately wanted us not to exist—or, if forced to acknowledge our existence, insisted on seeing homosexuality not as something that existed in itself, but as a privative form of heterosexuality. Like those theologians who saw evil as the absence of good, they saw homosexuality as an arrested case of heterosexual development, as an inverted form of heterosexual gender roles, as a bent form of the straight. In other words, we *still* didn't exist, only heterosexuality exists, and those poor, mangled forms of heterosexuality, one of which was homosexuality. This peculiar obsession goes very deep in heterosexual culture—all the way back to the medieval definition of homosexual acts as crimes not fit to be spoken about among decent men. This is *the definition*—repeated with minor variations again and again in theological and legal treatises—it is *defined* as that which is not to be talked about among decent people. Nutty as it sounds, it is defined as something the existence of which we must deny, hide, or ignore. Think about it.

Well, after Stonewall, it was clearly our task to talk about it—to try to imagine who we were before we were seen by them, so to speak. As the newly self-conscious gay writing began to emerge in the Seventies—to my mind, reaching its first high-water mark in '78, which saw the publication of Edmund White's *Nocturnes for the King of Naples*, Andrew Holleran's *Dancer from the Dance*, and Larry Kramer's *Faggots*—gay writers were claiming the right to define their own reality. That's why it seems to me that gay writing can never be seen as a mere variation—even an expansion—of the straight society's codification of writing as a cultural activity. Gay writing is a revolt against the internal colonization of the imagination, quite parallel to the experience of other colonized people politically dominated by European forms of culture. Gay writers were and are engaged in creating a cultural space, a clearing of the mind where we can imagine our own lives. But since, unlike other colonized peoples—and this is where that parallel ultimately breaks down—we live with and are dispersed among straight people, since we have no country of our own, but live in the same cities with them, this cultural space becomes precisely that opening where we can come together in each other's presence. The site where the gay community can happen and be real is the space created by gay culture. If this line of thought is correct, it would mean that all gay writing is intensely and inherently political. It would mean that the realm of the imagination opened up by gay writing is the space in which the gay community can come into existence. And it would mean that it behooves us to learn how to move with grace in this public and shared space of the imagination.

Unfortunately, as far as I can see, there are no gay critics of any stature on the scene who might be our teachers in this, who might show us how to interact with these books based on their knowledge of the proper relation between writing and life, which is the essential definition of cultural literacy, as Felice Picano said many years ago. The gay reviewing that goes on now, for the most part, exists on a generally abysmal level, full of petty spite, characterized by an arrogance matched only by ignorance, informed by a political consciousness whose central tenet seems to be "monkey see, monkey do," and displaying a sheer, breathtaking inability to read.

And the level of talk about these matters is important. I hope that the gay writers conferences, which are being held with increasing frequency and attendance, are a sign that things are changing and that we will begin to get a level of discourse about gay writing that matches the extraordinary possibilities that the present moment holds for us.

A Letter to Ed White, 23 December 1990

ONE EVENING ED White called and asked me for a few comments he could use for an article he was preparing for the *New York Times*. Being the Christmas season, it took me a couple of days to get back to him.

Ed White

Key West, FLA 33040

Dear Ed,

I should have asked you how fast you needed these comments. Hope this is not too late—been running around like crazy, as usual, doing my Christmas shopping at the last moment. I do believe it's done, so now I turn to this. The state of gay fiction, eh? Good luck, you're sure to offend multitudes, but that keeps the literary kettle boiling.

What's striking to me is that ten years ago, when the Eighties began, the idea that "gay literature" was a legitimate genre was fiercely contested and seriously doubted, even by some of those who are today considered among the leading practitioners of the genre, whose existence and legitimacy would seem to be no more open to doubt. I mean, *there it is*, tons of books are coming out each year, the number of gay bookstores has grown from eight to something like forty, and nobody I know can even keep up with it all nowadays (except maybe Richard Labonté).

Then, as the Eighties progressed and the magnitude of the historical catastrophe that is AIDS began to dawn on us, the possibility arose that this disaster could wipe out not only the newly emerging gay writing but the entire gay movement as well (this curious cultural movement that seemed bent on creating the first elective "ethnic" group, where you didn't inherit your "ethnicity" but freely chose to affirm your membership in the community). It soon became clear that more than half of the first generation of post-Stonewall gays in New York, San Francisco and Los Angeles were infected, and I suspect an even larger proportion of the first generation of post-Stonewall gay writers. Surprisingly, this threatened wipe-out did not turn out to be the case. Quite the reverse: the writers were among the first in the community to realize the extent of the disaster and rise to the occasion, in the process wrenching their practice of writing out of the traditional contexts of literary career and cultural creation that the society had provided and situating the act of the imagination within a new, existential frame (engagé, indeed!). Writers as diverse as Randy Shilts, Paul Monette, Larry Kramer, Allen Barnett, among so many others, placed the existence of gay literature beyond doubt.

It's important, I think, to note that AIDS did not create or provoke this literature, but it didn't derail it either; it merely deepened the imaginative commitment and the elective solidarity of this new group/community coming into existence.

Why this should be, I don't know. I'm not sure that upsurges of cultural creativity like this can ever be "explained" by causes, but only described, like other historical events of the first magnitude. (And this *is* an historical event of the first magnitude, perhaps the major historical event to happen domestically to this country in the latter third of the twentieth century.)

It has occurred to me that this does fit the pattern of how new writing has been arriving on the scene in America since World War II. Unlike the waves of modernism by which new writing emerged in the previous decades, since that war our writers have appeared on the scene "ethnically" as it were. If you look at the major writers in America from '45 to '65 or '70, the overwhelming majority of them were urban male Jews—Mailer, Miller, Bellow, Roth, Malamud, on and on. And I am convinced that when the histories of American literature in the later part of this century come to be written, it will be seen that the main event of the Seventies and the Eighties was the emergence of Black women writers in astonishing profusion and quality. And my bet is that the Nineties will be dominated by gay male writing (a proposition I used to think radical, but when I tried it out on James Atlas at lunch a few weeks ago, I was disconcerted by his instant agreement). Even I—having acted as a sort of cheerleader for this movement for a while now—am taken aback by the sheer number of talented younger gay writers coming up. I have been introducing one new gay male writer on each list (and we have three lists a year, not two) for a couple of years now, and I'm booked for over a year into the future. Who would have thought there were so many good ones out there? Of course, this does make some sense if you put it in the framework of the enormous social transformation of American society that the gay movement is actually achieving and which can be documented in just about every social category—politics, military, sports (the incredible growth of gay ones, I mean), professional associations, neighborhoods, etc., etc.

Nor will this gay literature be any less universal than is the writing of our urban Jewish male writers or our Black women authors, or any less relevant to the rest of us. It will be *particularized*, but this is not the same as parochial, as a second's consideration of Dostoevsky, Synge, or Flaubert should make instantly clear. When reviewers, especially reviewers for the *New York Times*, indicate they are getting tired of reading about gay life, they are in the same position Bill Moyers was when he asked August Wilson, "Don't you ever get tired of writing about Black life?" This was a stupid and racist question, and Wilson was too polite to say, "Would you ask Faulkner if he ever got tired about writing about White life, or Sophocles if he ever got tired of writing about Greek life?" Wilson writes about life as it happens to Black people in this country, just as gay writers write about life as it happens to gay people. The subject is inexhaustible and in no way limited. In fact, given the peculiar nature of the gay community, which is encapsulated in the we-are-everywhere slogan, it could never be true of us. Having just published a gay, Jewish, son-of-Holocaust-survivors writer (Lev Raphael), I have novels signed up by a gay writer from Mississippi who now lives in Toronto (both locales are the themes of his work), a young gay from Tuscaloosa, Alabama, and am reading manuscripts from a gay deaf writer and a Hispanic (actually, I know that term is no longer politically correct, he and his family immigrated from Bogota, Colombia, so Latino, I guess) Manhattan writer. My guess is that our literature will show *much* greater diversity than heterosexual white middle-class male writing, but perhaps I'm still too much in my militant polemical stance of the last decade.

Anyway, I don't know if any of this will be of any use to you for your *N.Y. Times* article. Feel free to use any of it; the only idea I'd like to be credited for is the urban-male-Jewish-Black-women-gay-men literature-arrives-by-ethnicity notion—since I'm using it in some of my own writing that hasn't been published and it'd be a bitch if people thought I'd lifted it from you—unless, of course, you already had it, in which case, what the hell.

I hope you and John have a nice time in Key West. John gave an absolutely wonderful dinner party the night we called you. I told him it was the best group of gay men, the nicest, I'd met in a while and that was a testament to him. I myself will be going to Fort Lauderdale in a couple of days and staying there until the 3rd of January. If, for any reason, you need to call, it's 305 --- ----.

Have a good holiday and a wonderful New Year!

Best,

PART 6

In the Gathering Darkness an Age of Heroes

1991–1996

By the times the Nineties began the future looked bleak indeed. Medical knowledge of the disease had grown, but only to convince all of us of the difficulty of ever finding a cure or a vaccine. When we had really understood how long the incubation period could be, when a person had no symptoms but could still be infectious and spread the disease, many of us came to the same conclusion Cleve Jones had when Dr. Marcus Conant first explained the disease to him, and how it was spread. "Well. Then we're all going to die."[1]

And the deaths came more rapidly now, with funerals and memorial services becoming a common and recurring event in our lives. In my journal I found this entry from March of '95:

At the memorial service for Stan Levanthal today, Felice Picano told me this story: For his 40th birthday (maybe 10 years previously) Vito Russo and Clovis Ruffin gave him a surprise party, inviting 72 of his "closest friends." Today, Felice told me, he's the only person still alive from that party—the other 72 gay men are dead.

---

1 Cleve Jones, *When We Rise*, p. 197.

At this memorial service, I was handing out flyers for the service we're having for Paul next Monday. Seemed a bit tacky, but it was efficient.

Two memorial services this week, while helping plan two others. Too much.

With a whole generation of gay men facing death, matters had taken their ultimate turn.

Eulogy for Allen Barnett: 1955–1991

MY FRIEND ALLEN Barnett died of AIDS on August 14, 1991. He was thirty-six years old. We held a memorial service for him at the Cathedral of St. John the Divine in New York City on 19 September 1991, where this eulogy was delivered in that soaringly beautiful space to a surprisingly large audience.[1]

Allen once said, "Writing is an act of moral responsibility about moral responsibility." Whether or not this is always so, it was utterly true in his own case.

Allen belonged to that generation of gay men who came of age as the Seventies drew to a close; he got his MFA in creative writing from Columbia in 1981 and left school just as AIDS was gathering the momentum that would soon achieve epidemic force as it broke over the gay community in New York. Like so many men of his generation, his first experience of true adulthood was a medical holocaust, a disease of almost unbelievable viciousness happening within a context of ignorance, indifference on the part of the medical, political, and media establishments, and the consequent disbelief and confusion within the gay community.

It was not a good time to become a man, but, of course, neither Allen nor his peers had any choice. It astonished me then and it astonishes me today that so many met the occasion with a display of moral responsibility that was as heroic as it was unexpected. Allen was one of the earliest volunteers for Gay Men's Health Crisis, a self-imposed task he kept at year after year; the Gay and Lesbian Alliance Against Defamation was founded one day at his kitchen table, and the last job he was able to hold was that of AIDS educator for the YMCA.

1 It was later reprinted in issue 165 of *Christopher Street*.

It took some kind of nerve for a young man in his mid-twenties who should have been out dancing and looking for love in the bars and the discos, to spend his evenings instead jumping up *on* the bar, uninvited, to demonstrate the techniques of safe sex with a condom and a banana to what must have been, at least in the early days, a somewhat unreceptive audience. It took some kind of nerve to care for and nurse men he had not known through the harrowing medical and spiritual emergencies that AIDS engenders. It took some kind of nerve to try to be a decent and mature gay man in the Eighties. And luckily for him, and luckily for us, Allen, and so many of his peers, had that kind of nerve and demonstrated that kind of moral responsibility in the face of the worst catastrophe that gay men have ever experienced.

When he left school, Allen's overriding ambition was to become a writer. In more than twenty years in publishing I have known few people who so loved the literary life. Victor Bumbalo told me last week at dinner that when Allen admired something you had written, the intensity of his enthusiasm was almost frightening. Writing was the center of Allen's life. In the last few months when he was often in the hospital in very bad shape, I discovered that the one thing that would revive his spirit and make the daily hospital visits a success was literary gossip. As I scrounged around for dish and offered him the latest news about what outrageous advance some fool had given a writer we both knew, or who had trashed whose book in some gay paper, his eyes would gradually focus, his face become animated, his speech clearer, and soon he would be sitting up, fairly cackling with cracks and opinions. Though he was in the hospital last June and not in good shape at all as the Lambda Literary Awards rolled around, there was simply *no way* he wasn't going to attend that ceremony, though we had to surreptitiously sneak him out of co-op care in a wheelchair without the hospital knowing and help him climb the three steps to the podium when he received the two awards that night he so richly deserved. At the time, when I was worrying about the wisdom of this illegal, and potentially lethal, escapade, Allen said to me, "I believe that when you have your health, you have everything; and since I don't have my health, I *want* those literary awards."

It has become a trope nowadays, at occasions like this, to lament the loss to gay literature of so many brilliant young writers cut down at the beginning of their career, to dwell on what they might have achieved had they only had the time. But I would rather consider what Allen did achieve, for I believe he did achieve the necessary thing for Allen Barnett. Though his life was stopped short, it seems to me that Allen did reach the goal, did become the person he was meant to be, did realize the idea God had in mind when he said, "And now let there be an Allen Barnett."

I don't think there is any question that had Allen been granted the normal span of decades to craft his works, he would have become a major writer of our time. But in my opinion there is no question that with his one book, he did in fact become a major writer. The stories in *The Body and Its Dangers* have the density of meaning, the musical finish of language crafted into beauty, and the depth of spirit that mark truly realized works of great literary art. Above all, these stories have the power that comes when the imagination is infused by a naked courage. I don't know if non-writers realize how much sheer courage a true act of the imagination requires. Churchill once said that courage is the pre-eminent virtue, for it alone can guarantee all the others, and all great acts of the imagination rest on the courage of he who dares to imagine.

Allen once wrote that rereading his own story "The *Times* as It Knows Us" was a harrowing experience—a description I agree with; the first time I read that story I almost couldn't breathe—but how much more harrowing must have been the act of writing it. In the dark times that descended on the gay community in the Eighties, the courage to imagine what was happening to us was the only guarantee that our literary art could be relevant and real and ring true. To me, these are the stories of a great writer. Sure, it would have been nice to have another dozen books from this man, but the point is that his work got to the place it needed to be.

As with the work, so with the life. In the last year, Allen got to lead the literary life he so cherished. In the notes for his talk at the OutWrite Conference in San Francisco last spring, he recounts the pleasure he had in meeting Geoffrey Woolf, one of his former teachers, when they were both on book tours of the West Coast, bumping into each other again and again in the lounges of radio stations and exchanging complaints about life on the literary road. He also mentioned how proud he was when Edmund White, another former writing teacher, invited him out for coffee. This was the life Allen had always dreamed of, and it was the life he was now living. No doubt he wanted it to go on and on, but the point is he had achieved it, he had in some sense gotten home, come safe to journey's end.

So for our friend Allen Barnett, the writer who believed writing was an act of moral responsibility about moral responsibility, we can use the old words, for they fit so perfectly:

> This be the verse you grave for me:
> *Here he lies where he longed to be;*
> *Home is the sailor, home from the sea,*
> *And the hunter home from the hill.*
>
> ROBERT LOUIS STEVENSON, "Requiem"

Honoring Richard Rouillard

ON OCTOBER 24, 1993, the National Lesbian & Gay Journalists Association held a formal dinner at the Century Tower Plaza in L.A. to honor Richard Rouillard, the editor of *The Advocate*, the national gay newsmagazine, and asked me to speak. I was delighted since Richard was still alive and relatively healthy at the time. I thought it only prudent that we start honoring our community's (many) heroes while we still had time.

In 1979 Richard had co-founded National Gay Rights Advocates of San Francisco, the country's first public interest law firm for lesbians and gay men. Two years later he moved to Los Angeles to become the editor in chief of *The Advocate*, where the circulation nearly tripled during his tenure. He also worked as society and style editor for the now defunct *Los Angeles Herald Examiner* and as a senior editorial consultant and contributor to the *Los Angeles Times Magazine*.

Richard always struck me as a perfect example of Vito Russo's theory of the spontaneously assumption of responsibility: a free agent all his life, Richard had consistently worked to further the gay movement. I thought with enough people like this, we've got to win.

In 2010 Richard would be inducted (posthumously—he died of AIDS in 1996) into the LGBT Journalists Hall of Fame by the National LGBT Journalists Association (of which he had been a founder).

I'm happy to get the opportunity to say a few words about Richard, the boy from New Jersey, who became Richard Rouillard, a source of great joy to his many friends. All of us have taken delight in Richard's humor, his joy in style, in an elegance slightly askew, his deep generosity, and his sheer delight in socializing, in sharing the world with his friends. Indeed, Richard has shown that homo-sociability can be taken to awesome lengths and can have a perceptible impact on the world.

But this energetic cloud of charm and humor circles a core of un-compromising straightforwardness, and, as a member of the first gen-eration after Stonewall, this has given Richard's life a deeply political dimension.

As a political phenomenon, Stonewall is somewhat odd. It led to an immediate flurry of activity and to some political organizing, but that mostly frittered out by the mid-Seventies. Stonewall's peculiar political reality was in the impact of the idea on the minds of lesbi-ans and gays scattered all over the country and across a diversity of jobs and professions. The Stonewall Riot was a call to the colors, and what made history was the fact that it was answered by a spontaneous and decentralized assumption of political responsibility by individuals here and there, and eventually everywhere.

For Richard, who found himself in the world of magazines and newspapers, the political challenge of being gay at this time had to be made concrete in his work, and this has had, and is having, a sizable impact on newspapers and magazines in this country.

When Richard took the helm of *The Advocate*, his intelligence and panache made it into a truly national publication that had a pro-active effect on the rest of the media. It was Richard's vision that led to the Advocate Book Project, which I have been working on intensively for the last few days. To be published next spring, it chronicles the first 25 years of openly gay history in some 400,000 words and nearly 1,000 photographs. The book's impact is overwhelming, but what be-came clear to me reviewing it is that the gay movement *consists* of indi-viduals like Richard, people who, *on their own*, set out to change things and who have changed things mightily.

And Richard being his exuberant gay self in the world of the print media had an impact on someone like me in the publishing world. Over the last two decades, one repeatedly became aware of individ-uals doing work for the gay cause in one or another field, and you felt strengthened, heartened to see these other travelers along the same path. And through the years it's often happened that we started meet-ing one another and forming these wide networks of friendship that seem to be the great strength of gay life. Indeed, that "band of cameradoes" Walt Whitman prophesized at the dawn of the modern gay world seems a vigorous and growing reality today.

You constantly hear calls nowadays for a national unified gay political leadership, and perhaps this is desirable though it's dubious whether it's possible. But I would like to point out that the gay movement *does* have a national leadership, and it is made up of people like Richard Rouillard, people who by their own spontaneous assumption of responsibility have, in one corner of the world after another, made a reality of the social change we know is necessary.

In honoring Richard we are honoring a whole generation, a heroic generation of friends and allies who have in fact created a social revolution, the generation that responded to Stonewall. And if this generation fulfills Whitman's prophecy of an "army of cameradoes," then the dashing Richard Rouillard is one of the guerrilla generals of that army. I will never forget the party Richard and *The Advocate* hosted last year at the '92 Democratic National Convention. Told by Richard it was going to be formal to the tits, Deborah Daly and I sent him a pair of white gloves for good luck. And when I arrived, betuxed, at the midtown hotel, I was greeted by a regal Richard in formal tux and white gloves. With such champions, the gay movement is in good hands.

Eulogy for Randy Shilts

RANDY SHILTS DIED of AIDS on February 17, 1994, in his home on the Russian River. He was forty-three. Our personal and professional lives had been closely and productively intertwined for almost twenty years. The loss was enormous; the tectonic plates of my world were shifting.

I delivered this eulogy at the Memorial Service for Randy held at Glide Memorial Methodist Church in San Francisco on February 22, 1994. It seemed as if the whole town had come out to honor this man: the church was full to overflowing, loudspeakers had been set up outside on several corners so the crowds in the street could hear, and all the flags in the city were flying at half-mast in honor of a favorite son.

But as we slowly made our way through the crowds to the Church the organizers seemed unusually nervous and kept listening to their radios. "The Rev. Phelps and his demented followers in the Westboro Baptist Church have flown in from Topeka," it was explained to me. "They plan to picket Randy's funeral with their hateful signs, and the radio's been following them ever since they arrived at the airport. That's why the massive crowds are here. They won't be able to get anywhere *near* the church, not within blocks." As we got to the church steps, the report came over the radio that the police had stopped the Phelps band, saying they could not guarantee their safety in the city, and escorted them back to the airport, to the cheers of the crowd.

This public display of respect and solidarity that Randy's beloved city put on that day for their hometown boy moved me immensely.

Randy Shilts was one of the truly great journalists of our time. Because the issues he chose to report on were gay topics the world has only belatedly begun to appreciate this fact. His career was a shining example of what journalism at its best can be and can accomplish, and I think he will be an exemplary role model for aspiring journalists for decades to come.

From the first time I met Randy, in the mid-Seventies, I was struck by his obvious and total commitment to journalism, its principles and its ethos. Along with his ebullient energy and boyish charm, he displayed what seemed to me an almost naïve belief in journalism as a profession, as Max Weber might have put it, which struck me as very Californian, very Lincoln Steffens. It has been a great pleasure, as well as an object lesson to me, to watch as he carried out that belief in action over the last fifteen years and proved that it wasn't naïve at all, although it was indeed idealistic.

From the time he left journalism school and accepted a job at *The Advocate* against the advice of friends who warned that it would kill his career, he has proven that idealism can still change the world, in this case the world of professional journalism. For make no mistake, by his work and by his example, Randy Shilts helped to change the face of journalism in America.

Randy's career can be neatly summarized in his three books. In the late Seventies when he became the first openly gay reporter on a major metropolitan daily, he was convinced that the emergence of the gay community, which he could concretely observe in the Castro, would become a major national news story. Everybody thought he was crazy, but that local reporting about what was happening in San Francisco became his first book: *The Mayor of Castro Street: The Life and Times of Harvey Milk*. In the early Eighties when he fought to cover the AIDS story full time for his newspaper, again people thought he was crazy, but, of course, that reporting led to *And the Band Played On: People, Politics and the AIDS Epidemic*.

In the late Eighties when he began to investigate the situation of gays and lesbians in the U.S. military, even Randy thought a book on the topic might be a little iffy, since at the time he couldn't imagine a lot of people being interested in the subject. But he couldn't resist what he thought was one of the best stories around, one that captured what was happening both to the gay movement and to America, and one that almost nobody was covering. Looking at our society through the prism of the military, Randy was convinced, would yield a definitive analysis of homophobia in America, while addressing the broader issue of the state of freedom in our supposedly free society. And that led to *Conduct Unbecoming: Gays & Lesbians in the U.S. Military*. And once again his intuition about what would be a good story, a story that would capture what was happening to his community and to his country, was sound.

In the last interview he gave, to *60 Minutes* a couple of weeks ago, Randy suggested that one could summarize his career by saying that, like any successful journalist, he had simply been in the right place at the right time with the right instincts. But I would add to that a couple of other qualities: independence of mind and the courage to pursue the truth and let the chips fall where they may. Randy has taken a lot of flak over the years from those (including a good number of my friends—and yours) who believed that public relations for the gay and lesbian community were more important than getting the story right. But Randy Shilts was always clear about the fact that he was a gay journalist and not a gay activist. And if journalism is going to be more than a job, if journalism is going to be a profession in Max Weber's sense, then it must be grounded in a commitment to the truth and energized by a faith that the truth can indeed change things. Yes, this is idealism, but after two decades of watching Randy at work, I am convinced that such idealism is not at all naïve, but, on the contrary, totally necessary.

Necessary Bread

GAY WRITING COMES OF AGE

IN THE MAY 1994 issue of *Forecast*, their in-house magazine, Baker and Taylor, the main supplier for libraries in America, offered me their column, "Publisher's Place," to highlight St. Martin's forthcoming list of gay and lesbian books. Although this is really an infomercial for the books, I tried to make it a short essay in gay history, particularly directed at librarians, and to express my appreciation and the appreciation of the whole gay community for the support their profession had provided gay writing from the very beginning.

This summer will mark the twenty-fifth anniversary of the Stonewall Riots, the event that is generally taken as the beginning of the contemporary gay rights movement in the United States. On the night of June 28, 1969, the police made a routine raid on the Stonewall Inn, a somewhat disreputable bar on Christopher Street in Greenwich Village. In the Sixties it was actually illegal in New York State to serve a drink to a homosexual, indeed it was then illegal for three or more homosexuals to congregate in a public place. Of course, such things could be gotten around, but evidently the mafia owners of the bar were behind in their payoffs to the police. At the time, all of this was routine; what was not routine was the response. As their friends were being hustled into the waiting paddy wagons, bystanders began hurling catcalls at the cops, then pitching pennies, then beer cans and bottles. As things escalated the cops retreated inside the bar for protection, while calling for reinforcements. Meanwhile, some demented queen managed to upend a parking meter and was using it as a battering ram to break down the bar's door. Thus began three nights of rioting in Greenwich Village that electrified homosexuals from one end of America to the other. It is this event that is commemorated every June in Gay Pride Marches across the country.

In the larger scheme of things twenty-five years is not a long time; but for someone who lived through that period the social changes that occurred beggar the imagination. Recently, the Publishing Triangle, a group of lesbians and gay men in the publishing business, and The Lesbian and Gay Community Services Center of New York opened the Pat Parker/Vito Russo Memorial Library, a lending library at The Center that is heavily used by teenagers, especially working-class, Latino, and African-American gay kids who find it unwise to hang out in their own neighborhoods after school. It is staffed entirely by volunteers, often members of SAGE (Senior Action in a Gay Environment). Imagine: in the Sixties, New York State had laws that would have made this public library illegal and prevented these kids from meeting their gay elders. This intergenerational alliance was totally unexpected when we were planning the library, but delighted us, for we remembered our own teenage years when the burden of being different was nearly unbearable and the fear of being the only one, of not finding others like you, was a torment.

It is this elemental emotional experience of all gay people—the realization that you are different and the fear that you are the only one—which I find very difficult to convey to my straight friends. I'm not sure they get it, even when I say, "Look, imagine you're Jewish, but being Jewish is a despised thing and you have to keep it a secret; then imagine that all Jews are raised in Christian families, in fact, in families that are pretty prejudiced against Jews, and you'll get some idea of where we start from." I think it's probably for this reason that the printed word has been so important to gay people. If you can't talk to your parents, and you can't talk to your friends, and you can't talk to your teachers, and you can't talk to your coach, you turn to books.

In fact, the gay movement has been particularly dependent on the written word, much more so than the Civil Rights Movement, in fact more than any social/political movement I know of, except perhaps the Women's Movement. Ever since the first "Iron Butterfly" pamphlets[1] began floating across the country in the autumn of '69, only

1 Mimeographed and stapled essays, printed on colored paper (pink or purple, as I remember), devoted to various strands of gay liberation (emanating, I believe, from New York City and the Gay Liberation Front).

months after Stonewall, and I found one in the bookstore at the University of Chicago, my identity as a gay man and the shape of my life have been hugely affected by what in effect was an immense public conversation held via the medium of the printed word. By way of the imagination, the printed word allows us to be in each other's presence, and it is this being in the presence of others that creates a public space and allows a community to emerge.

A year and a half prior to Stonewall, the nation's first gay newspaper, *The Advocate*, had been founded by a couple of guys in a Los Angeles basement. A quarter of a century later, the publication of *Long Road to Freedom: The Advocate History of the Gay and Lesbian Movement* will be a milestone for the gay community: half a million words and almost a thousand photographs document the first twenty-five years of gay history.

As *The Advocate*'s circulation broadened in the Seventies and as gay newspapers and magazines sprang up in various cities, a public space was opened and we began to see reflections of ourselves, to see who we were and what was happening to us; and it was only a matter of time before the writers and artists among us felt the urge to set all this down in fiction. In 1976 I was involved with a group of people in establishing the first gay literary magazine, *Christopher Street*, although even at that date friends in publishing took me aside and warned me my career would be dead if my name appeared on the masthead. And although I was fired shortly after the first issue came out, I was lucky enough to meet Tom McCormack and land a job at St. Martin's Press, the only publishing house that was willing at that time to even consider publishing gay books. During those early years the prospects for gay writing often looked grim: the gay press was small, irregular, and just emerging, and the mainstream media seldom deigned to review gay books. Those reviews that did appear tended to be sneering if not downright clinical, unless they were grudgingly kept at bay by overwhelming literary talent (if one was sufficiently literary one was allowed to be queer; after all, there was precedent). With only a half dozen gay bookstores in existence (today there are around fifty) and few mainstream bookstores willing to carry gay books, sales were minimal. Nor did *Christopher Street* magazine fare much better. We had made a mistake in believing that gay writers had all these unpublished manuscripts in their bottom drawers; but it turned out that, without anywhere to publish, gay writers had tended to avoid writing on gay themes and there was a dearth of material. I remember one issue in particular in which Ed White wrote four different pieces under four different names to fill up the pages.

One of the few bright spots for the magazine was the libraries, which were surprisingly supportive right from the beginning. And slowly that paid off; five or six years later I started meeting writers like Christopher Davis, who told me he had read every issue of *Christopher Street* from the very first issue when he accidentally discovered it in his college library, and it had a major influence on his decision to become a gay writer.

From the start, *Christopher Street* was a writers' magazine and its core group of writers in the early years were the members of what was known as the Violet Quill Club: Edmund White, Andrew Holleran, Felice Picano, George Whitmore, Robert Ferro, Michael Grumley, and Christopher Cox. Now fifteen years later, with the appearance of *The Violet Quill Reader: The Emergence of Gay Writing after Stonewall*,[2] the measure of this group can be taken for the first time, and it is my belief that they will turn out to be as historically significant as the Bloomsbury Group or the Gertrude Stein circle in Paris (two other groups of mainly gay artists, who affected the course of twentieth-century culture).

The members of the Violet Quill were among the first to use their fiction to investigate what it meant to be gay if it didn't mean the evil things we had been taught it meant. Their pioneering work and the courage of their example have indeed paid off with a flowering of gay writing that in its depths and richness has surprised even those of us who believed in it since the beginning.

St. Martin's own trade paperback line dedicated to gay and lesbian writing, Stonewall Inn Editions, now has in print more than sixty titles, both fiction and nonfiction, including works by Paul Monette,

2 Edited by David Bergman (St. Martin's Press, 1994).

Ed White, Ethan Mordden, Larry Kramer, Randy Shilts and a host of other exciting writers. And something like a third generation of gay novelists seems to be emerging with the work of young writers like Doug Sadownick, whose *Sacred Lips of the Bronx* breaks new ground for the gay novel, with his inspired use of magic realism to create a mythic love story in the age of AIDS that deserves comparison with Tony Kushner's *Angels in America*.

If fiction allows us to imagine what our lives have become in this terrible time of plague, then nonfiction is what allows us to mobilize our strength and address a world that needs changing. That's why we need books like Michael Nava and Robert Dawidoff's *Created Equal: Why Gay Rights Matter to America*. Using as their model John Stuart Mill's classic essay, "The Subjection of Women," these authors show that what is at stake in the struggle for gay rights is the heart of American constitutional principle: that the state serves to protect the liberty of the individual, including the liberty of gay individuals, free from the intolerance of religious zealots or majority opinion. And we need books like Brian McNaught's *Gay Issues in the Workplace* to learn how to cope with homophobia on the job. We need books like Susan Fox Rogers's *Sportsdykes: Stories from On & Off the Field*, an anthology of essays, stories, interviews, and cartoons that examine the central place of sports in lesbian life. We need books like Randy Shilts' *Conduct Unbecoming*, books that lay out the patterns of prejudice and discrimination that we're fighting against. We need books as we need bread, all sorts of books. We need entertainments like the mystery novels of Mark Richard Zubro, Phyllis Knight, Grant Michaels, and Randye Lordon, just as African-Americans need to read the mysteries of Walter Mosley—simply because one wants to read books about, and by, people like oneself.

It is because of the importance of books to us that last year the Publishing Triangle launched the first National Gay and Lesbian Book Month in June. Patterned after Black History Month, the event is designed to highlight gay and lesbian books in both libraries and bookstores across the nation. We hope to honor those writers who have helped free our imaginations, while at the same time making sure that all gay people, and especially gay kids, realize these books are out there for their use. Someone once said, "We read to know we are not alone." They are not alone. As librarians I hope you will bring this good news to your communities.

(p.s.: For more information about Gay & Lesbian Book Month, contact Michele Karlsberg of the Publishing Triangle at [address deleted].)

Stonewall

FROM EVENT TO IDEA

FOR THE SUMMER 1994 issue of what was then called *The Harvard Gay & Lesbian Review* (now *The Gay & Lesbian Review/Worldwide*), Richard Schneider asked Edmund White, Martin Duberman, Sarah Schulman, and myself to reconsider Stonewall on its twenty-fifth anniversary. This was my piece.

As we celebrate the 25th anniversary of the Stonewall Riots, much is being written about that now mythical event which is generally taken as the birth of the contemporary gay and lesbian rights movement. Much of what I have read strikes me as wrongheaded, especially the revisionist attempts by the currently politically correct to downplay the role of white males in that event. "Middle-class white men" is the term generally used, but considering the reputation of the Stonewall bar, or just glancing at the few photos left from that time and place, one wonders about the term "middle class"; one wonders, in fact, about the word "men." "Randy white boys" might be more accurate. Recently I read a manuscript proposal (generated by a PBS television series on gay rights) that asserted that "middle-class white men" had "stolen" (their word) Stonewall as an event, appropriating to themselves an action generated by lesbians, transvestites, and people of color. The authors offered no evidence for this statement, just blandly asserting this revision of history with the same smug and self-righteous certainty that Stalin's encyclopedists must have felt as they dutifully revised their history books decade after decade.

Personally, I doubt that the Stonewall Inn, while clearly a racially mixed bar, was ever a popular dyke hangout, or that its clientele was anything like equally divided between men and women. And while anyone who knew Marsha or Sylvia knew what a force Street Transvestite Action Revolutionaries (their term) could be in a confrontation with the cops, the contribution of either to the ongoing organizing of the gay movement is a different question.

But, in retrospect, all these squabbles to claim credit are not only petty but beside the point, except when they interfere with the attempt to ascertain historically what actually happened. They are beside the point because they misunderstand how an event like Stonewall actually comes to interact with history, becomes a part of history, or not. Stonewall was not the first time gay people had confronted the police, nor the first time we stood up for ourselves. John Preston once told me about a remarkably similar event that took place at a gay bar in Chicago a year or so earlier. The police were harassing the bar owners and made the patrons walk a long gauntlet of cops while being photographed entering and leaving the place. For the people involved, this confrontation was as harrowing and as heroic as Stonewall, but it had no echo across the country and is now almost forgotten. There had also been a similar confrontation in L.A.

So what made Stonewall different?

Kant wrote of the French Revolution that it was not so much the event itself that was going to change the world as the quality of attention paid to it by its spectators, by those observers across Europe who watched the unfolding events in Paris and knew that something momentous had happened. It was what the spectators made of the events of the French Revolution that would change history, not what the rioters in Paris had done. In other words, it is when an event is raised to the level of an idea that it has the power to alter history through changing the consciousness of people.

I would argue that something similar is the case with Stonewall. It was definitely not the first sign of the emerging gay revolt. A year and a half before Stonewall a couple of guys had started *The Advocate* in Los Angeles, and at about the same time Troy Perry had established the first of the Metropolitan Community Churches, today the largest gay organization in the world. Clearly, something was afoot with gay people even before the events at Stonewall. What was missing was any sense of possibility, any alternative to the oppression gay people faced daily everywhere they looked.

To get a sense of the mental oppression gays labored under, this lack of possibility that was so spiritually suffocating, one might look at Mart Crowley's play, *The Boys in the Band*, a much maligned work that precisely delineates the pre-revolutionary emotional situation that would lead to Stonewall. The play is about eight gay men and one straight; in essence the gay guys, who are very unhappy and bitchy, start the evening beating up on each other and progress till their anger is directed at the straight man. What is amazing in this play is that none of the gay characters has any sense of possibility, of any way out of the trap of gay life as it was then led. Although they are clearly angry to the point of fury, the idea of gay liberation is the furthest thing from their minds. As someone who remembers the years before Stonewall, I can testify that the very concept of gay liberation would have then struck most of us, even those of us who were intensely politically active, as absurd. Being homosexual was a psychological situation, maybe a medical situation, but certainly not a political matter.

Luckily for everyone, the Women's Movement came along and got us to consider the notion that the personal *was* political, a major step forward. Then what was needed was a crystallizing moment, and the four continuous nights of rioting that the raid on Stonewall provoked offered that moment. What was decisive was not the event itself, but how people responded, the immediate, spontaneous and utterly decentralized flurry of organizing, leafleting and pamphleteering that resulted (and that was so well documented in Donn Teal's 1972 book *The Gay Militants*, now reissued[1]). It was this response, and perhaps above all the late Craig Rodwell's determination to commemorate the event the next June with the world's first Gay Pride March, that made Stonewall the shot heard 'round the gay world.

The event had become an idea, the idea that gay people would fight back, would stand up for their rights. And ideas can change the world.

1 St. Martin's Press, 1995.

Three Takes on John Preston

BY THE TIME of his death in April 1994, at the age of forty-nine, John Preston had become a major presence on the national gay literary scene he had done so much to initiate and foster. Having published over twenty books of his own, he also edited another nine volumes focused on the central issues of the day (AIDS, hometowns, our natural families, the families we create, and—repeatedly—sex), books that introduced dozens of new and emerging gay and lesbian writers. That intensive editorial work (John started out as an editor at *The Advocate*) as well as his monthly column on publishing in the *Lambda Book Report* won him the respect, gratitude and affection of a whole generation of up-and-coming writers.

I met John in 1977, I think, one night after work in a trendy new bar/restaurant on 22nd St. near the Flatiron Building. I'd announced I was publishing gay books and John was interviewing me for *The Advocate* about my plans. Of course I'd heard about John, who was already a legendary top man in leather circles, but when I found out he had an MA in Sexology from the University of Michigan, I cracked up—"Nothing like professional credentials, hey?"—and started interviewing him. And that began an intense conversation that lasted about six hours, until the two gay owners of the place told us they wanted to go home. It turned out John was passionately interested in two things: sex in all its forms, and the business realities and social complexities of publishing. So, you can imagine. . . . Such absolutely instantaneous and deep contact has happened to me only a few times, and in each case that contact remained fast for life, interrupted maybe but never broken. And all one can do is say, with Montaigne, "If you press me to tell you why I loved him, I feel that this cannot be expressed, except by answering: Because it was he, because it was I."

John Preston was, for nearly two decades, one of my closest friends, the immediate witness to my life, and my closest professional

comrade-in-arms, and dealing with his death was difficult for me. I realize these three talks involve more than a bit of repetition (the first
two were delivered under the immediate impact of his death and close
to one another). I've let them stand as they were delivered because
they seem to me three takes on the same themes, like jazz riffs on the
same melody, each one more extended and developed than the last.

I.
Eulogy

JOHN PRESTON
DECEMBER 11, 1945–APRIL 28, 1994

THIS EULOGY WAS delivered at St. Luke's Cathedral in Portland, Maine, on May 7, 1994.

John Preston was a man of many talents, but the rarest and most valuable of these was his natural gift for friendship. John had more friends than most of us can even imagine. And he was wise enough to know that friendships, like gardens, need nurturing; in endless letters, phone calls and faxes, John tended to his friends.

For John, friendship manifested itself mainly in conversation, a way of sharing the world with others by talking about it. Conversation was important to him because it was how he came to know the shape of the world and to find his place in it. The series of anthologies he began editing with *Personal Dispatches* resembles nothing so much as one huge conversation among gay men and lesbians, a conversation about our place in the world and the people with whom we share it, our natural families and the families we create out of the fabric of friendship. Even his column about publishing in the *Lambda Book Report* was a way of talking to people he didn't know, young writers just setting out whom he wanted to help. For by the time he came to write this column, John had achieved success as a writer by anybody's definition, and he felt the pressing need to give something back to the community.

In retrospect it strikes me as ironic that this man who in the Seventies had an almost legendary reputation as a literary and erotic outlaw—and that in a community itself virtually outlawed—that this man's central theme, in both his life and his writing, was community. Virtually all of John's books, from *Franny, the Queen of Provincetown* to the forthcoming *Friends and Lovers* are, at bottom, about community. He was one of the few people I have known for whom the need for community was an immediate and tangible reality. He spent years moving from city to city until he realized that at heart he was a New Englander and he came to Portland, to be near his roots and his family. What was important about Portland was that here he could know by name the people who worked in the Post Office, here he was accepted by the guys at the barber shop, here he knew the Governor as well as the members of the leather fraternity, here he felt truly at home.

And it was here in Portland that John slowly—and much to his own amusement—came to the realization that he, this man of many masks and personas, was in essence a New England bachelor, a "curmudgeonly New England bachelor" in his own words.

Surrounded by young men who valued their connection with him as intensely as he valued his connection with the late Sam Steward, young men he took to calling his nephews, the transition was complete: the bad boy of gay porn had become the good uncle of the gay community, a trusted and respected elder whose help and guidance was eagerly sought and generously given. John had achieved a singular status within the national gay community, and his passing will be mourned from Portland, Maine, to Portland, Oregon. We want his family to know that not hundreds, but thousands upon thousands of gay people across this land feel their loss, for it is also our loss. As their family is diminished, our family is diminished. John was one of our leaders, one of our heroes, one of our storytellers, but above all he was one of our best friends.

II.
A Tribute to John Preston

LAMBDA LITERARY AWARDS, MAY 27, 1994

THE IMPACT OF John's death, his sudden absence from the world, paradoxically brought to light the impact his life had had on us, the difference his presence in the world among us had made. This can be seen clearly in the testimony of the twenty-seven writers contributing to *Looking for Mr. Preston: A Celebration of a Writer's Life*,[1] which came out a year later. But immediately Jim Marks of the *Lambda Book Report*, who was organizing that year's Lambda Literary Awards, asked me to deliver a tribute to John at the Lammies, the closest thing we had to a national convention of gay and lesbian writers, held that year only a month after John's death.

John Preston was a man of many accomplishments. In 1971 he helped to establish and then became the director of the very first gay community center in this country, in Minneapolis. In 1975 he was the editor of *The Advocate* where he gave Randy Shilts his first job after Journalism school. Already a legendary top man in S&M circles by the mid-Seventies, the publication of *Mr. Benson* serially in *Drummer* magazine established him as our leading pornographer, along with his good friends Sam Steward and Steven Saylor. Under a pseudonym, he was the author of dozens of mass market male adventure novels, as well as the creator, under his own name, of a gay male adventure series for Sasha Alyson, *The Mission of Alex Kane*. He became a frequent essayist as well as our leading anthologist, while remaining a political activist. The ad card we're putting into the new edition of *Franny, the Queen of*

---

1 *Looking For Mr. Preston: A Celebration of the Writer's Life; Interviews, Essays and Personal Reminiscences of John Preston*, ed. Laura Antoniou (New York: Richard Kasak Books, 1995).

Provincetown will list some thirty books that John either wrote under his own name or edited.

My friendship with John goes back seventeen years. It started over drinks one evening after work when John was interviewing me—for *The Advocate*, I think—and I was so amused when I found out that this legendary top-man had a Master's degree in Sexology—academic credentials, right?—that I started interviewing him. We talked until the restaurant closed, and that evening began what in retrospect seems to me a seventeen-year-long conversation.

John was a wonderful conversationalist. At the time he was in the process of deciding that he wanted to be a writer—and for John that meant quite concretely supporting himself from his writings and not taking a day job—and he wanted to know everything there was to know about the writer's life, agents, the publishing business. Since I was also trying to figure these things out for myself, John became the perfect interlocutor for me, for he was absolutely discreet. That gave me the freedom to discuss in total detail the literary quality or financial complexities of submissions I was considering, with perfect confidence that not one iota of the discussion would ever go any further. And it never did. They say all politics is local; well, all publishing is particular. When you discuss publishing in general, the talk turns vapid as fuzzy generalities bump against one another; but when you talk about publishing in particular, you tend to say things that could get you into trouble if they became known publicly, which is why most people in publishing tend to avoid speaking about particular books, unless they are success stories. With John I could indulge in the luxury of perfectly candid discussions about the most interesting and thorny problems I was running up against in my job. Nor was I the only one John had such conversations with; he discussed these matters with just about everyone he met who had anything to do with publishing, and as a consequence within a few years he soon knew more about how the business actually worked than any writer I have met.

Nor were our conversations limited to publishing. At one point we had on tape over fourteen hours of our discussions and arguments over S&M—we were planning some kind of joint project on the subject—but the highpoint of our early friendship was surely the night

we were both thrown out of the Mineshaft. Deep into a discussion of
S&M which by then had been going on for weeks if not months, we got
distracted from the original purpose of the evening, which was sex,
and kept pointing out to each other various tableaux that strengthened
some point one of us had been making. Unfortunately we were oblivious to the fact that we were ruining the atmosphere for everyone else
there, those who had not forgotten that the point of the evening was
not intellectual clarity. The management was forbearing—this was, after all, the author of *Mr. Benson*—but finally they had had it and told us
in no uncertain terms that our behavior was totally inappropriate and
rude. Since at the time we were standing between the area where the
slings were set up on one side and a bathtub where people were enjoying water sports on the other, this struck me as hilarious—"rude?"—a
reaction no doubt buoyed by whatever chemicals we were on that
night. For a moment, John's blue eyes flashed with fury at this *lèse-
majesté*, then he broke into a grin. We both apologized and, giggling,
took ourselves to the street where we started talking about rudeness
and the surprisingly elaborate code of politesse that held sway at the
trucks and why no one had ever written about it. I think we wandered
Greenwich Village 'til dawn talking, always talking.

For John, friendship manifested itself mainly in conversation, a way
of sharing the world with others by talking about it. Conversation was
important to him because it was how John came to know the shape of
the world and to find his place in it. The series of anthologies he began with *Personal Dispatches* resembles nothing so much as one huge
conversation among gay men and lesbians, a conversation about our
place in the world and the people with whom we share it, our natural
families and the families we create out of the fabric of friendship. Even
his column about publishing in the *Lambda Book Report* was a way of
talking to people he didn't know, young writers just setting out whom
he wanted to help. For, by the time he came to write this column, John
had achieved literary success by anybody's definition, and he felt the
pressing need to give something back to the community.

And the gay and lesbian population did finally have something like
a literary community, and John had contributed mightily to this de-

velopment. I think he never forgot his hurt at the standoffishness of New York's gay literati when I first introduced him around. He thought they looked down on him because he was a pornographer; I think they were intimidated by the fact that he was a famous hustler and top-man who was *also* a writer. In any event, he was determined never to act that way towards younger writers. He even proposed in his column the idea that every established gay or lesbian author should take on two or three younger writers in an explicit mentor role, advising them not only about their work but explaining the intricacies of publishing and helping them practically to get their work into print. John was constantly networking, and this networking was a significant contribution to the emergence of a literary community of our own.

In retrospect it strikes me as ironic that this man who in the Seventies had an almost legendary reputation as a literary and erotic outlaw—and that in a community itself virtually outlawed—that this man's central theme, in both his life and his writings, was community. Virtually all John's books, from *Franny* to the forthcoming *Friends and Lovers*, are, at bottom, about community. He was one of the few people I have known for whom the need for community was an immediate and tangible reality. He spent years moving from city to city until he realized that at heart he was a New Englander and he settled in Portland, to be near his roots and his family. What was important about Portland was that there he could know by name the people who worked in the Post Office, there he was accepted by the guys at the barber shop, there he knew the Governor as well as the members of the leather fraternity, there he felt truly at home.

And it was in Portland that John slowly—and much to his own amusement—came to the realization that he, this man of many masks and personas, was in essence a New England bachelor, a "curmudgeonly New England bachelor" in his own words.

Surrounded by young men who valued their connection with him as intensely as he valued his connection with the late Sam Steward, young men he took to calling his nephews, the transition was complete: the bad boy of gay porn had become the good uncle of the gay community, a trusted and respected elder whose help and guidance was eagerly sought and generously given. John had achieved a singular status within the gay community, and his passing will be felt from Portland, Maine, to Portland, Oregon.

In the last conversation I had with John, a few days before his death, after we settled the final details for the revision of *Franny* he wanted published, I told him I was having trouble believing that we might never again have such a conversation. I told him his friendship had been one of the great pleasures and honors of my life and had sustained me through many rocky times in the last decade or so. And I thanked him for seventeen years of the best conversation I have had.

I know that thousands upon thousands of gay people across this land feel the same loss I do, for we are all diminished. John was one of our leaders, one of our heroes, one of our storytellers, but, above all, he was one of our best friends.

III.
Inventing John Preston

THE NEXT YEAR, on October 6–8, 1995, thanks to a generous grant of $20,000 from John's good friend Anne Rice, we were able to hold a conference on John's work—"Flesh and the Word: A John Preston Gathering"—at Brown University. The speakers included Katherine Forrest, Michael Lowenthal, Michael Lassell, Dorothy Allison, Andrew Holleran, Michael Bronski, Christi Cassidy, Wickie Stamps, Steven Saylor and myself. Around four hundred gay and lesbian writers came from all across the country to spend three days celebrating John and discussing his work. There was also a staged reading of *Franny, the Queen of Provincetown* on Saturday night and an ongoing exhibit of John's work—manuscripts, various editions of his multiple books and some nice photographs—at the University's John Hay Library, which had acquired John's papers.

This was my contribution to the gathering.

About twenty years ago, in the mid-Seventies, Ed White remarked in one of his essays that post-Stonewall gay people were the true existentialists of our time. The riots at the Stonewall had shown clearly what Hegel called the great power of the Negative, expressed succinctly but no less philosophically by the folks in the streets as "No More Shit!" Stonewall was The Great Refusal, a deep, not fully understood, rejection of the way society both conceptualized and treated homosexuals, which is why it became the founding myth of the gay community. But if this rejection of society's construction of homosexuality was wildly liberating, it also presented those of us who lived through it with a perplexing question: just what did a non-repressed, non-oppressed, non-closeted gay person look like? There were no examples; there was no map. Thus, willy nilly, we all became existentialists, attempting to construct new identities, new forms of relationships, a new type of community, even new sexual acts, with precious little to go on besides the cautionary, somewhat negative examples of such heroic forebears as Quentin Crisp or Jean Genet. Of course, this led to a great deal of experimentation, not a few disasters, and many dead ends, all the while creating a sheer exuberant joy at being alive. And as the whole community gradually became involved with the great work of transformation—a part of the transvaluation of all values Nietzsche had called for almost a century earlier—it was only natural that our writers became excited about it and sought to document as well as participate in this great transformation.

Which only raised further questions. What was gay literature? What was a gay novel? Did gay culture even exist? In the early Seventies there was a very heated discussion among the writers and editors I knew about the very possibility of gay writing. In the immediate aftermath of Stonewall, many serious writers rejected the possibility and insisted that they were not gay writers but writers who happened to be gay. They wished to be judged on their writing, not on their subject matter. Unfortunately, they found that the only thing most straight editors could see *was* their subject matter. Felice Picano has testified that what brought the Violet Quill group into existence was the writers' need to have somebody who could read their writing without being blown out of the water by the subject matter, somebody who could actually see past the subject to the *writing*. So they turned toward each other and thus was the Violet Quill Club born.

Almost two decades later, with members of that group having achieved some literary and even occasionally commercial success, it has become customary to denigrate the importance and achievement of these "white gay men." This is understandable—every generation has to overthrow the preceding generation to come into its own—but it is a mistake. Actually, it's worse than a mistake, it's a cheap shot. These individuals—Ed White, Andrew Holleran, Robert Ferro, Michael Grumley, Felice Picano, Christopher Cox and George Whitmore—had the courage at a pivotal moment in gay history to risk their literary careers by forging ahead into uncharted territory. They did pioneering work in establishing the contemporary tradition of gay writing which all our writers draw on today. Six or seven years of furious discussion and experimentation bore fruit (so to speak) in 1978, a banner year that saw the publication of Ed White's *Nocturnes for the King of Naples*, George Whitmore's *The Confessions of Danny Slocum*, Andrew Holleran's *Dancer from the Dance*, Felice Picano's *The Lure*, Paul Monette's *Taking Care of Mrs. Carroll*, and Larry Kramer's *Faggots*. In 1978 I was convinced that we had passed a major milestone, that a new gay literature had announced itself and begun the struggle for recognition that continues to this day. (Actually, though I find it odd to say so, I think we can say today that this battle has essentially been won—even more reason to respect those who initiated the struggle.)

This was the literary situation for gay writers when John Preston arrived in New York in 1978 or 1979, I can't remember which. John had already done many different things: he had founded the first gay community center in Minneapolis, he had been the editor of *The Advocate*, and he had become a legendary top-man in S&M circles. When I first knew him, John was working any number of odd jobs—it always tickled me that he wrote most of *Mr. Benson* at the office while working as a temp secretary for the Women's Division of the World Council of Churches—and he was trying to decide whether he wanted to be a professional writer.

The gay literary world in New York was a rather small affair in those days; all the gay writers as well as the few gay agents, gay book editors and gay magazine editors could be and were found at the same parties. Again and again. In fact, my memory of those days is one of almost constant literary parties. Naturally, I took John around and introduced him to everyone, which did not go very well. John thought the Violet Quill folk were snobs, while they, I think, were intimated by John's sexual outlaw status and reacted to his ambition to be a writer as if they were threatened by unfair competition. No doubt this was to some degree a matter of personalities, but I think there was a deeper and more interesting distinction between John and the writers of the Violet Quill, a distinction that goes to the heart of the cultural strategies available to a gay writer at that time.

Since Ed White was always the foremost representative of this group, I will use him for simplicity's sake. White did not appear from nowhere; he too was preceded by a generation of what we might call proto-gay writers. In his case, the most immediate, persuasive and practical cultural influences on him in the middle and late Seventies were the examples of Richard Howard, Susan Sontag and Richard Sennett. These gay writers from the immediately preceding generation exemplified a cultural strategy that homosexual artists in America had used for almost two centuries and which is brilliantly examined in Robert Dawidoff's book, *The Genteel Tradition and the Sacred Rage*. This strategy rested on an elitist conception of art, fueled by a fear of the ignorance and intolerance of the democratic masses and a leaning toward the European literary and cultural tradition as pervasive and irresistible as phototropism. It is no accident, as old lefties used to say, that White's first claim to fame was Vladimir Nabokov's statement that he was the most interesting young American writer he had read, nor is it an accident that White would devote years of his prime as a writer to a biography of Jean Genet. This was, in fact, the dominant strategy for homosexual artists in America from George Santayana and Henry James through the early Thornton Wilder to Edward Albee and Gore Vidal—with the remarkable and startling exceptions of Walt Whitman and Christopher Isherwood and a few others. This Eurocentric cultural strategy exalted culture and literature to a pure realm of perfection, so far removed from ordinary reality that it made trivial the distinctions of race, class or sexual orientation. In the clear air of Parnassus, talent was judged purely and all prejudice was triumphantly overcome. I hasten to add that in certain historical circumstances this strategy can be not only valid, but downright progressive.

For various reasons of personality and education, John was not much inclined to this European strategy of high culture. Instead, he found himself drawn to another literary strategy—the underground tradition exemplified by the mass market pornographic novels of Sam Steward (aka Phil Andros) and the works of John Rechy. These novels not only provided completely democratic erotic stimulation to gay men, they managed to convey—in Steward's case, quite consciously— essential information to the isolated gay men of the Fifties and Sixties: where the hottest sexual cruising spots were in various cities, the classic types of police entrapment that could ruin lives, information on sexually transmitted diseases, etc. Working on the economically hard-pressed fringes of book and magazine publishing, this writing hearkened back to the classic British tradition of Grub Street, where professional writers worked their asses off to keep a roof over their head and pay the bills. Often denigrated as hacks, these writers were the polar opposite of the high culture authors whose creative writing would never be sullied by the commercial demands of the marketplace. Grub Street was a tradition John felt totally at home in.

I think the most interesting and important distinction between these two literary strategies lies in who the ultimate reader is seen to be, whose judgment the writer is aiming for and willing to accept. White, of course, has often said that his ideal reader is an educated and cultured woman of a certain age living in a small Midwestern city; someone, no doubt, who has read the same authors White has, with the same appreciation. And John's ideal reader is obviously a young and horny gay man, one of the boys in the bars. The writers of the Violet Quill Club—with, I think, the exception of Andrew Holleran—aimed at the traditional pantheon of European literary culture, hoping to take their place, great or small, in that distinguished line that is the backbone of western literature. Whereas the other, underground tradition of gay writing addressed itself directly to the newly emerging gay community and found validation in the impact that writing could have on gay men and their ongoing daily lives. Since that community was still coming into being in the Seventies, this Grub Street strategy implied a commitment to political and community work to insure that their audience existed, was in good shape and persevered. Thus, as a strategy, Grub Street is inherently more political than Parnassus. Although often dismissed as hacks for being slaves of the marketplace, these writers could legitimately claim to be trying to change the world, while the Parnassus wannabes are only trying to get the approval of the world.

When John made the decision to try to become a writer in 1979 or 1980, it was a truly existential decision. For John, "being a writer" meant living off the money that your writing brought in, no mean trick as any writer can tell you. Thus John refused to have any more day jobs to support himself, and even decided to forgo the benefits that his status as a sexual outlaw could have brought him. So John went from being poor to being ridiculously poor. I remember that first winter when he owned only two pairs of jeans, two white tee-shirts, a black leather jacket and black boots—very sexy, to be sure, but he seemed to be freezing most of the time. Luckily he was in town for the big dinner I threw on Christmas day, so I simply informed all my friends that I expected each to bring a present for John to be put under the tree and suggested that flannel shirts, warm socks, thermal underwear and gloves would be appropriate. I think I gave that man a flannel shirt every birthday and Christmas for the first three or four years I knew him.

But John's decision to become a full-time writer—risky as that is in every case—created a particular dilemma for me. We were close friends—we had become extremely close friends very fast—but I was also an editor by profession, and when John gave me something to read I had to decide whether to respond to him as a friend or as an editor. And, believe me, these would have been quite different responses. By then, I had been in publishing for a little over a decade, and it seemed to me that the success of any writer's career always depended on the particular mix of talent and character present. When I was a young and naïve editor I was inordinately impressed by literary talent and thought it was the all-important thing, but slowly I began to change my mind. I had seen so many talented people—and true talent I think is as obvious as a sixth finger—whose careers I had gradually come to realize were going to go nowhere, for they were lacking in the character half of the equation: they didn't have the steadfastness to press on, they were not organized enough to get the work done, they were not thick-skinned enough to withstand criticism and rejection, they drank or drugged too much, etc., etc. If I had started out thinking the equation should be 75 percent talent and 25 percent character, I had come to reverse that by the time I met John. Increasingly, I thought issues of character and determination were what would prevail. And while John was well endowed in the character department—he had the determination, the intelligence, and the practical street smarts to negotiate a tricky publishing world—it seemed to me that he had almost no natural talent.

By natural talent, I mean a gift for the language, an ear that hears the musical cadences in everyday speech, an eye for the telling detail that in two strokes makes a character come alive on the page, a creative imagination that is often far ahead of a writer's conscious intention. And John, I thought, had a tin ear, as well as a weakness for clichéd and conventional phrases, and no true feel for the language, or flair with metaphor and simile. If the writing career is the result of some combination of talent and character, then John's case might show just how far one could go on character alone, with virtually no native talent.

I've thought long and hard about making that statement publicly. The question of talent is, of course, taboo in our public discourse. Which is why I get the feeling that so many of the discussions we have at the annual OutWrite meetings are so phony. The question of talent, the question of quality, especially relative quality, can not be politely raised in public, and yet that question is at the heart of the matter. Talent, whether you like it or not, is there—or not there, as the case may be—and this is a relatively objective fact. Even worse, it seems to be very unequally distributed, which is quite frustrating to our feelings of justice and fairness. But so what? Physical beauty is just as random a gift, just as undeserved, but no one but the dementedly politically correct would deny that it's a fact of life.

I also realized that the question of talent or lack of it is really an essential—if not central—fact about John as a writer, especially if we are considering the act of self-creation that resulted in John Preston the writer. As far as I could see, John, when he made the decision to become a writer, had no talent, showed no particular gift, for writing.

Thus my dilemma. As a friend I firmly believed I should support John in his creative endeavors. As an editor, a professional whose judgment should be unmoved by friendship with the writer, I'd be less than honest if I didn't warn him that the chances didn't look too great. At the time I thought about this a lot, until I decided that my friendship with John was more important than my professional judgment, and I should support his endeavor wholeheartedly. When John gave me things to read and edit, I concentrated on doing whatever I could to make them better (and perhaps over the years I overdid it, judging from a wry acknowledgment in one of his late books thanking me for telling him each time I read something that it was the best thing he had ever written—of course, in the last four or five years that was true).

Luckily, John's writing in the beginning was mostly nonfiction essays or work in various genres from pornography to male action and adventure—the one place where intelligence, lack of ego, willingness to learn, and sheer good work habits can make a success. Then something truly interesting happened.

When the catastrophe of AIDS fell over the gay male community, John, as could be expected, rallied to the cause. What was unexpected—at least, by me—was that his writing style began to change. Under the pressure of this historic disaster, which first hit his community, then his friends, then his loved ones, then himself, John began forging a new, plain style, with no literary affectations and with a terrible clarity and urgency. And before my eyes he began to turn into a very moving writer, a very significant writer, even, I think all of us here would agree, a major writer for our community.

One of the most remarkable responses to the AIDS holocaust was the emergence of a group of heroic writers (and no matter what you hear, writers are seldom heroic; it doesn't come with the territory), writers like Randy Shilts and Larry Kramer and Paul Monette and John Preston. If ever the gay community needed heroes, it was when the AIDS crisis fell upon us, and these writers rose to the challenge. I believe this generation of gay writers—and there are many others whose names I haven't mentioned—will go down as one of the great moments in American literature. Truly, the only writers I can think to compare them to are the great Russian underground writers of the Twenties and Thirties and Forties—Akhmatova and Mandelstam and all the rest—whose record of spiritual resistance became a precious treasure for future generations of Russians, as well as all the rest of us. Just so, the examples and the works of these men will, I believe, come to be recognized as a shining moment when literature really did matter, when writing helped one to live. This is a precious legacy.

And so character was triumphant. John became the major writer he so much wanted to be. In fact, since John was actually, underneath it all, a modest man, I believe he became a much more important writer than he ever expected to be. John wanted to become the scribe to the gay community, and he did become that, even though it meant first doing all the heavy lifting to help that community come into existence.

In his posthumous book, *Winter's Light*, John at one point remembers when he "was a kid who belonged in my hometown. Generations of my mother's family had lived there. No one questioned whether I was part of the community." But as he hit adolescence he found himself "becoming something that could not exist in a New England town." It took him nearly three decades, but his physical and spiritual return to New England was a notable achievement, and it was *the achievement of a writer*, a man of words who had made a home for himself not only in the gay community he helped to bring forth, but even in his native New England where he liked to think the guys in the barber shop said "something like, 'He's a queer writer, but he's *our* queer writer.'"

This achievement was a *literary* achievement, it was done by his writing. John Preston did indeed invent John Preston, gay man of letters, public scribe to his community, public activist and respected elder, a Yankee queer. Anyone interested in the literary life can only be astonished by his achievement.

Food for Life

A DINNER PARTY IN TWO HOURS

The conversations I so valued with my gay friends often took place around the dinner table. Restaurants were okay for meeting one on one (especially if you were an editor and had an expense account) but didn't work so well for larger groups, if your purpose was to introduce people to one another. Home-cooked meals lead to a much more relaxed and convivial atmosphere. So it became important to develop a few standard dinners that could be made quickly on a work night, but were still reasonably pleasing.

In 1994 Lawrence Schimel asked me and fifty-two other gay and lesbian writers to contribute to *Food for Life . . . and Other Dish,*[1] a cookbook he was doing, all the royalties of which were to be donated to organizations providing food to homebound people with AIDS. It was amazing how people kept finding ways to fund what the government wouldn't but what was necessary to help our own. Given the cause and the company, I was more than happy to participate.

This is my ever-trustworthy plan for those harried evenings when I leave the office at five-thirty and know I have four to six people coming to dinner at eight. Though basic—even downright plain—it works, and it's fast. It also seems particularly popular with people with AIDS, who seem to do best with simple, non-spicy foods. It was Paul Monette's favorite meal at my house, one that he asked for each time he visited as if it were a gourmet treat.

The following shopping list provides the whole meal:

2 to 3 cans Campbell's tomato soup	Butter
A loaf of good, fresh bread	Parsley

1 Cleis Press, 1996.

4- to 8-pound chicken

2 to 3 Acorn Squash

Vegetable for steaming, such as Carrots or or Brussels sprouts

Dessert and Chocolate

Lemons

Honey

Lawry's Seasoned Salt

Raisins (optional)

Tomato Soup

Use Campbell's tomato soup—it's the best they make, though do add two tablespoons of butter and whisk briskly while heating. Serve with a few sprigs of parsley on top, with a very thin circular slice of lemon floating in the middle, and with the very best loaf of freshly baked bread your neighborhood offers. (Eli's sourdough baguettes for the Upper West Side of Manhattan.)

Roast Chicken

Wash the chicken inside and out in warm water, removing any innards; pat it dry with paper towels; massage the skin with half lemons and sprinkle (very) liberally with Lawry's Seasoned Salt. For extra juicy chicken, make tiny slits in the skin of the breast and thighs and insert small pats of butter under the skin. Put on a rack in a roasting pan, or better still, one of those vertical chicken-holder do-hickeys that lets all the fat drip off, and roast at 325 to 350 degrees for 18 to 20 minutes per pound. Basically, you shove it into the oven for an hour and 15 minutes, then look at it.

Acorn Squash

Cut each squash in half, scoop out the innards, perforate the flesh with a fork, drop a tablespoon of butter and a large dollop of honey in each hollow, then put them on a rack below the chicken and cook for an hour. (Squash is easy: 15 minutes more won't do it any harm; if the squash is done early, remove and cover with tin foil.)

Steamed Vegetables

Use a triple boiler with several steaming compartments. Cut carrots into 1-inch lengths and steam till slightly soft—say 45 minutes. (The smaller you cut them, the faster they'll cook.) You can add raisins if you want. Brussels sprouts will take about half an hour and will cook better if you remove the older outer leaves, cut off the stem and score it (cut an X into the stem). Both can be served with butter or lemon juice, or both.

Dessert

Take the easy way out and buy sherbet (or ice cream or frozen yogurt) and cookies (and make sure chocolate is somehow involved).

And that's it—all in under two hours.

Turning . . . Turning

THE BOYS IN THE BAND

I FIRST SAW the film version of *Boys in the Band* in 1970, on the Near North Side of Chicago. Struggling with my own issues of sexual identity at the time, I'd gone alone, almost surreptitiously, to the theater where I was first riveted then devastated by the story. It seemed to me an utterly accurate and completely depressing analysis of the situation of a gay man in the America of the Sixties. What was missing was any possible way out—there was no horizon of possibility which could give you hope. This was why the riots at the Stonewall resounded so loudly throughout the gay world. That was the great No!—the great refusal, the declaration that we weren't going to put up with it anymore.

John Harris, the editor of *Christopher Street*'s sister publication, *Theater Week*, who had heard me, on probably more than one occasion, defending the unpopular position that *Boys in the Band* was a gay work of major importance, mercifully offered me the chance to set forth my ideas in his magazine once and for all.[1] Or perhaps he was just hoping to shut me up. In any case, here's the result.

Mart Crowley's play *The Boys in the Band* opened in the spring of 1968, a little over a year before the riots at the Stonewall Inn changed everything. That next June 1969 became the great dividing line of modern gay history, separating everything into a before and after, and in our heady enthusiasm to explore the possibilities that a newly discovered gay liberation opened before us there was a strong tendency to consider anything written before that date as . . . well, dated. If the newly emerging gay community of the Seventies referred to Crowley's play at all, it was to cite it almost as a case study of the distortions of the psyche caused by a homophobic society, a theatrical illustration of "the

---

1 *Theater Week*, June 17–23, 1996.

havoc wrought in the souls of people who aren't supposed to exist" (Ntozake Shange). The one line that passed into general circulation— Emory's observation, "Oh, Mary, it takes a fairy to make something pretty!"—reeked of a pre-Stonewall consciousness, but its self-evident truth made it necessary and gave it the status of a proverb in the community.

Which is why it is surprising, on rereading the play, to find it so current. *The Boys in the Band* actually depicts, with remarkable precision, a pre-revolutionary situation: the emotional constrictions and outright misery of the eight gay characters churn the atmosphere with unfocused anger that slowly directs itself against the straight man. Much happens in the course of this play, but the essential action is twofold and intertwined: the closeted Michael stands up to his straight college roommate and close friend, Alan, and Hank and Larry openly avow their love for each other. What makes the play truly serious is that the author instinctively realized that these two actions are essentially connected.

Michael is the central character and the one who generates virtually all the action on stage. A man fighting alcoholism, who shops neurotically but can't pay his bills, his misery lashes across the set like a loose electrical wire flopping in a storm, scattering sparks whenever it hits. Michael is an unpleasant character, uncomfortable in his skin, who has found solace neither in drink, nor the church, nor fashion, three of the four traditional opiates of despised faggots (for obvious reasons the fourth—sex—couldn't be put on stage at that time, but Cowboy, the young hustler, stands in as a marker). As Harold, in whose honor Michael is throwing this evening's birthday party, points out to him, "I am turning-on and you are just turning," a word he repeats at points throughout the play—"turning, turning"—as Michael writhes in an existential pain that was the lot of most gay people before Stonewall. Harold sees right through Michael: "You are a sad and pathetic man. You're a homosexual and you don't want to be. But there is nothing you can do to change it. Not all your prayers to your God, not all the analysis you can buy in all the years you've got left to live. You will always be a homosexual. Always, Michael. Always. Until the day you die."

For Michael there is no way out of his misery. He thinks he can avoid it by living in the closet: "Well, even you have to admit it's much simpler to deal with the world according to its rules and then go right ahead and do what you damn well please." Simpler until the crunch comes, simpler until the evening when your best straight friend comes over while you're hosting a party with seven homosexuals, simpler until all hell breaks loose and you see that the liberal tolerance—Alan's "Oh, come on, man, you know me—you know how I feel—your private life is your own affair"—is only a mask for the truly murderous hatred straight society had for homosexuals: "Alan: (Lashes out) Faggot, fairy, pansy . . . (Lunges at Emory, grabs him, pulls him off the stool to the floor and attacks him fiercely) queer, cocksucker! I'll kill you, you goddamn little mincing swish! You goddamn freak! FREAK! FREAK!"

Alan's outburst of physical violence near the end of act I brings onto stage the surrounding reality of heterosexual America circa 1968, the implacable, unrelenting, nearly universal hostility this strange straight culture directed at homosexuals and homosexuality, a horizon of hatred that circumscribed gay life and bore down on those who lived it with the force of a pressure cooker. This omnipresent and socially approved hostility is why, when the apartment buzzer sounds, Emory yelps, "Oh my God, it's Lily Law! Everybody, three feet apart"; why Bernard responds to Michael's quip about fear of flying with "I'm scared on the ground"; why Cowboy agrees, "Me too. That is, when I'm not high on pot or up on acid"; why even Harold has been collecting enough pills to keep suicide a viable option; why Donald throws himself on his shrink's coach to "vomit-out how depressed I am"; why Michael turned first to drink and then to the Catholic church. The strange social hatred is so accepted as the norm that even though Alan is outnumbered eight-to-one he doesn't hesitate to attack one of Michael's guests; after all, the entire weight of social reality as he knows it is on his side.

If Crowley had left matters here, he would have had a striking play on the psychological distortions caused by homophobia; but the playwright sensed a change in the air and in act II he shows the audience something altogether new: for the first time we can see the beginnings of what could be considered fighting back. When Alan, having recovered from his fit of violence, comes down the stairs to leave, "Michael intercepts, blocking Alan with his foot, 'As they say in the Deep South, don't rush off in the heat of the day,'" he says, as Harold comments, "Revolution complete."

The worm has indeed turned, and Michael will not let Alan leave until they have played a parlor game, "Affairs of The Heart . . . a combination of both the Truth Game and Murder—with a new twist," a game in which the player has to call the one person he truly believed he'd loved, identify himself and say, "I love you."

At first this might seem like no more than ringing another variation on the old theme of the love that dare not speak its name, but two things are worth noting here. First, for those born after Stonewall, it needs emphasizing that the characters in this play *assume* that while a man might love another man, that could never be spoken. Indeed, in pre-Stonewall days, the mechanics of homosexual desire were self-defeating virtually by definition. If a gay guy found himself attracted to another man, he was generally attracted precisely by masculinity; most closeted gays in the Fifties and Sixties found themselves fantasizing about the captain of the football team, not the raging queen in the drama club. That is, precisely those who would be appalled to know about it and who would reject that desire with distaste. In the argot of the day, the queen was attracted by trade; if the trade experienced sexual desire for the queen, he wasn't trade, by definition, just another queen in disguise, another queen to be despised. The conundrum was so well established there appeared no way out. This, of course, is the experience of both Bernard and Emory, the first two to play the game.

The turning point comes when Hank calls the answering service he shares with Larry to leave the message "I love you." How radical that message sounded at the time is indicated not only by the answering service which couldn't believe it had heard right, but by Alan's totally shocked response:

ALAN: Why, Hank? Why did you do that?
HANK: Because I do love him. And I don't care who knows it.
ALAN: Don't say that.
HANK: Why not? It's the truth.

To which Alan replies, "I can't believe you," a denial the straight world would cling to for the next two decades until an exasperated generation of gays would stomp around yelling "We're here, we're queer, get over it!"

Hank and Larry's public avowal of their love is the political heart of this play, but note how the author has insisted that this happen in front of a straight man: this love must dare to speak its name not only among its own but in front of the others. It is this in-your-face attitude that marks the beginning of something new, something that barely one year later would burst forth at Stonewall. To be sure, lesbians and gay men had built communities of their own, circles of friends, groups around bars, havens in a heartless world. But these spaces were invisible to the world at large, as for the most part were the people who inhabited them. The mighty surge of cultural energy that would thrust so many out of the closet in the next decade has not yet arrived, though the first tremors of that great social upheaval can be felt in this play.

But the time is not yet. The play captures the moment before, and so ends on a dying fall: Michael, alone with Donald amid the wreckage of the party, the wreckage of his psyche, panicked and, yes, pathetic: "If we . . . if we could just . . . learn not to hate ourselves so much. That's it, you know. If we could just not hate ourselves quite so very much." But, of course, nobody is born hating himself. It is not a natural instinct to hate yourself. People learn to hate themselves because others hate them first. Michael must wrestle with the demons of self-hate because straight society hates what he is and he can't change it. Because Alan hates Emory to the point where he would kill him. Michael has not made that connection yet, but the play does, implicitly.

It is, finally, Michael's inability to make that connection that strikes a contemporary gay reader as so startling. All these internalized fights of self against self, all this internalized self-hatred that was so debilitating, had to be externalized. This psychologized issue had to be transformed into a political issue—not self against self, but us against them—before one could do anything about it. And this is precisely what the gay movement has done, and why the fights today are about gays in the military, gays in the priesthood, and gay marriage and parenting, accurately targeting the three main institutionalized sources of homophobia that had made our lives miserable: the military, the church, the family.

But in this play there is as yet no horizon of possibility for the characters, no way out of the emotional constrictions society has forced them into. The idea of gay rights is as totally alien to the characters on stage as it would have been to the members of its original audience, and without that idea there is no way out for these people. But surely astute gay men sitting in that audience must have sensed that something was happening, something was on the way, that the great work was about to begin.

A Mouthful of Air

THE CASE OF LARRY KRAMER

IN 1996 LARRY Mass invited me to contribute to a volume he was assembling, *We Must Love One Another or Die: The Life and Legacies of Larry Kramer*,[1] a welcome opportunity to consider the man and the writer.

By this time, well over a decade into the epidemic, Kramer's voice echoed loudly throughout the national gay community and beyond; he seemed everywhere, his words angrily agitating the air to mobilize us to action. To someone interested in the connection of writing with politics it was a remarkable performance, a rare instance of the political power inherent in the use of language alone. I could think of no other example where political action and writing were so completely fused.

> *They have spoken against you everywhere.*
> *But weigh this song with the great and their pride;*
> *I made it out of a mouthful of air,*
> *Their children's children shall say they have lied.*

> W. B. YEATS, "He Thinks of Those
> Who Have Spoken Ill of His Beloved"

Larry Kramer presents an interesting case to anyone curious about the interaction between writing and politics, two realms whose relations have been strained ever since Plato banished poets from his ideal Republic. No one today would deny that Kramer has been one of the major political players in the AIDS epidemic, as one of the founders of the Gay Men's Health Crisis (GMHC), the first and now the largest AIDS support organization in the world; as the man who called ACT UP into existence and tried to guide it through its early years; as the tireless agitator whose thundering diatribes and denunciations have shaped

---

1 London: Cassell, 1997.

the attitudes and politics of more than one generation of gay men. Few writers in our day have plunged into the political arena as deeply and as energetically, and even fewer have made their impact as widely felt as Kramer's, "whose pronouncements, ultimatums, vilifications, lampoons, and dramatizations seemed ubiquitous in the early years of the epidemic."[2]

What is interesting about Kramer as a political actor is the means he employed. After all, Larry Kramer represented no one; he had no constituency, no political following and no organization to back him up. Indeed, he was more or less thrown out of Gay Men's Health Crisis and, in its later years, attacked by various factions and individuals in ACT UP. In fact, after his first purely political statement, a 1978 op-ed piece for the *New York Times* called "Gay Power Here" which he wrote at the suggestion of the Random House publicity department to garner attention for his first novel, *Faggots*, he "received a number of phone calls and letters, all saying, more or less, 'Who the fuck are you and what right do you have publicly mouthing off?' Indeed, I was criticizing an entire community and its leadership that I hardly knew and that certainly didn't know me. 'Where have you been all these years, while we've been working our asses off fighting for the gay rights bill?' was screamed at me by not a few."[3] Three years later when he began to write about AIDS, he was still not a popular figure (to say the least) in the gay community. He had alienated many people with *Faggots* and its satirical portrait of a gay world delirious in its pursuit of sex. Having taken what was widely viewed as an anti-sex stand in that novel, Kramer was not a person most gay men were willing to listen to easily. And in the years ahead we found that he was never easy to listen to, but listen we did. And the fact that we did listen is remarkable and worth looking into.

For Kramer had nothing but his mouth. It was only his stunning ability to use language, to speak in public and to write in fury, that gave

---

2 David Bergman, "Larry Kramer and The Rhetoric of AIDS," in *Gaiety Transfigured: Gay Self-Representation in American Literature* (Madison: University of Wisconsin Press, 1991), p. 123.

3 Larry Kramer, *Reports from the Holocaust: The Story of an AIDS Activist* (New York: Stonewall Inn Editions, St. Martin's Press, 1994), p. 6.

him any political position at all. This strikes me as remarkable. Not since Emile Zola's *J'accuse* has the sheer power inherent in the written word been as effectively deployed for political ends. Who would have thought that one man raising his voice—loudly and repeatedly, then more loudly and repeatedly, then, when you thought he couldn't, *still* more loudly and repeatedly—that one man could mobilize an entire community, could force the media and the politicians to pay attention, could call into existence the major activist organization of the 1980s with a single speech at one public meeting? We have seen many instances of grassroots political initiatives, of clever media campaigns, of relentless lobbying, but nothing quite like this in a very long while. Kramer presents us with a remarkable example of the political power that can be generated by language alone—one man raising his voice—and this, it seems to me, should be of intense interest to anyone concerned with language and its uses.

Many people, trying to define Kramer's role in the gay community during the great catastrophe of AIDS, have used the word "prophet" and referred back to the Old Testament, and it is not an inappropriate comparison. A prophet is a person who becomes a hero to the community—at least in the retrospective view of history—by speaking out and telling people what they don't want, but need, to hear, which was certainly the case with Kramer. Furthermore, it is generally true of prophets that they get no respect in their own country or in their own time. From the beginning—from the first piece of writing he ever did about AIDS, which provoked a blistering response from the playwright Robert Chesley: "Read anything by Kramer closely, I think you'll find the subtext is always: the wages of gay sin are death."[4] Not only was his message rejected, but his motives were called into question; he's saying these awful things because he's fanatically anti-sex, because he's on a demented ego trip, because he hates gay people.

In retrospect it is startling how little credit this man was given for the now quite obvious concern for the gay community that animates everything he ever wrote. Unlike John Preston or Paul Monette, writers also mobilized by AIDS but whose dedication to the community was

4 Kramer, *Reports*, p. 10.

acknowledged and appreciated, Kramer was viewed as a divisive and destructive force. His trenchant satire of the gay world of the 1970s, like all satire, was the work of a moralist, a man committed to strengthening, to reforming, the gay community. If he attacked the extreme value placed on sex, it was to make room for love and friendship; but few readers saw this at the time. As a prophet, Kramer got precious little respect, but he was right. At each and every point, Larry Kramer was right. What appeared to most to be wildly exaggerated scenarios of doom turned out to be accurate, sometimes even conservative, predictions, utterly borne out by events. Kramer outraged people by public speeches in which he asked the right half of the audience to stand up and then bluntly told them they'd be dead, half the room would be dead, in ten years. Of course, in New York City the number turned out to be more like 75 percent—three-quarters of the room *was* dead after ten years—but who could have believed that at the time?

And here the figure of the Old Testament prophet gives way to the image of Cassandra—"I wanted to be Moses, but I could only be Cassandra," says Ned Weeks in *The Destiny of Me*[5]—Cassandra who saw so clearly the terrible vision of the destruction of her beloved city, who tried to warn her fellow citizens of their impending doom, but whose prophesies failed to avert the destruction of Troy. Cassandra was right, but it didn't matter, Troy still fell. Like Cassandra, Kramer failed. Larry Kramer failed to stop the AIDS epidemic, a point not often stated for obvious reasons, but worth pausing over for a moment. Kramer failed, just as the movement against the war in Vietnam failed to halt that bloody conflict, a fact—an essential fact, one would think—that tends to be overlooked when memory turns to the anti-war movement of the 1960s.

Whatever the retrospective view of Kramer as a political figure may eventually be, that central point—the bitter knowledge that all his efforts judged against their original purpose, ended in failure—is starkly clear to Kramer himself. He records it, repeatedly, in *Reports from the Holocaust*. Gay Men's Health Crisis, founded to alert the gay community to the clear and present danger and mobilize the nation's political

---

5 Larry Kramer, *The Destiny of Me* (New York: Plume, Penguin Books), p. 87.

and health establishments to come to our aid, became a social welfare organization that helped people with AIDS die, alleviating the pressure that otherwise would have been felt by the federal, state and city authorities. ACT UP had perhaps its greatest success in twice forcing the pharmaceutical companies to reduce the price of AZT; only in retrospect would many come to believe that tens of thousands of people had died not from AIDS but from AZT. When Kramer wrote his first piece on AIDS there were 120 cases in the United States; with more than 500,000 cases in America today and estimates of more than 20 million worldwide, the point should not need driving home, but it does: However heroic, the effort to stop the AIDS epidemic was an utter failure. We lost the battle against AIDS, no matter how noble that battle was, and this failure began to be apparent even in the heyday of ACT UP. What is impressive about Kramer is that he began to recognize this, in public and private conversations, even then, although it didn't stop him for years and years.

You're probably objecting that this is too harsh a judgment, that it is utterly unreasonable to think that any one individual could have stopped this disastrous epidemic. Yet I am only giving due respect to the motives that propelled Kramer into action in the first place. It is utterly clear that he had one overriding purpose in all his writing during the 1980s and that was to stop the epidemic before it wiped out the entire gay male community. As he testified at the time, "I don't consider myself an artist. I consider myself a very opinionated man who uses words as fighting tools."[6] The point was not to produce writing— "I am no longer interested in plays and movies and books"[7]—but to have an effect on the world. But Kramer was caught in the same irony that Randy Shilts laid out with such bitter clarity in his essay, "Talking AIDS to Death,"[8] which described the enormous success of *And the Band Played On* and his own total failure: He had set out to change the world, to end the epidemic, but he only produced a best-seller.

Of course, in the political realm, success or failure is not the final

6 Kramer, *Reports*, p. 145.

7 Kramer, *Reports*, pp. 145–46.

8 Randy Shilts, "Talking AIDS to Death," *Esquire*, vol. 111, no. 3 (March 1989): pp. 123–35.

word in judging any action or actor. Since the Greeks, since Herodotus announced he would relate the great deeds of the Greeks *and* the Persians alike, and Thucydides decided to tell the story of the Athenians and their enemies equally, the victors *and* the vanquished, we have realized that in the political realm success cannot be the sole standard of judgment. When it comes to action what is important, what is worthy of praise and memory, is not the outcome of the act but some inherent quality that shines forth and is illuminating and inspiring to future generations. As Hannah Arendt taught us, action can reveal a certain kind of greatness that is quite independent of success or failure. For the sobering truth is that almost all the great acts of history, almost all the great historical actors, were, in their own terms, failures. What makes them still worthy of memory is that which shines through the act, that greatness of spirit that can inspire future generations by its example.

My hunch is that future generations will find this kind of greatness in Larry Kramer's mighty but ultimately futile efforts to stem the tide of this epidemic; that Kramer will be judged a true hero in a time when catastrophe threatened to destroy a gay community that had barely emerged into the light of history. And, although the battle to prevent the AIDS epidemic from overwhelming us was indeed lost, the fight to resolve it, to find a cure, remained fully engaged and was doggedly led by Kramer, when so many others considered talk of a cure to be wildly optimistic. And now, in no small measure because of his efforts and his vision, that goal may be truly in sight for the first time. Kramer's insistence that the focus be kept on finding a cure struck many as reckless, and there *is* a quality of sheer recklessness in Kramer, in both his writing and his actions—in setting himself against this epidemic!—which combined with a nearly unbelievable relentlessness has made him a hero, one of the founding fathers of the community and the culture, the major voice of resistance during its darkest hour.

But what about the writing? After all, what is unique about this case is that Kramer's political impact was the result of his writing and speaking, his use of language, and when all is said and done and suffered through and the AIDS epidemic has become another episode in the nightmare of history, what will be left are the words on paper.

How do we judge Kramer's writings?

Oddly enough, though many people willingly give him credit for much in the political arena, when it comes to the man's writings, considered solely as writing, the enthusiasm diminishes. Although most of my friends and acquaintances have eventually come to have great respect, and even affection, for him, they seem to shy away from discussing his work and would be taken aback were one to claim that Kramer is one of the most important *writers* of our time. Perhaps this is because we are so used to thinking of politically motivated writing as the realm of the second-rate; after all, books like *Uncle Tom's Cabin* or *What Is To Be Done* seldom head our lists of favorite literary works. Such books are honored in the canon, but more for their extra-literary merit than for their intrinsic worth as writing. In the western tradition, the vast majority of those considered to be great writers tend, when not being totally apolitical, to be conventional and conservative in their politics, if not downright reactionary or simply loony; while the writers admired for their politics, their commitment to a cause or a community, tend to be distressingly mediocre.

If this is indeed the case, the prospects for Kramer's literary reputation do not look bright, for all the writing he has produced is intensely political, more so, in fact, than any other contemporary American writer I can think of. Consider each of his works:

Faggots may have shocked his contemporaries into apoplectic fits of fury, but it is pure, if savage, social satire in the tradition of Jonathan Swift. One critic, describing it as "a phantasmagoria of rape, incest, drug addiction, coprophilia, pedophilia, and torture," confessed to having "difficulty imagining how Kramer expected readers to find the mordant comedy he intended."[9] Of course, the Irish readers of Swift's "A Modest Proposal," and perhaps even the English, might have experienced the same difficulty. Successful satire is not nice, and never polite; it aims to draw blood. With *Faggots*, Kramer clearly intended to jolt his readers into reconsidering the lives they were leading.

The Normal Heart is, arguably, one of the most successful pieces of

---

9 Bergman, *Larry Kramer and The Rhetoric of AIDS*, p. 126.

agitprop theater ever produced; unabashedly a propaganda play, it set out to instruct and arouse its audience to political passion and political action, and it worked remarkably well, much better than most such attempts. "When I wrote *The Normal Heart*," the author states, "I knew exactly what I wanted to achieve: to hear my words screamed out in a theater, and to hope I'd change the world."[10]

Reports from the Holocaust: The Story of an AIDS Activist is a book crafted from Kramer's political writings and speeches, pieces mostly written to have an immediate practical impact, which even the author originally doubted had any lasting literary merit. Indeed, it took several months to convince him to run them out of his computer so they could be read together to see if they would make a valid book. The resulting work still has the capacity to rouse the activist instincts of any reader not clinically dead and is intensely admired by young Black students who gather after Kramer's college lectures to discuss with him how to write in outrage and anger without being consumed by those emotions.[11]

With *Just Say No: A Play about a Farce*, Kramer used the form of the classic French bedroom comedy to skewer the Reagan Administration's hypocrisy and deceit, while lambasting their indifference and neglect of the major public health threat facing the country. "The style is classic farce," wrote one reviewer, "with roots in Swift ... and Restoration comedy. *Just Say No* does not merely drop names. It flings them, usually into the mud."[12] And another critic applauded "Kramer's lonely frontline commitment to theater as a political instrument."[13]

In *The Destiny of Me*, the author puts onto the stage the public and highly politicized figures of Larry Kramer and Tony Fauci, head of the National Institute of Allergy and Infectious Diseases, to act out the complex tragedy of gay men in the AIDS epidemic. A classic family play, yet it is enmeshed in the politics of the moment.

10 Kramer, introduction to *The Destiny of Me*, p. 2.
11 Personal communication from Larry Kramer.
12 Linda Winer, *Newsday*, quoted on the back cover of the paperback edition of *Just Say No* (New York: Stonewall Inn Editions, St. Martin's Press, 1989).
13 Gordon Rogoff, *Village Voice*, quoted on the back cover of *Just Say No*.

And in his currently uncompleted epic, a historical novel called *The American People*, Kramer seeks the roots of the disease of homophobia, tracing the growth of this sickness through the course of American history.

It is hard to imagine a more intensely political oeuvre, and impossible to find a comparably political writer among contemporary gay authors, or anybody else for that matter. Yet what saves this work from being consigned to the dustbin of agitprop theater and second-rate propaganda work is the paradoxical fact that it is at the same time *intensely* personal. *Faggots* is the story of Kramer's own unhappy love affair, a revenge novel to be sure, but virtually every fact, character, incident and institution is taken directly from life, and with much less exaggeration dolloped in than anyone who didn't live through the gay scene in New York in the 1970s could imagine.[14] In *The Normal Heart* and *The Destiny of Me*, Kramer put chunks of his intimate personal life on stage to capture the great tragedy his generation of gay men was living through. In *Reports*, Kramer's anger and outage are so personal and particular, especially his obsession with Mayor Koch and *The New York Times* and the huge and ever increasing list of his dead friends, that some readers thought he was on an ego trip of monumental proportions. And finally, the sheer venom and stinging bitchiness of *Just Say No* are as directly personal as the slanderous assaults of political theater have ever been since the days of Aristophanes.

In the realm of literature, the political is hardly ever personal—think of *Uncle Tom's Cabin*, think of *What Is To Be Done*—and, contrary to popular wisdom, the personal is seldom political. But in this case, at any rate, the personal and the political have been smashed together to the point of fusion. If Kramer is the most political of all contemporary gay writers, he is also the most immediately and unguardedly personal. And it is this remarkable fusion, I believe, that will allow Kram-

---

14 Kramer himself has written "Some readers tell me my novel *Faggots* is about as surreal a portrayal of the gay world as could be, but it was all the real McCoy to me," in the introduction to *The Destiny of Me*, p. 3.

er's writing to escape the dreary fate of so much politically inspired literature.

Reading Kramer's various works, what is striking is how remarkably *alive* his writing remains. His three plays possess a taut immediacy and dramatic urgency that not only hasn't diminished but seems to have clarified and concentrated over time, convincing me at least that his position in the history of American theater is secure. The three plays cohere so remarkably it is almost as if Kramer had intended to write a trilogy—two tragedies followed by a satyr play—in a modern update of the ancient Greek tradition.

Faggots is as outrageously funny as a Marx Brothers movie dreamt up by a queer Philip Roth, a linguistic farrago barreling ahead at an unsafe speed. With his very first book Kramer placed himself in the mainstream of postwar Jewish American humor, in the tradition of Philip Roth and Woody Allen, as well as the great television comedy writers of the 1950s. *Faggots* is written in a classic New York yiddisher, faegele voice that is utterly hysterical when read aloud—when the reader really *hears* it as voice—the narrator is a stand-up comic in the Borscht Belt tradition, a sort of Jack Benny afflicted with logomania, as his torrent of words cascades over the reader with the relentlessness of Niagara Falls. From its opening page the author lets us know that he is addressing grand themes and addressing them with a writerly amplitude that sometimes threatens to drown the reader: "There are 2,556,596 faggots in the New York City area," the first line announces sweepingly, going on to break down the numbers by borough and suburban area before continuing, "There are now more faggots in the New York City area than Jews. There are now more faggots in the entire United States than all the yids and kikes put together. (This is subsidiary data, not overtly relevant, but ipso facto nevertheless.) The straight and narrow, so beloved of our founding fathers and all fathers thereafter, is now obviously and irrevocably bent. What is God trying to tell us . . . ?" Like a latter-day Sid Caesar, armed with patter, dropping asides left and right, the narrator stands stage left and introduces the narrative. The voice is grandiloquent, even operatic at times, gliding easily from stage declamation to whispered asides to muttered meditations to sweeping arias, and this narrative voice vibrates with sympathy, sympathy even for the furniture of the world, the buildings—the sexual haunt of the piers off Christopher Street gets a direct address worthy of Whitman[15]—and sympathy for the characters it evokes with clouds of words before directing our attention to the often vaudevillian scenes about to take place on the page before us. Kramer's language is simply extraordinary and while its voluminousness at first seems excessive, a closer look shows how much information and atmosphere is conveyed in a style that might be described as loquaciously concise. Just try to unpack the information conveyed in that ode to the piers, for instance, as the narrative voice slides seamlessly into the consciousness of the main character, and see if you don't end up with many more words than Kramer used. So much for the temptation to say, "Too many notes, Mr. Mozart."

But perhaps most surprising is how alive the language remains in *Reports from the Holocaust*, essays and speeches written on the spot for specific occasions and specific effect which years later retain their impact. The voice—which is again operatic, as critic David Bergman has noticed[16]—is urgent, personal, demanding, exasperated, loud and absolutely unrelenting. The presence of the author haranguing you is almost physically palpable; indeed, Kramer seems to have a patent on what might be called the Ancient Mariner ploy: you feel like you have to break free of his hold every time you put the book down. Which might have made for an uncomfortable read if Kramer had not added the second, more meditative, occasionally rueful, voice that appears in the interstitial material that introduces and frames each piece, giving its occasion and commenting on its impact, as he rounds out a story which takes us from sheer activism to the philosophical question of evil and personal responsibility in our time.

It is precisely these qualities of his language—the fact that it *is* so personal, urgent, extreme, unrelenting and intimate—that accounts for both the immediate political impact it had and the tendency of some to dismiss it as not serious "literature." Critic David Bergman is

15 See *Faggots* (New York: Random House, 1978), p. 102: "Ah home away from home, ah black hole of Calcutta. . . . *Play, Guts, Ball!*"
16 Bergman, *Larry Kramer and The Rhetoric of AIDS*, p. 128: "The voices of the family float up."

a perfect example of both these reactions: "Kramer's habit of responding to political events as personal affronts, of transforming impersonal
bureaucracies into individual bogeymen, of subsuming all conflicts
into a version of the Freudian family romance is the source of both
the power of his political polemics and of the problems with them."[17]

While I agree with Bergman about the "source," for the life of me I
can't see the "problem." The "political event" Kramer is talking about
is AIDS, and the man is HIV-positive and, until recently at any rate,
expected to die of it relatively soon—if that's not as personal an af-
front as fate can hand one, I don't know what is. Nor can I see what's
wrong, in this situation, with "transforming impersonal bureaucracies into individual bogeymen" (though "bogeymen" is an unneces-
sarily loaded term)—I'm pretty sure it's what Hannah Arendt would
have advised; but if Bergman has a better political strategy for dealing
with such a situation, which one might call genocide by bureaucratic
indifference, incompetence and folly, I'm open to hearing it. And as
for "the Freudian Family romance"—"Kramer's tendency to place the
gay community within the bosom of the heterosexual family"—that, it
seems to me, is precisely where the gay community is situated, as the
catastrophe of AIDS made abundantly clear to us. The illusion that the
gay world was totally separate from the straight world, the fantasy of
the ghetto, was only the wishful thinking of the 1970s and was hardly
tenable then, since we all come from straight families. In any event,
it was totally demolished with the advent of the AIDS epidemic in
which we realized that we were inseparably (intimately and sexually)
connected to the rest of the world, and that we needed the rest of the
world, and its social and scientific resources, to survive as individuals
and thus as a community.

Confronted by Kramer's writings it is clear that this is not strong
emotion recollected in tranquility, it is strong emotion being thrown
in your face. Kramer is not interested in the making of well-wrought
urns, he wants to hurl well-aimed bombs into your consciousness. And
this, I think, gets us to the root of the problem. It is Kramer's apparent disregard for form, for the classic forms of literature, that inclines

17 Bergman, *Larry Kramer and The Rhetoric of AIDS*, p. 128.

people to dismiss him as a serious writer, and to categorize his work as "rhetoric."

Of course, such critics are, oddly forgetting that for two thousand years rhetoric was considered not only legitimate but one of the highest forms of literary art. Some of the most respected authors of western literature—Cicero, for instance—were revered precisely because they were masters of rhetoric. Today, on the contrary, rhetoric carries the overtone of *merely* rhetoric or *empty* rhetoric. In an age when the private and the intimate seem the only guarantee of authenticity and sincerity, rhetoric seems bogus almost by definition. The more public the speech, the less we trust it; only what is intimate is true and sincere. But rhetoric, as one critic has said, transforms texts from something legible (to be read) to something audible (to be heard), it restores to language an acoustic dimension—and, as we know, Kramer was definitely heard.

And, with a brilliant stroke, he abolished the dichotomy between private and public. By smashing together the private and the intimate with the public and the political, he has found a way to bring rhetoric back to life as a legitimate, indeed inspired, capacity of language. His startling use of the personal insult and abusive street language so shattered the general conventions of the day that the protective shield most of us have against public and political speech disappeared. And this, in turn, allows him to employ many of the classic tropes of rhetoric to great effect. Kramer's use of repetition, for instance, or the simple list, are astonishingly effective in piece after piece. And who would have thought that the thundering rhetorical question—**"DO YOU WANT TO DIE???!!!"**—could actually viscerally enrage audiences today? It would be interesting to see a scholarly analysis of all the classic tropes of rhetoric Kramer uses, for it might go some way toward showing there is more literary structure there, a curiously organic structure, than is at first apparent.

Be that as it may, it is nonetheless true that form is not Kramer's strong point. His aim when he puts pen to paper is not to construct a perfect object, but to release energy into the world through his readers. It is not form but voice that is the touchstone, providing the unity and aesthetic coherence in his various writings. Here Kramer joins a tradition that stretches through Allen Ginsberg all the way back to Walt Whitman—also criticized for his neglect of form, for his long-windedness, and for putting himself so viscerally into his poetry. What Whitman said of his work—"Who touches this book, touches me"—applies to Kramer with a vengeance. And, as in the case of Whitman, the voice is the secret of the vitality, the aliveness of the writing. Kramer is an absolute master at the use of voice, and it is his brilliant fusion of the public voice with the personal voice that makes him one of the most remarkable writers at work today.

This voice was called forth by the great catastrophe that overtook the gay community at the beginning of the 1980s: Larry Kramer raised his voice in response to the onslaught of the epidemic. (Of course, *Faggots* was written four years before AIDS emerged; but in an uncanny way that novel now seems to anticipate the crisis—the wages of gay sin are death, indeed.) For gay writers or writers with AIDS, the personal and social catastrophe of this epidemic forced on the mind radical questions about the act of writing, its nature and its purpose and the standards by which we judge its inherent quality, while at the same time offering the opportunity to look afresh at the deepest roots of this cultural act. When you are facing death, when all your friends are dying, why do you write? So posterity might have a few more well-wrought urns? I don't think so.

Kramer responded to the harsh challenge history presented him with using the only tool at his disposal, language. In the midst of such a total disaster for the gay community and this particular gay man, silence did indeed equal death. In such circumstances what is required is speaking out, talking back, not finally because such action will solve the crisis—as we know, nothing stopped this epidemic—but because if speech does not equal life, it does equal dignity. As Mark Doty says in his magnificent memoir of the devastation AIDS wrought on his life, "The deepening of the heart, the work of soul-making, goes on, I think, as the world hammers us, as we forge ourselves in response to its heats and powers."

Through his spirit and his language, Kramer has crafted a testimony that runs alongside the disastrous reality his words are responding to. And I believe that this voice and this catastrophe will be yoked together for as long as people remember these dark days and as long as people value the power of language to keep our spirit alive through the tragedies of history.

To quote Hannah Arendt once again, "Man cannot defend himself against the blows of fate, against the chicanery of the gods, but he can resist them in speech and respond to them, and though the response changes nothing, neither turning ill fortune aside nor prompting good fortune, such words belong to the event as such. If the words are of equal rank with the event, if, as is said at the end of Antigone, 'great words' answer and requite 'great blows struck from on high,' then what happened is itself something great and worthy of remembrance and fame. Speech in this sense is a form of action, and our downfall can become a deed if we hurl words against it even as we perish."[18]

Precisely.

---

18 Hannah Arendt, *The Promise of Politics* (New York: Schocken Books, 2005), p. 125.

Key West Seminar

IN MID-1996 MILES Frieden, director of the Key West Literary Seminar, invited me to take part in their fifteenth annual session entitled "Literature in the Age of AIDS," to be held January 9–12, 1997. Who gives up a chance to visit Key West in January? Besides I thought I was witnessing a unique situation in the history of writing, a truly rare occurrence when the act of writing and the implacable fact of death faced one another head-on, and in that confrontation a clearing emerged which revealed the roots and essence of all writing, of all culture.

As I reread this piece today, I see that my minor irritation with the way the seminar question had been posed concealed a deeper dissatisfaction with the underlying assessment of the cultural situation we were in. I had come ready to share my enthusiasm, even awe, at the literary and cultural feats gay writers had been accomplishing in spite of an unbelievably difficult and hostile situation. And I thought that hostile situation was mainly caused neither by homophobia nor by AIDS phobia (both social attitudes) but by the cruel physical reality of the disease itself as it impacted our bodies and the bodies of our loved ones and brought death to a whole generation of gay men. I came ready to celebrate our triumphs, rather than lodge complaints about society's indifference or hostility.

But I have to admit that in the discussion that followed I did not carry the audience with me—even though that audience included many of the writers I was talking about! Another instance of my being too early? Or was I deluded, too close to the scene, too involved to render a sound judgment? Only time will tell, I suppose.

The question posed to us for this seminar was "What's it like to write (publish) about AIDS in a phobic culture?"

First, I'd like to say that I have a problem with the title of this seminar. (Don't you just love people who start out this way? It's so academic.)

Not with the question "What's it like to write or publish about AIDS," which I think is an interesting question, but with the phrase "in a phobic culture."

This could mean "in a homophobic culture" or it could mean "in an AIDS phobic culture." If it's the first, "What's it like to write about AIDS in a homophobic culture," then I would say it's a lot like writing about Black life in a racist culture. In a nutshell, it's an uphill fight. But if the question is "What's it like to write about AIDS in an AIDS phobic culture," I would say it's a lot like writing about sex in a sex phobic culture, or writing about death in a culture that does everything it can to avoid thinking about that rather elemental fact. In a nutshell, it's an uphill fight.

With any luck some of the other panelists will find something interesting to say about the phrase taken in either or both of these meanings. Perhaps it's my perversity, but to me what's interesting about this homophobic, AIDS phobic culture of ours is the fact that it hasn't prevented the production of a rather large amount of first-rate work being written, published, reviewed, sold, put on the boards, and filmed—perhaps I go too far here—and all in less than fifteen years since this epidemic first announced itself. Compare this to what was written, produced, etc., about the Holocaust fifteen years after the beginning of that event, i.e., by 1957. Some few things to be sure, but I suggest nothing like the amount of work that has been produced about AIDS—in the theater by playwrights such as Bill Hoffman, Larry Kramer, Tony Kushner and others; in the autobiographical writings of Paul Monette, Mark Doty, Fenton Johnson and many, many others; or in the enormous amount of fiction and poetry that AIDS has occasioned. If writing about AIDS in a homophobic, AIDS phobic culture is an uphill fight, it's a fight that many, many creative people have *won*. And not only won, but been crowned with laurels for winning. Admittedly, only laurels and not the royalty income of Anne Rice, but still, laurels are laurels and they were good enough for Pindar.

So I would point out that this homophobic, AIDS phobic culture of ours has witnessed an astonishing cultural production of work about AIDS, work that has often been honored and celebrated throughout the land, even by the dominant culture, something that I, for one, would never have imagined possible in 1983 or 1984. But it's a fact, as

Paul Monette's *Becoming a Man: Half a Life Story* winning the National Book Award for Nonfiction in 1992 or the enormous success of Tony Kushner's *Angels in America* in 1993 can attest to. So I don't think we should go around bemoaning a hostile situation.

So much for my problems with the phrase "in a phobic society." I'm sure this will get me into hot water with some of the other panelists, which should make for a lively discussion. Now, I'd like to turn to the main question: What's it like to (in my case) publish work about AIDS.

It's weird, it's stressful and it's unlike any other type of publishing I've ever experienced. I know other editors who have had the experience of trying to get a book out before the author died, but this used to be a rare occurrence. Now I found myself working, *for years*, under the pressure of trying to publish books, or at least get to the galley stage, before the author died. Time after time I stood before the salespeople at a sales conference to pitch a book to them and had to end my presentation by saying that the author had died or was too ill to do publicity for the book. I don't know if I can convey to you how depressing this was after a while, although it did get their undivided attention. And I think this experience points out one of the unique aspects of AIDS writing. All writing about AIDS that I know of, at least until now, has been produced under the direct impact of the event on the writer. Writers were writing about their own illness, the death of their friends and lovers, their own approaching end. And the real audience they were writing for was not posterity, but other people similarly threatened by the epidemic. This is not writing after the event, as for instance is most of the writing done about World War I; it is as if the poems of Siegfried Sassoon were written in the trenches, produced in the trenches, to be read by other men in the trenches and under fire. This was not the case with most of the poetry written about the First World War, and definitely not the case with the writing about the Holocaust. The diary of Anne Frank may have been written during the event, but it was published, reviewed and read after the event when one could do nothing to change the course of history. It seems to me that this unique situation we found ourselves in brought up radical questions about why one writes and how one judges what is written.

Most of the writers I have known personally who wrote about AIDS were not into the production of aesthetic objects. They could care less about adding another well-wrought urn to that imaginary museum in the sky we call culture. The source of their writing was much deeper than that.

This is a rare occurrence—thank God!—in the history of writing, but it seems to me one of great importance, for it brings us back to meditate on the original purpose and cause of writing, why writing is important to the life of the spirit and to the continued existence of the community.

PART 7

Reconsiderations

1996–2014

In 1996 the triple therapies came in, and for the first time in a decade
and a half there was medical hope. The pills began to work, people on
the verge of death started improving, getting out of their beds, eating,
walking—disoriented and in somewhat of a daze over this unexpected
turn of events. AIDS was over as an epidemic; it had become, at least in
the first world, a manageable, if dangerous, disease.

For the first time in a decade and a half of misery and death it felt
like we could exhale. The storm was over and now we had to live with
the damage, those of us who were still alive. Which turned out to feel
like a very small remnant, very few of my old friends survived, leaving
me with more grief than I knew how to deal with.

But evidently we *had* survived, the gay community and gay identity
had survived, even if indelibly changed by the catastrophe. As Cleve
Jones has said, "Before AIDS, the notion of an LGBT community was
just that, a notion. But AIDS proved us. . . . AIDS created a militancy
and political power that first expressed itself in the powerful street theater of ACT UP and continued to a new generation with Queer Nation, Housing Works and Health GAP. . . . AIDS also changed the way
we viewed marriage. . . . now understood as a vital, even life-saving
right. We looked around us, at the lives we were living. We saw the
loving partners caring night and day for their dying lovers, dressing the
wounds, emptying the bedpans, changing the IV lines. We saw their

devotion and said, *What do you mean this isn't a real marriage? Fuck you. This is exactly what real marriage looks like.*"[1]

More surprisingly gay men continued to exuberantly celebrate the erotic, both on the dance floor and in the bedroom, as Peter Staley's memoir *Never Silent* and Sarah Shulman's massive documentary *Let the Record Show* make perfectly clear; and not in spite of the crisis but immediately face to face with it and seeming to draw energy from the very situation they were fighting.

Thus, as the Nineties came to a close, we were ready for the next fight, the fight for full equality, from the Marines to marriage. The great political awakening that started to unfold before AIDS side-tracked us all returned in full force. And the surprising triumph of gay marriage and gays in the military seemed to herald a new chapter in gay history, bringing to a close the thirty-year era of gay liberation that we had just lived through.

And meanwhile it was time to take some account of its impact on our lives, a process I suspect that will go on for quite some time.

1 Cleve Jones, *When We Rise*, p. 248.

Hymn to the Gym

IN LATE 1996 Walter Armstrong, an editor at *POZ* magazine, called to say that a forthcoming issue would be devoted to the theme of beauty and he wondered whether I would be interested in writing about the Chelsea Gym, which in the Eighties had become the epicenter of male beauty in the gay world of New York City and of which I had been an early member. He was interested in whether the standards of beauty in the gay world had been affected by the AIDS epidemic—or not, a question that interested me also. *POZ* cut the piece for length, but this is the original version.[1]

After fifteen years of the Plague, at a time when the optimists among us are announcing the beginning of the end of AIDS and even the pessimistic would admit to coming to the end of the beginning, it is perhaps time to try to assess the damage this historic catastrophe has wrought on the gay male community. What has AIDS done to the spirit of gay men; how has it affected the way the gay male community imagines itself?

And this is no small question, the question of how we imagine ourselves. Immediately after the Stonewall Riots, an event that took by surprise even those who participated in it, the search was on for an image, a look; what *did* a liberated gay man look like? Just as we borrowed our politics from the left-leaning civil rights movement of the late Sixties, we at first borrowed our self image from the hippie movement: long hair and an androgynous prettiness commanded attention in the bars and marches of the early Seventies. Only slowly did it dawn on us that it was precisely masculinity we were attracted to; we were men and we wanted to have sex with men. Thus was the famous clone look born: 501 jeans, tee-shirt and black leather jacket. It was easy, it was cheap and it had two great advantages: it obscured class lines totally (as long as you kept your mouth shut) and on the street it made us visible to each other and to the straight world.

An army of clones started gathering in the streets of the West Village and the Castro in the mid-Seventies, as gay boys first discovered the Nautilus machines—which delivered visible results in a few months—and then graduated to pumping iron. In this new democracy of beauty *everybody* could—and soon did—have muscles. Disco music blared, The Saint opened, drugs went down, shirts came off and by the early 80s the great halcyon days of gay liberation were in full swing.

We had passed through the looking glass and entered PornoLand; dweebs, loners, sissies and fatties, one by one, we passed through the narrow gate of the gym and emerged on the dance floor and the beach looking like porno stars. One Saturday afternoon in 1980 at Tea Dance in the Pines I looked around and simply marveled, not at the fact that Peter Berlin, Cal Culver and several other porn stars were shaking their booty within ten feet of me, but at the fact that they weren't even the hottest men on the dance floor. "We have," I shouted to my partner, "*arrived.*"

And indeed as the new decade opened it seemed that gay men had embarked en masse on an unprecedented social experiment: we attempted to unleash the erotic into our everyday lives by becoming our own objects of desire. We would become as hot as the men we fantasied about and lead lives of Dionysian abandon that hitherto had only been the stuff of our erotic fantasies. Beauty and brotherhood, muscles and the manly love of comrades would define the new gay male culture, with brunch thrown in for good measure. In 1983 Norm Rathweg, who had helped design and build The Saint, opened the Chelsea Gym, which immediately became the temple of beauty to which aspirants flocked and gay life looked good as gay men looked better and better.

The first time I walked into the Chelsea Gym in 1983 I felt much as Alice must have when she stepped through the looking glass. It seemed to me I'd walked into a Tom of Finland drawing: the pornographic dreams his images had sparked in my soul as an adolescent had become a reality—a sweating, straining, gorgeous reality on a bench not five feet away. With the sound system pumping in "I Will Survive" and the last light of day bouncing off the mirrors that covered every wall to illuminate some of the more outrageous workout costumes outside an *International Male* catalogue, this was a disorienting, not to say intimidating, experience.

Those days, to work out at the Chelsea during peak hours was a remarkable experience, as crammed with the erotic—and as crowded—as the dance floor at the Ice Palace in Cherry Grove on a July weekend. There on the incline press, surrounded by friends, was the most stunning blond on the beach, a tall, perfectly proportioned and gorgeous boy-man whose beauty was almost beyond belief. "Pinch me," whispered Bambi, my longtime gym buddy, "I want to be sure this isn't just a drug flashback." On the bench press was a young Latino who looked like a painting by Quaintance, sweat sliding down his arms, arteries throbbing as he pressed 240 pounds. In the beginning our workouts were almost as hard on our egos as they were on our bodies.

In the early '80s the gym was well on its way to replacing the bar as the central institution of gay life for a large number of guys in New York City. For many of us the gym had become a kind of community center, the hub of overlapping circles of friendship, sex, and romance, a way of keeping track of events in our social milieu. One might even say the gym had become what Joseph Campbell called a sacred space: "A room, a certain hour or so a day, a place where you can simply experience and bring forth what you are and what you might be, a place of creative incubation." Like the beach and the dance floor, the gym had become a place where we called forth the ideal, actualized the images that stirred our souls and celebrated the values that made us gay in the first place.

But the gods are fickle. First came that small report on page 40 of the *Times*—some kind of "gay cancer"—and then Larry Kramer started yelling at us. Who could believe this disease? It was like an evil metaphor: a disease that not only targeted gay men, but zeroed in on sexual activity? Give me a break! But, of course, no one gave us a break, and by 1985 you could look around the Chelsea between pec sets and spot the telltale lesions, hear the plaintive beepers go off, calculate the weight loss of the most beautiful blond on the beach. Slowly the full magnitude of the catastrophe dawned on us, as death began to sweep away our friends and lovers and buddies and tricks.

I remember one night in 1987 coming into the Chelsea late after spending several hours in the hospital trying to coax a pathetic amount of food down an ex-boyfriend's throat, surveying the scene and wondering if this gay worship of the body and its beauty that we had embraced with such intensity would vanish like the morning dew. Perhaps Tom of Finland's vision was nothing but a *fata morgana*, a mirage our desire had conjured up amid the aridity of straight culture. At this rate, I thought, the Chelsea Gym would be empty a decade hence, a mere memory of a wildly optimistic time.

But this did not turn out to be the case at all. The notion that these circles of gym buddies and disco friends would be scattered by the first winds of winter proved utterly untrue. These were the men who appeared in hospital rooms to rally 'round sick friends, creating ad hoc care groups that were remarkably effective. The social networks we had forged at the beach and on the dance floor, at brunch and in the gym, proved to be strong and supportive in this time of crisis.

At the gym itself people were fairly open about their illness and were quite prepared to work out with a Hickman catheter, even if that did make bench pressing a bit tricky. At the Chelsea one saw KS and weight loss to be sure, but what was more impressive—and surprising— was the dedication these guys showed to working out. Only days out of the hospital they would be back at the gym, tentatively exploring what their bodies could still do as they eased back into a lighter routine. *Village Voice* writer Robert Massa worked out right up to the end, and when the gym posted a copy of his ID photo and an obituary on the bulletin board over the water cooler, as had become their custom for any member who died, it startled those of us who had seen him at the gym scarcely a week before.

Now, one could say this only shows that gay men are afflicted with terminal shallowness in addition to this miserable disease, but that misses an important point my current ex-lover brought up recently: "One of the reasons I'm still healthy is my vanity. *That's* why I work out—not for all the 'good' reasons. But the gym taught me what feeling healthy felt like, and that was useful when I got sick. It taught me health is an act—something you *do*. And for people with AIDS, muscle mass is money in the bank."

The values that touched our gay souls in Tom of Finland's drawings, the celebration of the male body in all its erotic beauty, the exuberant and playful enjoyment of male camaraderie, have survived this medical catastrophe. And they still point to the deepest roots of the gay male psyche. These are not superficial values at all; or rather, they are values that ennoble the surface, that remind us that life itself is lived on the surface, the point of intersection between us and the world.

AIDS Books

IN 1999, AS the AIDS crisis began to subside, the *Lambda Book Report* asked me to write an overview of AIDS books for their publishing column. I thought it was a good opportunity to take stock of what had been done, to review whether those of us in publishing had been able to mobilize the full resources of our industry to confront the AIDS epidemic.[1] In my own mind I was reporting back to Vito.

When asked to write a short piece on where AIDS books have been and where they're going, seen from the publishing perspective, I had to explain that working editors have precious little *perspective*. Yes, we read almost constantly, but we seldom read books between covers. I read proposals and manuscripts submitted to me, manuscripts that friends of mine write, manuscripts that editor friends of mine are publishing, but I seldom get the time to read already published books. It's one of the ironies of the job, a sort of functional illiteracy caused by the very profession I'm in. Who has time to read the new gay book everyone is talking about? I *buy* those books, but most often they sit on the radiator next to my dining room table waiting for that mythical weekend when I'll have the time to look at them. So, while these comments are indeed from a publishing perspective, be warned that perspective is a very narrow and skewed one.

It seems to me three types of books have been generated in response to the AIDS epidemic: non-fiction books meant for use, first-person accounts by PWAs (people with AIDS) and those who care for them, and literary attempts to come to terms with what's happened to us by means of poetry, drama, stories, novels and history.

Use books are those works of non-fiction which deal with health and

---

1 *Lambda Book Report*, February 1999.

medical issues, financial and legal matters, and the psychological and spiritual conundrums this epidemic has generated. To my mind, publishing has done well in this area. Ever since the very first AIDS book, Dr. Kevin Cahill's collection of scientific papers, *The AIDS Epidemic*,[2] appeared in 1983, only two years after we first became aware of this new disease, publishing has produced a mountain of such books, providing people with information and advice of all sorts. The tricky part of this sort of publishing is deciding when such material is best served by being published in book format, as opposed to magazine articles, medical journals or specialized newsletters. While it all seems urgent and this can often be a perplexing question in any given instance, my impression is that all these forms of publishing have done a good job of serving the community affected by AIDS.

The second category of books—and one that is strikingly evident in the AIDS arena—consists of first-person narratives by those immediately affected by this disease, whether they be PWAs, their loved ones or the people who care for them. These are individual accounts of illness or of taking care of someone who is ill, and they are legion. I couldn't begin to estimate the number of manuscripts I've read that recount one person's struggle with the disease or tell the tale of a loved one or relate the experiences of someone working professionally in this area. The only publishing parallel to this I know of is the plethora of accounts of Holocaust survivors. These works are really testimony, people wanting to leave their story on the public record.

Such manuscripts create problems for people in publishing. While those written with the most literary skill often become successful books—think of Paul Monette's *Borrowed Time*, Fenton Johnson's *Geography of the Heart*, or Mark Doty's *Heaven's Coast*—only a relatively small number of these stories will actually get published. And probably no one outside of the publishing would ever believe how *many* such accounts are written. And one doesn't feel easy turning them down. These stories *should* be on the public record, yet 95% of them are not commercially viable as book projects. We need someone to figure out a sort of literary equivalent to the AIDS Quilt, perhaps special

2 Kevin Cahill, *The AIDS Epidemic* (New York: St. Martin's Press, 1983).

libraries or a project like the WPA's collection of the narratives of former slaves done in the 30s, some way to house these testimonies for future generations. In this area, I would have to say I don't think we have been successful.

And finally, there are, of course, what most people probably think of when they think of AIDS books: books of poetry, drama, novels and history which attempt to come to terms with this disaster using the power of the human imagination and the literary genres that imagination has invented. This is probably what the *Lambda Book Report* was thinking of when they asked me to write this. But this is also the area where my professional illiteracy comes to the fore—I have an entire bookshelf of such books that I haven't gotten around to reading yet.

But even from my narrow and skewed perspective in the trenches I have recently noticed some interesting straws in the wind. Fiction responding to AIDS seems to be more ambitious lately, to have greater scope and reach, to be seeing this epidemic in the wider context of humanity and history. Last spring Keith Kahla published *An Arrow's Flight* by Mark Merlis, the same season I published Rabih Alameddine's *Koolaids: The Art of War*. Both novels are experimental, hugely ambitious and place AIDS in a wider historical context, ancient Greece in the case of Merlis and the Lebanese civil war in Beirut in the case of Alameddine. Both novelists remind me of the great Latin American masters of fiction, writers who confront the concrete historical dilemmas of their own people with a soaring, almost metaphysical imagination that irradiates the ultimately particular with universal meaning. All of which tends to convince me that the great surge of creative energy that empowered gay writers to respond to and resist this historic catastrophe continues to course strongly through our artistic community. When history looks back, I suspect that the extraordinary creative response to this crisis will be seen as the foundation of what will be recognized as an authentic gay culture.

As we look back now over almost two decades, I think we can say that the publishing response to AIDS has been both timely and effective. The book world has produced both those books of non-fiction that brought desperately needed information and advice to beleaguered people as well as the creative works of poetry, fiction and drama that strengthened our spirits and gave solace to our souls as we endured this particular nightmare of history. Now what remains is to find some way to collect and preserve the first-person testimony of eyewitnesses, our friends and lovers, our families and doctors and caregivers. For these voices will be as important to gay culture in the future as the slave narratives are to African-Americans today or the testimony of Holocaust survivors to Jews everywhere.

Affectionate Men

WHEN PATRICK MERLA, who had been variously editor of the *New York Native* and *Christopher Street* magazine, later became editor of the *James White Review*, he had the brilliant idea of offering a page to working editors and agents who wanted to discuss a book they were particularly excited to be publishing. (Why don't more magazine editors think of this? After all, it's free copy.)

I had just published a book of images of male couples, from the 1850s to the 1950s—daguerreotypes, ambrotypes, tintypes, cabinet cards and ordinary Kodak prints and photographs. For some time now, I had become enamored of the craft needed to produce beautiful art books, and this venture I thought was particularly successful. And since the more I thought about it, the more *visibility* seemed somehow at the center of the gay movement, these images held a particular value for me. In a way, it's a bookend to the first gay book I published, Alan Ebert's *The Homosexuals*, a visual response to the voices raised in that book.

My piece appeared in the Winter 1999 volume of the *Review*.

When the first finished books of *Affectionate Men*[1] landed on my desk I took a copy home and after dinner sat down to look through it carefully, page by page, as I try to do whenever a project I've worked on first comes through as a bound book. Partially I do this out of a sense of relief; there are so many moments in the publishing process when you almost lose faith that one day all this will actually become a real book bound between two covers, that it's reassuring to handle the physical object. But partially I do it because I've come to feel that the core of an

1 *Affectionate Men: A Photographic History of a Century of Male Couples (1850s to 1950s)* by Russell Bush, book design by Ron Lieberman.

editor's job may be simply to give a book the only perfect reading the book might ever get (or the closest approximation I can manage).

With *Affectionate Men* this was a pleasurable experience because it was one of those rare cases when the book had come out utterly perfect, precisely the way I had imagined it when the author pitched it to me. I spent about an hour and a half perusing its pages and found myself immensely moved. With photo books you never quite know what you have until the finished object is finally in front of you, and this book had a strange emotional power I hadn't quite expected.

In reflecting on it, I realized that Russell Bush and his designer, Ron Lieberman, had created a wonderful artifact—a gay male family album stretching back to the mid-nineteenth century. Browsing among these pictures, noticing details of body posture and facial expression, wondering exactly what these guys were like and what their relationships were, gives you a strange feeling, a feeling, I suddenly realized, much like the one I got when I inherited the family album after my mother's death and spent an evening engrossed in it. Gay men *qua* gay men start out to some extent always alienated from our immediate families, an alienation that with any luck we manage to overcome as our biological families come to know and value our gay friends and our gay family. What Russell Bush has created here is the album of that other family, the family of gay men we feel an immediate kinship with once we have come out. Here are guys like us, couples mostly, from the 1850s to the 1950s, who not only tantalize our imagination with their untold stories but also confirm our being somehow with their message: "Yup, we were here. Whether they noticed it or not, we were here."

And yes, I know that not all these men were gay, that it would be an anachronism to read modern homosexuality into images caught as far back as 150 years ago, that what we have here is a remarkable manifestation of Walt Whitman's "dear love of comradoes" rather than a modern catalogue of homosexuals. But I defy anyone to spend an hour or two with these photos and not feel the commonality that links us modern gay men to these affectionate "friends." In fact, the great virtue of this book is that it points out this commonality without making the mistake of trying to define it. You *recognize* these people, sometimes to the point of laughing out loud when you see the utterly familiar under the costume of history. Essentialists and Social Constructionists can argue till the cows come home, but I know my kind when I see them and these are my kind. And I was grateful to Russell Bush for excavating the historical record and putting these images into a family album that we can enjoy and pass on.

Last Letter to Paul Monette

PAUL MONETTE DIED of AIDS on February 10, 1995. He was fifty years old. He had been one of the first members of the post-Stonewall generation of gay writers, having published *Taking Care of Mrs. Carroll* in 1978. The appearance in 1988 of *Borrowed Time: An AIDS Memoir* and his extraordinary poem cycle *Love Alone: Eighteen Elegies for Rog* established his position as one of our leading writers and spokesman; in fact, when he won the National Book Award in 1992 for *Becoming a Man: Half a Life Story*, many of us felt it was a belated recognition of the enormous impact of those two books. He had, by this time, achieved in the national gay community the rare status of respect and affection enjoyed, for instance, by Vito Russo.

In the last decade of his life he had become a very close friend as well as an invaluable comrade-in-arms in the fight against AIDS. On both counts his loss was monumental. My world suddenly became much smaller, and colder.

Ten years after his death there was a conference on his life and work entitled "One Person's Truth," held at UCLA's Charles Young Research Library (October 14, 2005), and Winston Wilde asked me to speak.

So Paul is sixty today. I hadn't realized he was two years younger than I am, but who's counting? These ridiculous numbers make us just about perfect contemporaries anyway. I remember the last letter I wrote to Paul, a few days before Christmas in 1994, right after he'd called to tell me he had decided to go off all medication. We both knew what that meant. But still, it wasn't a grim conversation. Paul had a way of always keeping things light, a trait my morose, black Irish ancestors had lost somewhere along the way. He was hoping that, with those awful medicines out of the picture, he and Winston might yet have a few clear days to be with each other. And, as it turned out, the gods smiled and actually granted them a number of weeks, weeks in which Paul felt better than he had in months, maybe years, but I didn't know this yet. So I went morosing 'round the apartment after hanging up the phone, until I decided that I had better sit down *right now* and write him a letter, saying at least some of those things that somehow, at least if you're Irish, you never get to say in person or on the telephone, but things that ought to be said while there is still an open channel. Like the last letter I wrote to my Dad about being his son and being gay, which thankfully got to him before the cancer completely obscured lines of communication.

It was a letter of thanks really, although I admit it took me a while to become clear on what I was thanking him for. "We've never had models," I wrote, "you and I and the rest of the gay men in our generation, models of what a decent, mature, reasonable gay male adult would look like." We were, after all, a generation that had come of age before Stonewall, the last generation to come of age before that great divide in our consciousness, and for the most part, the elders we found already inhabiting the gay world—at least, the ones who were visible to us—did not provide workable role models for us.

"And so," I continued, "I think we have tended to use each other as models, or at least I have you." With almost no exemplary individuals in sight in the vertical direction (although, hey, we should never forget Christopher Isherwood), we glanced sideways, like two-year-olds in a sandbox, playing by themselves but checking out the others playing by themselves, not as role models maybe, but for some general reassurance in this strange new world. Oh, *that's* the way to do it. And we were lucky to be part of a truly remarkable generation, the first generation whose task was to figure out what the Stonewall Revolution really meant. What did this gay liberation translate into concretely? And as the Seventies deepened, what we saw—besides a lot of really good sex, I mean—was a remarkable and widespread and spontaneous assumption of individual responsibility, one person after another deciding, quite independently really, to try to implement the truth that had become visible, to make the gay revolution a reality, each in our own backyard.

There was Vito Russo who used to have us all over to his apartment on Sunday afternoons to watch old movies, deciding to get it all down in a book, the history of gays in Hollywood. And there were the gay psychiatrists who decided to clean up their own profession, and the gay lawyers, and—like the decade, the list could go on, but Winston said to keep it short. Maybe we didn't, in those early years, join political parties in mass numbers or organize and lobby the power structure in a disciplined way—for which we would soon be severely yelled at by Larry Kramer—but this was really a remarkable phenomenon. Pervading the whole society, at all levels, utterly uncoordinated (the so-called "national gay leadership" always had a hard time keeping up with their supposed followers), enduring and even growing through the decade with what seemed to be an unstoppable momentum—these were the signs of a true social revolution, and this decentralization would prove to be a great strength in the trying years that were to come.

When the great historical disaster of AIDS first struck our community, like a tidal wave, like a storm of death that seemed unstoppable, gay people responded on every level, doing whatever they could on their own home ground, and the response of gay writers, the group I found myself among, was something you could be proud of. AIDS runs like an earthquake through gay writing in the Eighties, and what Paul said of his own work is true of so many other gay writers: "One thing is abundantly clear. The difference between the first half of my career (the nice part) and the war work of AIDS is like two sides of a chasm, with no rope bridge connecting."[1] You hear the same story from writer after writer, AIDS burning though literary conventions, corroding the forms that had bewitched our minds, leaving behind the raw power of the act of writing. In his three volumes of autobiographical memoirs Paul managed the only human response to tragedy, which is an act of language. And in his two volumes of poetry, Paul showed that acts of language could also be acts of a warrior.

But if Paul became the committed model of the great gay cultural fighter, along the way his writing also disclosed other identities. Paul

---

1 Paul Monette, *West of Yesterday, East of Summer: New and Selected Poems* (New York: St. Martin's Press, 1994), p. xix.

was a great romantic, a great lover, someone whose life, as well as his work, made everyone, even the cynical queens among us, believe in the seriousness of love all over again. In addition to romantic love, Paul also reveled in Whitman's "dear love of comrades," concretely in friendships and the literary celebration of friendship.

Warrior. Lover. Comrade. These were the roles that Paul modeled so well for his friends and that shine through his writing. *That's* what an adult gay man should look like, *that's* the way to do it. "And what I want to say," my letter went on, "is that I feel incredibly lucky to have met you, to have known you, to have been your friend for these last ten years. Our friendship has meant an enormous amount to me. Your spirit and elan have helped me through many a dark time since this holocaust hit home. I can't imagine how I would have gotten through it without you and John Preston as friends and comrades. . . . I want to thank you. For being around in my life I want to thank you. I don't know what life will be like without knowing you're out there in that wonderful house on the hill, but one thing I do know is that I will miss you terribly.

"So thank you for being here, thank you for being you—I loved it. I love you both and I think of you two every day, and I hope that this last time you have to be together will be wonderful.

"You sure done good. Done good by me, done good by all of us. Much, much love."

That is what I was so grateful for then, and that's why I miss him today. I would love to see Paul at sixty, see how he'd model the role of gay elder. That's something we're going to have to make up from scratch.

Looking Back

Don Weise, a younger gay editor I'd known for a decade or two, interviewed me on June 20, 2014, for the Lambda Literary Foundation's website. This conversation was really the first time I'd taken the opportunity to think about these years systematically, and it changed my attitude toward the writings sitting in my file drawer. So I went back to read them again. Acknowledging to myself finally that the era was truly over, I found that I wanted these voices to come alive again, so this particular generation's great public conversation would not be lost. So Don's initiative was really the proximate cause of my decision to assemble these pieces into a book.

And as for my worry that the story I wanted to tell would be too particularized by my own limited experience, putting together this book I realized that while history is general, it can only be experienced and lived by individual people, and individual people live utterly specific lives, uniquely situated in time and space and society. The great waves of history are, like the wind, invisible and can only be seen in their impact on individual lives. But from hearing many particular accounts, we can begin to see what happened. And as an increasing number of reports come in from members of this generation—Sean Strub's *Body Counts*, Mark Segal's *And Then I Danced*, Cleve Jones's *When We Rise*, Peter Staley's *Never Silent*, just to mention books that came out while I was preparing this one—we get to see, from various individual perspectives, the huge wave of social and spiritual transformation that was going on throughout the gay world, a truly remarkable phenomena that spun our lives in new directions.

It's to this tapestry of voices that I add my account.

Don Weise Interview

DW: Since book editors don't typically grow up wanting to be editors and many have never taken an editing class, or in some cases even

Photo © Jessica Lehrman

been formally trained in the field [I'm speaking for myself here], what led you to become a book editor?

MD: In '71, as a result of Stonewall, I moved to New York City, mainly to be gay. I didn't have a job or an apartment or even a concrete plan, so the first few months were difficult: sleeping on friends' couches, walking to job interviews since I didn't have subway fare, watching my few dollars shrink. Among other things I tried for publishing jobs since I'd worked half time for two years at the University of Chicago Press. When a friend told me he was leaving his editing job at the old Macmillan (at 3rd Ave. at 53rd St. then) to go to Paris and be a poet, we arranged it so I came in for an interview a couple of hours after he handed in his resignation. On paper we looked like the same person (except that I did have some experience in publishing), and they hired me. It was an accident really, I was just desperate for a day job.

I thought it was a bit of a coup since I skipped the usual step of first being an editorial assistant. But in retrospect that was a mistake. The wear and tear of the first few years, when I had to figure out what the job was while actually doing it, was enormous, and in retrospect I don't think it was worth it. I think the only way you really learn this job is by watching someone else do it for some time, like an apprentice, since it actually is a craft skill.

DW: I really identify with your comments because the same thing kind of happened to me. I got started because I'd moved to San Francisco with no job or apartment and needed work desperately. So much so that I went to the local Pepsi plant, thinking they'd have to have jobs, willing to take anything. They had nothing, but there I was with my suit on and resume in hand. I was heading back to the freeway when I came to a stop sign, looked to my left, and there were the words on the side of a warehouse: Publishers Group West. I was an English major so thought this might be a fit. I went in and the receptionist was a shave-headed dyke, who saw the words "gay and lesbian" on my resume, took it personally to the HR guy, who was also gay, had me interview the next day for the orders department, and I started work a couple days later. Like you, I did not plan for it to last as long as it has.

Like you, no one trained me at all to be an editor, I just did it. I felt *like a fraud*.

MD: (Laughs.) I certainly knew that feeling my first few years. So in the beginning it was just a day job, so I could live here. I never thought it would last. In the early 70s at the old Macmillan everyone wore suits, white shirts and ties and had two martinis at lunch—I mean, it was 1972, only a couple of years from *Mad Men*—while I had spent the 60s at the University of Chicago being an intellectual hippy and a political activist. I thought the job would only last a few months, until they discovered who I really was. But by then at least I'd be able to collect unemployment! It amazes me in retrospect that I lasted thirty years in corporate publishing. What happened was I got involved with a couple of books that really intrigued me and gradually realized that one might be able to do something interesting in publishing.

DW: I'm curious about those suit and tie/two-martini days of publishing: what was it like being an openly gay man in that old school world?

MD: It wasn't exactly the case of "being an openly gay man." In the early 70s, in spite of the fact that there were quite a few gay men and lesbians working as editors, it was something never spoken about. I swore to myself I wouldn't lie about it or try to hide it, but on the other hand I didn't go out of my way to broadcast it either.

I remember the first time I had to confront that decision. It was at the Christmas party my second year working there. In the 70s publishing companies had these really terrible Christmas parties where everyone got drunk out of their minds and all sorts of indiscreet things got said (and done). Anyway, at this one the head of Macmillan's warehouse and inventory control, a short, really feisty Puerto Rican dyke whom I liked a lot, came up to me, clearly very drunk, and asked if I was bisexual. When I said "No" her face really fell and she realized she'd gone a step too far, but then I added, "I'm gay" and she broke into this terrific smile. And she was one of my best allies in the company from then on.

I suppose I really came out to the whole company because of a book by Alan Ebert, the first gay book I ever published, called *The Homosexu-*

als: Who and What We Are. Great title, right? (Laughter.) By publication we had changed the subtitle to "The First Book in Which Homosexuals Speak for and about Themselves." I was actually fired over it, when the CEO of the company, a twisted little man named Raymond C. Hagel, found out about it as we were preparing for an upcoming sales conference in Phoenix. But after I was fired every other editor, right up to the editor in chief, refused to present the book, and since Legal told the company they were obliged to publish it, they ended up hiring me back—really, just to present one book! (Laughter.)

Anyway, one of our New York sales reps, who was a friend of mine, had been reading the manuscript, I think in order to support me from the floor. And he had come to an interview with a gay Rabbi who, among other things, described fist fucking. And the guy didn't believe there could be such a thing as a gay Rabbi, or that fist fucking was physically possible. This was a question from the floor, and I'm standing on stage at the microphone in front of 250 people. It was one of those moments when you just wish the earth would open up and swallow you. I had a split second to make a decision and I realized that the whole credibility of the book—as well as my own—depended on the answer.

So, I took a deep breath and said, "Chuck, you know that bar at the very western end of 14th Street (his territory was lower Manhattan), on the south side of the street in the triangular building? It's a gay bar (it was the old Anvil) which, among other things, has sex acts performed right on the bar. It's a place I've been to a few times and I can assure you that it's physically possible," and I held up my right hand and with my left measured off about halfway up my forearm and said, "You can get it in about this far." The silence in that room was palpable; as they say, you could have heard a pin drop. (Laughter.) "And as for the Rabbi, I happen to know him socially and I guarantee you he's a real person. I can introduce you to him, if you want." So the cat was definitely out of the bag.

And you know one of the interesting things: all the salesmen of that era—and they were all men, no women, we're talking 1973-74 here—were culturally 1953 jocks.[1] And it was traditional at sales conferences

---

1 I suppose only people of my generation will understand this reference.

that you had to drink with the sales guys late into the night if you wanted to do any bonding at all, and I noticed that even when totally plastered these guys were careful never to say anything that would embarrass or offend me. And that was touching.

DW: As a follow-up question, in reference to the books that interested you, what did you acquire and edit initially, and how long was it before you decided there was a market for LGBT lit?

MD: That took a while—I was a bit dense, I guess. The first books that really hooked me on publishing were political. I might not have known much about editing or publishing, but politics was what I knew from the 60s and the earliest books I really got involved in were political.

First, there was a book on the architecture of public housing called *Defensible Space* by Oscar Newman (1972), which I had inherited from another editor who told me I should just cancel it, it was hopeless (in those days the junior editor was the low man on the totem pole and all sorts of difficult projects got dumped on him or her). But when I read it, the material was incredibly interesting. At the time there was a dispute going on all over the country about using high rises for public housing and Oscar had proved that it was a disastrous choice. Unfortunately, the man couldn't really write and I ended up reworking and restructuring the book with him, virtually sentence by sentence.

And then there was an interesting struggle: at the time there were court cases all over the country about high rise public housing, and HUD (the cabinet department then called Housing and Urban Development, headed by George Romney, Mitt's father) was afraid that the book would be used as evidence against them, so they tried to suppress it and failed. They sent in six experts who demanded to review it. I wouldn't let them have a copy of the manuscript, but I let them read it in the conference room. I said they could take notes but not Xerox anything and either my assistant or I had to be present. And they came back to my office at the end of the second day triumphant: they had found 384 errors in the book and they proudly handed me a list of them.

Really, I couldn't believe they were so dumb! I pretended to be concerned as I showed them out and said I'd respond after I had a chance to review these "errors." Then I immediately went back to my office and called Oscar and said, "Get up here, we're got to fix these things," and we worked almost to midnight going through them. They were all tiny factual or statistical things, really petty, easily corrected; and they didn't affect the over-all argument of the book at all.

I finally wrote a letter to Romney suggesting, in essence, that if HUD acclaimed the publication of the book, then the book couldn't really be an attack on them, could it? (Laughing.) All they had to do was reverse their position 180 degrees! Which I didn't say directly, of course. And so it happened that HUD gave a press conference to herald the publication of the book—in the Senate Cloak Room at the Capitol no less!—and the book got wide media coverage and sold much better than anyone had expected. (And HUD reversed their policy on high rises.)

The second was a book by Jack Chen, a friend of Mao and Zhou Enlai, and the first Chinese to come west after the Cultural Revolution. At the time New York had a Senator James Buckley, brother of the writer William Buckley, and the two of them tried to drive Jack, whom I had signed up to do a book, out of the country. But Senator Buckley's bill in the Senate went down to defeat, 98-to-2—he only got one other vote! And again, with all this fuss the book got a good deal of attention, virtually all of it positive.

So now I was seeing that this could be an interesting job and I started feeling my way into it. I published Susan Fromberg Schaeffer's first novel *Falling* and her second book of poetry and then her amazing novel of the Holocaust, *Anya*. Buckminster Fuller's magnum opus, *Synergetics*, got dumped on me as "the mother of all problem books" and I managed to bring it to successful publication. (It's too complex to go into; there's a whole book written about the writing and publication of that book, *Cosmic Fishing* by Ed Applewhite, which I also published at Macmillan, just to spite them, but I don't think anybody noticed.) And there were other books, the most significant of which was probably *for colored girls who have considered suicide / when the rainbow is enuf.* It was actually Ntozake Shange who raised the issue of gay books with me, saying, "You're publishing all these women's books and Black books, how come you aren't publishing more gay books?"

Which was a good question.

In New York City at the time (say '72 to '75) there was an intense discussion going on among gay people as to whether or not there was such a thing as gay literature, or gay culture in general. I'd gotten involved at the Firehouse (the first gay community center down in Soho) with a bunch of guys from the Communication Committee (I think that's what it was called) of the Gay Activists Alliance and in time we'd started our first gay magazine, *OUT*, in '73 or '74, but it only lasted two issues before folding. During that period I'd gotten close to a young kid just out of grad school in Kansas named Chuck Ortleb and we continued that discussion—intensively!—for the next couple of years. These discussions with Chuck ended up convincing me there was such a thing as gay literature and, more importantly, that a change of consciousness, a change in our imaginations, had to be the first step in fighting for gay rights, and that the best way to do that was a literary magazine. I mean, zaps were fine as political theater but they didn't change things,[2] and electoral politics was not at all a promising avenue at the time. Reminds you of the Irving Howe quip, "When intellectuals can do nothing else, they start a magazine." So we ended up founding *Christopher Street* in '76, one of the first gay literary magazines, and that got me fired for good from Macmillan.

At that time, I was a hot young editor, my books were getting a lot of attention and, more importantly, making good money, and I had, if memory is correct, 47 job interviews. (It's hard to remember but in the mid-Seventies there were something like 280 publishing houses in Manhattan. Today there are five, and a handful of small presses.) At each one I'd put a copy of *Christopher Street* on the table and say, "Look, I'm gay and publicly involved with this gay literary magazine, so if that gives you a problem we should just forget about the job and

2 Wrong again, as I learned from working on Mark Segal's autobiographical memoir, *And Then I Danced*, which showed just how far you could go with zaps.

enjoy lunch, since this is a very good restaurant and you're paying for it." (In those days they always took you to these incredibly fancy restaurants for the interview.) And they would say, "Oh no, no," picking up the magazine and leafing through it, "how interesting . . . interesting."

And of the 47 interviews, I got exactly one call back, from a guy named Tom McCormack who was running a small place called St. Martin's Press down in the Flatiron building, at the time in the middle of nowhere. I mean, I had never even been at that subway stop! When I first worked there, we used to have to go to the Village or midtown to have lunch! Most of my publishing friends had never heard of it. I only knew it because they had published a couple of the earliest gay books (Weinberg's *Society and the Healthy Homosexual* and Liege Clark and Jack Nichols' *Roommates Can't Always Be Lovers* and *Fire Island*). I ended up having five interviews with the man, telling him that I was convinced there was a new market for gay fiction and I wanted to try to publish to it—without there being a huge hullabaloo every time I tried to sign up a gay book. And keep up my mainstream publishing as well. And, finally, he went for it. So I moved to St. Martin's in '76 or '77.

If I hadn't run into Tom, I don't think I ever would have had a career in publishing; it would have just been a five-year adventure in the business world.

DW: My next question would be, who came before you? I'm less interested in small presses or the gay and feminist presses. I'm curious to know who in corporate publishing, straight or gay, was known for LGBT titles?

MD: In corporate publishing? Nobody. I mean, we're talking mainstream New York publishing here, I don't know about the rest of the country, but in New York publishing there was no one who was out. There was Tom McCormack, who is straight and who did publish three gay titles, but otherwise, nobody in mainstream publishing; they weren't publishing anything gay. Which is why it was such a big deal when I came out publicly. And there were no small gay presses at the time, the mid-Seventies, maybe with the exception of *Gay Sunshine* magazine which put out a couple of gay books. Interestingly enough there were already several lesbian/feminist presses—Daughters in Vermont and a couple of others. One of the things that motivated me was that I had several very close lesbian friends and I saw that they had several presses, and a number of magazines and other institutions like The Sagaris Institute, but by 1976 we gay men had virtually nothing, except *The Advocate*.

Of course, lesbians had the advantage of the Women's Movement. Those presses, for instance, were basically lesbian (in most of their personnel and an awful lot of what they published) but were presented to the world as feminist presses. That's why at the time lesbian litera-ture was way ahead of gay literature; they had an allied audience of straight women interested in the work of lesbians, which made publi-cation of such books and magazines financially viable, if limited. But gay men had no such allies who could augment the audience for gay books, so there were no small gay presses. Sasha Alyson only started Alyson Books many years later and when he did, he came to me for advice.

DW: So what was it like, initiating the publishing of gay books in the mainstream?

MD: I think I made the same mistake at St. Martin's that we initially made at *Christopher Street*. Knowing there was some samizdat gay lit-erature going around (W. H. Auden's "Ode to a Blow Job," for instance, and other stuff), we assumed that gay writers had all this material in their bottom drawers because there was no outlet for publishing it, and it would come gushing in. But gay writers are no dummies; since there hadn't been any outlets, most didn't waste their time writing stuff that could never be published. This we discovered to our chagrin at *Chris-topher St.*, where we were always scrambling to fill up the next issue. Once Ed White wrote I think four different articles, under four differ-ent names, to fill the issue at the last moment, although I think the prize goes to Andrew Holleran who once did five articles under five aliases. (Laughter.) If we'd known anything about magazine publishing, we would never have tried to start *Christopher Street*, which, mind you, lasted for over twenty years.

So anyway, when I went looking for gay books, the pickings were slim. There was Wallace Hamilton who had published a novel called *Coming Out*. He wrote a Biblical, historical novel for me about King David and Jonathan (*David at Olivet*), and Pete Fisher and Marc Rubin (old friends from the Gay Activist Alliance who had worked on *Out* magazine) wrote *Special Teachers/Special Boys* about a gay high school teacher. Now you could say that this was ideological fiction, akin to the old socialist realism school of fiction, you know, "Man meets tractor, man falls in love with tractor, man marries tractor" sort of thing. But you had to start somewhere. You had to show that gay books could be published if you wanted to encourage gay books to be written.

Then Ed White's *Nocturnes for the King of Naples* came along. Ed's first novel, *Forgetting Elena*, had been published by Random House and then in paperback by Penguin and had gotten rave reviews, and, in a comment endlessly repeated in publishing circles, Nabokov had declared Ed the best young American novelist (or something like that). So it was a scandal that he couldn't find a single publisher willing to take on his second novel because it dealt with homoerotic love (although the beloved was safely dead and gone, which should have made it easier for straight people to deal with). So I published it in 1978, to rave reviews I might add. And quite decent sales for a literary book.

In fact, 1978 was a banner year for gay writing; it really marked the dawn of the new gay literary movement that would swell into a torrent over the next fifteen or twenty years. In that year were published Ed's *Nocturnes*, Andrew Holleran's *Dancer from the Dance*, Paul Monette's *Taking Care of Mrs. Carroll*, Larry Kramer's *Faggots*, and Felice Picano's *The Lure*. (And my own *Lovers: The Story of Two Men*, which I wouldn't put in the same category but wanted to remember.) Anyway, basically after that we were off and running, and ten years later enough gay books were being published that I could start a new paperback line, Stonewall Inn Editions,[3] totally devoted to gay writing, both fiction and nonfiction. And later start a Stonewall Inn Mysteries line.

---

3 See appendix A for a list of the titles in Stonewall Inn Editions.

DW: I'm curious to know what impact your coming out had on the company?

MD: Well, that's a funny story. After I'd been in my new office for a few weeks, Tom McCormack, the CEO of St. Martin's, stopped by while I was on the phone with an author or agent or someone, so he signaled me to keep doing what I was doing and dropped into a chair. I managed to get off the phone pretty quickly, figuring I was in trouble. But Tom said he'd just stopped by to see how I was doing. "Since you're the only gay person working here, I wanted to make sure everything was going O.K." And I burst out laughing and said, "Tom, I'm not the only gay person working here. Believe me. Give it six months to a year and they'll be coming out of the woodwork." And he looked surprised, which actually surprised me.

And, of course, that's what happened, if a bit slower than I'd anticipated.

Then there was my assistant, Paul Dinas, who was 24 or so, and a very good-looking guy. So, of course, everyone thought he was gay. Finally, Paul, who was straight, single and wanted to date, had a tee-shirt made that said on the front: MICHAEL IS and on the back: BUT I'M NOT. And he wore it at work for a week. The whole company was startled. I thought it was a riot. And it worked: he got dates.

Then there was an effect that I didn't actually notice for a few years. As you know, there's an enormous turnover of young people in publishing, not only among editorial assistants who change every 2 or 3 years, but in copy-editing, production, design, publicity, art. And slowly I noticed that an awful lot of the young people in the company were gay or lesbian. Got to be I figured roughly half of the entry level people were gay. And openly so, which was new. And after work they went out to bars with the straight kids—lesbian bars no less!—and they roomed with each other. It turned out that St. Martin's got so much publicity about its gay publishing—I mean, I had to do something, I didn't have big advertising budgets to get these books noticed, so something had to be done—that young people just coming into the book business who were gay or lesbian saw the company as a really desirable place to work.

So we were achieving equality and visibility in the workplace, which satisfied my 60s progressive soul. In fact, progress came so fast it was a bit unnerving, especially when you've braced yourself into a militant stance for the duration. Jane Rotrosen, one of my oldest friends in publishing, laughs when she reminds me that at publishing parties in the Seventies, I'd introduce myself to people, saying "Hi, my name's Michael, and I'm gay." Especially when we went to events together; I didn't want anybody thinking I was straight! As I say, progress can be unnerving . . . not to say surreal. I remember one Christmas party the company had. It must have been 3 or 4 years after I'd been there, say 1980 or so, disco was still supreme and we'd rented one of the hot discos in midtown for the party. And there was great drinking and great music and everyone was dancing. And I loved to dance in those days; I was one of the original members of The Saint and went dancing a lot. So I'd come prepared and under my jacket and shirt and tie was one of the guinea tees I danced in on the weekends. And as the dancing got hotter, the jacket came off, the tie was loosened, the tie came off, the shirt was unbuttoned, the shirt came off—unfortunately, unlike at The Saint where you could dance in your underwear, it had to stop there. But still, it seemed to give everybody permission to dance more sexily, more wildly. And the best dancer there—aside from me, of course— was Charlie, the new head of our sales department, who was about 28, looked like a young Paul Newman (and I mean, *really* looked like), and was the Young Lochinvar of publishing in those days. And—

DW: Wait! wait! Who, or what, is a Young Lochinvar?

MD: Oh, sorry. A Don Juan figure, only more romantic. It was a phrase of my mother's. It's from a poem by Sir Walter Scott. Do kids nowadays still read Walter Scott in High School? I doubt it. Anyway. So finally we both realized we'd been dancing next to each other, his shirt was now off (but his respectable tee-shirt had sleeves, diminishing the effect) and we had started competing with each other, as males will, in dirty dancing. Finally he turned and started dancing *with* me. This was not only a straight guy, he was *famously* straight, his love affairs among the young women in publishing were already legendary. And he was a very good dancer. At one point he slipped the belt off his pants and put it around my neck. Very S&M-y, very hot. And we were dancing not eight feet from the table where the CEO was sitting with his wife, watching. Coming home in the early hours of the morning I thought, somewhat confusedly, that there'd been some kind of break-through that night.

You know, you take these little incidents that happen to you as markings that change might really be happening, although you can never be sure. The one that really stands out for me was a few years later when I was presenting one of Buckminster Fuller's major books, *Critical Path*, at a sales conference and I had Bucky come and address the gathering. I don't know whether you ever heard Bucky speak, but it was a remarkable thing, this thinking out loud he did. Mesmerizing. Anyway, at the end of his talk he said that in his first book, *Nine Chains to the Moon* (1938), he'd made a set of 24 predictions for the future, and that 23 of them had come to pass, "but the 24th—that there'd be no change in the ways of a man with a maid, well, Michael has shown me that was not true." For me, that neatly matched that early sales conference when I'd presented *The Homosexuals* and had to explain fist fucking. And I thought, okay we're getting somewhere.

DW: And the effect of your coming out on publishing at large?

MD: As I used to say: the main point was all I had to do was stand there and not get hit by lightning. Not be fired. Show publicly that you could be openly gay and still work successfully in publishing. I always insisted on taking boyfriends to company events and parties, and when I didn't have a boyfriend at the moment, I'd press one of my exes into service, using a political argument: "Hey, it's for the Revolution!" (Laughter.)

It gave new people coming into publishing cover not to be closeted about their gay life. I think it had a pretty immediate impact on new people just coming into publishing. You just had to break the taboo publicly and that was it. With the people who were already there it took much more time, years. For instance, Bill Whitehead, a beloved editor who is mainly known today through the Bill Whitehead Award the Publishing Triangle gives out, turned down John Fox's first novel,

The Boys on the Rock, a really superb gay novel, because he was already publishing Ed White's *States of Desire* (1980) and one other gay writer and he didn't want to become known as a gay editor. Of course, he moved beyond that position, but it took a few years.

What Bill feared was that one would be typecast, able *only* to publish gay writing. So I had to prove that wrong too. And I did. I kept publishing mainstream books like Judith Thurman's biography of Isak Dinesen, which won the National Book Award, as well as the poetry and novels of Ntozake Shange, and the books of Buckminster Fuller. I even developed a sort of minor specialty in books by superbutch men: *Will*, the autobiography of G. Gordon Liddy, Mr. T's autobiography, even a science fiction novel by L. Ron Hubbard, *Battlefield Earth*. And let me tell you, dealing with those Scientologists was like trying to herd cats. Impossible. Although L. Ron himself, as an author, was not a problem at all—he'd started out as a hack writer and he appreciated good editing.

The upshot was essentially that being gay in publishing or publishing gay books (which the straight editors at St. Martin's started doing) became normalized; it was no big thing. And *that* was a big thing, because invisibility and silence had been the chief means of gay oppression. And we were dealing with that.

(Laughs.) You know, when I started this I did an interview with John Preston for *The Advocate*, in 1977 I think, and I laid out the whole rationale for what I planned to do and I thought it would take five years or so. Well, it really took about twenty years, but except for the time factor, I still think my analysis of the problem and how to change it was pretty good.

DW: And what was the impact on gay writing, gay literature?

MD: Well, by the early 80s, there was this remarkable flowering of a new literary culture. And everybody everywhere was busy building the necessary infrastructure. When I started there were something like 8 or 9 gay bookstores; within a few years there were 45 of them. And my sales people loved them, they were among their best customers. People were creating new magazines, new local gay newspapers—

which were a fabulous review media for these gay books. I could get 20 or 30 reviews for a first gay novel and a bunch of author interviews, whereas publishing a first novel by a straight person you might gather 4 or 5 reviews—if you were lucky! National gay literary conferences like OutWrite were started, and all sorts of new organizations. David Groff and I and a bunch of other people founded The Publishing Triangle, a professional networking organization for gays and lesbians working in mainstream and gay publishing. Then we went on to establish the Publishing Triangle's gay literary awards—because publishers just love awards. They'd print award medallions on their covers or ship stickers to the bookstores to be put on the books, which helped both sales and review attention. In the Seventies gay liberationists had urged us to "make the revolution" a sort of transvaluation of values. As I saw it, that could only be realized concretely, in steps like these, taken in your own backyard.

Before the threat of AIDS started darkening our horizon, there really was a halcyon moment that's hard to remember today. It reminds me of the last scene in the documentary film about Fire Island, *Where Ocean Meets Sky*. The film ends with the first White Party on the beach at the Pines, a stunning scene that beautifully captures the sense of new possibility, of a whole new world aborning, that animated us all at the time. (Laughs.) It was morning in gay America, for sure.

You can get some sense of the times if you look at the three collections we published out of *Christopher Street* during those years. *The Christopher Street Reader* (nonfiction, 1983) is an exuberant exploration of the new world then emerging, in vigorous, impassioned essays. And the two fiction collections—*Aphrodisiac* and *First Love/Last Love*—introduced writers like Robert Ferro, John Fox, Brad Gooch, Andrew Holleran, David Leavitt, Ethan Mordden, David Plante, Felice Picano, Christopher Bram, and, of course, Ed White. By the way, we also published three volumes of gay cartoons from the magazine, and I think we were the only magazine that had a cabaret act—Chuck Ortleb and Tom Steele wrote songs together about gay life and Tom, also a pianist, performed them in local gay bars, making for wonderful social evenings. They even put out two cassettes.

The point is, there was this huge social movement going on; gay people were emerging everywhere and organizing into coherent communities, into neighborhoods, into professional associations, religious associations, athletic associations. There was a cultural revolution going on, and the emergence of the new gay writing was an exuberant manifestation of that. I think Ed White's *States of Desire* (1980) captures the spirit of the times best. Just before the first appearance of AIDS he travelled all over the country, in '78 and '79, and was reporting back on what can only be described as the awakening of the gay community.

But I think this historical moment, say '77 to '83, has been so overshadowed by the catastrophe of AIDS as to be nearly forgotten. It needs a name, a label, something better than borrowing "morning in gay America" from President Reagan. If you were considering the history of gay writing, you'd have to break it into two periods here: the dawn, the new beginning, post-Stonewall/pre-AIDS, and then the writing that arose as a response to the great disaster of AIDS.

DW: Well, you've dealt with the first period . . .

MD: Yes, so let's face . . . the darkening plain. (Pause) You know the first public notice of this new disease appeared in *Christopher Street*'s sister publication, *The New York Native*, two or three weeks before the first report in the CDC's *Mortality and Morbidity Weekly Report*, which was then picked up by the *New York Times*, in a little article on page 18, I think. And, as I think everyone would agree today, the *Native* continued to have the best medical as well as political coverage of the new disease for the first five or so years of the epidemic, when the national media tried to avoid the crisis—"Silence=Death" indeed. Chuck Ortleb should be proud of that. I am for him.

Anyway, by 1983 it had become utterly clear: AIDS was a catastrophe, an epidemic, an event unleashed like a hurricane, and this event threatened the very existence of this new community, of this new feeling of identity that was just emerging and beginning to consolidate at the end of the 70s. You know, I was reading a review of Sean Strub's new book, *Body Counts*, in the *G&L Review/Worldwide* last night, and the reviewer said—here, let me find it—"It was only on reading Strub that I understood how fragile and experimental gay legitimacy was 35 years ago."

AIDS seemed so unbelievable at first; it looked like a metaphor for the homophobia of the whole society—but reality isn't supposed to come prepackaged in metaphors, I kept muttering. Larry Kramer's great 1983 essay, "1,112 and Counting," ended all that for me and I think for an awful lot of gay men across the country. (After being published in the *Native*, that essay was reprinted in virtually every gay newspaper and magazine in America, one of the most successful pieces of political rhetoric ever seen.) After two years of confusion, denial, evasions, fear and growing panic, we realized that AIDS was going to be the major event of our time; that it threatened our continued existence, not only as individual gay men but as a community, as a culture, and that we had to mobilize every resource within our power against it.

And in that moment of crisis it was the gay writers who, disproportionately, led the way—who sounded the alarm, who told the stories of what was happening, who tried to repeat in the imagination the desperate lives we found ourselves living. And I think this is a very unusual event in the history of writing. Writers have a spotty history in terms of political involvement, if they get seriously involved at all. But, for once, a community's writers turned all their energies, their resources, their talents, their work, toward a political end, mobilizing the community against an ultimate threat. We can't go into it in detail here, of course, but I think the gay writers of the 80s rose magnificently to the challenge history had presented us with. To my mind, it made a whole generation of writers heroic and raised some of the most elemental questions about the nature and value of writing that I've ever encountered in my publishing career.

And again, to my astonishment, I think this whole remarkable episode has been forgotten, has slipped under the waters in our historical wake. I mean, a few academic books have been published about this AIDS literature, but mostly it seems to be forgotten as we've waded further into the "post-AIDS" period, which you can probably date from 1996, the year they discovered the triple therapies, the year it went from being an epidemic to being a so-called manageable condition.

So maybe both these episodes of gay history and of gay writing will be forgotten. Or maybe it will be like the Harlem Renaissance, whose writers seemed to disappear in the 40s, 50s and 60s, only to be unearthed again, initiated by Alice Walker and her small press in California. We'll see.

DW: So where do you think gay writing is going today?

MD: Lord only knows! (Laughter.) Let me tell you about the last two gay books I published, just before losing my perch in corporate publishing for good. This was 2002 and I thought they reflected where we were at the time as a community. There was *An American Family* by Michael and Jon Galluccio, with David Groff, two gay men in New Jersey who became foster parents and fought, successfully, for the legal right to adopt their child, and later for marriage equality. And there was David Nimmons' *The Soul Beneath the Skin: The Unseen Hearts and Habits of Gay Men*, brilliantly marshaling evidence of the social sciences to argue that gay men had since Stonewall created new and valuable forms of community, relationships, and masculinity. One essentially wants to assimilate to the dominant culture; the other wants to change it radically (the liberationists).

As anyone can plainly see, the assimilationist wave has been dominant for the last decade, balancing the first decade (the 70s) dominated by the liberationists—the middle two decades essentially devoted to the fight against AIDS. I suspect these two poles of the culture will always be with us. Which is the right strategy depends on the historical moment. We'll see what emerges.

DW: And for you, what emerged after corporate publishing?

MD: A surprisingly soft landing. Besides giving me a plethora of business and literary adventures which I really enjoyed, thirty years of this work had given me the opportunity to thoroughly develop and hone a craft skill.

And that is what manuscript editing is, what the academics call a praxis, an art, knowledge as something you do, not as something you know. And craft skills can only be developed by actual practice, preferably a couple of decades' worth. Malcolm Gladwell has calculated in one of his essays that mastering a skill—violin playing, tennis—takes approximately 10,000 hours of actual hard practice. Which seemed about right to me—and that would be, say, twenty years as a working editor.

And, given how corporate publishing has evolved, there is a great need for free-lance manuscript editing these days, as so much more of it is being done outside of the publishing houses. So I get to keep doing what I always loved best, working with writers and their manuscripts. And get paid for it. What's not to like?

Appendix A

OUT MAGAZINE

Just for the record:

Out magazine was to my mind the first flash appearance of what would emerge as *Christopher Street* three years later. The preview issue of *Out* was published in December 1973. According to the "General Information" sheet released by the magazine, "*Out* was conceived by four members of The Gay Activists Alliance[1] who published that organization's journal—*The Gay Activist*. *The Activist*—a modest publication of 24 pages without cover or binding sold 3,000 copies monthly (nearly all through subscription). Because of its inexpensive format, ad rates were low but it raised several hundred dollars revenue monthly for GAA. Based on letters received, demographics on other gay publications and the continuing media interest in the Gay Movement, the decision to publish a sophisticated gay publication was a logical venture. Because of our association with *The Gay Activist* and many of the gay groups throughout the United States, we were able to gather the support of outstanding contributors who are now donating their services to help support the publication."

The Editor in Chief was Ernest Peter Cohen, the Art Director was David Jones, and the Associate Editor was Chuck Ortleb. Editors included Martin Duberman, Peter Fisher, Vicki Richman, and Marc Rubin; assisting editors were Gerry Geddes, David Hathwell, John Maiscott and Brad Mulroy, with Richard Howard as the Poetry Editor, George Dickinson covering Rock, Rodney Ritter covering Photography, and Olaf Odegaard and Krista Van Laan as illustrators.

The Preview Issue contained articles by Andrea Dworkin, Chuck Ortleb, Arthur Evans, and Arthur Bell; a play by Martin Duberman, fiction by Pete Fisher, reviews by Richard Gollance, Michael Shepley

---

1 Not named here, they were: Ernest Cohen, Arthur Bell, Pete Fisher, and Marc Rubin.

and George Dickinson, and columns by Arthur Bell and Pete Fisher/ Marc Rubin.

As Ernie Cohen was my boyfriend at the time—I had met him either at GAA's Thursday night meetings at the Firehouse or at the Saturday night dances there—and I was already working in publishing, I got involved in the magazine. Ernie's best friend was Arthur Bell, the openly gay journalist of the *Village Voice*, who himself had a new boyfriend at the time, a twenty-one-year-old blond boy named Chuck Ortleb who had left grad school in Kansas to join the revolution in New York, and the four of us spent a lot of time together. When the magazine folded after its second issue, and after a great deal of effort and time, most of us were dispirited and lost faith in the project. But Chuck kept insisting that a magazine was what was politically needed at the moment, that cultural politics were more promising right then than other avenues for advancing gay liberation. This led to an ongoing and intense two-year discussion between Chuck and me about gay culture and gay fiction (it helped that he was a terrific dancer and loved to go to the dance bars, which Ernie did not). And the end result of Chuck's fierce determination was ultimately *Christopher Street* magazine in 1976.

Appendix B

A FEW WORDS ABOUT *CHRISTOPHER STREET*'S FINANCES

Again just for the record (since I have seen in print a number of totally wrong accounts of the origin of *Christopher Street*, and especially its finances):

A couple of years after the demise of *Out* magazine, Chuck Ortleb founded a company TNMI (That New Magazine Inc.) that would own *Christopher Street* and eventually its sister publications. The company was controlled by its five board members who were its principals: Chuck Ortleb, Paul Baron (who was Chuck's roommate and the magazine's treasurer), Dorianne Beyer (Chuck's close friend and our lawyer), myself, and Byrne Fone, a young gay academic whom we recruited to be the magazine's editor.

The magazine was started by selling non-voting stock at $200 apiece, mostly to our friends and a number of gay writers about town. I don't think anyone bought more than 3 or 4 shares; I bought, Chuck bought, Arthur Bell bought, Ed White bought, my straight grad school roommate bought, a whole lot of people bought stock. And when we had $10,400 (if my memory is right), Chuck made the (in retrospect, reckless) decision to start the magazine. Since it was all non-voting stock, the five principals totally controlled the company and the magazine.

Byrne was supposed to be editor, but although he had collected some pieces, he did not have a whole issue as our publication date was rapidly approaching. Furthermore, the articles he had collected were out of sync with what the rest of us thought the magazine should be. I think Byrne really wanted to start an academic journal of gay scholarship (articles about gay love poetry from monks in the Middle Ages, that sort of scholarly thing, rather than current creative writing)—you can see from his later work what he was really interested in (cf. his *Columbia Anthology of Gay Literature*). But that was never what *Christopher Street* was intended to be. If you look at the two issues of *Out*, you can see that the approach is totally congruent with *Christopher Street*, an attempt to more or less do a gay version of *The New Yorker*. This led to a split on the board about the nature of the magazine and four of us voted him out (not just Chuck).

Having started with so little working capital to begin with, *Christopher Street* was constantly on the verge of bankruptcy for its first five years. After a while we were dangerously in debt and Chuck and I spent a good deal of time trying to convince a somewhat older, enormously successful gay man to invest. But he was too good a businessman; although he fully supported the project, he couldn't convince himself that it could be made to work economically, consequently he couldn't bring himself to invest. Instead, he made the following offer: if Chuck and I would come to dinner one night a month at his place for conversation, he would give us a check for $10,000, and he would do so for twelve months. It was a zero interest loan, with no due date (he would ultimately forgive the whole $120,000, and presumably write it off as a bad loan on his taxes). We were somewhat dubious, but our backs were against the wall economically and he promised no editorial interference with the magazine, so we accepted (it was order-in-Chinese in his beautiful modern townhouse in the West Village). And he was as good as his word; although our monthly conversations were always lively, and occasionally quite heated, he never attempted to exert any influence on what we were publishing. Nevertheless, this has led to some ridiculous rumors of a dark angel manipulating us; all untrue, this man generously backed us and asked for nothing in return but conversation.

This kept us going for a while but wasn't a permanent solution. In fact, after the first year or two, I spent a good deal of my time trying to sell the magazine in order to insure its survival, first to Don Embinder, the owner of gay hotels and nightclubs in Fort Lauderdale and Atlanta and publisher of the gay magazine *Blueboy*, and then to David Goodstein, who owned *The Advocate*. But after an enormous amount of negotiation, both attempts failed, and after five years I thought the magazine was doomed.

At this last moment, Chuck came up with the idea of starting a gay newspaper (which became the *New York Native*—we originally wanted to call it *Native New Yorker* until lawyers for that song's copyright holder threatened a lawsuit). I was dubious since we were already massively in debt, but Chuck argued it would only cost $640 dollars to print 8,000 copies of the first issue (we had no idea newsprint was so much cheaper, in fact at the time we knew nothing about starting a magazine; had we been better informed, I think we might have started *Christopher Street* on newsprint, imitating a cross between the *New York Review of Books* and Andy Warhol's *Interview Magazine* rather than *The New Yorker*). I finally agreed on the condition that unless the first issue brought us $1,280 in income there would be no second issue. Of course, this meant that the staff (maybe ten people at the time) in addition to producing the magazine each month would now have to produce, in addition, two newspapers (the *Native* was a bi-weekly)—all, of course, for the same salary. After a meeting that lasted until 2 or 3 in the morning, everyone agreed and we were off.

And since a newspaper offered the possibility of local vernacular advertising (local gay bars, restaurants, shops, etc.) which was not available to a national gay literary magazine (which could only count on publishers' ads for gay books, which were mighty few), the newspaper saved the magazine financially, and Chuck was able to keep the company going—and growing, with eventually three more publications—for twenty-two years. Which still astonishes me.

Appendix C: The Stonewall Inn Editions

MICHAEL DENNENY, GENERAL EDITOR

(In order of publication in this line)

Buddies by Ethan Mordden
Joseph and the Old Man by Christopher Davis
Blackbird by Larry Duplechan
Gay Priest by Malcolm Boyd
Privates by Gene Horowitz
Taking Care of Mrs. Carroll by Paul Monette
Conversations with My Elders by Boze Hadleigh
Epidemic of Courage by Lon Nungesser
One Last Waltz by Ethan Mordden
Gay Spirit by Mark Thompson
As If After Sex by Joseph Torchia
The Mayor of Castro Street by Randy Shilts
Nocturnes for the King of Naples by Edmund White
Alienated Affections by Seymour Kleinberg
Sunday's Child by Edward Phillips
The God of Ecstasy by Arthur Evans
Valley of the Shadow by Christopher Davis
Love Alone by Paul Monette
The Boys and Their Baby by Larry Wolff
On Being Gay by Brian McNaught
Parisian Lives by Sam Steward
Living the Spirit by Will Roscoe, ed.
Everybody Loves You by Ethan Mordden
Death Takes the Stage by Donald Ward
Untold Decades by Robert Patrick
Reports from the Holocaust by Larry Kramer
Gay & Lesbian Poetry in Our Time by Carl Morse & Joan Larkin, eds.

Personal Dispatches by John Preston

Tangled Up in Blue by Larry Duplechan

How to Go to the Movies by Quentin Crisp

Just Say No by Larry Kramer

The Prospect of Detachment by Lindsley Cameron

The Body and Its Dangers and Other Stories by Allen Barnett

Dancing on Tisha B'av by Lev Raphael

The Arena of Masculinity by Brian Pronger

Boys Like Us by Peter McGehee

Don't Be Afraid Anymore by Reverend Troy D. Perry, with
    Thomas L. P. Swicegood

The Death of Donna-May Dean by Joey Manley

Profiles in Gay and Lesbian Courage by Reverend Troy D. Perry &
    Thomas L. P. Swicegood

Latin Moon in Manhattan by Jaime Manrique

On Ships at Sea by Madelyn Arnold

The Boys on the Rock by John Fox

Tom of Finland by F. Valentine Hooven III

Created Equal by Michael Nava and Robert Dawidoff

Gay Issues in the Workplace by Brian McNaught

Sportsdykes by Susan Fox Rogers, ed.

West of Yesterday, East of Summer by Paul Monette

The Dream Life by Bo Huston

End of the Empire by Denise Ohio

Sacred Lips of the Bronx by Douglas Sadownick

I've a Feeling We're Not in Kansas Anymore by Ethan Mordden

Sudden Strangers by Aaron Fricke and Walter Fricke

Sweetheart by Peter McGehee

Winter Eyes by Lev Raphael

The Listener by Bo Huston

Labour of Love by Doug Wilson

The Long Road to Freedom by Mark Thompson, ed.

The Violet Quill Reader by David Bergman, ed.

The Love Songs of Phoenix Bay by Nisa Donnelly

Franny, the Queen of Provincetown by John Preston

The Gay Militants by Donn Teal

Under the Rainbow by Arnie Kantrowitz
Late in the Season by Felice Picano
Show Me the Way to Go Home by Simmons Jones

(After 1995, the line went on with Keith Kahla as the General Editor.)

Another Mother by Ruthann Robson
Close Calls by Susan Fox Rogers, ed.
How Long Has This Been Going On? by Ethan Mordden
My Worst Date by David Leddick
Girljock: The Book by Roxxie
Pawn to Queen Four by Lars Eighner
Coming Home to America by Torie Osborn
The Necessary Hunger by Nina Revoyr
Call Me by P. P. Hartnett
My Father's Scar by Michael Cart
Getting Off Clean by Timothy Murphy
Mongrel by Justin Chin
Now That I'm Out, What Do I Do? by Brian McNaught
Some Men Are Lookers by Ethan Mordden
A/K/A: A Novel by Ruthann Robson
Execution, Texas: 1987 by D. Travers Scott
Gay Body by Mark Thompson
The Venice Adriana by Ethan Mordden
Women on the Verge by Susan Fox Rogers
An Arrow's Flight by Mark Merlis
Glove Puppet by Neal Drinnan
The Pleasure Principle by Michael Bronski
And the Band Played On by Randy Shilts
Biological Exuberance by Bruce Bagemihl
The Sex Squad by David Leddick
Bird-Eyes by Madelyn Arnold
Out of the Ordinary by Noelle Howey & Ellen Samuels, eds.
The Coming Storm by Paul Russell
The Salt Point by Paul Russell
Walt Whitman Selected Poems 1855–1982, ed. by Gary Schmidgall